ORSON WELLES
AT WORK

Phaidon Press Limited
Regent's Wharf
All Saints Street
London, N1 9PA

Phaidon Press Inc.
180 Varick Street
New York, NY 10014

www.phaidon.com

ISBN 978 0 7148 4583 8

A CIP catalogue record for this book
is available from the British Library

Translated by Imogen Forster,
Roger Leverdier and Trista Selous
Original design by Paul Raymond Cohen
and adapted by Bianca Wendt

Printed in Italy

Cover illustrations:
Portrait of Welles (front)
On the set of *Citizen Kane* (back)

Endpapers:
A promotional still for *The Lady from Shanghai*

ORSON WELLES

AT WORK

Jean-Pierre Berthomé & François Thomas

INTRODUCTION

There was no single Welles method, only Welles methods – almost as many as the films he made. His gargantuan appetite for work, willingness to experiment and ability to adapt to any set of circumstances never flagged. The particular task of the present book is to examine the stages of Welles's development as a filmmaker, and particularly the ways in which they were disrupted, for his films were not made according to a logical and regular pattern but were often the product of chance or unforeseen circumstances.

Previous pages:
Shooting *Citizen Kane*.

Opposite page:
Promotional portrait
of the young Welles.

IN PRAISE OF OVERWORK

The American press dubbed Orson Welles 'Public Energy Number One' during his first years in Hollywood. His strength lay in his hyperactivity, which enabled him to create a body of work so vast that it would take several lifetimes to research. Making his debut as a professional stage actor in 1931 at the age of sixteen and as a director five years later, he went on to produce and direct for radio until 1946, worked in the theatre until 1960, staged magic shows and made recordings. He played over sixty character parts in films for other directors and appeared in numerous television productions. He delivered a wide variety of speeches and lectures, published several books and wrote dozens of prefaces and articles. In the mid-1940s, contemplating a career in politics as a Democrat, he penned a daily column for a major New York newspaper. And, of greatest importance for this book, he left us twelve completed feature-length films, twenty television programmes, as many short films made in various circumstances and twelve unfinished works for the small and big screens.

Turbulence was essential to the way Welles worked and to the success of his artistic ventures. He wrote a vast number of scripts and could always substitute one project for another, or pitch ten stories to a producer rather than one. According to his assistant Richard Wilson, one of his closest collaborators during the 1930s and 40s, 'Orson was absolutely awful when he was confined to a single project. He stalled and wouldn't give it his attention. He needed the constraint of having to do several things at once.' In a letter to cameraman George Fanto, whose support as manager he was seeking in 1950, Welles claimed he needed to work 'a minimum of eighteen hours a day'. His collaborators were expected to follow his example.

But Welles's hyperactivity also jeopardized some of his projects. He often committed himself to new projects while underestimating the time needed for the one in hand, and would accept impossible deadlines. Once the total immersion in a shoot was over, the prospect of new ventures would soon lure him away from the editing process, even if that meant having to work more frantically than ever when he returned to it.

THE ART OF THE PROTOTYPE

Welles never managed to regain his position in the film industry after the acrimonious break with RKO, his first Hollywood employer, in 1942. Saddled with a reputation for indiscipline a year after the critical triumph of *Citizen Kane*, he was forced to seek independence by working as a director, and whenever possible as a producer, for various production companies, or by founding a company himself. Throughout his entire career he never knew which of his projects would come to fruition and always kept several options open. He was capable of inventing a project on the spur of the moment, but usually tried to keep relations with backers on an even keel by submitting a long-term production programme, although most of his work was prototypical. In effect, Welles was primarily an experimenter, as much in terms of his working methods as of the aesthetic results he was looking for. Every project was a matter of planting a flag on an undiscovered island or an unconquered summit. There is an element of bravura in much of his work: this is what you can do with a low budget when working for a B movie studio (*Macbeth*), with a crane (the opening of *Touch of Evil*), with an editing table and odd bits of film (*F for Fake*). Apart from *The Stranger*, deliberately undertaken in a bid to regain Hollywood's favour after a period in purgatory, *Mr Arkadin* was the only film on which Welles abandoned his fondness for experimentation. But even here, saddled with a crew that seemed to be on a different wavelength, he managed to draw something fresh from his actors and composer.

Welles was also capable of varying his methods on a single film. According to the first editor employed on *Touch of Evil*, Welles worked alongside him every night, yet one of his replacements claimed that the director never set foot in the editing room and preferred to view the rushes on a big screen before issuing instructions for the next few days.

Shooting *The Lady from Shanghai*.

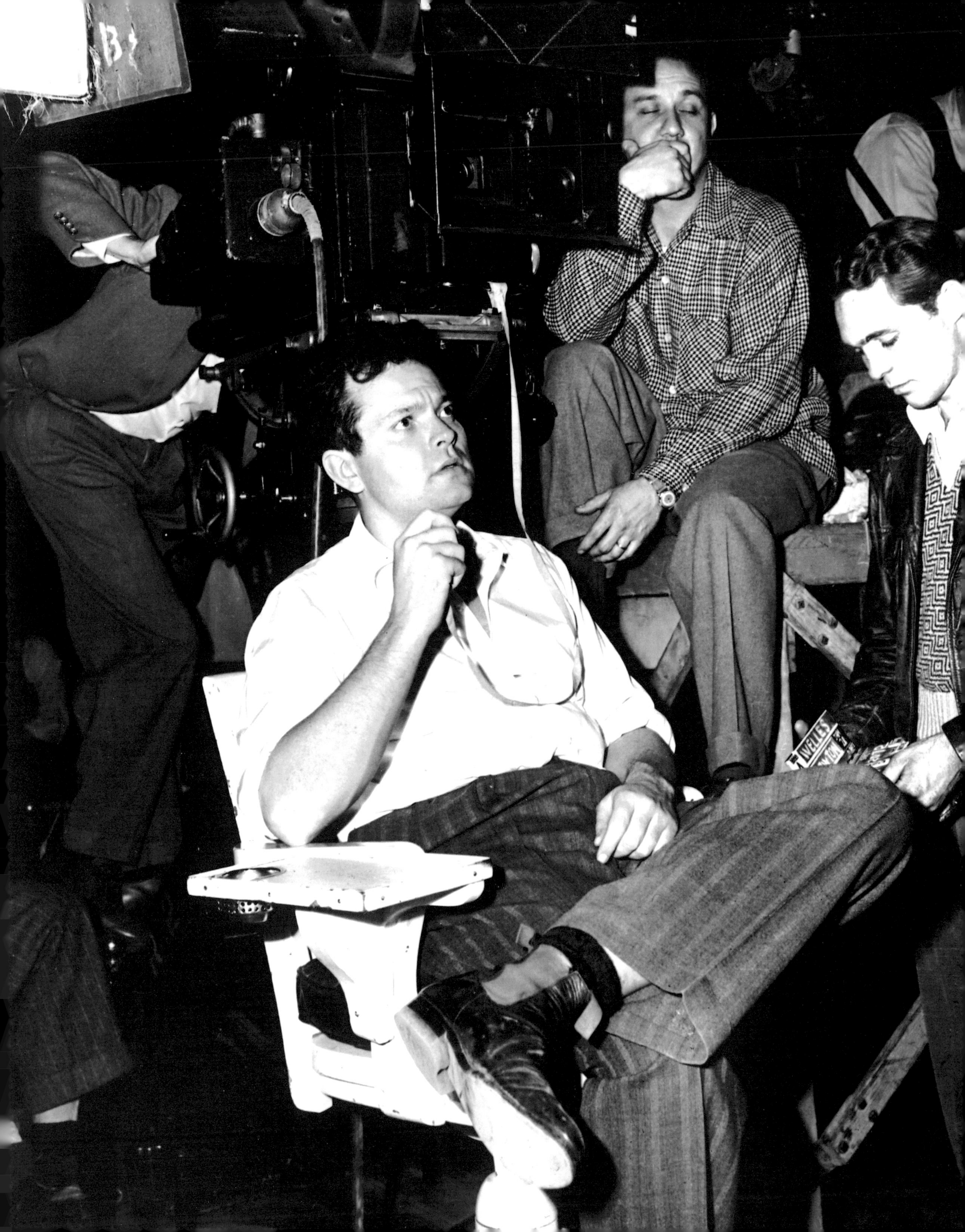
WELLES

ADAPTING TO CONSTRAINTS

The working methods were often dictated by the aesthetic envisaged for the project. In many cases they evolved through the need to adapt to constraints. Welles deplored the way that the Hollywood of the golden period devoted so much effort to controlling every aspect of a film's production: 'For the cinema, accidents are sublime.' He prepared his own films in minute detail, but displayed extraordinary flexibility when confronted with adversity or struck by sudden inspiration. When Columbia, unhappy with many of the scenes in *The Lady from Shanghai*, dictated the way they should be reshot, he still managed to infuse them with an unorthodox style. Welles frequently resorted to extraordinary working conditions in order to keep several projects on the boil. In 1947, for example, he left Hollywood in the middle of editing *Macbeth* in order to set up projects in Europe, but arranged for his American editor to join him in Italy, where he finished the film and recruited Jacques Ibert, a French composer living in Rome.

Welles's working principles were therefore never clear-cut. Take the example of whether to shoot on location or in a studio: *Citizen Kane* and *Macbeth*, to be sure, embody the studio aesthetic, but everything depended on the type of project and its financial and logistical possibilities. In 1939, Welles intended to ignore Hollywood practice and film part of his first project, an adaptation of Conrad's *Heart of Darkness*, in the swamps of Florida or in Panama. There were also plans to use the rivers and impenetrable jungles of South America for other films in the early 1940s. In 1942, he travelled to Brazil for the anthology film *It's All True*. And in 1949, when the money for *Othello* failed to materialize, he simply adapted to the circumstances: if he could not get access to a studio, he would film it wherever he could (Italy and Morocco in this instance), and drastically alter his shooting strategy by replacing long takes with rapid cross-cutting. There were various ways of achieving the same ends: the labyrinthine aspect of *Macbeth*'s décor was created on a single studio stage by means of interconnecting sets; the look of *Othello* owed much to the various locations linked together at the editing table.

Welles had a habit of revising a script in the middle of shooting. When working in Europe he constantly tinkered with the structure and details as he cut the film. Yves Deschamps, an editor on the unfinished *The Other Side of the Wind* in 1973 and 1974, recalls one striking instance. Welles devised a virtuoso long take in which the trendy young filmmaker played by Peter Bogdanovich is mobbed by reporters and turns in a clockwise direction to offer their cameras his best profile, while Welles's camera moves in the opposite direction. Instead of selecting one of the ten or so takes, he chopped the scene into several segments, shattering its continuity to still more spectacular effect.

The European films represent a clear departure from the earlier working methods. The shift had been anticipated to a certain extent during the shoot of *It's All True* in Brazil in 1942, but with *Othello* the rules changed abruptly: the script had become a pretext for far bolder experiments. Demonstrating considerable flexibility once again, Welles adapted his shooting schedule on the spur of the moment, rejected direct sound in order to speed up the shoot and gave himself much more room for manoeuvre at the editing stage. *The Other Side of the Wind* illustrates another development, although this was perhaps less apparent as it was chiefly confined to the unfinished films. In the last fifteen years of his life, Welles found it so difficult to finance his projects that he often put up the money himself or worked for minor sponsors. Filming in short bursts with a small but dedicated crew and a regular cameraman, he definitely established the primacy of the editing process.

FROM ORCHESTRA LEADER TO ONE-MAN BAND: THE ROLE OF THE COLLABORATORS

The Orson Welles at work in this book is first and foremost Orson Welles the director. However, for us the director is inextricably linked to the producer. The power Welles enjoyed on his arrival in Hollywood stemmed from his status as a producer. After the split with RKO, he attempted to regain this status by working for other companies, and often achieved his aim in Europe by financing his own films when there seemed to be no other solution. Welles was also a screenwriter (usually adapting material), and a star. But the one-man band did not stop there. His name appears on the credits as art director and costume designer and even, as in the 1956 television drama *The Fountain of Youth*, as musical arranger. However, a mention on the credits is of less significance than his true ability to undertake many of the tasks assigned to his collaborators.

Welles arrived in Hollywood after a brief but intensive career in theatre and radio and a little dabbling in amateur filmmaking. During his first months there he underwent a rapid initiation into cinematic techniques. He was not about to allow the assistant director or cameraman to dictate his choices when he started shooting. On the contrary, once he had grasped the rules he would be in a position to change them. Throughout his life, Welles maintained an ambivalent view of the medium and made many contradictory statements that ranged from attributing the art of filmmaking to a single individual to attacking the cult of the director.

During the sound post-production of *Citizen Kane*.

Welles was quick to praise his actors and could wax eloquent on the skills of his technicians. He bought full pages of advertising space in trade journals in order to thank the cast and crew of *Citizen Kane*, particularly his make-up artist, who had been denied a credit by RKO. He shared *Citizen Kane*'s final credit with cameraman Gregg Toland, thus implicitly designating Toland as co-author. In 1973, when French public television asked him to appear in a documentary, he insisted that Adolphe Charlet, his camera operator on *The Trial* and *Falstaff*, should also be interviewed.

In fact, Welles learned a great deal from his early collaborators, beginning with Amalia Kent ('best script girl that ever existed') who helped him to structure the shooting scripts for the early unrealized projects before going on to *Citizen Kane* and *The Magnificent Ambersons*. Toland and Perry Ferguson, the art director on *Citizen Kane*, showed him how to construct a specific image for the screen and how to integrate the set design into the overall *mise en scène*. In the late 1940s, Alexandre Trauner, art director on several unfinished projects as well as on *Othello*, encouraged him to turn poverty into a virtue by teaching him simple tricks of perspective as well as other purely makeshift solutions. Several composers contributed to his musical education, particularly Virgil Thomson, who wrote the music for *Macbeth*, his theatrical debut in 1936, and Bernard Herrmann, with whom he made dozens of radio shows and his first films.

Welles also picked up a great deal from some of his cameramen (he often mentioned Russell Metty, Edmond Richard and Willy Kurant), although he had very clear ideas about the photography when he began shooting a film. Richard, cameraman on *The Trial* and *Falstaff*, recounts how Welles, when framing the action, would decide the lens and camera position with the naked eye, always accurately. His cameramen were selected more for their innovative approach than for any innate aesthetic sensibilities they may have possessed. He was unable to secure the services of a cameraman close to his style only twice – *The Lady from Shanghai* and *Mr Arkadin*. On the other hand, Welles restricted the set designer's role, despite his admiration for the finest of them. Accustomed to designing sets and costumes when working in the theatre, he gladly assumed the burden of these tasks on *Macbeth* (1947) and particularly on the European films, leaving the designers to carry out his instructions.

Welles claimed even greater control over the editing process: 'If there's something another fellow can or should add to your picture after you've made it, then it doesn't seem to me that you're really in command of your work.' It is probably fair to say that none of Welles's editors made a significant contribution to his films. He reduced them to assistants, either because he had already planned everything during pre-production and on the set or, conversely, because he was reluctant to delegate the editing of so much material when he alone held the key to it. The editors of his European films were subordinates: some resented this status, while others were enthusiastic and unconditionally devoted. Welles sang the praises of most of his composers, at least those who had not been foisted on him by his producers. However, his European periods were marked by the constant re-editing that took place after the music had been recorded, a process that often led to the stitching together of brief fragments from various pieces the composer had written so that they could be heard as single passages.

The logical outcome of the later phases of Welles's career was a series of artisanal films created by a small team. They were shot and edited wherever the director happened to be as he roamed various countries while still hoping to regain a foothold in the production system. Despite the difficult circumstances, Welles made every effort to support those of his collaborators who demonstrated loyalty, competence and flair.

Throughout his career in film and television, Welles frequently resorted to the 'first person singular' technique, using off-screen narration to introduce films, devising spoken credits and periodically addressing the viewer directly. This highly distinctive approach did not prevent him from denouncing the cult of the director and indeed, in *F for Fake*, he concluded his meditation in front of Chartres cathedral, the work of thousands whose names were never recorded, with 'Maybe a man's name doesn't matter that much'.

With camera operator
Philip Lathrop on
the set of *Touch of Evil*.

FIRST STEPS IN THEATRE & RADIO

1936—1939

From 1936 until his departure for Hollywood in the summer of 1939 – and for some time after that date – Welles worked intensively as a producer-director for stage and radio. He familiarized himself with the material, actors and collaborators he would use for his films and also sketched out many of the working methods he would bring to the cinema, for he believed that these art forms were inextricably linked.

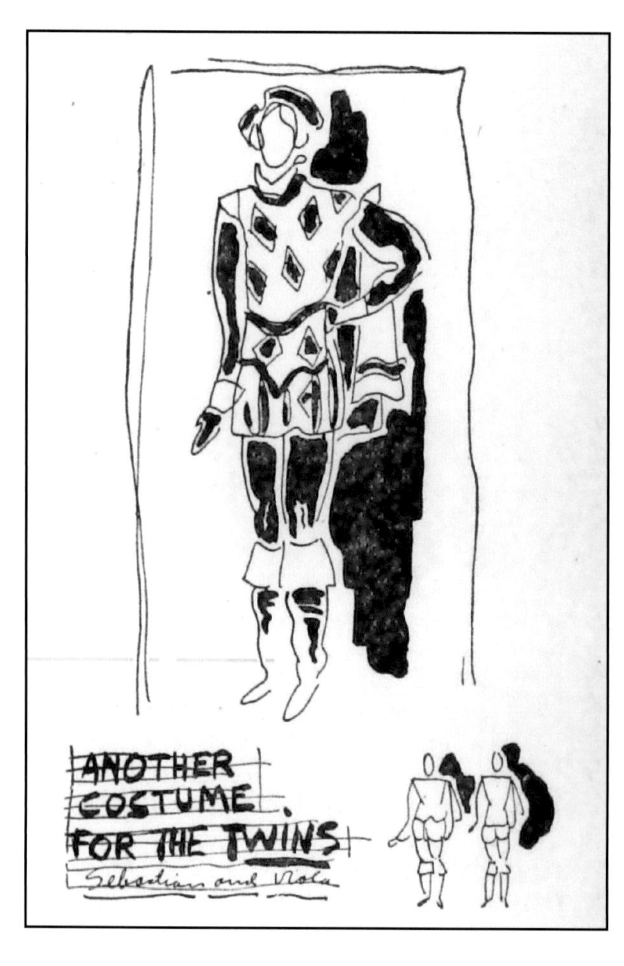

Previous pages:
Welles (left) in an unidentified play.

Left:
An illustration by Welles for *Twelfth Night* in *Everybody's Shakespeare* (1934).

Opposite page:
Welles and John Houseman (standing) during rehearsals for their adaptation of *An Italian Straw Hat* (1936).

A DAZZLING DEBUT

Welles was born in the small town of Kenosha, Wisconsin, in 1915. A multi-talented child prodigy and a precocious traveller, he would later depict himself as both a Peter Pan figure who refused to grow up and an adult who had never known childhood. His involvement in amateur dramatics, chiefly at the private school he attended as a teenager, provided an early opportunity to combine the tasks of adapter, director, scriptwriter and actor. During a trip to Europe in 1931–2, the sixteen-year-old Welles made his professional acting debut at Dublin's Gate Theatre. On his return to America in 1933, he toured with a repertory company led by the distinguished actress Katharine Cornell. He wrote one play and co-wrote another (both unstaged), and co-authored an annotated and illustrated edition of three Shakespeare plays designed for schools, universities and amateur theatre groups.

In the spring of 1936, the twenty-one-year-old Welles became a professional director in New York thanks to the producer John Houseman, with whom his career would be associated for the next four years. Houseman headed one of the units of the Federal Theatre Project, created by the US government in 1935 to provide opportunities for artists during the Great Depression. The Project would be the first and last example of subsidized theatre in American history. Houseman, impressed by Welles's performance in a contemporary play, suggested that he stage something with an all-black cast. The novice director chose Shakespeare's *Macbeth* and transposed the action to nineteenth-century Haiti. For what became known as the 'voodoo' *Macbeth*, Welles found himself in charge of 140 actors, extras and technicians. Further productions for the Federal Theatre followed, including a very loose adaptation of Eugène Labiche's *An Italian Straw Hat* and Marlowe's *Doctor Faustus*.

But the staging of one of the first American operas, *The Cradle Will Rock*, Marxist composer Marc Blitzstein's account of the rise of labour unions in the steel industry, led to problems with the federal authorities. In July 1937, Houseman and Welles founded their own company, the Mercury Theatre. Houseman raised funds through sponsorship and rented a Broadway theatre. The Mercury was a 'people's theatre' that offered a repertory programme at modest prices. For a time, it satisfied the appetite that the young Welles had already developed for constantly interweaving the various stages of the creative process: he could keep several plays in rehearsal, rehearse one play during the day, act in another at night and alternate performances.

Houseman and Welles complemented each other. Houseman, a cultivated man and a capable organizer, shielded his associate from outside interference and helped to recruit actors and collaborators. Welles was the adapter, director and general actor. The Mercury Theatre proceeded to stage five very different plays: Shakespeare's *Julius Caesar*, an Elizabethan comedy by Thomas Dekker, a 'fantasia' by George Bernard Shaw, a farce by William Gillette and Georg Büchner's *Danton's Death*. These productions immediately ensured the Mercury a significant position in the history of American theatre. The early plays, like those for the Federal Theatre, were acclaimed, but the last was such a resounding failure that the eighteen-month-old company was forced to give up its theatre. In early 1939, the Mercury joined forces with the more conventional Theatre Guild to mount *Five Kings*, a composite of scenes from seven Shakespeare history plays, although only the first of the two parts was ever performed. Welles played Falstaff, a role that he would reprise for the big screen twenty-five years later. Unable to control the escalating budget, the Theatre Guild withdrew from the project in the middle of the trial run performances, thus ensuring that the play could not be staged in New York.

Welles had also been in great demand as a radio actor since 1935, particularly for *The March of Time*, which re-created the most significant news stories of the day in the form of live sketches. The show gave him the chance to perfect his talents as an impersonator, playing prominent figures such as Haile Selassie and Victor Emmanuel III. For three years he managed to continue his theatrical activities while dashing from one New York studio to another, often doing more than ten broadcasts a week (and sometimes combining several roles in a single show) for the major networks CBS, NBC and Mutual. He made his debut as an occasional radio drama director in 1937, just as American radio was entering its golden age.

Between 1938 and 1940 Welles made nearly eighty one-hour radio programmes, some of which were the most inventive of their era. In July 1938, CBS gave him a weekly show, *The Mercury Theatre on the Air*, for the summer season. Delighted with its success, the network offered him his first exclusive contract as producer, director, presenter, narrator and star. As long as he kept to the budget, he could do as he wished. Resisting the trend for theatrical adaptations, he turned to novels and short stories by authors such as Chesterton, Dickens, Schnitzler, Stevenson and Dumas. Still busy with his stage work, he seldom wrote the script himself but trained Houseman, and later others, to write for radio, although he was always careful to set the tone and style. He directed the shows by donning headphones and cueing the actors, soundmen and orchestra leader while he performed his own part. In October 1938, the broadcast of H.G. Wells's *The War of the Worlds* created a panic: over a million listeners were convinced that Martians had landed in New Jersey and had destroyed the country in a mere thirty minutes. Welles's reputation received a tremendous boost and won him sponsorship from the Campbell Soup Company, providing a much larger budget for his show, renamed *The Campbell Playhouse*. This time there were a few strings attached: he would have to adapt plays, films and best-sellers, and invite guest stars who did not necessarily blend in well with the regular cast. Although hired by the Hollywood studio RKO in July 1939, Welles continued work on *The Campbell Playhouse* until March 1940, four months before shooting began on *Citizen Kane*.

Theatre and radio gave Welles the opportunity to operate in many capacities. He was surrounded by an industrious swarm of artists and managers and had a press office to promote the company and its leader. Most of the members of the Mercury were very young and believed they were participating in a unique period in the history of American theatre. In interviews given at a later date, some took the view that the company was designed to glorify its autocratic leader, while others remembered it as a close-knit family. Welles, on the other hand, described himself as a charismatic guru and claimed that the troupe made a vital contribution to the creative process. He spoke in terms of 'we' rather than 'I' ('we at the Mercury'), and implied that, artistically, there was no conflict between the collective spirit and his overarching control.

THE ART OF ADAPTATION

The Welles of stage and radio was essentially an adapter, a speciality that he carried over into film, since, whether he liked it or not, almost all his original screenplays remained in the drawer. His entire career was founded on a refusal to distinguish between high and low culture, between art and entertainment, a principle that allowed him to pass easily from canonical works to detective stories and farces. Adaptations of Rostand, Tolstoy, Saint-Exupéry, Mérimée, Wilde, Pirandello, Tennessee Williams, Homer, Gogol, Dostoyevsky, Poe, Henry James and Graham Greene featured among the screenplays he never filmed, as well as work by twentieth-century popular novelists. His career during the 1930s gives an early indication of the kind of material that would later receive such unique treatment in both the finished films and the various unrealized projects. Shakespeare, of course, was the primary source (Welles broke new ground when he took the Mercury troupe into a studio to make a series of recordings based on *Everybody's Shakespeare*). The radio adaptations included Conrad's *Heart of Darkness*, Verne's *Around the World in Eighty Days* and several novels by Booth Tarkington, including *The Magnificent Ambersons*. He delighted in taking a classic text and experimenting with its form.

Welles's adaptations were very short and dynamic. He reduced novels of several hundred pages to one-hour broadcasts; his plays rarely exceeded ninety minutes and were often much shorter. He had a keen sense of structure and of the ways in which existing material could be transformed. Not content with simply excising great chunks of text, he wielded the scalpel on every page. The films would owe a great deal to the techniques of adaptation he developed when writing for stage and radio, and the theatrical adaptations laid the foundations for the Shakespearean projects.

Welles manipulated the text in a variety of ways: changing the order of events, rearranging the order of lines within a scene and introducing lines from several other scenes, or even from several acts. He passed dialogue from one character to another, and sliced up lines and verses, scattering the fragments among several characters.

The radio adaptations provided a foretaste of the treatment that Welles gave to the literary material he would adapt for the cinema. His radio plays delegated descriptive or explanatory passages to a first-person narrator (usually himself) and inserted the dialogue scenes between them. In general, the language of the original was transferred with very few alterations, since Welles was always careful to retain its literary qualities. The broadcast took the form of a storyteller who addressed each listener personally, taking them by the hand, involving them as a witness and implicating them in the drama. Welles's introductions and conclusions regaled the listener with anecdotes, and he read the credits with great verve and relish. He was about to become one of the first filmmakers to favour off-screen narration, a technique rare in American cinema before 1939. Many of the unrealized screenplays reveal a clear debt to the years in radio. The combination of tasks – producer, director, presenter, narrator and actor – on *Heart of Darkness*, the first Hollywood venture, was a natural extension of his work as a broadcaster. The same could be said for *The Magnificent Ambersons*, the television adaptation of John Collier's *The Fountain of Youth* in 1956, and Karen Blixen's (writing as Isak Dinesen) *The Immortal Story*, all of which scrupulously respected the language of the author.

Above, left:
Welles in costume as Marlowe's *Doctor Faustus* (1937).

Above, right:
At an anti-fascist meeting in New York, November 1938. Welles's sympathies lay with the radical left and he was always eager to take part in political debate.

MERCURY THEATRE ACTORS IN WELLES'S FILMS

	William Alland	Edgar Barrier	Ray Collins	Joseph Cotten	George Coulouris	Agnes Moorehead
THEATRE (1937–9)	4 plays	3 plays	–	4 plays	3 plays	–
RADIO (1938–40)	34 broadcasts	32 broadcasts	60 broadcasts	11 broadcasts	22 broadcasts	21 broadcasts
CINEMA	*Citizen Kane* *The Lady from Shanghai* *Macbeth* *F for Fake*	*Journey into Fear* *Macbeth*	*Citizen Kane* *The Magnificent Ambersons* *Touch of Evil*	*Citizen Kane* *The Magnificent Ambersons* *Journey into Fear* *Touch of Evil* *F for Fake*	*Citizen Kane*	*Citizen Kane* *The Magnificent Ambersons* *Journey into Fear*

On the other hand, when adapting popular fiction in such films as *The Lady from Shanghai* and *Touch of Evil*, Welles would not hesitate to transpose the plot and invent most of the dialogue. *The Trial* could be regarded as an intermediate example: Welles modified the conception of the characters, added new characters and scenes and wrote much of the dialogue himself, but he still managed to retain a great deal of Kafka's words.

SETTING UP THE TROUPE

At the beginning of his career, Welles benefited from large casts (even experienced actors were paid little more than half the minimum union wage when working for the Federal Theatre). He had already developed a mistrust of English actors and 'American stage English', and attempted to invest canonical texts with a more contemporary resonance. Most of the black actors chosen for the 'voodoo' *Macbeth* were not familiar with the standard repertoire. In his later Shakespearean work for stage and screen, he preferred to work with Scottish, Welsh and especially Irish actors, and frequently commented on the beauty of Gaelic diction. When Welles and Houseman founded the Mercury Theatre, they recruited some of the company from the Federal Theatre, but focused mainly on the outstanding radio actors with whom Welles had been working on a daily basis.

Most of the cast of *The Mercury Theatre on the Air* were already working in radio, while a small but select number came directly from the stage. Every week, Welles would assemble a cast that offered new roles for the vocal chameleons Ray Collins and Frank Readick, as well as George Coulouris, Agnes Moorehead, Everett Sloane and others who would later appear in his films. *The Campbell Playhouse* had already taught him the art of directing Hollwood stars such as Katharine Hepburn, Walter Huston, Margaret Sullavan and William Powell.

Welles mixed the personal and the professional by giving small stage and radio parts to Virginia Nicolson, whom he had married at the age of nineteen in 1934; the couple had a daughter, Christopher, four years later. In Hollywood he worked with a partner and his second wife, both of whom were leading actresses: Dolores Del Rio appeared in *Journey into Fear* and Rita Hayworth, from whom he was separated at the time, starred in *The Lady from Shanghai*. The Pygmalion tendency re-emerged when he gave his future third wife, Paola Mori, her only starring role in *Mr Arkadin*. Similarly, Oja Kodar, his partner in later life, appeared as a star only in Welles's films. Welles's own performances encompassed an extraordinary range of styles, ranging from tragedy to burlesque. He was especially keen on playing characters much older than himself, even octogenarians.

The Mercury Theatre mounted six plays between 1937 and 1939. *The Mercury Theatre on the Air* and *The Campbell Playhouse* comprised seventy-eight broadcasts. Thirteen of these appear to have been lost, including four for which no source gives the cast. Ray Collins, Everett Sloane and Paul Stewart went on to act in plays Welles staged after *Citizen Kane.*

Frank Readick	Erskine Sanford	Stefan Schnabel	Everett Sloane	Paul Stewart	Richard Wilson	Eustace Wyatt
–	4 plays	2 plays	–	–	4 plays	4 plays
28 broadcasts	4 broadcasts	4 broadcasts	40 broadcasts	10 broadcasts	31 broadcasts	21 broadcasts
Journey into Fear	*Citizen Kane* *The Magnificent Ambersons* *The Stranger* *The Lady from Shanghai*	*Journey into Fear*	*Citizen Kane* *Journey into Fear* *The Lady from Shanghai*	*Citizen Kane* *The Other Side of the Wind* *F for Fake*	*Citizen Kane* *The Lady from Shanghai* *The Other Side of the Wind* *F for Fake*	*Journey into Fear*

On radio, he played characters at different stages of their lives, which accounted for the ease with which he later handled the role of Charles Foster Kane. He often undertook both the starring role and an anonymous supporting role, a pleasure he rediscovered when using his own voice to dub supporting actors in some of his films.

DIRECTING ACTORS

The direction of actors was thoroughly integrated into the *mise en scène.* When working in the theatre, Welles encouraged his actors to attend rehearsals even when they were not involved in the scene. On stage they were expected to synchronize their performances with a multitude of extremely precise visual and sound effects. In one instance he even asked his actors to work to a metronome, and was known to record a lengthy Shakespearean funeral oration so that the participants in crowd scenes could rehearse their reactions. His own stage performances were unpredictable and liable to change from one night to the next. After his debut at Dublin's Gate Theatre, Welles had adopted an Irish accent for several months in order to complete his integration into the troupe. The years in radio honed his skills as an imitator of regional and foreign accents; he constantly adopted different accents himself and encouraged his actors to do so in his films, even if it meant changing the nationality of the characters in the play or novel he had adapted.

Welles was the first American theatre director to use overlapping dialogue in the Shakespearean repertoire, although a few of his colleagues had recently adopted the practice in modern comedies. The actor no longer had the right to end his sentence without interruption from his fellow performers. The successive drafts of his adaptations contain examples of shortened and interwoven lines that sometimes amount to two or three columns of simultaneous dialogue. He rehearsed his actors to the syllable to ensure that the competing lines would not drown each other out. The technique would be carried over to some of the radio shows and would feature prominently in the films.

SETS AND LIGHTING

A Welles production was an extremely complex undertaking that demanded minutely detailed adjustments and the perfect co-ordination of actors, sets, lighting, music and sound effects. A director fascinated by machinery and special effects, Welles devoted particular attention to sets and lighting. He provided his designer with detailed sketches that left very little room for manoeuvre. An article he wrote in 1938 contains some harsh comments on the role of the designer and also claims that the director has a better grasp of this element: if the director can't build and paint a set, he should find another job.

In fact, Welles developed a highly assertive concept of set design for most of his plays. When staging *Doctor Faustus*, he exploited the light-absorbing properties of the black velvet used to drape the stage, lighting it so that the dark surfaces could not be distinguished from one another and thus depriving the audience of a sense of depth and perspective. Inspired by his beloved magic shows, he had tubes of black velvet suspended from ropes, and rigged lamps directly above each of them to create vertical columns of light. When the curtains suddenly rose or fell, the characters appeared or disappeared in total silence, as if by magic. In *Five Kings*, a huge revolving platform containing several sets created a fluid transition from one scene to the next as the actors, in full view of the audience, shifted from one set to another in a movement contrary to that of the turntable.

The lighting arrangements were equally precise and made great use of the recently developed dimmer bank. Welles's working notes for the 'voodoo' *Macbeth* provide an early indication of his ability to work with complex lighting plans and create a variety of effects, although he still relied heavily on the expertise of professional technicians. According to Abe Feder, the lighting designer on *Doctor Faustus*: 'In the past, light had been the tool to illuminate what was to be seen; now light itself was to take the place of the object that was to be illuminated.'

WELLES AND HIS COMPOSERS

For his stage productions, Welles relied on a tightly-knit group of young American composers – Marc Blitzstein, Paul Bowles, Aaron Copland, Lehman Engel and Virgil Thomson – some of whom had a classical musical background while others tended towards a more contemporary and popular style. Some advocated a purely American style; others looked to France and England. However, they all shared a distaste for the German romanticism that was exerting increasing dominance over Hollywood films during that period. Although Welles did no film work with any of these composers, he worked in the same spirit whenever he was in a position to control the score of his films.

Welles had very clear-cut ideas about music. On occasion he would leave it to the composer, but the general rule was total control. Thomson, the only member of the group in his forties, remarked that when confronted with the younger man's demands and musical expertise during *Macbeth*, he preferred to arrange existing pieces rather than 'humiliate myself to write so precisely on his demand'. Engel claimed that Welles virtually dictated his work on *The Shoemakers' Holiday*, tapping out the rhythms and indicating the type of melody and number of bars required. Even at that early stage, Welles was suspicious of the strings sound and preferred light orchestration or small and constantly changing instrumental combinations to signal the transitions from one scene to the next.

Welles met the composer-conductor Bernard Herrmann when working for radio. The slightly older Herrmann had been with CBS for four years and went on to become the musical director of Welles's broadcasts. Given the tight deadlines, he was often forced to arrange standard pieces or draw from a catalogue of his own themes, which he then had to revise for each new assignment. He also wrote some original scores that formed the basis of his future style: short phrases which could easily be adjusted to match script or editing revisions, fleeting transitional pieces, a predilection for the extreme registers of instruments, hesitant tonalities, and slow, melancholy waltz tunes. Herrmann was adept at revising to order and, if necessary, could do so minutes before the show went on air. His collaboration with Welles would lead to triumph in the cinema.

Welles was also one of the pioneers of sound effects in the theatre. He loved creating echoes in different parts of the auditorium as well as devising off-stage soundscapes and shock effects. He attempted to forge unbreakable links between sound effects, music and dialogue, particularly in his Shakespearean productions, which were characterized by the careful timing of sound effects or percussion to match the sinuosity of the lines. He would spend hours experimenting with new effects for radio, constructing a multi-layered soundscape or slowly varying the volume of a single, haunting sound. He was not afraid to overlay the dialogue with a howling storm, forcing the characters to shout against the wind and the audience to listen intently for the almost inaudible lines. All these effects would find their way into his films.

REHEARSALS AND THE RACE AGAINST TIME

The battle against time ranged across two fronts: union rules and tight deadlines. Welles rehearsed late into the night, often relying on the patience and loyalty of his actors and technicians, and putting in sixteen- or twenty-hour days in the theatre. Such schedules were tolerated by the Federal Theatre, which did not pay overtime, but they were ruinous for the Mercury Theatre and caused the co-producer of *Five Kings* to withdraw from the project.

Welles's plays were the product of urgency and chaos. He constantly modified the order of the scenes and the continuity of the lines, which in turn required changes to the lighting, music and sound effects. Drastic, last-minute revisions were legion, and the openings of most of his plays were postponed more than once. In the case of *Five Kings*, such practices sparked the director's first violent confrontation over deadlines and the ultimate failure of an under-prepared play: the joint backer, the Theatre Guild, pulled out, refusing to countenance any further delays and costs. Welles refused to abandon the project completely and stored some of the sets in a repository for nine years, a fate that also awaited the reels of some of the unfinished films. The fear of not meeting the deadline also hung over the radio shows, which had to be written, rehearsed and broadcast within the space of seven days. Turmoil and no safeguards demanded constant alertness from actors, soundmen and musicians alike, for success rested on the perfect synchronization of a plethora of sound effects, music and razor-sharp dialogue.

DELEGATION

As the Mercury's leader, Welles assumed responsibility for a vast number of enterprises. His appetite for work stood him in good stead, but he also had the ability to delegate. He was content to supervise others as long as he would remain the source of inspiration: individual projects were less important than the overall production programme. In 1937, when a music school commissioned a few performances of Aaron Copland's opera *The Second Hurricane*, he realized he had accepted too many simultaneous commitments and quickly delegated its direction to his assistant. Radio writers received no on-air credit at the time, but Welles dictated the style of the adaptation and his directives and revisions were often those of a co-author.

Welles, Dan Seymour, Richard Wilson, Arthur Anderson, William Alland, George Coulouris (half-hidden) and Bernard Herrmann (at the back) at the close of a *Mercury Theatre on the Air* broadcast (July 1938).

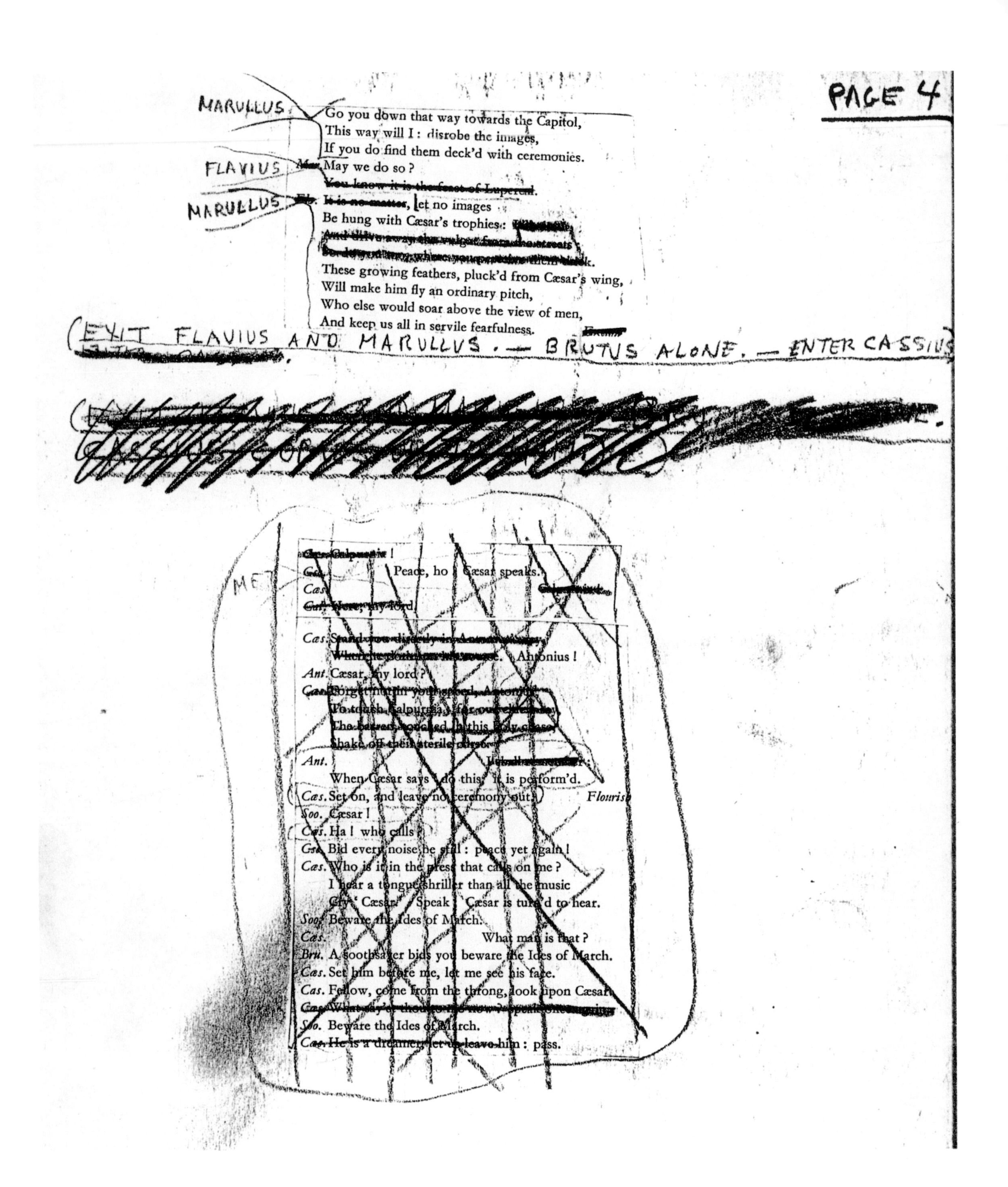

PAGE 4

MARULLUS Go you down that way towards the Capitol,
This way will I: disrobe the images,
If you do find them deck'd with ceremonies.
FLAVIUS May we do so?
You know it is the feast of Lupercal.
MARULLUS It is no matter, let no images
Be hung with Cæsar's trophies:
These growing feathers, pluck'd from Cæsar's wing,
Will make him fly an ordinary pitch,
Who else would soar above the view of men,
And keep us all in servile fearfulness.

(EXIT FLAVIUS AND MARULLUS. — BRUTUS ALONE. — ENTER CASSIUS

Cæs. Calpurnia!
Cas. Peace, ho! Cæsar speaks.
Cæs.
Cal. Here, my lord.
Cæs. Stand you directly in Antonius' way,
When he doth run his course. Antonius!
Ant. Cæsar, my lord?
Cæs. Forget not in your speed, Antonius,
To touch Calpurnia; for our elders say,
The barren, touched in this holy chase,
Shake off their sterile curse.
Ant. I shall remember:
When Cæsar says 'do this,' it is perform'd.
Cæs. Set on, and leave no ceremony out. *Flourish*
Soo. Cæsar!
Cæs. Ha! who calls?
Cas. Bid every noise be still: peace yet again!
Cæs. Who is it in the press that calls on me?
I hear a tongue shriller than all the music
Cry 'Cæsar!' Speak; Cæsar is turn'd to hear.
Soo. Beware the Ides of March.
Cæs. What man is that?
Bru. A soothsayer bids you beware the Ides of March.
Cæs. Set him before me, let me see his face.
Cas. Fellow, come from the throng, look upon Cæsar.
Cæs. What say'st thou to me now? speak once again.
Soo. Beware the Ides of March.
Cæs. He is a dreamer; let us leave him: pass.

Opposite page:
Welles prepared his adaptation of Shakespeare's *Julius Caesar* (1937) by annotating a copy of the text.

Left:
Welles as Doctor Faustus (1937).

Above:
Label for one of the 'Mercury Text Records', 1939

Below:
Arthur Anderson (Lucius) and Welles (Brutus) in *Julius Caesar* (1937).

Left:
Agnes Moorehead, Welles, sound mixer John Dietz (back, right) and George Coulouris in the CBS studios (1938).

Opposite page:
First significant film direction, filming the prologue for *Too Much Johnson* (July 1938).

After the first few weeks of *The Mercury Theatre on the Air*, he would sometimes work relentlessly on every aspect of a particular show. At other times, he would leave the preparation to Paul Stewart, his right-hand man, who directed the early rehearsals before the master took over and altered the concept completely if he thought it necessary. If the pressure was too great, Welles would simply assume his own role just before going on air.

WELLES AND HIS BACKERS

Welles had the good fortune to start work in conditions of which most people could only dream. As the Federal Theatre had been designed as an element of social policy, production costs were very low. He enjoyed total freedom as the Mercury Theatre's producer, while Houseman, anxious to get the show on the road at all costs, took care of the management side. Throughout this entire period Welles, who as a radio actor earned twenty-five times the union minimum wage, paid certain expenses out of his own pocket in order to overcome bureaucratic lethargy. He was openly suspicious of the Theatre Guild, his first independent backer, and refused to allow its officials to attend rehearsals. In the world of radio, *The Mercury Theatre on the Air* offered him total artistic control. However, there were soon bitter arguments with the sponsor over every episode of *The Campbell Playhouse*, although Welles sometimes took advantage of the absence of its usual representatives and smuggled some daring ideas into the show.

Welles had New York at his feet throughout this period, and his finest moments – both of them acts of defiance – came within eighteen months of each other. In June 1937, four days before the première of *The Cradle Will Rock*, the US government refused to allow the Federal Theatre to stage any new productions before the start of the tax year, a move that was interpreted as a disguised censure over the opera's pro-union stance. On the opening night, a belligerent Welles and Houseman, happily abandoning the maze of mobile glass partitions that gave the set its kaleidoscopic effect, defied the government and led the cast and audience on foot to another theatre. At that time the actors' and musicians' unions refused to let their members work outside the terms of their contracts, but a makeshift solution was found: the opera would be performed on a bare stage, with the composer playing the piano and singing all the parts himself. It was not long, however, before the actors, who were all present in the audience, courageously rose from their seats and began to sing their parts. The following day, Welles was headline news.

In October 1938, the radio broadcast of *The War of the Worlds* took the form of a series of fake bulletins and newsflashes. Welles, in the interests of maintaining the illusion of truth, had ignored certain conditions laid down by CBS. Not wanting his audience to catch on too quickly, he deferred the obligatory station identification announcement by several minutes. The resulting furore propelled Welles into the headlines once again, and rekindled the interest of Hollywood producers.

FILM: THE FIRST TENTATIVE STEPS

Before being hired by RKO in July 1939, Welles had made minor but significant forays into filmmaking, mostly linked to his theatrical activities. The initial steps were modest. In 1933, the eighteen-year-old Welles filmed a series of silent, static takes – a distillation of scenes from Shakespeare's *Twelfth Night* – which he had staged at an amateur dramatics festival. The following year he teamed up with a student friend and co-directed a one-reel 16 mm silent piece, *The Hearts of Age*. The film was a free improvisation shot in one or two afternoons, a parody of the French avant-garde interspersed with allusions to Robert Wiene's *Cabinet of Doctor Caligari*, with Welles appearing in heavy make-up as an elderly personification of Death.

In the summer of 1938, still working with silent 16 mm film, Welles shot some more ambitious footage to provide a prologue and linking episodes during set changes for the stage production of William Gillette's *Too Much Johnson*. In this 1899 farce, a rake (Joseph Cotten), pursued by a cuckolded husband, flees New York and embarks on a ship bound for Cuba. On arrival, he assumes the identity of a planter and is constantly caught out by his lies. The prologue takes the form of a madcap, Keystone cops-like chase over rooftops, through streets and around the waterfront. The footage, distinguished by its enthusiasm, was a Mercury family enterprise, the only professional collaborator being a newsreel cameraman.

Welles spent ten days on the film, shooting on locations in and around New York and in a makeshift studio. It was so freely improvised that the press compared it to the work of the earliest silent directors. Combining living quarters and workplace, a practice he would frequently resort to from the 1950s onwards, he set up an editing table in his hotel room.

Various problems prevented him from finishing the editing, but he had already caught the cinema bug. In May and June 1939, he toured the vaudeville circuit with an abridged parody of William Archer's melodrama *The Green Goddess*. Once again, he assembled a brief and unpretentious silent prologue (a plane crash) using archive footage augmented with some inserts that he shot himself.

Hollywood had been following the young prodigy's fortunes for two years. In the spring of 1937, the independent producer David O. Selznick had asked Welles to take charge of his story department. Selznick was also interested in his possibilities as a screen actor, as were Warner Bros. (a Warner screen test has been preserved), MGM, and Goldwyn. But Welles, holding out for autonomy as a producer-director of his own projects, had rejected all offers. RKO finally succumbed to this extraordinary demand from a twenty-four-year-old novice: Welles was given total artistic control over his first films.

CONQUERING HOLLYWOOD

The young Welles arrived in Hollywood in 1939 with a determination to stake his claim as a producer who also wrote, directed and acted in his own films. Despite his total lack of professional film experience, he sought to control every aspect of his first project *Heart of Darkness*, from beginning to end. Although never shot, it was the most thoroughly prepared film of his entire career.

A STATE WITHIN THE STATE

Welles owed his Hollywood debut to the smallest of the five major companies, RKO, which combined production, distribution and exhibition. George Schaefer, RKO's new president, had decided to change the studio's image by inviting screenwriters, theatre people and celebrated European artists to join it as associates or form their own production units within it, managing films on a day-to-day basis. Established in-house teams would be on hand to initiate the newcomers and provide intensive training in every aspect of the Hollywood industry.

Welles and John Houseman seized the opportunity to create Mercury Productions, with which Welles would be associated throughout his years in Hollywood. In July 1939 he signed a series of exceptionally advantageous contracts with RKO. These agreements guaranteed Welles's control over his films from beginning to end and gave him access to the equipment, personnel and financial backing of a major studio. In return, over the very short period of seventeen months, he was required to produce, write, direct and act in two feature-length films. As the distributor, RKO were to approve the screenplay and a reasonable budget, but otherwise Welles was free to do as he wanted on the set as long as he adhered to the terms of his contract.

He was obliged to screen the rushes for RKO's representatives and to discuss the final cut with them, but he retained the final say on the edit intended for the domestic market, an unprecedented privilege for a novice who some believed would throw in the towel before he had shot a foot of film. In addition to his director's fee, Welles would draw a salary as a star. Above all, however, he saw the Hollywood contract as the means with which to relaunch the Mercury Theatre and ensure a triumphant return to Broadway with a repertory season. He envisaged six months' work in Hollywood followed immediately by a theatrical season in New York, after which he would return to Los Angeles to make the second film. With his own production unit and an office within RKO, Welles, the head of a state within a state, was surrounded by a small team of managers, production assistants, researchers and the various aides who ensured the co-ordination of his enterprises. He hired a personal press officer to manage his public image.

Welles settled in Hollywood during the summer, while *The Campbell Playhouse*, his New York radio show, was off the air. But the show was due to resume in mid-September and the sponsor was trying to pressure him into breaking his contract with RKO. He spent two months shuttling between the West and East coasts every week in order to fulfil his radio obligations, before obtaining permission to broadcast the last thirty shows from the CBS studios in Hollywood. His intensive work on some of these shows did not prevent him from devoting most of his time to learning the ropes in Hollywood.

Eager to familiarize himself with the various branches of the industry and to gain an insight into the way a Hollywood company functioned, Welles made lengthy visits to all of RKO's artistic and administrative departments. He was introduced to the mysteries of electrical equipment, the sound archive and special effects. The company put together a technical manual illustrated with photographs of sets, drawings of set designs and strips of printed film, which helped him to absorb the language and technicalities of camera angles, shot scale and focal range. He watched many American, English and French films, studying style and technique, evaluating and re-evaluating performances and selecting jungle shots that might be useful for his first project.

THE HEART OF CONRAD

Welles persuaded RKO to begin their association with *Heart of Darkness*, an adaptation of Joseph Conrad's novella published in 1902. He had already made a thirty-minute version for radio, as part of a broadcast containing two adaptations. Marlow, a merchant navy officer, is hired by a colonial ivory company to venture into dense jungle and retrieve its most efficient agent, Kurtz, who has broken off contact. Kurtz has become a tyrant, using his rhetorical skills to dominate both his subordinates and the indigenous tribes over whom he rules with ruthless methods or, as Marlow later remarks, no method at all. During the slow voyage up-river, broken only by the occasional landing at the company's trading posts, Marlow meets some of Kurtz's disciples and enemies and discovers evidence of unspeakable atrocities. When he finally locates his prey, he finds a sick man protected by cannibals. Kurtz dies on the return journey, but not before telling Marlow that they are not so unlike each other.

The adaptation was ambitious in three respects: it had to measure up to a monument of English literature; it contained a politically controversial element, given the isolationist stance maintained by the United States at the time; and it involved an experiment with form.

With the model of Marlow's paddle steamer for *Heart of Darkness* (1939).

Welles made Marlow an American, brought the story up to date and invested it with a contemporary political resonance, as he had done before when his theatrical production of *Julius Caesar* established a parallel with Italian fascism. In his version, the ivory company becomes the tool used by a totalitarian Germanic government to penetrate a British protectorate, while Kurtz unifies the tribes inhabiting the unexplored part of the jungle. As for formal experimentation, Welles intended to use the subjective camera – something that had never been attempted for almost the entire duration of a feature film – and first-person off-screen narration in the style of his radio programmes. The film would thus chime with Marlow's point of view. Rather than to persuade the viewer to identify with Marlow, the goal was to create a mood that constantly shifted between identification and estrangement so that the narrator never lost his air of mystery: 'The desire to know more about him,' notes Welles in a portrait of the character, 'must be sustained throughout and never satisfied.' Welles had played Kurtz on the radio, but originally considered playing both roles (despite an age gap of fifteen years) on the screen, thus reinforcing the growing identification between the hunter and his prey.

Houseman was asked to write the script, but soon realized he was not equipped for the task. Welles took over and began by pasting pages from the novel on to sheets of paper, which he then annotated, indicating cuts, alterations and additions. He adhered closely to the text, but invented a great deal of the dialogue, although the seams are barely visible. He strengthened the gallery of bizarre characters that Marlow encounters, expanded the role of Kurtz's fiancée and drew parallels between Kurtz and his European counterpart (a transparent allusion to Hitler), whose failure Kurtz predicts. Amalia Kent, the production secretary and script supervisor who would join him on some of his later RKO films, helped to convert the screenplay into a shooting script. Three versions were written during November, the last dated the 30th.

The shooting script of *Heart of Darkness* is faithful to the Mercury radio outline in every respect: Welles, the host and narrator, opens the proceedings with an address to the viewer; the adaptation then unfolds, alternating between frequent passages of narration and dialogue scenes. After the RKO logo and the title, the screen fades to black as Welles's voice launches into a lengthy and didactic introduction to the subjective camera. He adheres to the credo developed for the radio shows: talk directly to each individual viewer, rather than to an undifferentiated audience.

After dividing the audience into two parts ('you and everybody else in the theatre'), he suggests that the viewer may want to close their eyes and open them again when requested to do so. He wields the power of an illusionist or a hypnotist, like Kurtz himself. When he judges that the viewer, called upon to imagine himself as a canary in a cage, is resisting the order to sing, he points a gun at him and pretends to shoot. The viewer is thus subsumed into the story – indeed, he becomes its protagonist: 'Of course, you're not going to see yourself on the screen, but everything you see on the screen will be seen through your eyes and you're somebody else.' According to the shooting script, Welles then briefly introduces Conrad's novel before handing over to Marlow the narrator, or, rather, to himself. Initially heard as an off-screen voice, as he begins his story Marlow is shown leaning against the mast of his boat in New York's port, then is once again reduced to a voiceover. But the narrator does have some visibility: he reappears in outline at certain points, but in flashbacks is perceived only as a shadow, a reflection in a mirror, or as a hand entering the frame. At the very end, however, he stares directly at the camera – 'straight into the eyes of the audience' – as he wonders whether he was right to conceal from Kurtz's fiancée the truth about the man she loved. Kurtz himself looks 'into Marlow's eyes' several times, which means, of course, that Welles looks into the eyes of Welles. Once the contract was signed, Welles, anxious to preserve the singularity of his project, decided against casting familiar faces from the studio stable and gave almost all the parts to members of his Mercury company. He also reassembled many of the actors he needed for his radio broadcasts in Los Angeles.

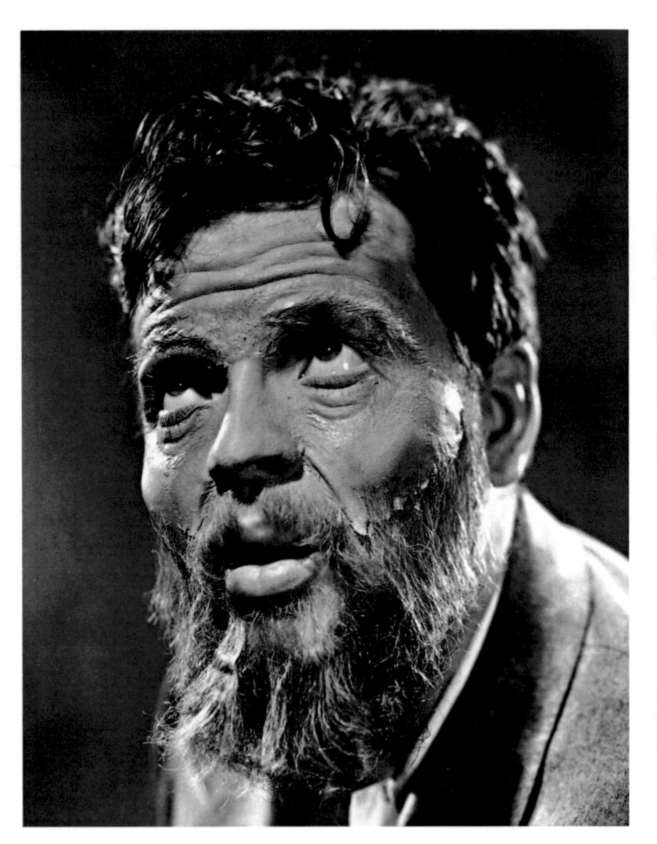

K
THE HORROR! — THE HORROR!

~~GREAT MODERN SHORT STORIES~~

time—his death and her sorrow—I saw her sorrow in the very moment of his death. Do you understand? I saw them together—I heard them together. ~~She had said, with a deep catch of the breath,~~ 'I have survived' ~~while~~ my strained ears seemed to hear ~~distinctly, mingled with her tone of despairing regret,~~ the summing up whisper of his eternal condemnation. ~~I asked myself what I was doing there, with a sensation of panic in my heart as though I had blundered into a place of cruel and absurd mysteries not fit for a human being to behold. She motioned me to a chair. We sat down. I laid the packet gently on the little table, and she put her hand over~~ it. . . . 'You knew him well,' ~~she murmured, after a moment of mourning silence.~~

"'Intimacy grows quickly out there,' ~~I said~~. 'I knew him as well as it is possible for one man to know another.'

"'And you admired him,' ~~she said~~. 'It was impossible to know him and not to admire him. Was it?'

"'He was a remarkable man,' ~~I said, unsteadily. Then before the appealing fixity of her gaze, that seemed to watch for more words on my lips, I went on~~, 'It was impossible not to—'

"'Love him,' ~~she finished eagerly, silencing me into an appalled dumbness~~. 'How true! how true! But when you think that no one knew him so well as I! I had all his noble confidence. I knew him best.'

"'You knew him best,' ~~I repeated~~. And perhaps she did. But with every word spoken the room was growing darker, ~~and only her forehead, smooth and white, remained illumined by the unextinguishable light of belief and love.~~

"'You were his friend,' ~~she went on~~. 'His friend,' she repeated, a little louder. 'You must have been, if he had given you this, and sent you to me. I feel I can speak to you—and oh! I must speak. I want you—you have heard his last words—to know I have been worthy of him. . . . It is not pride. . . . Yes! I am proud to know I under-

Triumphant darkness — from which I could not have defended her — from which I could not even defend myself.

Above, left:
Welles made up as Kurtz in *Heart of Darkness* (1939).

Above, right:
An RKO artist's version of the ivory company's first trading post.

Left:
Adapting *Heart of Darkness*: Welles transposed the dialogue from one page to another, attributing lines to the protagonist Marlow (M) and to Kurtz's fiancée, whom he named Elsa (E).

Opposite page:
Kurtz's temple.

The newcomers had little experience of working in cinema, but this was an advantage for a director who did not intend to follow the conventions when shooting began. On the other hand, the discipline his actors had acquired through their work for the stage, and particularly for radio, had equipped them to meet the harshest demands. Moreover, they trusted their leader, whereas most seasoned actors would probably have had little confidence in an inexperienced director. Some of the cast – Ray Collins, George Coulouris, Everett Sloane – would go on to act in *Citizen Kane*; others would have to wait longer or would never act in a Welles film. Welles had already established one of the principles that would guide the rest of his career in America: the actors he worked with in radio and theatre would also appear in his films. This gave him the opportunity to maintain permanent contact with his company and harmonize the various activities undertaken by Mercury. The only notable deviation from the '100% Mercury' rule was the unsuccessful attempt to obtain the German actresss Dita Parlo (who had impressed him with her performance in Jean Renoir's *La Grande Illusion* and other European films) for the role of Kurtz's fiancée. Welles also secured the services of Bernard Herrmann, his radio composer, who would be on hand for both the film and the Los Angeles radio broadcasts. According to the terms of the contract, Welles's first film should have been wrapped up by 31 December 1939. The actual footage for *Heart of Darkness* amounts to nothing more than a few tests shot in late November and early December, but preparation was so thorough that the project indisputably represents the first major stage in Welles's search for working methods for the cinema.

THE DREAM OF TOTAL CONTROL

Welles's desire to plan everything at a very early stage may be explained both by his desire for control and by the novice's concern to avoid, whenever possible, being caught out in the heat of the action. The most conventional aspect of this intensive preparation was the set design, for which Welles used Walter E. Keller, an RKO designer previously confined to low-budget productions. Welles planned to move out of the studio and shoot some of the film in the swamps of the Everglades in Florida or perhaps in Panama, but his location scouts concluded that the logistical problems were insurmountable. He worked with illustrators who came up with a graphic depiction of the river, the surrounding jungle and the wooden temple to the glory of Kurtz which stands on pilings in a lake. Unlike Conrad's simple ruin, the inside of the temple was entirely covered in human skulls and bones. Welles ordered scale models of Marlow's paddle steamer, the temple and the colonial waterfront buildings. Aided by a small periscope, these small models enabled him to visualize the movement of the camera and actors on the set.

The shooting script is impressively meticulous, setting out camera movements and a variety of special effects in minute detail. It indicates sound effects, pauses, silences and the frequent use of overlapping dialogue, signalling precisely at which word – and indeed at which syllable – one character's line should overlap the line delivered by another. It defines what Welles expects from Herrmann's music. The menacing sound of jungle drums harks back to the 1938 radio adaptation, in which the native drumming, orchestrated by the same Sierra Leonean choreographer and troupe leader from the 1936 'voodoo' *Macbeth*, often overwhelms the dialogue.

The need to control everything at a very early stage stemmed partly from the decision to employ the subjective camera technique and the visual choices this involves. In effect, Welles conceived the film as a series of long takes (at one point he considered using an entire reel of film, enough for eleven minutes of footage). The total number of shots would therefore be unusually low – about 170. He rejected the traditional laws of shot breakdowns at the outset, refusing to film the same action from different camera setups or to frame it differently; this would have given him a margin of safety at the editing stage, but it would also have given the producers room for manoeuvre. There would be no use of shot-reverse-shots, intercutting or cutaways. As a matter of fact, all his early films would be made in such a way that, whether using long takes or some other technique, a sequence containing several shots from the same angle constituted a rare occurrence.

Two factors were primarily responsible for sinking the project before filming had begun. Forty per cent of the scenes required special effects (scale models, painted mirrors, process shots), but Welles decided to reverse standard practice and create them before, rather than after the shoot. Furthermore, forty per cent of the shots had to be linked to the following shots by 'feather wipes'. This technique, which required pinpoint precision, involved panning the camera to a fixed point and then, for the next shot, starting from exactly the same spot at exactly the same speed; editing would ensure that the link between the two shots remained invisible. The film would seem as if it were composed of no more than a hundred shots, all joined by dissolves. The technique, worked out with RKO's camera department before a cameraman had been hired, posed a number of technical problems. The studio was willing to adapt its equipment to accommodate the novice's innovative concept (Welles often claimed that his innovations were the product of innocence) and agreed to fit a camera with a double viewfinder, thus enabling Welles and the operator to control the frame during the technical rehearsals and takes. It was also rigged with a gyroscopic head to give it the necessary flexibility when Marlow passed through doorways, stood up or sat down. Further work was needed to improve hitting the marks when the mini-crane had to be used for the feather wipes.

Several days were devoted to test shots: these established the project's feasibility, but also revealed the extent of its technical challenges and its costs. The special effects alone would require twelve to fourteen weeks' work before the fourteen-week shoot could begin. Besides incurring a budget overspend, it would not be possible to alter the shooting script once the special effects were underway. Moreover, the takes were so complex that the dialogue would have to be rehearsed to perfection. Welles dictated an analysis of all the characters, describing not only their psychological traits but also their physical appearance, clothing and props. He did a number of rehearsals, striving for an ensemble performance based on mutual respect and a shared understanding of the issues in the script. Some of the rehearsals were recorded at the CBS studios. The actors, all experts at overlapping dialogue, became so familiar with their roles that they could always improvise lines during a take if necessary. In addition, Welles wanted to model the rhythm of the film in both off-screen narration and dialogue at the earliest possible stage. He was expecting Herrmann to use the sound recording as he wrote the score, so that the music would be organically timed to the dialogue.

With all these arrangements in place, the editing would be largely a matter of respecting the preconceived design; a mere four weeks were set aside for the process. As a statement of intent makes clear, the film could only be shortened by removing an entire sequence.

FROM 'HEART OF DARKNESS' TO 'CITIZEN KANE'

In early December, a budget estimate drawn up on the basis of the final shooting script came in at over one million dollars, more than double the sum agreed. In addition, RKO had lost some of its European markets due to the outbreak of war and had decided to cut its costs. Rather than cancel *Heart of Darkness* altogether, the studio was willing to postpone it as long as costs were slashed and a low-budget project was filmed beforehand. In exchange, Welles, to the outrage of colleagues and agents alike, offered to shoot the new project for nothing, and take a percentage of any profits it made. But he would still owe RKO the two films he had agreed to make when he signed the contract six months earlier. The postponement of *Heart of Darkness* weakened the Mercury's position and led to a row with Houseman, who left the company. There were a few brief reunions, but the Welles-Houseman partnership was to be terminated eighteen months later. Welles then embarked on the script and shot breakdown for *The Smiler with the Knife*, an Americanized adaptation of a recent suspense thriller by the British writer Nicholas Blake. The story centres on a woman who pretends to separate from her husband in order to infiltrate a crypto-fascist organization and foil its plans for a *coup d'état*. Welles turned it into a spy thriller interspersed with comic episodes, and cast eight Mercury actors, who would move on to *Heart of Darkness* within a few weeks of finishing the film. The budget was much smaller than that for *Heart of Darkness* or any of the films that Welles would later make for RKO. But because of apparent disagreements over casting the female lead or because the project seemed too run of the mill for the exalted Welles-RKO partnership, the studio cancelled it before he could make inroads on the technical preproduction.

The decision to abandon *Heart of Darkness*, ratified only after *Citizen Kane* had begun, was probably based on a number of factors, including the size of the budget and the fear of alienating foreign markets (some of which might have banned it for its anti-Nazi references). According to Richard Wilson, the adaptation's formal properties also constituted a drawback: Welles was officially informed that contemporary audiences were not ready for the subjective camera or 'first person singular' narration. He resuscitated some elements of the script in a thirty-minute radio programme in 1945, but never made a serious attempt to return to *Heart of Darkness*. What he had learned from it, however, would serve him well on other films, beginning with *Citizen Kane*.

Welles and his assistants Edward Donahoe and Fred A. Fleck with the model of the ivory company's first trading post. Donahoe is holding the periscope, a tool for visualizing angles prior to shooting.

KANE

CITIZEN KANE

1941

With *Citizen Kane*, Welles, enriched by the experience gained on *Heart of Darkness*, was less intent on controlling every aspect of the project from the outset, although his first feature film still represents a triumph of meticulous preparation that left little room for improvisation. Taking full advantage of the pool of talent placed at his disposal by RKO, he surrounded himself with seasoned and innovative collaborators, kindred spirits who were ready to challenge the routines of classical Hollywood cinema. At every stage of its creation, *Citizen Kane* combined the reliability of a finely tuned studio system with the creative flair of its cast and crew.

Previous pages and opposite page:
Public and private life, Welles and Ruth Warrick (Kane and Emily, Kane's first wife).

Left:
Xanadu, the setting for Kane's death in the film's opening moments.

THE RELUCTANT SCRIPTWRITER

After the experience of writing the *Heart of Darkness* script unaided, Welles played it safe and hired a professional screenwriter, Herman J. Mankiewicz, a run-of-the-mill plot merchant but a brilliant dialogue writer who had already revised the screenplay for *The Smiler with the Knife*. Mankiewicz agreed to write a biography of a fictitious press magnate. Fiction had its limits, however, as the character would be secretly based on William Randolph Hearst, a press and radio station tycoon whom Mankiewicz knew well, having been part of the charmed circle invited to Hearst's palatial Californian dwelling at San Simeon.

Early in March 1940 Mankiewicz shut himself away in Victorville, 150 kilometres north-east of Los Angeles, and stayed there until early May. He was accompanied by John Houseman, the former president of the Mercury Theatre, who had been enlisted to help him structure the plot, although Welles was also relying on Houseman to curb the writer's excessive drinking. Welles himself remained in Hollywood, dividing his time between preparing the film, making a recording of *Macbeth* with his Mercury players and giving a series of lectures on 'The new actor'. In mid-April, Mankiewicz sent him the first draft of a script provisionally entitled *American*. It contained all the principal ingredients of *Citizen Kane*, but there were too many events and their organization was uninspired.

The film opened with the press tycoon Charles Foster Kane dying alone in his palace, Xanadu, and then cut abruptly to a long newsreel obituary. Curious to know more, a newsreel editor sends a reporter, Thompson, to interview Kane's friends and associates and to discover the meaning of 'Rosebud', the dying man's final utterance. This was followed by five portraits of Kane drawn by those – guardian, employee, friend, wife and butler – who had known him at various stages in his life. The 'Rosebud' enigma derived its power from the fact that once Kane's death had been established and the broad outlines of his life

THOMPSON SEES BERNSTEIN
(KANE'S LATEST OFFICE)

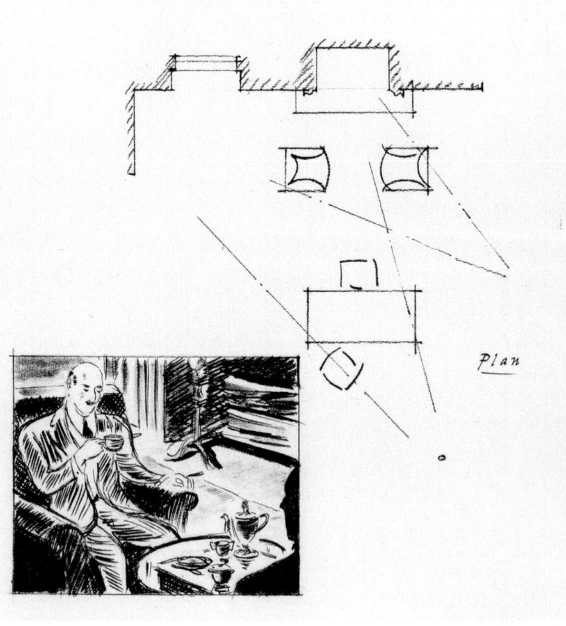

Above:
Sketch (attributed to Albert Pyke) for the parlour of Mrs Kane's boarding house. The child is already present behind the window, but the organization of the rooms in a line from the window has yet to be decided.

Left:
Storyboard for Thompson's visit to Bernstein.

Opposite page:
In the film the spatial arrangement was modified by the removal of the two armchairs under Kane's portrait and the decision to shoot from a single angle towards the right instead of to the left.

Left:
Welles, Erskine Sanford (Carter) and Joseph Cotten (Leland). The scene is set in 1890, but Kane's clothes have a distinctly 1920s cut, thus emphasizing the character's modernity.

Opposite page, top:
Kane hurls curses at the back of the departing Gettys after the confrontational scene in Susan's apartment.

Opposite page, bottom:
Welles setting up the scene at the foot of the staircase.

revealed in the newsreel, all that remained was to investigate the meaning of his last word. But Mankiewicz's somewhat pedestrian original version (which would have resulted in a three-hour film) was hampered by apparently irresolvable structural problems such as the evocation of Kane's youthful escapades in Italy (which slowed down the narrative), and his marriage to his first wife, Emily (if Kane was dead and Emily – still alive in this version – refused to talk about him, who would provide an account of their life together?).

Mankiewicz and Houseman completed a second draft and delivered it at the beginning of May. Although a great improvement on the first version, the main problems had still not been resolved. RKO's technical departments then began estimating production costs and preparing a shooting schedule. Welles thoroughly revised the script over the next few weeks, frequently resorting to 'montage' sequences in order to speed up the slowest scenes. He also deleted entire episodes and amalgamated others in order to simplify and revitalize the story. Welles was therefore directly responsible for the third (early June) and fourth (18 June) drafts. The fourth draft was the first to bear the title *Citizen Kane.*

This draft was considered the final version, but Welles and Mankiewicz (back on the payroll on 18 June after six weeks on another assignment) worked together on three further drafts, finishing the last on 16 July. Kane and Emily's breakfast scene, for example, an elegant rendering of the decline of a marriage over a twelve-year period, did not appear until the sixth draft (2 July). Every change was designed to simplify, tighten and speed up the action by reducing the number of sets and actors to the minimum, for the mid-June budget estimate was still too high.

The guiding principles changed between the first and final drafts. Many of the structural flaws in *American* arose from the fact that the witnesses could only recount what they knew from their own experience. Welles rejected this approach and replaced it with two others: dramatic continuity would be ensured by linking sequences dealing with the same issues (beginning with the origin and management of Kane's fortune, and following on with the *Inquirer* newspaper, the marriage to Emily, political activity, the marriage to Susan, etc.), while most of Kane's biography would unfold in chronological order. Although the newsreel constantly shifted back and forth in time, the witnesses who followed it retraced Kane's life in a linear fashion, beginning with the guardian who knew him as a boy and ending with the butler who worked for him during his final ten years. Two striking deviations from the general rules would be enough to create the illusion of a non-chronological puzzle. The first involved one of the witnesses referring to events that had occurred forty years before those described by the previous witness. The second, an even more radical departure, concerned Susan's account, which opened with a scene set slightly before the one that had concluded the previous account. This offered another version of the disastrous opening night of the opera *Salammbô* experienced not from the point of view of the drama critic Leland but from that of the reluctant prima donna.

Nevertheless, the 16 July shooting script was still a provisional document. All the brainstorming of the previous few weeks had been conducted with the close involvement of the cameraman and art director, whose innovative technical solutions had persuaded Welles that further improvements could be gained by adjusting his shot breakdown. Besides the newsreel, which gradually took shape as editing progressed, certain scenes were heavily revised as they were filmed and new episodes added, almost all of them inspired by the constant desire to convey the passage of time as economically as possible. Some changes took the form of quasi-autonomous sequences, as when Thatcher fulminates against the *Inquirer* headlines, or when Kane is forced to sell his newspapers to his former guardian. Others involved a series of moments that are clearly separate in time, such as the progression of short scenes from the boarding house where Susan first plays the piano for Kane to the political rally in Madison Square Garden, which encompass the apartment where Kane has installed Susan, now his mistress, and Leland's street-corner electoral harangue. The Welles–Mankiewicz partnership made for a rich and ambiguous film.

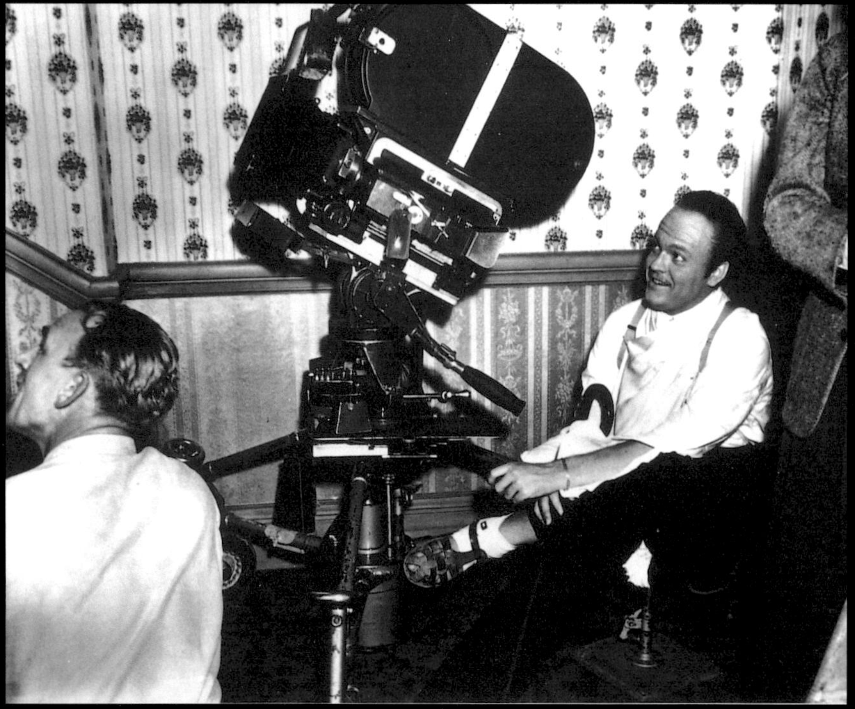

Everett Sloane, Welles
and Joseph Cotten.

KANE MEETS SUSAN · #1 · SEE OTHER CARD FOR PLANS

EXT. DRUG STORE & STREET - WEST SIDE - N.Y. & INT SUSAN'S 1ST APARTMENT.

FADE IN ON SUSAN COMING OUT OF DRUG STORE HOLDING FACE BECAUSE OF TOOTHACHE (WET STREETS - R.K.O. RANCH) SHE STARTS TO

WALK TOWARD HER APARTMENT AND AS ARRIVES IN FRONT

KANE COMES FROM OPPOSITE DIRECTION - STEPPING ON

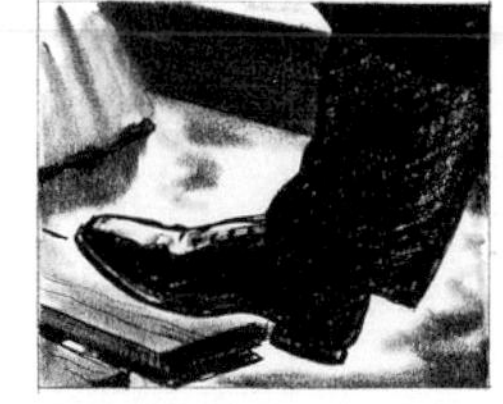

AS LOOSE BOARD PUT THERE TO BRIDGE A MUD PUDDLE IT

FLYS UP SPLATTERING HIM WITH MUD AND AT ONE AND

THE SAME TIME BUMPING INTO SUSAN - SHE INVITES HIM IN TO GET CLEANED UP

AND THEY ENTER APARTMENT HOUSE

PICK THEM UP ABOUT TO GO INTO THEIR DOOR AND CUT TO

INSIDE APARTMENT AS THEY ENTER FOLLOW AS

KANE GOES TO BUREAU - EXAMINING THIS AND THAT - SUSAN IN BATHROOM IN BACK G

SHE BRINGS HIM WATER IN BASIN AND THEY DO BUSINESS OF CLEANING UP - DISSOLVE TO

SHADOW OF DUCK ON WALL PULLING BACK SHOWING KANE DOING TRICKS

FOR SUSAN - FROM HERE GO TO PIANO SEQUENCE AS

SUSAN SINGS FOR KANE AS MA PERKINS ENTERS FROM REAR -

DIALOUGE BETWEEN THE THREE END WITH BEER NOTION - (CONTINUED)

Opposite page, top:
Two drawings for Kane's visit to the newspaper office after the opera performance.

Opposite page, bottom:
Joseph Cotten and Everett Sloane act the scene under the watchful eye of script supervisor Amalia Kent.

Above:
Storyboard for Kane and Susan's first encounter.

Left:
Welles and Dorothy Comingore.

Overleaf, left and right:
Joseph Cotten, Welles and Everett Sloane.

One believed in 'Rosebud', while the other did not. For Mankiewicz, Kane's last utterance served to explain the course his life had taken. For Welles, it was simply a dramatic device, the kind of fake argument that Hitchcock would later call a 'McGuffin'. Instead of resolving anything, the film's ending offers a number of contradictory conclusions. Some seem to tie up all the threads, while others suggest that Xanadu's secrets will remain impenetrable. Welles contributed so much to the successive stages of the script that at one point he considered taking sole credit for it, as the terms of Mankiewicz's contract allowed him to do. However, he abandoned this idea in the face of vehement protests from his co-author, who would later himself claim sole credit.

The budget ($723,800) received final approval on 2 July. This was much less than the initial estimates and represented a relatively modest sum for such an ambitious production, although it was still higher than the agreed figure. Welles would manage to keep the overspend down to twelve per cent.

THE FIRST TEAM

Welles recruited most of his collaborators from within RKO. He was now sufficiently familiar with the studio and knew which of its technicians would respond to his desire for innovation. He rejected the services of a veteran editor and opted for the younger Robert Wise. Most of the crew were aged between twenty-five and forty. When preparing *Heart of Darkness*, Welles had not had the opportunity to work with a cinematographer. On this occasion, however, he was able to benefit from the expertise of Gregg Toland, a cameraman with a reputation for speed and inventiveness, who had joined the project at an early stage. Welles had asked RKO to borrow Toland from the independent producer Samuel Goldwyn, who had given Toland the freedom to develop his own ideas. Toland was heavily involved in pre-production two months before shooting started, working closely with Perry Ferguson, an art director noted for his ability to come up with original solutions and reduce expenditure on major productions. Encouraged to use their initiative, Toland and Ferguson collaborated with the director on a detailed strategy that had to be strong enough to guarantee visual consistency and originality, and flexible enough to adapt to the contingencies of the shoot.

When assembling his cast, Welles focused on newcomers to the screen, almost all of whom were recruited from his Mercury players in New York; he also hired several radio actors he had worked with in Los Angeles. Like Welles himself, the character actors Joseph Cotten (Leland), Everett Sloane (Bernstein, Kane's business manager) and George Coulouris (Thatcher) would all be called upon to play men at different stages in their lives. They were assisted by Maurice Seiderman, a twenty-five-year-old make-up artist with no formal experience but a flair for designing and perfecting new processes and materials, many of which would find their way into the film. Welles would ask for Seiderman's services in some of the later films he acted in. The only real outsiders were the actresses who played Kane's two wives: Ruth Warrick (Emily) had never appeared before the camera and Dorothy Comingore (Susan) had played only minor parts. Bernard Herrmann, the Mercury composer, was also brought on board.

Welles's strength lay in the fact that once his collaborators were under contract, they answered only to their director. He often defied the RKO studio heads, shooting scenes under the guise of 'tests', or bringing work to a halt when studio representatives walked on to the set. He set a furious pace, racked up the overtime, often filmed at night and would work round the clock. There were very few protests: his enthusiasm and energy were contagious, and it was abundantly clear that his stylistic daring required more than adherence to routine practices.

ABANDONED STORYBOARDS

The storyboard, one of the keys to the film's pre-production, was standard practice in the major Hollywood studios. Since the early 1930s specialist illustrators had been employed to create hundreds of drawings that break down the action and narrative progression. This method enabled the director and his crew to identify those parts of the sets that would appear on the screen and thus avoid any unnecessary set construction. Storyboards also enabled the director and cameraman, who were often assigned to the project after the main choices had been made, to plan the principal angles of a scene, check its continuity and agree on the lighting options.

Top:
The set for the Great Hall at Xanadu.

Above:
The sketch for the set by Claude Gillingwater, Jr.

Right:
A publicity photograph reveals the face (which the viewer never sees in the film) of the reporter Thompson (William Alland), shown here with Raymond (Paul Stewart).

The importance of what were then known as 'continuity sketches' was particularly evident when a project was entrusted to an inexperienced director, as was Welles at that time. They were not meant to provide a model for the *mise en scène* – the anonymous illustrators were simply carrying out instructions – but to act as a visual guide for the scenes that had been suggested by the script and further developed in the shooting script and at pre-production meetings.

A number of the *Citizen Kane* storyboards have been preserved. Based on the second draft of the script submitted to the studio at the beginning of May, they often illustrate scenes that were later abandoned; but they also provide a vivid demonstration of the freshness of Welles's approach whenever he chose to follow a different course. In effect, the storyboards tend to reflect a conventional *mise en scène* based on shot breakdown and the fragmentation of space. After close consultation with Toland and Ferguson, Welles decided to ignore the storyboards, going on to devise astonishingly simple solutions which, in every case, attempted to preserve the spatial and temporal continuity of the scene in question.

The storyboard for the scene in Mrs Kane's boarding house depicts the mother turning away from the window, then joining her husband and the banker Thatcher on the right-hand side of the frame in order to continue their discussion before exiting through the adjoining hall. This version, which breaks up space and has the action moving parallel to the back wall, suggests the traditional resort to editing to recall the presence of the young Kane standing outside the house. When, in actual fact, Welles shot the scene, he preferred to set the camera in front of the window and film the action in a double movement, the camera dollying back then advancing, while the child outside remains visible. This long take is echoed in the following shot which, in contrast to the storyboard, is filmed from outside, portraying the mother in a reverse shot before she emerges into the snow-covered courtyard.

Similarly, the storyboard for the first encounter between Kane and Susan is divided into half a dozen different shots, while Welles would only film two shots: one in the street showing Susan leaving the drugstore and passing the already mud-spattered Kane; the other showing the couple entering Susan's apartment. Here again, Welles's choices demonstrate his desire for rigorous continuity. Both shots also simplify the sequence by deleting superfluous sets (the hall of the apartment house, the bathroom), and even the minor character of the landlady.

DEEP FOCUS

Since the late 1920s classical Hollywood filmmaking had favoured an extremely softly-lit image that contained very little depth. There was a simple reason for this: the sensitivity of the film stock was so poor that cameramen were obliged to work with very large lens apertures in order to capture the maximum amount of light. In order to restrict the distortions that resulted when fully open, these lenses were usually of average focal length (32–40 mm), which limited the amount of space that could be encompassed and reduced the depth of field. Close-ups, a key element of the classical aesthetic, were idealized by the blurred area surrounding the actor. Space, limited in scope when using lenses of average focal length, had to be divided into complementary points of view by way of using the shot-reverse-shot pattern and then reunified through editing.

With Toland's agreement, Welles opted for a deep focus image in which everything, from foreground to background, would be equally sharp. Toland had already experimented with the concept in recent films such as William Wyler's *Wuthering Heights* and John Ford's *The Long Voyage Home*. He systematized it for Welles, who was also the first to fully grasp its implications for the language of film. To achieve the required result, Toland and Welles had to rent a Cooke lens with a very short focal length (24 mm, the widest angle available), which offered an exceptionally great depth of field: 55 cm to infinity for a focus adjustment at 1.20 metres. However, optics of this kind distorted the image, precluding the use of close-ups (there are very few in the film) and meaning that nothing of importance could be positioned at the sides of the frame, where the spatial curve was most pronounced. The choice of a wide-angle lens immediately became a key element in the creation of a film in which the action always seems to be drawn towards the background. In many scenes the action in the far background assumes as much importance as the events taking place in the foreground. This is apparent, for example, in the arresting scene that places Kane prominently in the foreground so that he dwarfs the tiny figure of Susan, lost in the depths of Xanadu's vast hearth. It is also apparent in the spatial organization of the scene in which Kane fires Leland: Kane, in the foreground, occupies a third of the frame; in the background, the small figure of Bernstein stands out in the illuminated doorframe; Leland, in the middle ground, leans towards Kane over a wooden railing, thus emphasizing the depth of field.

ARC LAMPS MAKE A COMEBACK

In order to create a deep focus image, there had to be some means of ensuring that all spatial planes were sharply defined. The classical Hollywood image offered no precedent, as its composition required the use of tungsten lights to soften outlines and balance the lighting systematically, thus avoiding areas of shadow. Once again, Welles and Toland came up with their own solution.

To obtain the desired depth of field, they had to close the lens stop to the maximum. In other words, they had to reduce the quantity of light allowed in at risk of under-exposing the image. To avoid that, they adopted the multi-layered anti-reflective lenses that had recently come on to the market, which restricted the loss of light and simultaneously enhanced the sharpness of the image. Welles and Toland also opted for a new type of film stock, Eastman Kodak Super XX, which was four times more sensitive than the Super X generally in use. But rather than take advantage of the enhanced sensitivity to reduce the lighting, as many other filmmakers were doing, they re-introduced the powerful arc lamps that the studios had more or less abandoned ten years earlier, using them to light the action in a highly directional way, usually from the sides of the set.

Arc lamps played a significant role in the construction of a deep focus scene. They emphasized the successive planes of which the scene was composed, and added visual drama to the characters' movements by making them pass through areas of shadow and light as they moved back and forth in the axis of the camera. When Kane gives up his press empire to Thatcher, his retreat to the background reveals the vast dimensions of the set; when the old man returns towards the camera, the successive areas of light and shadow add rhythm to his passage.

Previous pages:
Dorothy Comingore in the Great Hall at Xanadu.

Right:
Make-up artist Maurice Seiderman modelling a plaster head of Kane, which will be used to devise the make-up.

Below:
The set of the bedroom Kane is about to destroy was constructed on a platform so that two cameras could shoot simultaneously from a low angle.

HEAVY CEILINGS

The lateral lighting ploy was also justified by the impossibility of placing projectors above the sets, the usual practice at the time. Short focus does more than expand the angle of the shots horizontally: it also augments them vertically, so that floors and ceilings, which were usually cut out, appear in the frame. The ceilings that Welles and Perry Ferguson built on a number of sets were important in three respects. First, they contributed to the dramatic effect by accentuating the impression of the characters' confinement in a tight space. Second, they had a physical function, as the beams and other supports heightened the impression of depth by establishing a line of markers that guided the eye towards the background. Third, the muslin sheets stretched between the beams prevented any lighting from above (which would make them translucent), but they allowed microphones to be placed above the action, thus decisively solving the problem of recording sound in confined spaces, in which the cumbersome microphones tended to cast shadows.

Ceilings were systematically employed on sets of average height – the boarding house, the *Inquirer* offices in New York and Chicago, the love nest in which Kane installs his mistress. They were also used to great effect in the two scenes shot entirely from an extreme, almost vertical, low angle: the confrontation between Leland and Kane after the electoral defeat, and Kane's destruction of Susan's bedroom in Xanadu. In the latter case, the ceiling, adorned with images of familiar animals, is the only indication that the bedroom is not so much Susan's as the room designed for the child the couple were unable to have. In both scenes, the low angles required to produce grotesque distortions of characters consumed by anger and loss were so crucial to Welles's vision that floors had to be built to a considerable height so that the crew would have enough room to work between set and studio floors.

SIMULATING OPULENCE ON SET

In terms of expenditure on sets, *Citizen Kane* seemed well on its way to setting a record. The story constantly shifted from one place to another, never staying in one location for more than a few minutes. There were thirty-five main sets covering a period of seventy years, and another sixty secondary sets which, although appearing on the screen only briefly, were still absolutely essential to the film. Further complications arose from the fact that the script demanded several sets of immense proportions – Thatcher's library, Bernstein's office, and especially the interiors for Xanadu, the opulent but glacial palace Kane had erected to his own glory. Nevertheless, set construction costs were remarkably low – at barely seven per cent of the overall production costs, they amounted to half the sum anticipated. Welles, Toland and Ferguson achieved savings by preparing everything in minute detail, determining what was indispensable and devising the cheapest way of obtaining it.

The general rule governing set design was that sets would be filmed from a single angle whenever possible, the angle being indicated on all the preparatory sketches. Set construction was therefore limited to whatever would be visible in the frame, although this restricted camera movements and Welles would not be able to change his mind at the last minute – there would be no opportunity for reverse shots.

The set for Thatcher's library is thus not the one depicted in the storyboard, but a reduced area encompassed within the angle formed by the statue's massive pedestal, the desk beneath it, the great door in the wall, the long table aligned behind it and, at the very back, the safe built into a second wall. The angle is only reversed in the final shot of the sequence, which reveals the large portrait of Kane hanging on the other side of the door.

For the more complex sets, or for those that could not easily be designed on such a straight line (the opera house and the Madison Square Garden conference hall, for instance), Welles filmed limited portions of the sets (stage, lectern, audience), which were not physically connected to each other but linked through a network of visual and sound effects during the editing. The great hall at Xanadu was reduced to a few specifics (the staircase, the jigsaw-puzzle table, the hearth) which were linked by an assortment of architectural elements in order to create an illusion of profusion.

A RIOT OF SPECIAL EFFECTS

Special effects were used to create the more imposing elements of the scenery. RKO was noted for its high-quality special effects, having acquired exceptional expertise in the use of matte paintings (chiefly the work of Mario Larrinaga) and optical tricks (devised by Linwood G. Dunn) ten years earlier, when Ernest B. Schoedsack and Merian C. Cooper began work on *King Kong*.

Toland was reluctant to use effects over which he had no control and preferred to concentrate on those he could create himself with the aid of his camera. The final segment of Susan's suicide attempt, for example, which places the young woman in a shadowy area between an equally sharp foreground and background, was the fruit of two successive exposures of the same strip of film: one a shot of the glass in the foreground and the other a shot of the door through which Kane would burst. However, as filming progressed, Welles entrusted more and more special effects work to the capable hands of studio technicians. This would account for considerable overruns, in terms of time as well as budget, during post-production.

The film benefits from the full panoply of optical special effects, from the simplest (the occasional use of back projection, for example) to the most complex. At the time the most common technique was the matte shot, which enabled a painted set and live action to be combined during post-production. Welles made spectacular use of it, beginning with the opening advance to the single illuminated window at Xanadu: although the angle never varies, every shot of the enormous building reveals some new aspect that situates it differently, so that its shape changes constantly in relation to its surroundings. The blatantly obvious resort to *trompe-l'oeil* actually enhances the prologue's sinister and fantastical atmosphere. Matte shots were later used in the more conventional invisible manner for inserting a group of (real) journalists into a window on the *Inquirer* office's (painted) facade, for adorning Xanadu's great hall with huge gothic windows, and for replacing the Californian hills with Florida's flat landscape when Kane and Susan depart for the picnic.

Left:
Welles with Buddy Swan (Kane as a child).

Below and opposite page:
Shooting the final scene.

Welles was quick to appreciate the endless possibilities of Dunn's optical printer, a projector coupled to a camera loaded with new film: once shot, footage could be manipulated in any number of ways. He used the printer to achieve the enormous close-up of Kane's lips murmuring 'Rosebud' (a simple enlargement of one part of the image), and the fake travelling shot that homes in on the name on the burning sledge (a series of images shot as the frame tightens around the subject). It also gave him the opportunity to create opposite effects: the sudden animation of the photograph of the *Chronicle* reporters (a transition from the result – the fixed image – to the moment the photograph was taken), and the facade of the love nest, which turns into a newspaper photograph (a real image becomes a printed illustration). Many of the film's extraordinary visual transitions were created with the aid of the optical printer.

Some of these transitions are deliberately designed to be seen, as with the dissolve that ends the picnic scene and unites Susan's eye and the eye in a stained-glass window at Xanadu. Others rely on total invisibility, as with the wipes that sweep away one shot and replace it with another. The technique is unremarkable when used simply to ensure a smooth link between two scenes in the editing process, but in Welles's hands it acquires a unique versatility. For example, a single, seemingly continuous pan connects the statue of Thatcher (a small-scale model) to its massive (full-size) pedestal. The technique works even more impressively when Leland describes Susan's opera debut: once again, Welles resorts to inconspicuous wipes and makes us believe that the camera starts from the singer's open mouth, before it soars up to the wings to reveal the disapproving stagehands. What appears to be a single shot is actually five, all welded together by various tricks, including two successive wipes that maintain the illusion of continuity. The stage set is real, as is the stagehands' catwalk; the ascending pan that links them is achieved by means of a model of the machinery cables – in the camera's illusory upward trajectory, the shot of the stage gives way to a shot of the cables, which in turn gives way to a shot of the wings. Welles demonstrates an extraordinary awareness of what can be achieved with these effects, as well as an inexhaustible ability to find new uses for them and an exceptional mastery of the ways in which they can be integrated into other images. His handling of special effects confirms what we have already learnt from his work with framing, lighting and sets: Welles, conducting his first proper experiment with the cinematographic image, immediately identified it as something that had to be created rather than reproduced.

SEAMLESS EDITING

Leaving aside the prologue of Kane's death in Xanadu, which ends with a fade to black, the transitions from one sequence to the next are so adroit that the film unfolds as a seamless series of images. This flawless continuity is all the more remarkable as the film is composed of relatively autonomous segments that displace the action in place and time, and presuppose large gaps in the narrative thread.

While Welles had encouraged Toland and Ferguson to use their initiative, he was not about to let his editor, Robert Wise, tamper with his first film. Wise had to follow the instructions laid down in a shooting script that had been implemented after minute pre-production: it restricted angles, envisaged most of the transitions and included a large number of long takes. The concern to set the editing style at an early stage is particularly apparent in the transitions from one sequence to another and in the almost systematic recourse to dissolves based on incredibly precise visual links. At their simplest, these take the form of the blank page Thompson finds in the manuscript of Thatcher's memoirs, which becomes the snow in which the child Kane is playing. A much more complex example is the shot of Kane's head at the end of Susan's opera performance, which becomes the photograph of Leland that accompanies his review of *Salammbô* in the following day's newspaper. Moreover, long takes offered the editor no opportunity to introduce his own ideas. This is a risky approach for a novice director, especially when his cast is not familiar with the techniques of the medium. In fact, it calls for a complete mastery of every element of the sequence, and total confidence in the way in which each of them can be slotted into the broader continuity. Scorning the conventional breakdown indicated by the storyboards, Welles increased the number of long takes and became so fond of them that he would not hesitate to fake their continuity by stitching them together with invisible seams, as in the apparent pan from Susan's mouth to the stagehands in the wings.

Welles's initiation into the mysteries of editing left him with much more than a knowledge of the mechanics of transitions, for the method could be honed to perfection if the shooting script left no room for last-minute innovations. He had experienced the exhilaration of the long take; and the godlike power of creating something perfectly formed.

THE ACTOR AND HIS TROUPE

The tight grip Welles exercised on composition and editing presented the actors with several challenges demanding an extraordinary degree of precision. Long takes were complicated by the frequently overlapping dialogue and the actors' tendency, when positioned behind each other in the frame, to encroach on each other or move out of the light. Welles stepped up collective readings before the shoot. He devoted yet more time to on-set rehearsals, working out the actors' relative positions and giving the actors the chance to discover from within themselves the nuances of the role rather than impose his own interpretation. He was constantly attentive to his cast's reaction and would overturn a lighting or dialogue instruction in order to make an actor feel more at ease, or modify his concept of a character if an actor brought something new to the role.

On the other hand, once the scene had been worked out, the restrictions imposed by the lighting, positioning of actors and delivery of lines left no margin of flexibility. Welles would then become intransigent and shoot as many takes as necessary to obtain what he wanted. Paul Stewart (the Xanadu butler) recalled one instance: the continuous scene in which Kane gives up his press empire to Thatcher. The scene is very long (just over two minutes) and particularly complicated, focusing first on Bernstein alone, and then on Bernstein and Thatcher, before introducing Kane, who moves towards the background before advancing to take a seat in the foreground. Throughout the first part of the take, the camera strategy relies on the appearance of characters who had previously been concealed by a prop, or by another character who has to move aside. The co-ordination of all these elements was so complex that an entire day was lost in trying to perfect it. Welles was forced to give up after more than a hundred takes, which, according to the all-or-nothing logic of the lengthy shot, were not worth printing. But he stubbornly returned to the fray the following day and filmed until he got what he wanted.

Difficulties arose during rehearsals because the director was also the leading actor in most of the shots. When he had to direct himself he began as an actor, feeding a line to his partners and determining their positions. Once satisfied that everyone was on the right marks, he had himself replaced with a double while he discussed the camera movements and lighting with Toland. He then returned to act the scene for the camera, but would accept only the judgement of his most trusted technicians when deciding what was good enough to send to the lab.

Extending the boundaries of a technique that Frank Capra, Gregory La Cava and Howard Hawks had already used to great effect in their comedies, Welles turned overlapping dialogue into a personal trademark. Apart from its influence on the density and vivacity of the film (and on the overall structure, as Welles used different rhythms of dialogue for different scenes), the overlapping lines created a spirit of rivalry among the actors and enhanced the group dynamic. As Welles remarked: 'It can be taught in about two hours. We need three very good actors and a little exercise in it ... You have to drill them so that the right syllable comes at the right moment. It's exactly like conducting an orchestra.' His assistant, Richard Wilson, confirmed that Welles would rehearse to the syllable rather than the word. In *Citizen Kane*, the overlapping lines are far from inaudible; they emerge with greater clarity thanks to their contrasting rhythms and the vocal range employed in their delivery. Even when three characters are talking at once, every line is sharp and intelligible. The secret was probably at least partly due to Welles's insistence that one line should never cut into another in the middle of a syllable, the overlap had to occur either between two words or between two syllables of the same word. He also used the technique as a tool in the power relations between characters, letting them assert dominance by interrupting their interlocutors and blocking any attempt to get back into the discussion.

INTERWOVEN SOUND

The sound in *Citizen Kane* is just as innovative as the photography. Welles refused to let dialogue take precedence over sound effects and music, but attempted to create a mosaic of all three elements, so that they constantly overlapped and sometimes even replaced each other, only to spin off in another densely interwoven pattern. Many of the sound transitions that inextricably bind one sequence to another were established during the scriptwriting phase.

Brimming with the confidence derived from his theatrical and radio experience, Welles reversed roles and became a mentor to James G. Stewart, the imaginative head of sound post-production at RKO. He also hired his chief sound effects man from CBS, Harry Essman, who would be responsible for some of the more stylized effects. He ensured that Stewart's

The figures of Welles (top) and Dorothy Comingore (bottom) reveal the vast dimensions of the sets.

6.

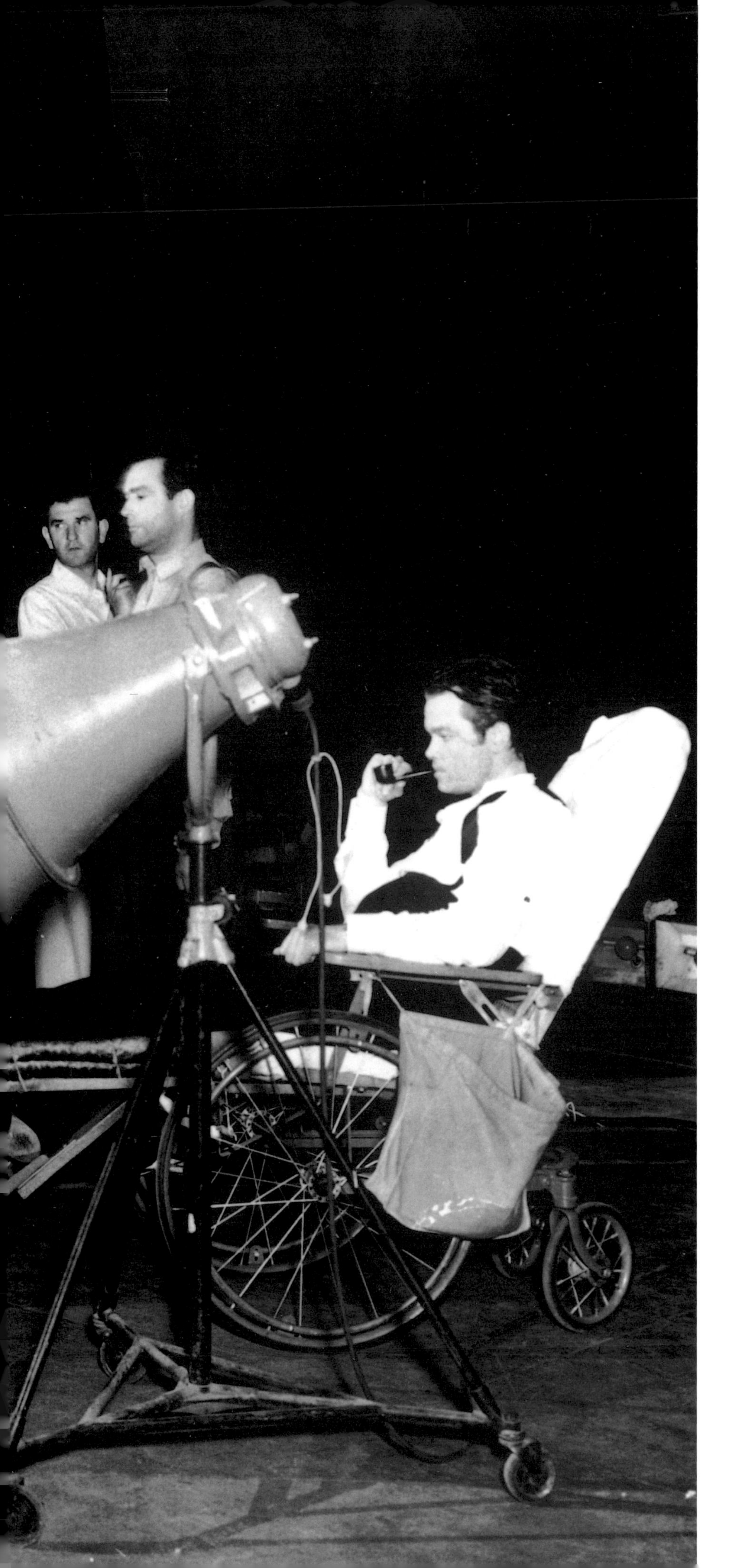

Immobilized with
a sprained ankle,
Welles directs Dorothy
Comingore (Susan)
as she makes her debut
as an opera singer.
Gregg Toland crouches
beneath the camera.
The French lyrics of the
aria from *Salammbô* are
written on the blackboard
opposite the actress.
A loudspeaker in the
foreground is ready
to broadcast the pre-
recorded aria.

Left:
Welles and Bernard Herrmann, who, after *Citizen Kane*, became one of the most sought after composers in Hollywood.

Opposite page:
Harry Shannon (Kane's father), George Coulouris (Thatcher), Agnes Moorehead (Kane's mother) and Buddy Swan (Kane as a child).

unit had the means to work on a given sequence until it was completely satisfied with the result. Although most of the dialogue was recorded live, Welles familiarized himself with post-synchronization techniques, which enabled him to construct a soundscape by adding elements in post-production. He looked for ways – echo and reverberation, footsteps that varied according to the surface of the floor – to express the sensation of space, whether claustrophobic or vast. He sometimes used a single sound to add colour to a scene, or would graft a number of different sounds on to the dialogue or music simply to punctuate a line or fill the pause between two sentences. For example, the rasp of a horn from a passing car mockingly completes the empty threats Kane hurls at Gettys (Ray Collins), his political enemy. And in a street scene we hear no traffic, but when Gettys asks Emily if she has a car, the toot of a horn underlines his question; another punctuates Emily's affirmative response; and a final toot triggers the music that introduces the following sequence. Here, and indeed throughout the entire film, all the sounds are perfectly meshed.

THE MUSIC: CONSTANT REFINEMENTS

Thanks to Welles, Bernard Herrmann, making his cinematic debut with *Citizen Kane*, enjoyed working conditions of which most professional screen composers could only dream. Herrmann was on the payroll for fourteen weeks instead of the usual four to six. This gave him the opportunity to orchestrate and conduct his score as well as compose it – a marked departure from standard Hollywood practice, which usually entrusted these tasks to separate figures. Herrmann was present as the final drafts of the script were delivered and wrote the music as the shoot progressed, rather than after completion of the editing. The music plays a major role in defining the film's structure, particularly with regard to transitions between sequences, flashbacks, and 'montage sequences' like those of Kane and Emily at the breakfast table.

Welles issued Herrmann with extremely detailed instructions for the music arising from the action itself. In the *Salammbô* sequence, for example, the curtain rises and Susan begins to sing an aria which, by means of discreet dissolve, continues over the entire course of the opera, ending when the curtain falls less than three minutes later. Welles also suggested the use of existing melodies, some of which were arranged by studio composers.

As for the original music, Welles had very clear-cut ideas about the effects he wanted from it, about its position in relation to the editing and the principles of its orchestration. Herrmann and Welles reserved an identifiable symphonic texture for the ending, and opted for a constantly renewed selection of small instrumental combinations. They experimented with the highest and lowest registers of various instruments, as in the first sombre bars of the prologue, where the woodwind and brass descend to the limits of their possibilities. Their background in radio also gave them the idea for the five- to twenty-five-second bridges between sequences. On the other hand, the interweaving of recurrent themes and their role in the overall musical structure was largely the composer's responsibility. Herrmann based his score on two themes, each initially consisting of five notes. One, derived from the *Dies Iræ* of the Gregorian Mass for the Dead and probably owing something to its constant evocation in Rachmaninov's *Isle of the Dead*, signifies Kane's 'Power'; the other discreetly signifies 'Rosebud'. Owing to their brevity, they could easily be refashioned to fit the demands of mood and timing. Closely interwoven at first, they become separate after the boarding-house scene when the Rosebud motif, in the guise of an oboe solo, is cut short by its rival as the mother grabs the boy after he strikes Thatcher with his sledge, and leads him towards the banker who will take him away from her. Herrmann stresses the malleable Power theme, allowing the sinuous flow of its entrances and exits to overlay the more elusive Rosebud, which signals the moments when Thompson walks past a clue to the enigma. The Rosebud theme assumes its most melodic form just before the dying Kane utters his last word. Having accompanied the shots of the sledge with its label obscured by snow, and the various appearances of snowballs or glass balls associated with the memory of Kane's mother, it eventually comes to the fore in the protracted sequence accompanying the final exploration of Xanadu's treasures, swelling to a climax in the close-up of the sledge being consumed by flames, although we can make out the name inscribed on it.

The brevity of the themes enabled constant revision. Welles cut certain sequences to fit the recorded score, but in other cases the composer had to revise the music to conform to the editing strategy. Almost all the cues were shortened, and some reduced to their most basic form. Herrmann attended the mixing sessions to ensure that the logic of the music would not be jeopardized by any last-minute adjustments.

PROMETHEUS UNBOUND

Welles made a spectacular Hollywood debut with his first film, which also launched the screen careers of Bernard Herrmann, Joseph Cotten and several other actors who were soon signed up by major companies. He had earned a reputation for discovering talent and, despite the delays on his initial projects and the relative failure of *Citizen Kane* at the box office, had proved that a writer-producer-director-actor could prevail.

Welles had also demonstrated, with considerable flair, that he had grasped the full potential of the supremely efficient Hollywood studio system. *Citizen Kane*, however, was merely the first step, enabling him to explore every aspect of the system, including its limits. There was still room for improvement, both on the set and in the editing suite, but it was simply a matter of consolidating the fundamental lesson he had learned from *Citizen Kane*: a film resists its creator and demands a life of its own.

THREE FILMS ON TWO CONTINENTS
1941–1942

Welles filmed almost continuously from late October 1941 to late July 1942, interweaving the making of *The Magnificent Ambersons*, *Journey into Fear* and *It's All True* to such an extent that the fate of each film affected that of the others. Having initially encouraged this frenzied activity, RKO eventually realized it was losing control and reined in its unpredictable (and now unwanted) young prodigy. *Citizen Kane*, released with great fanfare in May 1941, was immediately acclaimed by American critics as one of the greatest films ever made. But William Randolph Hearst's powerful press empire regarded the portrait of Kane as a frontal attack on its founder and attempted to prevent the film's release, running a campaign of intimidation against RKO and threatening to extend it to every Hollywood studio. Hearst's newspapers refused to advertise the film and some cinema chains, fearing reprisals, chose not to show it.

By the end of its first run *Citizen Kane* had lost eighteen per cent of its investment, although this in itself was no great cause for alarm – every studio had its good years and bad years; if a film died at the box office, the volume of production would cover the losses. The disappointing returns weakened Welles's position at RKO, but not as much as the costly postponements and cancellations that had marked his Hollywood debut – of the two films planned before the end of 1940, only one had been delivered.

Previous pages, left:
With Tim Holt during the filming of *The Magnificent Ambersons.*

Previous pages, right:
Paul Stewart, Everett Sloane and Welles during rehearsals for *Native Son* (1941), adapted from the novel by Richard Wright. Welles staged the play in New York immediately after finishing *Citizen Kane.*

Above:
With John Barrymore, Dolores Del Rio and George Schaefer, president of RKO, at the premiere of *Citizen Kane* in Los Angeles.

Opposite page, top:
The cast of a patriotic show broadcast the week after the bombing of Pearl Harbor. Standing: Welles, Rudy Vallee, (unidentified), Bernard Herrmann, Edward G. Robinson, (unidentified), James Stewart, Norman Corwin, (unidentified) and Edward Arnold. Seated: Lionel Barrymore, Marjorie Main and Walter Huston.

Opposite page, right:
Welles and some of *The Magnificent Ambersons* crew: camera operator Jim Daley, editor Robert Wise, production assistant Richard Wilson, cameraman Stanley Cortez and gaffer Jimmy Almond.

However, RKO had no reason to break the contract with its brilliant producer. During the winter and into the spring of 1941 Welles, involved in the early stages of other projects and rehearsing a Mercury play in New York, also prepared an anti-fascist suspense thriller, *The Way to Santiago*, a loose adaptation of an English novel, which he had restructured around one of his favourite themes – amnesia. He planned to shoot the exteriors in Mexico, with Perry Ferguson as set designer and Gregg Toland behind the camera, and to star opposite him his new partner, the leading actress Dolores Del Rio. The project proceeded in fits and starts for the best part of a year, plagued by logistical problems and bogged down in negotiations with the Mexican government. Welles planned either to direct the film himself, or entrust it to low-budget specialist Norman Foster. In effect, Welles's contract had been amended to reduce the number of functions he was required to fulfil. On the one hand, this strengthened his position as a producer: he could nourish his dream of a long-term production unit and initiate projects without having to direct all of them. He envisaged an alternating programme of original screenplays, adaptations of the western literary canon and lighter material such as detective stories and spy thrillers. On the other hand, the postponement of the shoots he had already lined up meant that he would not be paid until one of the projects came to fruition. Faced with constant financial problems, Welles had been forced to take a decision which, in the long run, precipitated the decline of his relations with the studio: in order to gain a breathing space and avoid a decisive parting of the ways, he sacrificed his most valuable asset – the right to the final cut. According to the new agreement, RKO retained the final say on the budget and casting, but Welles now had to accept that beyond the first cut, the studio also had the right to 'subtract from, arrange, rearrange, revise and adapt [...] the picture in any manner.' Once an almost completely free agent, he had been reduced to an employee.

During the summer, he began working on three different projects: *The Magnificent Ambersons*, from a novel by Booth Tarkington; the anthology film *It's All True*; and, at the insistence of RKO, *Journey into Fear*, an adaptation of an espionage thriller by Eric Ambler. Welles wrote the *Ambersons* script himself, commissioned screenplays from different writers for the second film, and co-wrote the third. RKO began preparing all three films simultaneously. In mid-September, Welles also started producing and directing a weekly radio programme, *The Lady Esther Show*, with Bernard Herrmann overseeing the music. Always eager to cross-promote Mercury's activities, he invited the cast of *The Magnificent Ambersons* to appear on the show a week before filming began.

As time went on, the three films became increasingly entangled. In late September, after involvement in the location scouting and preparation, Welles sent Foster to Mexico to direct the first segment of *It's All True.* In late October, he began shooting *The Magnificent Ambersons.* In December, half-way through the shoot, the Japanese attack on Pearl Harbor had a direct impact on all his projects. Welles had obtained deferment from the draft on the grounds that he was an employer on whom the members of the Mercury Theatre company depended for their livelihood; he also could hope to be classed as medically unfit for military service. A US government body, the Office of the Co-ordinator of Inter-American Affairs (CIAA), asked him to participate in the war effort by serving as a goodwill ambassador to South America, where the Roosevelt administration was keen to counter the influence of the Axis powers.

Given the situation, it was agreed that the other segments of *It's All True* would be replaced by new stories that could be filmed in Brazil. As one of these centred on the Rio carnival, which was to take place in mid-February 1942, Welles had to postpone his efforts on *It's All True* earlier than planned. The only way he could free up time without abandoning the third project, *Journey into Fear*, was to start shooting it in early January, while he was still at work on *The Magnificent Ambersons*, and entrust the direction to someone else. Welles opted for Foster again, and brought forward his own scenes as an actor. His workload allowed him two weeks' respite between his final day on a Hollywood set and his first day of filming in Rio. During the first months of his stay in Brazil, he shot one film, edited two others from a distance of 2,000 kilometres by mail and telephone, and ran his cultural embassy. As producer and/or director, the boywonder seemed on course to release three films in 1942.

Citizen Kane had escaped the test screenings Hollywood studios often organized in order to gauge audience reaction and recut a film accordingly before giving it a general release. However, in line with the amended contract, RKO ran previews of *The Magnificent Ambersons* and *Journey into Fear* in Californian towns in March and April 1942: their reception was decidedly cool. This was a cause of deep concern to RKO, as both films had gone over budget. Moreover, Welles was overrunning on the *It's All True* schedule in a way that was impossible to control, nor could the studio do anything about the film's content, largely improvised in situ, which focused on race and poverty, issues that would simply alienate the less tolerant element in American society. Many feared that Welles's unit would bring about the collapse of RKO. Studio head George Schaefer continued to defend his protégé against their common enemies, but asked Welles to respect the laws of the business in future: 'Educating the people is expensive, and your next picture must be made for the box office.' Given the deteriorating relationship and the inefficiencies arising from long-distance communication in a time of war, the company took over the editing of *The Magnificent Ambersons* and *Journey into Fear.* Welles was told to finish the final segment of *It's All True* with very poor means. On 26 June 1942 Schaefer's enemies at RKO, who had gradually gained the upper hand in recent months, obtained his resignation. As Mercury Productions had neglected to sign an umpteenth supplementary agreement authorizing the latest postponement of delivery, RKO's new bosses argued that Welles's contract was null and void and did their best to discredit the undisciplined and extravagant filmmaker who, for his part, spent another month trying to finish *It's All True.*

As with all Welles's subsequent Hollywood films apart from *The Stranger*, the studio made little attempt to promote the release of *The Magnificent Ambersons* or to ensure its wide distribution: it was already regarded as a commercial failure. In the short term, the film regained no more than forty per cent of its costs. The release of *Journey into Fear*, however, was postponed. Shortly after Welles's return to Los Angeles at the end of August, RKO asked him to revise the editing, an offer perhaps partly motivated by the desire to put him in a good mood before the final negotiations over the future of *It's All True.* But the company remained sceptical of his ability to finish the anthology film and keep costs down. Welles saw his authority on *The Magnificent Ambersons* and *Journey into Fear* crumble due to an unfinished film, the rushes of which he never had a chance to see.

A BUSY FIFTEEN MONTHS: THREE FILMS IN PARALLEL

1941	*The Magnificent Ambersons*	*Journey into Fear*	*It's All True*	Other activities
June		29: Option on the rights to *The Captain's Chair* by Robert Flaherty (unfilmed)	20: Mercury Productions registers a project for a film about Landru with the Motion Picture Association of America	
July	End of month: Welles begins writing the script	Middle of month: Welles announced as producer/director 19: Synopsis 30: First script	29: *It's All True* title registered	
August	15: Estimating script 16: First actors' screen tests	1: Second revised budgeting	4: Contract with Duke Ellington to co-write *Jazz Story* (unfilmed) 8: First draft continuity of the *Love Story* episode written by John Fante (unfilmed)	21 & 23: Versions of script for the short patriotic film *V&W* (unfilmed) 29: Requests permission from the Mexican authorities to film *The Way to Santiago* (unfilmed)
September		30: Intermediate version of script	4: Welles joins director Norman Foster in Mexico for several days' location scouting for *My Friend Bonito* 25: Shooting begins without Welles	3: Performs as magician at the Sacramento Fair. 15: First of the weekly broadcasts of *The Lady Esther Show* (every Monday until 2 February 1942)
October	7: Final script Rehearsals begin 28: First day of shooting			
November				10: Master of ceremonies at a political fundraising evening
December		22: Norman Foster returns to Hollywood. Welles appoints him director	11: Decision to travel to Brazil in time for the Rio carnival in February Around 18: *My Friend Bonito* shoot interrupted 7 & 15: Takes part in three radio broadcasts	

1942	*The Magnificent Ambersons*	*Journey into Fear*	*It's All True*	Other activities
January	22: End of principal photography 31: End of additional shooting by Welles		2: Final shooting script 6: Shooting begins	22: First contingent of technicians leaves for Rio 25: Takes part in a radio broadcast for the Red Cross
February	4–6: Welles's final work on the editing in Miami	1: Welles's last day on the set	2: Welles meets the CIAA in Washington 8: Welles arrives in Rio 14: Filming begins on the Carnival segment	
March	15: Welles receives a print of the rough cut in Rio 17 & 19: First previews in California	12: End of shoot 26: End of first cut	6: Welles leaves Rio for a week's preparation on the *Jangadeiros* segment in Fortaleza Middle of month: shoots the arrival of the *Jangadeiros* in Rio bay 30: Welles prepares the second-unit shooting for *Jangadeiros* in Minas Gerai	
April	17, 18, 20 & 22: Retakes filmed in Welles's absence	17: First preview in California	10: Carnival starts shooting in the favelas of Rio	14 & 18: Takes part in two Brazilian radio shows broadcast in the United States 20–22: Mission to Buenos Aires
May	4 &12: Further previews 19: Last retakes filmed in Welles's absence			
June	4: Final version printed	16: RKO confirms its refusal to hand over control of editing to Mercury Productions	8: Filming of Carnival episode ends. Most of crew return to the United States 13: Welles leaves for Fortaleza to film opening of *Jangadeiros.*	29: Mercury Productions begins to leave its offices at RKO
July	10: Cinema release		14: Welles leaves for two days' shooting in Recife, followed by a week in Salvador de Bahia 24: Filming ends	29: Leaves for cultural mission in various parts of Latin America
August		End of month: RKO postpones release to following year		22: Return to United States

THE MAGNIFICENT AMBERSONS

1942

The Magnificent Ambersons marks a shift in Welles's working methods, due partly to his simultaneous involvement in *Journey into Fear* and *It's All True.* As with *Citizen Kane*, he held lengthy rehearsals with his actors, determined the look of the sets in minute detail and was involved with the music almost from the outset. However, he did not write a detailed shooting script on this occasion, while the lighting style was decided during the shoot in collaboration with a cameraman who had been hired at the last minute. Welles was also more willing to delegate some of his responsibilities, allowing a second unit to shoot certain scenes and leaving the post-synchronization work to his dubbing mixer. More significantly, he gambled on completing the editing while shooting another film in Brazil.

INTENSIVE REHEARSALS AND IMPROVEMENTS ON THE SET

The Magnificent Ambersons was based on a Booth Tarkington novel published in 1918. Welles had adapted it for radio in 1939 while preparing *Heart of Darkness*, although the result was distinguished more by the inventiveness of its script than by the quality of its production, which bore the signs of hasty and cursory supervision. The bittersweet, elegiac chronicle of an aristocratic family whose grip on a Midwestern town is threatened by the advance of industry provided Welles with the kind of ambivalent framework of which he was so fond: a new world which can only come into being by destroying the old, and the nostalgia we feel for the past as we erase it. Tarkington interweaves the old and the new through a complex dynamic of familial and romantic issues. During the era of horse-drawn carriages, the young Isabel Amberson is courted by the automobile inventor Eugene Morgan, but rejects him when he makes a fool of himself in public. Isabel marries a dull businessman, Wilbur Minafer, and has a son, George, on whom she dotes.

Previous pages:
George (Tim Holt) under the watchful eye of his mother Isabel (Dolores Costello).

Opposite page:
Isabel (Dolores Costello) and her two suitors, Wilbur (Don Dillaway) and Eugene (Joseph Cotten).

George (Tim Holt)
and Aunt Fanny
(Agnes Moorehead).

Above:
The end of the ball, ground floor of the Amberson mansion.

Right:
Storyboard for the ball on the first floor.

46-AH. GEORGE - "A YACHTSMAN."

46-AI. DISSOLVE

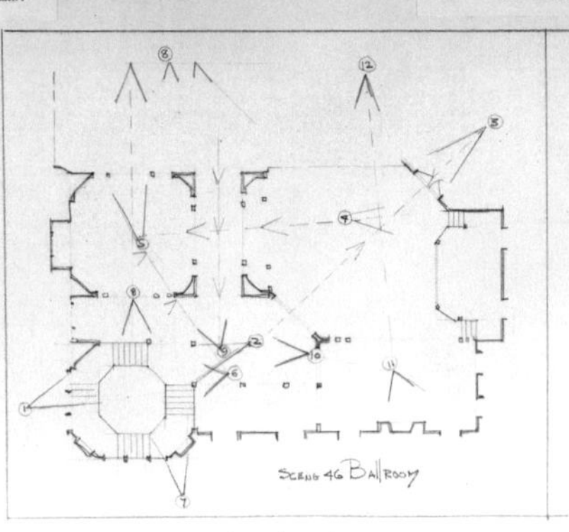

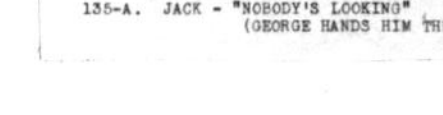

Above:
Uncle Jack (Ray Collins) and George (Tim Holt) saying goodbye at the station.

Left:
Storyboard for the above scene. The drawing indicates that the decision to evoke the station using a trick shot of its high vaulted ceiling, represented in *trompe-l'oeil*, has already been taken.

After an absence of twenty years, Eugene, a widower, returns to the town and builds a factory that quickly prospers. After Wilbur's death, George prevents his mother from marrying Eugene, thus sacrificing his own relationship with Lucy, the inventor's daughter. Meanwhile Wilbur's sister, Fanny, an old maid with a secret passion for Eugene, stirs up conflict. The automobile is one of the causes of the Ambersons' ruin; having invested their money unwisely, they gradually lose their dominion as the town succumbs to modernity, its languid existence shattered by milling crowds and the obsession with speed.

Welles, occasionally taking inspiration from the radio version, wrote two screenplays (dated 15 August and 7 October 1941), but lacked the time to prepare a proper shooting script. He took many of the scenes directly from the novel, and much of Tarkington's dialogue survived intact. The few alterations usually entailed a shift from third-person narration to direct speech. Welles added very little to the story, apart from the short scene in which Eugene tries to persuade Isabel to speak to George about their love for each other. Even so, there were permutations of episodes and other manipulations. The cast was drawn from the Mercury players and a pool of well-known actors. Joseph Cotten (Eugene), Agnes Moorehead (Fanny) and Ray Collins (Jack, Isabel's brother) had already appeared in *Citizen Kane*. Dolores Costello, a star of the silent screen and early talkies, was cast as Isabel. The thirty-seven-year-old Costello was called upon to portray a character who aged from adolescence to her forties as the story unfolded. Several young actresses were tested for the part of Lucy before Anne Baxter was cast at the last minute. But Welles's most significant casting decision, taken before the screenplay was written, was to forego playing George himself (he preferred to avoid younger roles; the 1939 radio adaptation – and other radio shows – confirm his uneasiness in such parts). He offered the role to Tim Holt, a star of western films who had impressed him with his performance in John Ford's *Stagecoach* two years earlier. This was to be Holt's first leading dramatic role.

Of all Welles's films, *The Magnificent Ambersons* was probably the most thoroughly rehearsed, certainly as far as the principal actors were concerned. Formal rehearsals, paid for by the production company, apparently ran from 7 to 25 October, three days before shooting started. These round-table sessions, rare in Hollywood practice, reinforced the team spirit. They were not designed to work out gestures and movements, but to explore the psychology and motivations of each character as they appeared in the text. The actors familiarized themselves with the general style in order to be ready for the long takes, which would present technical challenges and require close co-ordination. Welles rewrote lines according to the way his actors reacted, worked with them to refine the overlapping dialogue and initiated the newcomers into the technique. Returning to the experimental approach adopted during the pre-production of *Heart of Darkness*, he recorded soundtracks of some of these rehearsals and of his own third-person narration: these established both a model and a point of departure that enabled the actors to analyse and refine their work. The actors could also listen to the recordings during the shooting of certain scenes, as Welles had them played through loudspeakers on the set.

Despite these intensive preparations, the rehearsals were not meant to dictate what would take place on the set: they were simply a stage in the process, and the screenplay was not set in stone. The two annotated scripts that have been preserved – the script supervisor's copy and Welles's own copy (although the annotations are not in his handwriting) – reveal the way in which the dialogue was enriched on the set.

Welles kept adding lines as he shot the film; most were taken directly from the novel, although some were lifted from a different chapter or given to another character. He sometimes rewrote turns of phrase – in fact he invented freely – but never introduced a false note. The ballroom sequence, in particular, was revised to notable effect. Welles based his *mise en scène* on continuous dialogue: the lines create an unbroken rhythm as the actors, shot from a distance, pass in turn before the moving camera.

Sometimes he modelled the movements of the actors and camera on the dialogue; more often, he re-inserted lines to match human movement, thus creating a fluidity, playing on the separation of the actors in deep focus and ensuring their constant interaction. Conversations intermingle in an entirely natural manner as the camera moves through the set. Characters talk to one another then break off to address someone else, exchanging a greeting before resuming the conversation and eventually drifting from one group to another. Some of the last-minute additions were quite long; others extremely brief, as when George, standing in front of a buffet and smitten with Lucy, endeavours to elicit her first name. Her father, Eugene, standing behind them, moves forwards to answer the enquiry himself before making his exit, to the great indignation of George, who takes him for a complete stranger.

The screenplay contains a brief exchange taken directly from Tarkington's novel:
Lucy: What are you studying in school?
George: College! Oh, lots of useful guff.

On the set, however, Welles reinforced both the young man's sense of self-sufficiency and Lucy's conciliatory nature:
Lucy: What are you studying in school?
George: I beg your pardon?
Lucy: What are you studying in school?
George: College!
Lucy: College ...
George: Oh, lots of useful guff.

When shooting the scene in which George bickers with his aunt in the corridors after the ball, Welles again departed from his script and inserted off-screen lines: up in his room, Uncle Jack complains about the noise and jokingly announces his intention to move to a hotel. The lines set up a powerful reverberation throughout the house, which seems to come alive. As filming progressed, Welles used the existing dialogue as a working model, constantly tightening it and always returning to Tarkington's novel or style when looking for a solution.

Welles also constantly urged his actors to try different approaches to their roles. Agnes Moorehead recalled the four and a half minute long take – in which the mortified Aunt Fanny confesses to George that her savings are gone and that she can no longer afford to pay the rent – which required twelve takes: 'The first time I did it, he said that was all right, now we'll do it as a little child would do it. And the next time, he said to do it as an insane woman and the next time as a drunk.' Each off these approaches drew out nuances that could be fused together to form an interpretation rich in tonal disjunctions. On another occasion, Welles took three and a half hours of rehearsals and two hours of photography to sketch out the kitchen scene in which Fanny, fearing that Eugene has resumed his courtship of Isabel, interrogates George on the subject of Eugene's travels.

Top:
George (Tim Holt) examines the portrait of his father. The scene was cut from the final version.

Middle:
Tim Holt and Agnes Moorehead. Welles and cameraman Stanley Cortez shot the scene of George's return on 30 and 31 December 1941, using a specially constructed kitchen set on stage 7.

Bottom:
A month earlier, on 26 November, Welles and Cortez had filmed the scene of Fanny's despair in the same kitchen, built this time on stage 11, so that the four and a half minute single shot that started on the extinguished boiler could then move, without interruption, across the entire ground floor, finishing in the salon.

Overleaf:
A long scene cut by RKO. George (Tim Holt), Fanny (Agnes Moorehead) and Isabel (Dolores Costello) on the porch at the back of the mansion. The scene was lit by cameraman Harry Wild, who replaced Stanley Cortez.

Above:
Tim Holt and Anne Baxter with, beyond, Dolores Costello and Joseph Cotten.

Right:
Cameraman Stanley Cortez and Welles consulting the storyboard file.

Below:
Storyboard for the discussion after the ball and sketch of the ground floor. The staircase as shown would be built for the film.

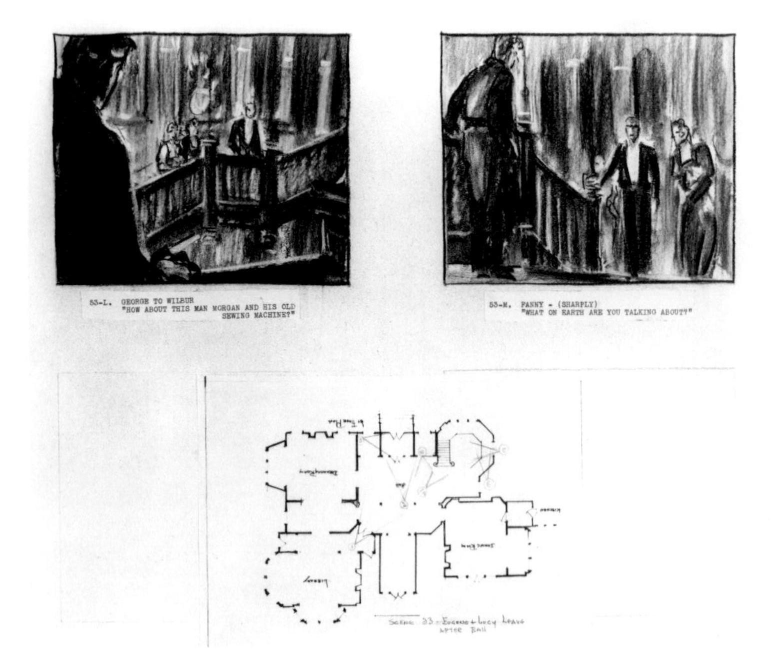

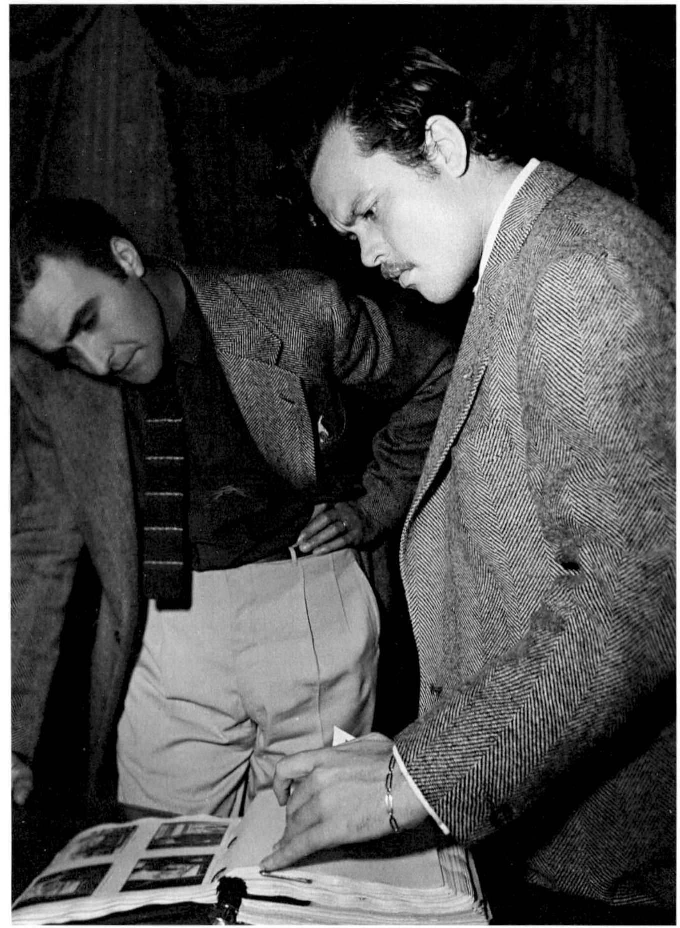

As she watches her nephew wolf down the dessert she has prepared for him, Fanny's speech is punctuated by a growing number of pregnant pauses. Taking inspiration from a simple line in the novel – George praises his aunt's cooking – Welles and the actors, whom he has encouraged to devise part of the text, create an entire block of secondary dialogue about the strawberry cake, thus heightening the tension of a scene that lasts almost five minutes.

METICULOUS SET DESIGN

The preparations for the set design were equally painstaking, although Welles was unable to reassemble the crew that had contributed so much to *Citizen Kane*. Van Nest Polglase had just resigned as head of RKO's set department, while his right-hand man, Perry Ferguson, had already moved to Goldwyn's company. Welles therefore had to work with a newcomer to the studio, Mark-Lee Kirk, a veteran designer but less imaginative than Ferguson. The importance of the sets to the overall *mise en scène* was acknowledged at a very early stage, at least in terms of the interiors. Welles ordered small-scale models of the various levels of the Amberson mansion and used them to map out his framing and camera movements, occasionally employing a rudimentary periscope to assess the view from the inside of a model. Meanwhile, illustrators were busy preparing countless storyboards. That they represent the future sets so precisely and conform so perfectly to the eventual shooting script is testimony to a *mise en scène* developed through a process of mature reflection (many of the *Citizen Kane* storyboards were little more than standard studio work).

Welles's and Kirk's choices were markedly different to those adopted for *Citizen Kane*. Instead of creating dozens of sets that would appear on the screen only briefly, they had to make a whole building that would see service throughout the film. Over half the scenes took place within its walls, and its gradual deterioration also served as a metaphor for the decline of its inhabitants. There could be no resorting to tricks of perspective and special effects to convey the impression of space this time: with a few exceptions, most of which concerned the facade of the house, the sets had to be full-size and three-dimensional. Rather than create a sense of magificence by opting for monumental simplification, the impression of opulent splendour would be conveyed through an abundance of detail. This proved to be extremely expensive; set construction consumed an unusually large slice of the budget, almost twice as much as for the previous film.

Most of the money was spent on the two great interior sets for the Amberson mansion, constructed on two stages in the old Pathé studio in Culver City. The vestibule, great hall, dining room, library and salon on the ground floor were built as a single set on stage 11. All areas were provided with wide doors or openings so that the camera could pass freely from one room to another. A reduced version of the back of the kitchen, where the boiler was located, was built behind the dining room to enable the camera to traverse the entire house – from kitchen to dining room to hall to salon – at the end of the long take in which Fanny confesses her ruin to George. The first-floor set, built on stage 3, contained the ballroom and reception rooms, which were also designed to allow the camera free movement. Both sets, vast horizontal expanses, were organized around the imposing, richly decorated octagonal staircase, the dominant feature of the house. Its flights of steps and short landings were ideal for punctuating the actors' movements and allowing them to observe the activity below.

Once the ballroom scene had been filmed, the first-floor sets on stage 3 were replaced by those of the second floor, where the staircase, still *in situ*, was surrounded by bedrooms and bathrooms. For the scene where George gorges on cake in front of his aunt, the kitchen was entirely rebuilt on another stage, possibly because there was not enough room for it in the completed ground-floor set or, more likely, because photography was two weeks behind schedule and stage 11 had to be vacated immediately.

The *Citizen Kane* sets formed a puzzle whose pieces could not be fitted together, or a series of partially-constructed areas that could only be filmed from a given angle. The set strategy devised for *The Magnificent Ambersons* took the opposite approach: each area was complete in itself and constructed in such elaborate detail that the camera could explore it from any direction. Costs mounted as the library had to be completely furnished, although it only appears in an extreme low-angle shot, from the point of view of the coffin containing George's father. The crumbling salon, shown only at the end of Fanny and George's passage across the entire ground floor, required similarly detailed fittings. But the sets allowed Welles to manage space in any way he chose, as can be seen from the long take in which George invades and is then driven from the house of an overly garrulous neighbour.

The rare outdoor scenes in the previous film had all been studio-based and had often required special effects. The *Ambersons* exteriors, much more numerous, were shot at RKO's ranch in the San Fernando Valley, where the facades for the buildings lining the town's main street were erected. The set for the sleigh ride, with its track, slopes and snowdrifts, was built entirely within the confines of an ice factory, where the temperature was so low that breath could be seen steaming from the actors' mouths.

WELLES AND CORTEZ: AN UNCOMFORTABLE PARTNERSHIP

Welles was unable to do much in the way of advance preparation for the photography. His original choice of cameraman, Gregg Toland, had other commitments. Rather than settle for one of RKO's contract technicians, he took another chance on youth and hired Stanley Cortez. Cortez, not yet thirty, had done little apart from a few undistinguished mass-produced films for Universal, and Selznick had recently asked him to light some actors' screen tests. The choice of a virtual unknown is all the more surprising given that it was made at the last minute, two or three days before 28 October, the start of a shoot that had already been delayed by six weeks. Returning from New York on a Monday, Cortez met Welles that same evening on the sets he would begin photography on the next day.

Besides working with an unfamiliar crew and conforming to pre-production decisions in which he had played no part, the newcomer also had to improvise appropriate technical solutions to the many problems arising from the director's choices. In effect, Welles had opted for deep focus once again, but had planned to increase the number of camera movements, particularly in the long ballroom sequence. The lighting had to be subtle enough to bring out the opulence of the scenery and still ensure that the characters' comings and goings in vast spaces were sharply defined. Cortez, like Toland, adopted short focus lenses (often using 30 mm lenses, which were less extreme than those selected for Citizen Kane) and laterally-positioned electric arc lamps, although the film's overall tonal quality limited the scope for the dramatic contrasts that Toland had enjoyed. As the period in which the film is set was characterized by dim, flickering gaslight, Cortez favoured chiaroscuro and deliberately plunged faces and figures into darkness.

50 (CONTINUED)

MAN WHO JUMPED

Look at that! Look at that boy!

(calls after George, not too loudly)

Sorry, Your Highness!

Eugene and Jack have come up behind them at the end of the man's speech. They pass by, or through them, on their way to the buffet table, the CAMERA PULLING back in front of them.

JACK

(laughing a little)

I can't see why Isabel doesn't see the truth about that boy!

EUGENE

What's the matter with him?

JACK

Too much Amberson, I guess, for one thing. And for another, his mother just fell down and worshipped him from the day he was born. I don't have to tell you what Isabel Amberson is, Gene. She's got a touch of the Amberson high stuff about her, but you can't get anybody that ever knew her to deny that she's just about the finest woman in the world.

EUGENE

No, you can't get anybody to deny that.

51 They have come up to the buffet table which is now cut in in the extreme f.g., and busy themselves with putting food on plates during the following action and dialogue.

JACK

Well, she thinks he's a little tin god on wheels. She actually sits and worships him! You can hear it in her voice when she speaks to him. You can see it in her eyes when she looks at him. My gosh! What does she see when she looks at him?

(CONTINUED)

Opposite page:
A page from the script, annotated by the script supervisor. Six musicians were brought on to the set to provide the music for the ballroom sequence. This particular passage (cut by RKO) was accompanied by *Estudiantina*, a waltz by Waldteufel.

Above:
Welles directs Bobby Cooper (George as a child) and Erskine Sanford (Bronson), watched by cameraman Harry Wild (wearing the hat).

Left:
This scene briefly reveals the back of the Amberson mansion and its porch. The house is represented by a not too convincing back projection. (Richard Bennett, Bobby Cooper, Dolores Costello and Don Dillaway.)

CAMERAMEN FOR THE MAGNIFICENT AMBERSONS

Scene	Cameraman
Opening: a town and its ruling family	Cortez, Wild (matching shots by Metty, McKenzie)
The Ambersons' ball	Cortez (one matching shot by Wild)
The end of the ball and departure of the Morgans	Cortez
Nocturnal arguments on the first floor	Cortez (one matching shot by Wild)
The ride in the snow	Cortez
The death of Wilbur Minafer	Cortez
The conversation in the kitchen	Cortez
The visit to the automobile factory	Cortez
Eugene and Isabel: should George be told they plan to marry?	Cortez
Lucy and George in the buggy, Major and Jack in the carriage	Wild
A spoiled lunch / George and Fanny on the staircase	Cortez
Visit to a gossip	Cortez
Arguments with a tap	Cortez
George dismisses Eugene	Cortez, Wild
Jack returns / George and Fanny on the staircase	Cortez
Eugene's letter: writing and reading	Cortez, retake by Musuraca (directed by Fred A. Fleck)
George and Isabel: how to react to the letter?	Cortez, retakes by Musuraca (directed by Fred A. Fleck)
Lucy and George: farewell in the street	Wild
Jack at the Morgans	Cortez (matching shot by Metty for exterior scene)
Isabel's return to town	Cortez (exterior), Wild (interior)
Eugene's last visit	Retake by Musuraca (directed by Fred A. Fleck)
George at Isabel's bedside	Cortez, Wild
The death of Isabel	Wild
The Major lost in thought	Cortez
Jack and George: farewell at the station	Wild
Lucy and Eugene: a walk in the garden	Cortez
George and Fanny in the empty house	Cortez, retakes by Musuraca (directed by Fred A. Fleck and Jack Moss)
At lawyer Bronson's	Wild
The last walk / George prays	? (exterior), Cortez (interior)
George's accident	Wild or Metty
Lucy and Eugene: reactions to the accident	Retakes by Musuraca (directed by Fred A. Fleck)
Reconciliation at the hospital	Retake by Musuraca (directed by Fred A. Fleck)
End titles	? (and microphone shot by Wild for the US *Citizen Kane* trailer)

Finished scenes shot by cinematographer Stanley Cortez, his replacement Harry Wild, Nicholas Musuraca (responsible for the retakes ordered by RKO), Russell Metty and Jack McKenzie (both of whom did some matching shots). The table does not include scenes shot by special effects cameramen.

RKO RADIO PICTURES, INC.

PRODUCTION REPORT Date Jan. 14 1942

Title MAGNIFICENT AMBERSONS

Pict. No. 340 Cameraman Wild

Director O. Welles Soundman Fesler

Location Stage 9 Pathe Set. No. 61 Description Int. RR Station

Stage 3 Pathe 60 Int. Pool Room

Company Called 8:00 a.m. Time Started 11:37 a.m. Time Finished 6:30 p.m.

	Number of Scenes	Number of Set-ups	Time Recorded	Negative Report	Sound Report
Shot Today	1	3	0:45	6590	6280

Scene No. 111

Scene No.

Add. Scenes 135J-K

Total Scenes

TALENT (Over $16.50 per day) or on weekly)	Worked—W Hold—H Off—O Ill—I	Time Called Studio A.M.	Time Called Studio P.M.	Time Report on Set	Dismissed On Set A.M.	Dismissed On Set P.M.	Arrived Location A.M.	Arrived Location P.M.	Dismissed Location A.M.	Dismissed Location P.M.	Time Arrive Studio	Minutes Mid-Day Travel	Tomorrows Call A.M.	Tomorrows Call P.M.	Date Started	Date Finished
T. Holt	W	8:00		8:00		4:15								2:00	10-11	
R. Collins	W	"		"		"								"	"	
A. Baxter	I														"	
R. Bennett	O												8:00		10-12	
D. Costello	W	Worked with other unit											8:00		12-29	
G. Schilling	W	10:00		10:00		6:30									1-13	1-14
W. Knudsen	W	7:00		7:00		4:15							7:00		10-28	
B. Adair	Wff														"	
D. Lawrence	W	7:00		7:00		4:15								1:30	11-1	
J. Lyons	W	Worked with other unit											7:00		12-29	

CORTEZ UNIT

Pathe Stage 3 - Pathe Stage 11. Ext. Window - Int. Library.

Called - 8:00 am. St. Shoot - 2:30 pm. Finished - 6:30 p.m.

D. Costello	W	9:30		9:30		6:00	(Lunch - 12:30		
J. Lyons	W	9:00		9:30		6:30			1:30

Delay caused by Ann Baxter being ill.
Company call changed at 8:30 am.

EXTRAS

Number	Time Called	Time Dismissed	Rate	Amount	Overtime Number	Overtime Check	Overtime Amount
21	7:30a	16-4:15	10.50	220.50			
30	9:30a	9:30a	10.50	78.90	Dism. on 1/4 ck. a/c Baxter's illness.		
		5-6:30p			4	1/4	10.50

MUSICIANS

Number	Occupation	Session From	Session To

SHOOTING SCHEDULE

	Original Schedule Date	Original Schedule Days	Present Estimate Date	Present Estimate Days
Start Rehearsal				
Finish Rehearsal				
Start Photography	10-28		10-28	
Finish Photography	1-7	62	1-23	77

Number of Days on Picture Including Today—Total 69 Worked 66 Idle 3 Hol

Time Status: Ahead-Behind Schedule 14 & 1 Sun Days Behind

SUMMARY

	Shot to Date	Budget
Negative	264,200	215,000
Sound	267,985	210,000
Time	122:55	
Scenes	112	

Lunch Out 12:55 In 1:55
Dinner Out In
Midnight Out In

Reasons for Delay:

Finished with Set:

Live Stock:

Autos Used:

Retakes:

Lunches:

F. Fleck

Signed

Assistant Director.

The production report of 14 January 1942 (according to the shooting schedule, filming should have finished on 7 January). Welles and cameraman Harry Wild reshot parts of scene 135 with Tim Holt and Ray Collins (George and Uncle Jack saying goodbye at the station), and then some of scene 111 with Gus Schilling (cut during editing). The original cameraman, Stanley Cortez, had joined the second unit, working with Dolores Costello and her double Joan Lyons on the ground floor of the Amberson mansion.

According to the daily production reports, the first month of shooting proceeded fairly smoothly, although there are frequent references to the amount of time Cortez needed to light the sets, as well as comments on Welles's lengthy rehearsals with his actors. On 7 November, the cameraman spent four hours composing the lighting for a ballroom scene, while four days later the director spent most of the day rehearsing a two-minute shot for the same scene, which he only managed to capture in the last thirty minutes. The situation deteriorated at the end of the first month, when filming started on the ice factory set. Scheduled to take three days, the unit spent twice that much time on it, achieving less than a minute's worth of satisfactory footage each day. The delays accumulated until by the end of December the film was two weeks behind schedule. Welles blamed Cortez and was particularly impatient as he was about to start shooting *Journey into Fear* and had just committed himself to being free one month later in order to begin filming *It's All True* in Brazil.

On 2 January 1942 Cortez was replaced at the head of the photography unit by Harry Wild, an obscure cameraman who had spent ten years with RKO and had shot some minor linking footage for *Citizen Kane* in Toland's absence. The final three weeks of filming under Wild's direct responsibility involved fifteen minutes of footage that found their way into the final cut, including four important scenes. Wild shot the long-take sequence in which Aunt Fanny tells George that his mother has died, and the scene in which George and Uncle Jack say goodbye at the station. More significantly, he was also responsible for two discreet but virtuoso travelling shots in the town's main street: one tracks the tilbury in which George presses Lucy to marry him; and the other, shot from the opposite direction, depicts the youngsters' last meeting. The evidence suggests that Wild was more comfortable with exteriors and sunlight than with interiors, for which he was bound to re-create his predecessor's sophisticated lighting effects with absolute precision. On the other hand, some of the exterior trick shots devised by Cortez lack the bravura quality of his work in the Amberson mansion. Cortez gained sole credit, although the final cut includes less than an hour of his photography. None the less, *The Magnificent Ambersons*, together with Charles Laughton's *Night of the Hunter* thirteen years later, remains his principal claim to fame.

WELLES DELEGATES: A BUSY SECOND UNIT

On 7 January, Welles, pushed for time, took advantage of the conventional division of labour in Hollywood and delegated some of the work to a second unit. He had by this time given up the idea of exercising total control over each and every image, but had dictated the overall style in such detail that he could accept, on occasion, leaving some of its execution to others.

The second unit was given three main tasks. It would film exteriors for which no actors were needed, or which involved fairly simple action. Trick shots were often involved, and would be handled by special effects technicians. The unit would also shoot non-dialogue scenes with actors. Cortez had already devised a number of tricks to disguise Costello's age, such as the spider's web lighting that falls on faces and bedding as George sits at his dying mother's bedside. He was therefore recalled for another six days' work (7–14 January) on Costello's solo scenes (when Isabel reads Eugene's letter imploring her to resist her son's hostility to him, for instance) and for a lengthy tracking shot in the deserted house (which Welles rejected before the first cut). Finally, after the end of the principal photography on 22 January, the second unit would complete the additional dialogue shots entrusted to various cameramen.

The actors involved in these scenes had been thoroughly rehearsed and knew what was required of them, although in the absence of Welles some had difficulty in finding their marks. Who directed them? First-hand accounts tend to contradict each other on this point, and the production reports do not indicate when a cameraman worked with a replacement director. On occasion, the reports suggest that Welles was working with both units simultaneously, which is not as far-fetched as it seems if they were operating on neighbouring stages. The director would sometimes shoot one scene and, while waiting for the next scene to be lit, join the second unit to direct operations. Welles certainly allowed editor Robert Wise to supervise the scene, lit by Cortez, in which Isabel reads Eugene's letter. And it is highly likely that the scene depicting Major Amberson (Richard Bennett) lost in thought as death approaches was filmed twice: once by Welles and once by Wise. The film may have lost something of its perfect visual cohesion, but the reorganization succeeded in avoiding further delays.

EARLY POST-PRODUCTION

As filming progressed, Welles edited the footage with Robert Wise, edited and re-recorded the sound with James G. Stewart and discussed the score with Bernard Herrmann. In each case, work proceeded rapidly thanks to the habits established during the making of *Citizen Kane*. Once again, the editing was largely implied by the filming. The opening, an eight-minute alternation of off-screen narration and dialogue cut into silent vignettes and then into playlets (the shortest of which are composed of single shots), is a clockwork mechanism that gained some of its inventiveness during the editing process, when the order and duration of a scene can be easily revised. The film then unfolds essentially as a succession of dialogue scenes, each of which forms an autonomous whole, often shot in long takes. Welles supervised the sound editing and pre-mix of edited sequences. Given the complexity of the takes, he was reluctant to waste time and did not always insist on live sound. An unprecedented amount of dialogue – almost all of it in fact – had to be re-recorded, which tripled the sound budget. Preoccupied with a great many other matters, Welles let Stewart work with the cast, but the post-synchronization had to be expressive and he constantly demanded improvements. For the winter outing scene, which ends with a hubbub of voices and song as six people ride in an early automobile, Stewart recorded each actor separately before adding a richly textured soundscape.

Welles listened to it and complained that the voices did not convey the jolting of the vehicle. Stewart later explained that he positioned each actor on a plank, sat on the other end himself and rocked it, trying to synchronize the voices with the car's jolting motion. The film represents Welles's first attempt to improve the overlapping dialogue during post-production: he often added lines to scenes in which the characters stood at some distance from the camera, or were seen from the rear or in three-quarters shot. He created layers of sound by combining a conversation in the foreground with another in the background and also used sound effects to express the evolution of the town as it slipped from the Ambersons' grasp. As the years go by, the street sounds change to indicate the rise of the automobile, the symbol of modernity.

Tim Holt (George) and Anne Baxter (Lucy).

Welles had enlisted Herrmann's services well before shooting began. As the production advanced, he asked him to record the dance numbers for the ball and to start thinking about the structure for the original music. The score was partly inspired by a waltz from Émile Waldteufel's *Toujours ou jamais suite* (1877), which the two men had used for a radio adaptation of *Peter Ibbetson* in 1939. This waltz *con tenerezza* ('with tenderness') opens the film and is re-introduced during the ballroom sequence. Herrmann wrote a number of increasingly bitter-sounding and distorted variations designed to accompany the collapse of the Ambersons' world. His music is perfectly attuned to the nuances of image and dialogue, and consolidates the dramatic structure; the principle of symmetry is underlined by the very titles – such as *First Reverie*, *Second Reverie* – of certain matching cues. Most of the score had been recorded by 29 January, just a week after the end of principal photography. There was still room for last-minute revisions, but the music had played its part in dictating the final form.

Above:
Joseph Cotten.

Below:
Joseph Cotten with Tim Holt, Anne Baxter, Dolores Costello and Agnes Moorehead.

Right and opposite:
Filming the long take of Lucy and George riding in the carriage.

BILLIARD HALL

On 2 February, two days after filming the last matching shots, Welles left Hollywood to embark on the *It's All True* venture, although *Ambersons* still required a month of post-production work. He paid a brief visit to Washington to meet officials from the Office of the Co-ordinator of Inter-American Affairs before travelling to Miami, where Robert Wise joined him for three days of intensive work on the existing material, planning what had to be done. Welles also used the opportunity to record his narration and the spoken credits. Despite the frantic schedule, his voice betrays no sign of fatigue.

LONG-DISTANCE EDITING AND REVISIONS

The release date for *The Magnificent Ambersons* had not yet been decided when Welles flew to Rio de Janeiro. As his cultural mission was to last several months, it seemed likely that the release would take place before his return to the United States. He therefore had to relinquish the day-to-day supervision of his film, but his contract allowed him to oversee the finishing touches, at least until the first previews. Despite his limited availability and the inevitable delays that shipping the reels to Brazil would entail, RKO agreed to let him finish the work. This was considerably more than most Hollywood directors could hope for.

Welles began viewing the reels of *The Magnificent Ambersons* and sending his instructions by cable, telephone and radio, although communications had deteriorated since America's entry into the war. Given the circumstances, delegation was unavoidable: at the end of February he asked the studio to shoot some minor additional shots. In early March he decided to cut a continuous block of almost fifteen minutes from the middle of the film (thus proving that he did not consider his own material indispensable), and asked Wise to film a short scene to weld the dislocated sequences together. Welles was also counting on a more hands-on approach, as Wise was supposed to join him in Rio in due course, bringing a print of the film as well as retakes and soundtracks, all of which would give him greater latitude. But civilian flights were restricted because of the war and Wise could not obtain a visa from the US government. However, on 15 March Welles received a 131-minute print, which had to be shortened even further.

It was at this point that Welles's struggle to maintain control of the revisions approved by studio head George Schaefer commenced. On 17 March, Schaefer organized a preview of a version from which he had asked Wise to cut three sequences. The audience, which had come to see the patriotic musical comedy that formed the first half of the programme, was decidedly unenthusiastic. Two days later, without consulting Welles, a hastily revised version was screened to a more sophisticated audience and garnered more favourable comments. Nevertheless, RKO agreed with the initial criticisms: the film was too long and too slow (it was shorter than *Citizen Kane*, but its plot centred on the process of gradual decline); it was perceived as too mannered; its plot, lighting and music were all too sombre; George was odious and Aunt Fanny too strident. Wise again requested a visa so that he could join Welles in Rio and work on a solution, but was unsuccessful.

The following four weeks were a time of acrimonious but well-intentioned negotiations. Welles was still in a position to exert some influence over the fate of his film. He suggested a thorough and extremely detailed overhaul which would address and remedy the studio's objections. Besides manipulating the existing material, he called for retakes and amendments to the dialogue (and even asked the studio to telephone him so that he could demonstrate the correct intonation of certain lines). He recorded an additional voice-over passage and sent it to Wise. But Wise was already restructuring the film in collaboration with two of Welles's deputies – his old friend Joseph Cotten and Jack Moss, the Mercury's manager and acting producer in the director's absence – both of whom shared the studio's reservations. Welles, who considered the trio's ideas nonsensical, had run out of allies. Cabling long lists of changes was all very well, but they had to be justified and he had no means of explaining their value apart from the telephone. Wise, however, was little inclined to listen.

In mid-April, Welles learned that Schaefer had disregarded his suggestions and had given the go-ahead for retakes, including entirely new scenes. The additions (eleven minutes of footage) were written by Cotten and Moss, lit by a new cameraman, Nicholas Musuraca, and directed by first assistant Freddie Fleck (Moss would shoot a few final scenes in May). Holt and Moorehead maintained the quality of their performances, but without Welles there to direct them, the other actors were rigid. Schaefer made some attempt to discuss the situation with Welles but a turning point had been reached – when the director could not be contacted, the studio simply coped without him. Welles was powerless to prevent cuts, the fragmentation of long takes, the reinsertion of scenes that he had removed and changes to the dramatic structure. Sound effects were sacrificed, resulting in the clearly uneven quality between sequences. Half the score disappeared (Herrmann had his name removed from the spoken credits) and a studio composer, Roy Webb, was enlisted to write new music. After a struggle, Welles managed to obtain a few concessions, chiefly the last-minute salvage of the kitchen scene where George eats under the watchful gaze of his aunt. The finished film ran for a mere eighty-eight minutes. Schaefer tried to preserve the most significant work prints, but in December his successor ordered the destruction of all the out-takes and negative trims.

During the final weeks of filming *The Magnificent Ambersons*, Welles, alert to the increasing urgency of the situation, had delegated work to a second unit and had requested the filming of additional shots in his absence. When he left for Brazil, therefore, his position still seemed relatively secure. His undoing came about through a combination of circumstances – the preview screening system, the impossibility of fighting a battle from a distance of 10,000 kilometres while directing another film, the fears raised by *It's All True* and the internal strife at RKO. Having some of one's film shot by others and taking no part in its editing was par for the course in Hollywood, as many of his fellow directors could confirm. But Welles, having enjoyed the right to the final cut on his first film, was now facing the prospect of working as a producer-director for people who would not tolerate his tendency to deviate from the established practices of a major studio.

Joseph Cotten and Agnes Moorehead in the film's final scene, which was replaced by a sequence shot in Welles's absence.

ROOM

JOURNEY INTO FEAR

1942

Journey into Fear, his third film for RKO, offers a convincing demonstration of how easily the twenty-six-year-old Welles could have fitted into the Hollywood system as the head of a production unit. In later years, he regularly attributed *Journey into Fear* to its nominal director, Norman Foster. But Foster, a modestly talented and unpretentious man, was simply a hired hand. Welles, originally assigned to direct it himself, ensured that the film bore his stylistic imprint.

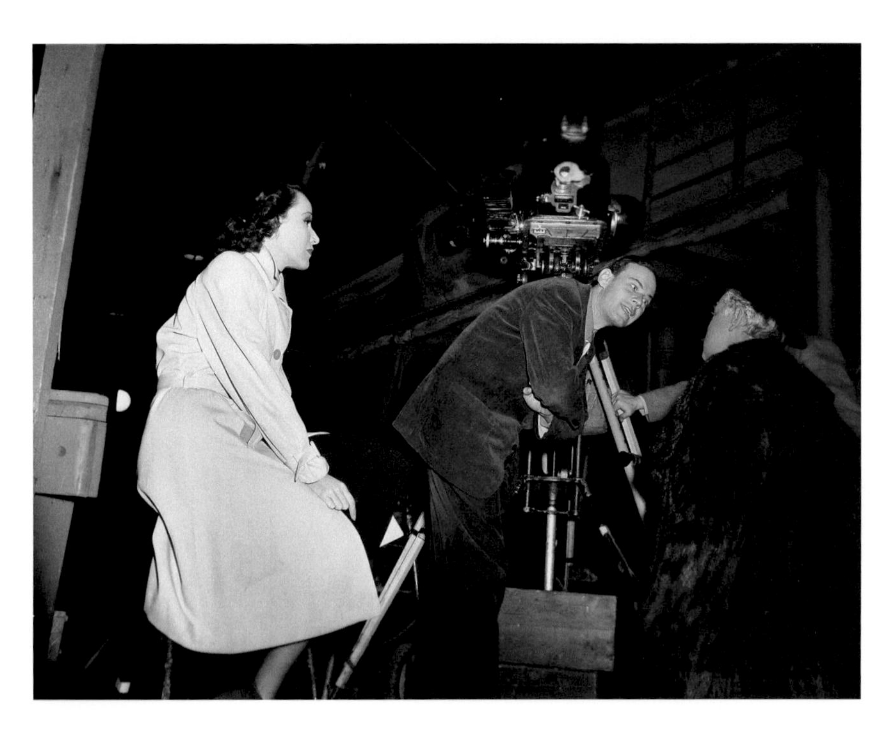

Previous pages:
Joseph Cotten (Graham) and Jack Moss (the killer) and, sitting, Agnes Moorehead and Frank Readick (the French couple) and Dolores Del Rio (Josette).

Left:
Dolores Del Rio, director Norman Foster and his actor-producer, Welles.

Opposite page:
Welles (as Colonel Haki, without the moustache) and Ruth Warrick (Stephanie).

PRE-PRODUCTION: A CHANGE OF DIRECTORS

In April 1941, RKO suggested that Welles play a character part in an adaptation of Eric Ambler's anti-Nazi espionage thriller, published the previous year. The story centres on a British engineer (Americanized and renamed Howard Graham for the film), who arrives in Istanbul to assist the Turkish armament programme, although he himself cannot even handle a pistol. After an attempt on his life by Nazi agents, the Turkish police hustle him aboard a small steamer before he even has a chance to contact his wife. At sea, he quickly realizes that his life hangs by a thread. Welles was soon involved as a producer, and probably saw an opportunity to notch up a credit for the kind of light entertainment, a blend of suspense and comedy in the Hitchcock manner, which could be slotted between more ambitious projects. The pot-pourri of accents and languages (the secondary characters were Turkish, Greek, French, German and Russian) suited his taste for cosmopolitan subjects. Welles asked two new scriptwriters, Richard Collins and the brilliant short story writer Ellis St Joseph, to overhaul the structure. Rejecting the studio's choice of director, he asked the actor Thomas Mitchell to make his debut behind the camera. He did not restrict his own prerogatives, however, as is clear from a letter he wrote to one of RKO's vice presidents: 'It is my policy to work with art directors a little longer than most producers since I find that great savings can be effected by thorough and adequate preparation.'

By July he allowed himself to be convinced that he should direct the film himself. He began intensive work on the script with Joseph Cotten, who was cast as Graham and who had never written anything for the screen. One of Cotten's letters dated March 1942 refers more broadly to his experiences with Welles and conveys the tone of their master pupil relationship: 'I have often been wrong in discussing scripts and plots with you, and I agree that I'm wanting in intellectual concept and understanding of art. I do, however, have reliable instinct.

16G. OO LANG SANG BEGS GRAHAM TO ASSIST HIM WITH THE NEXT TRICK. SHOOT TOWARD BAR.

16H. GRAHAM IS FASTENED TO THE CROSS. SHOOTING TOWARD ENTRANCE.

16I. OO LANG SANG GETS INTO COFFIN.

16J. MRS. OO LANG SANG MOTIONS FOR BLACKOUT.

95. EXTERIOR FIFTH FLOOR LEDGE - NIGHT -(RAIN)
MATTE SHOT - ANGLE UP FROM STREET.
GRAHAM ON LEDGE.

96 & 99. CLOSER SHOT.
GRAHAM STARTS TO MAKE HIS WAY AROUND A PILLAR.

102. BANAT COMING THROUGH FRENCH WINDOW FROM GRAHAM'S ROOM.

103-104. BANAT SEES GRAHAM.

Opposite page:
Storyboard for the conjuring trick. The killer stalks the hero on the ledge. As with *The Magnificent Ambersons*, the storyboard artwork is based on pre-designed sets. The finished film created the vertiginous effect with overhead shots rather than the pronounced low-angle shots indicated on the top left drawing.

Right:
Joseph Cotten, Everett Sloane (Kopeikin) and Ruth Warrick in a scene that RKO reduced to banality in the editing room.

And as often as I have been wrong about actual ideas, I have been right about audience reactions.' The first complete script was ready by 30 July. Shooting was planned to start in September, which meant that Welles would be working on three fronts, since he was also preparing *The Magnificent Ambersons* and *It's All True*. At that stage, working documents attribute both the supervision (the producer's role, in other words) and the direction to Welles.

With the hiring of many collaborators from *Citizen Kane* and *The Magnificent Ambersons*, the takeover of *Journey into Fear* by the 'Welles unit' was virtually complete. Welles selected almost all the actors from the Mercury troupe. Joseph Cotten's timid anti hero appeared in almost every scene and acted as a foil for a gallery of eccentrics. Always keen to bring new faces to the screen, Welles managed to enlist several of the actors who had worked with him in New York but had not yet made their screen debuts. Frank Readick was cast as the timid Frenchman who claims socialist values in order to distance his broad beamed, wart ridden spouse, played by Agnes Moorehead. The troupe expanded with the casting of Ruth Warrick (the first Mrs Kane) as Graham's domineering wife and Richard Bennett (also playing Major Amberson) as the doddering ship's captain, a character invented for the film. Welles, adhering to a practice inaugurated in his first film, also cast some of his collaborators in minor roles. Mercury manager Jack Moss played a mute contract killer hired by the Nazis to kill Graham. Robert Meltzer, an *It's All True* writer, and Herbert Drake, the Mercury press officer, were given walk on parts. Welles himself took a supporting role as Colonel Haki, the head of the Turkish secret police. The French actress Michèle Morgan, then a refugee in Hollywood, had been scheduled to play the French cabaret dancer Josette before Welles took over, but as she was no longer available the role went to Welles's current partner, Dolores Del Rio. Some of the principal technicians – art director Mark Lee Kirk, costume designer Edward Stevenson, make up artist Maurice Seiderman – had also worked on the first films for RKO. The only significant newcomer was the cinematographer Karl Struss, borrowed from Paramount for the occasion. Struss would soon disagree with the Wellesian camera and lighting style.

When Welles and RKO decided to bring forward the filming of *Journey into Fear* so that he could play Haki before flying to Brazil for *It's All True*, they needed another director for what was, after all, a relatively minor project. Welles found his straw man in Norman Foster, his elder by fifteen years, who had been churning out episodes of the low budget Mr Moto and Charlie Chan series for 20th Century Fox. He had already discreetly given up the direction of the Mexican segment of *It's All True* to Foster, who was ordered to return on 22 December, before the shoot had finished. Foster was then in the predicament familiar to many Hollywood directors. He had to take over the reins at the last minute and shoot a film that had been prepared by department heads and producers. He inherited a screenplay in which he had little faith, the sets were up and the storyboards completed. The final shooting script is dated 2 January 1942; shooting began on 6 January. His position was further weakened by the fact that his producer had a part in the film (and Welles was receiving a salary five times greater than his own). RKO press releases stressed the novelty of Welles's double function as producer and supporting actor: 'This is probably the first time in cinema history when the producer of a film also played an almost secondary part in it.'

THE PRODUCER'S INFLUENCE

Welles and Foster held last minute discussions on the overall style, but it is unlikely that Foster made any creative decisions at the pre production stage. Those who worked on the film are almost unanimous in attributing its paternity to Welles, even though his presence was limited to occasional appearances on the set during the first few weeks of shooting. Welles devised a timetable that allowed him to move from one stage to another, but could not participate in the shoot on a regular basis. During the first two weeks, he had to finish filming *The Magnificent Ambersons*, supervise its editing, and later return to it for matching shots. He also had his weekly radio broadcast, *The Lady Esther Show*. On 2 February, shortly before flying to Rio, he left Foster in sole charge of the shoot, which was wrapped up on 12 March.

Despite the limited amount of time Welles spent on *Journey into Fear*, his stylistic imprint extended beyond his own scenes, and his influence is often indicated in contemporary sources and first hand accounts. The most obvious signs are the tilts and powerful low angle shots, but in certain scenes his influence is even more pronounced in other domains. The lighting, for example, plunges vast areas into darkness, and creates a flickering play of light and shadow on the faces of actors in motion. And there are unobtrusive but complex camera movements, such as the measured dollying back as Graham and Josette stroll through the steerage compartment, and the crane shot that follows them from steerage to the wheelhouse. In contrast, long static takes create a sensation of unease, as in the dialogue of the deaf between Graham and the purser and captain, who refuse to believe that his life is in danger; or Graham's discovery of the body of a Turkish secret agent in a cabin. Welles may not have co directed in the strict sense of the term, but Foster was always under the supervision, both stimulating and stifling, of a producer.

PRODUCTION-LINE EDITING AND RE-EDITING

If Welles had been able to co ordinate the editing and sound post production, *Journey into Fear* might have emerged as a minor key companion to his first two films, at least stylistically. However, the studio, eager to complete the film, would not await his return from Rio, and he was unable to view more than a few reels. RKO's assumption of the task did not signal the emancipation of Foster, who was allowed little direct input. The first cut (entrusted to Mark Robson, an assistant editor on the previous two films) was finished around 26 March, after which Foster was off the payroll and called back only occasionally. On 17 April, a provisional 102 minute version was given a preview and failed to impress the audience – half the comments were either lukewarm or unfavourable. On 21 April, Foster summed up the situation in a letter to Welles and suggested cutting fifteen to twenty minutes and shooting retakes. Some of these would require half a dozen new or rewritten lines. The retakes were meant to clarify situations. In one example, the scene in which the secret agent's body is discovered, filmed entirely from a low angle, would be interrupted by shots of Graham and reverse shots of the victim (Foster believed that the victim should be instantly recognizable). On the other hand, modifications of this kind risked disrupting the fluid continuity and the coherence of the editing style. Further previews were held. In June, RKO, whose leadership had gradually changed during the making of the film, sidelined Foster and Welles's deputies and took over the editing.

The absorption of *Journey into Fear* by the Mercury unit could not be considered complete without Bernard Herrmann. But as Herrmann was in dispute with RKO, the studio passed the score to Roy Webb, who had written additional material for *The Magnificent Ambersons*. As for the sound mixing, James G. Stewart was forced to work fast and could bring little imagination to the task; nor could he incorporate any of Welles's inspired ideas such as the din raised by the cattle (Graham's incongruous shipmates), which was ultimately reduced to a few muffled bellows.

The film, now shortened to seventy-one minutes was shown to the press in August; the reaction was so disappointing that RKO postponed its release. In October, Welles set aside his quarrels with the studio and agreed to reshape it, but the job had to be completed in fourteen days (only one of which would be devoted to filming) with the aid of a standard RKO crew. Foster played no part in the revisions. A new version, shortened by another three minutes, was released the following year (the seventy one minute version resurfaced in the 1980s). Welles received no credit as writer or producer. Given the tight deadline, he had no choice but to endorse the version that had been put together in his absence. He hardly changed the cutting of individual sequences and was forced to accept the dissonance introduced by the belated retakes. His contribution was chiefly confined to tinkering with the overall structure. He added an off screen narration that owed nothing to Ambler's novel – a letter in which Graham tells his wife why he disappeared from Istanbul. The wordless scene in which the contract killer loads his gun while listening to the scratchy record that will become his signature tune was shifted to precede the titles. He deleted two sequences and restored another, a long take of which only the opening had been retained. However, he did shoot a new ending that allowed him, despite everything, to re appropriate the film.

THE ELUSIVE ENDING

The denouement in Georgia, after the fight between Graham and Banat on the rain soaked hotel ledge and the killer's fatal plunge, had always been the weak spot of the script. In the earliest version, written by Welles and Cotten, the film came to a rapid conclusion: Graham's bird's eye view of the crowd reacting to Banat's death. Each later version indicated that the tag was yet to come. A portion of the final cost estimate had been set aside for it when shooting began, but by March no decision had yet been taken.

On 4 April, Welles, then based in Rio, suggested adapting to the circumstances. His solution called for the construction of two very basic hotel sets: one in Hollywood for a scene with Cotten and Warrick; and the other in Rio for a scene with Welles and three members of the *It's All True* unit. Haki collapses after Banat's death, creating the impression that he might have been killed or injured by the assassin. He reappears in a corner of the lobby, where reporters fire questions at him in a babble of Russian and English. Cut to another corner of the lobby, as Graham finally shows his wife who's boss. Cut to Haki's statement to the press, a simple announcement that Josette will be joining him for dinner. Welles then reverts to the role of ringmaster, Haki enters the lift, turns to look straight at the camera and calls out to the disappointed reporters: 'But I sincerely hope it's a good enough end for the story.' Maintaining eye contact with the audience, he signs off with 'Goodnight, everyone!' The lift doors close. Fade to black.

Foster thought the ending too protracted. In a letter dated 21 April he suggested that the character played by his producer needed more depth, and asked Welles to write a short final scene featuring either Josette and Haki (which would mean filming Josette's scenes in Mexico, where Del Rio was currently in residence) or with Haki alone. Foster finally avoided the issue altogether by shooting a tag of his own devising, in which Stephanie, standing outside the hotel, shouts to her husband: 'Howard Graham ... You come right down off of that ledge out of that rain before you catch your death of cold!' The anti hero, having emerged victorious from his confrontation with the Nazis, shrinks back against the hotel facade, unable to face his nagging wife.

When supervising the re edit, Welles had decided to write and direct a new ending set in the hotel's deserted bar. In the first version, Graham, afraid his wife won't let him into her room, finishes his letter to her. When a bellboy arrives and announces that she is waiting for him, Graham tears up the letter, throws the shreds in an ashtray and leaves the room. The bellboy picks up the pieces and puts them in an envelope which he places in his pocket. The second version, a two shot scene lasting just over a minute, was actually filmed by Welles. It attempts to bolster Graham's character at the last minute and consolidate the role of Haki, one of whose scenes had disappeared in the restructuring. A Russian speaking bellboy arrives with a message from Stephanie; Haki, also present in the room, acts as interpreter. Graham, regenerated by his adventures, discovers his conjugal authority, terminates his letter with an emphatic full stop, tears it up and vigorously explains where he found the courage to confront an armed killer with his bare hands: 'I got mad. Spent too much time running away.'

THE INTERVENTIONISTS' CLUB

Foster's letters to Welles during the post production of *Journey into Fear* were always cordial, and with the Mexican episode of *It's All True* Welles had given him the most ambitious material of his career to date. But the producer was not about to relinquish his hold – his decisions were final. There was no element of contempt in this. It was simply a manifestation of power, a demonstration that Welles was just as capable of playing the omnipotent producer as anyone else in Hollywood. Zanuck and Selznick, figures of immense influence and discernment, were primarily men of power while Welles was a creative artist. It is clear, however, that all three producers were cut from the same cloth.

Joseph Cotten and Welles.

IT'S ALL TRUE

1942

The anthology film *It's All True* underwent a number of urgent re-adjustments, particularly between its conception in July 1941 and the political and financial guarantees put up by the Office of the Coordinator of Inter-American Affairs at the end of that year. As time went on, a prestigious and logistically complex production deteriorated into an enthusiastic but decidedly shoestring effort. *It's All True* marked a radical turning point in Welles's career as a filmmaker and presented many of the challenges he would later enjoy in Europe: natural settings, a rough outline rather than a screenplay, a shooting schedule that changed from day to day, no synchronized sound and a mountain of footage that would have to be subjected to draconian editing. In this instance, however, RKO had already turned its back on the film which he was not allowed to complete.

Previous pages:
Welles among the crowd at the Rio carnival.

Left:
Welles meets Brazilian president Getúlio Vargas.

Opposite page:
In the fishing village of Fortaleza for the *Jangadeiros* segment.

A CONSTANTLY EVOLVING PROJECT

When Welles registered the title *It's All True* on 29 July 1941, he had in mind a film composed of four autonomous segments linked by a common thread, a rare approach in Hollywood cinema. Two of the stories had already been confirmed, as indicated in a letter to Joseph Breen, RKO's production head, dated 10 July. Besides expressing a desire to work with cameraman Gregg Toland again, Welles suggested that Mercury Productions negotiate contracts with Duke Ellington, Louis Armstrong and Robert Flaherty. The two musicians would appear with other leading jazz artists in a story to be written in collaboration with Ellington. Welles also wanted to buy the rights to *Bonito the Bull*, a short story about the friendship between a young boy and a fighting bull he saves from the arena, which Flaherty, the acclaimed director of *Nanook of the North*, had written twelve years earlier. The third segment, *Love Story*, the tale of an Italian immigrant couple in the San Francisco Bay area, would be written by Welles and the young novelist John Fante. An adaptation of one of the stories from *The Captain's Chair*, a 1938 novel by Flaherty based on his experiences in the Arctic, was a possibility for the final segment.

The idea was further evidence of Welles's fondness for the short form; he had exploited it intensively in his dramatizations for radio and would continue to do so when he would begin working for television. The paradoxical link between the four very dissimilar stories of *It's All True* stemmed from the identity of their heroes, all of whom – from Mexico to the Yukon – were far removed from the traditional Hollywood models. Their diversity formed a mosaic of ethnic and cultural minorities that the cinema had previously tended to ignore.

The project underwent radical revision after the attack on Pearl Harbor in December 1941. Nelson Rockefeller, a major RKO shareholder and director of the Office of the Coordinator of Inter-American Affairs (CIAA), spotted the film's potential for furthering President Roosevelt's 'good neighbour' policy in South America. Rockefeller came up with an offer that was too good to refuse: not only would the CIAA throw its full weight behind the film, it would also provide up to $300,000 to cover the studio against any losses the film might sustain at the box office. In late December Welles, then in the middle of filming *The Magnificent Ambersons*, completely revised *It's All True*, for the CIAA deal meant that all four stories had to be set in Latin America. There were other, more personal, reasons for the enthusiasm with which he set about the task, including his support for Roosevelt and his desire to take an active role in domestic politics. It is also likely that the twenty-six-year-old director saw the project as a way to deflect criticism over his exemption from military service.

Life Goes to Rio Party

Orson Welles frolics at famous Mardi Gras

By far the biggest frolic in all Latin America is Rio de Janeiro's annual *Carnaval* which runs from the Saturday to the Mardi Gras (Fat Tuesday) before Ash Wednesday, which begins Lent. For those four days the 2,000,000 citizens of Rio go mad, after preparations and build-up lasting most of the preceding year. On the following pages LIFE tries in color to give some of the inexpressible quality of this mass outburst.

A sharp observer at this year's carnival was Hollywood Director Orson ("Citizen Kane") Welles, intent on catching the carnival with cameras for a "goodwill" movie about Latin America. The movie, tentatively named *It's All True,* uses local amateurs and professionals to act out native legends and historical events, such as the 1,600-mile trip last year of four Brazilian raft-fishermen. For Welles's cameramen, his characters whooped their way through the four days of carnival.

Welles and his characters and crew were literally caught up in pandemonium. They were jostled, serenaded, squirted with perfume by prancing, singing columns of *blocos,* groups who had spent half the year arranging a song, a theme, costumes, banners. They rode with carloads of the costumed upperclass, inching through jammed streets. Welles tried to catch the look and sound of all the varieties of samba, furious, melting, warlike and in march time. He learned, like carnival columnists, to call everything "*empolgante*" (terrific), "*assombrosa*" (stunning) or "*encantadora*" (enchanting). Like everyone else, he was amazed to discover that there is almost no licentiousness, pugnacity or crime in Rio's carnival.

SWEATING LIKE ALL CARIOCAS, ORSON WELLES AIMS A 16-MM. CAMERA AT REVELERS

WELLES (FOREGROUND) FEELS GOOD AT ONE OF THE LOW-CLASS "PEOPLE'S DANCES"

POOR WHITES AND BLACKS ARE TOO DAZED TO RESPOND TO WELLES'S DIRECTION

WELLES SQUIRTS ETHYL CHLORIDE FROM VIAL AT GUEST AT COPACABANA PALACE

GUEST RESPONDS WITH HIS OWN VIAL. WELLES AND HIS COMPANION DUCK IN HASTE

1. What is a jangada?
2. Launching of the jangada.
3. Fishing sequence.
4. Drowning of the boy.
5. Lowering of the sails and return of the jangadeiros.
6. Selling of the fish and news given to family.
7. Finding of the body.
8. Funeral?
9. Meeting and decision.
10. Departure.
11. The journey itself.
12. Arrival.

ITEMS NOT INCLUDED IN THE STORY LINE ITSELF

1. Wedding
    a. Find out about a jangadeiro wedding.
    b. How extensive is it?
    c. Where held?
    d. How are bride and groom dressed?
    e. Is it likely that they be photographed? (Can be – could be)
2. Dying the clothes
    a. Our bride does this.
    b. Do we present this under the heading of clothes dying, or as incidental business for presenting her?
3. Necessary shot
    a. Bride making lace, preferably with type from Iracema and other Iracema characters to round out cast.

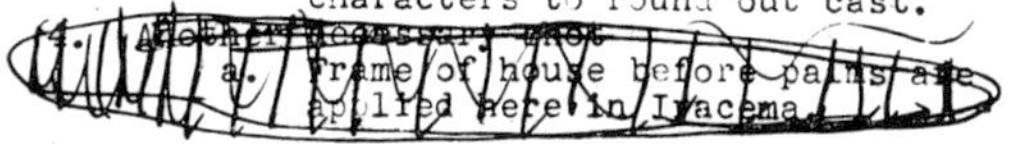
4. Another necessary shot
    a. Frame of house before paints are applied here in Iracema.

Opposite page:
The 18 May 1942 edition of *Life* magazine devoted a whole page to Welles in Rio and followed it with a two-page colour spread featuring the carnival attractions.

Top right:
Sketch for the *Jangadeiros* story line, probably written after Welles's first visit to Fortaleza.

Right:
The fishermen re-create their life in Fortaleza for the camera

Below:
The arrival of the *Jangadeiros* in Rio.

Near-documentary images of some of Brazil's poorest people.

The *Bonito* segment, already underway, had a Mexican setting and thus met the new criteria. The CIAA imposed no demands other than that the opportunity should be seized to include colour footage of the Rio carnival, which took place in February. Fortuitously, the news provided Welles with another Brazilian subject: in early December 1941, the American press reported the odyssey of four *Jangadeiros* – poor fishermen from north-east Brazil – who had sailed a primitive raft 2,500 kilometres down the coast, a sixty-one-day voyage, to present their grievances to President Vargas. As the fishermen's saga would be shot in Brazil, Welles decided to kill two birds with one stone and replace the jazz segment with a samba story, thus extending the carnival footage. Little thought had as yet been given to the final segment, but the conquest of Peru was considered as a way of completing the focus on South America.

There was still no screenplay apart from that for the Mexican episode. A few days before his departure for Rio on 4 February 1942, Welles spoke to a reporter and admitted that he had 'no script, no actors, no preconceived ideas. I'm going down there with a camera, and I hope to record something that will be of interest to the people of all the Americas'. Once in Brazil, he would also have to devise the structural link between segments. For the two Brazilian episodes at least, he could achieve it with a trick that became standard practice in his later television documentaries. By acting as an on-screen presenter he could justify abrupt shifts in the action: he could say goodbye to the fishermen in the hotel, for example, and then join them at the carnival.

MEXICAN INTERLUDE: 'MY FRIEND BONITO'

Welles had made good progress on the Mexican episode, which Norman Foster was scheduled to direct, well before the CIAA arrived on the scene. Adapted by Welles and Fante, *My Friend Bonito* was to be filmed entirely in Mexico, and Welles had accompanied Foster on a location scouting trip in early September 1941 before returning to Hollywood for the last weeks of pre-production on *The Magnificent Ambersons*. The project was unusual in three respects: it would use a non-professional cast recruited locally; it would be shot entirely on location and in near-documentary conditions; and it would employ the brilliant cinematographer Floyd Crosby, who had earned his reputation filming with the documentary-makers Robert Flaherty, Joris Ivens and Pare Lorentz.

The *My Friend Bonito* shoot began at the end of September and lasted ten weeks, far longer than had been expected for just one of the film's four segments. Welles recalled Foster to Hollywood before the shoot was over in order to put him in charge of *Journey into Fear*. The three hours of rushes were assembled into a rough cut but none of the footage was ever screened, not even as a short film, which might at least have given RKO the chance to recoup some of its money.

Little is known about the shoot itself, and it is still a mystery why Foster, a specialist in rapidly filmed, low-budget productions, took so long over it, especially as his cameraman was accustomed to working in the unsettled conditions of the documentary genre. It is even harder to understand why no one was sent to Mexico to finish the shoot – everybody knew the difficulties of resuming it at a later date, particularly as the film's young hero would have grown. The surviving footage contains some striking, almost pictorialist compositions that may have been influenced by the visual style Eisenstein employed for *Que viva México!*. They certainly owe much less to Foster than to Welles himself, who adopted a similar style for the few films of his in which landscape is an important factor – the *Jangadeiros* segment of *It's All True*, *Othello*, *Don Quixote* and *Falstaff*.

A FATAL LACK OF PREPARATION

Once in Rio, Welles had only six days in which to prepare for the carnival, which took place between 14 and 17 February. During this limited period he was expected to familiarize himself with Brazil (a country of which he knew nothing), establish the necessary local contacts, scout locations and deal with the urgent and major problems that cropped up every day. The first unit, led by faithful production assistant Richard Wilson, had arrived the week before. It had brought the cameras and film, but the ship carrying the lighting equipment had been delayed. This equipment was vital: most of the festivities took place at night, and RKO and the CIAA insisted on filming them in Technicolor, a process which demanded an enormous amount of light. In desperation, the unit appealed to the Brazilian army, which, in the spirit of pan-American friendship, provided six specially adapted anti-aircraft searchlights.

Welles was therefore forced to film the carnival in extremely difficult conditions, amongst the heaving throng of festival revellers, with some eighty soldiers placed under the orders of the unit's electricians. He captured whatever he could rather than what he wanted, and his troubles were exacerbated by the need to duplicate all the colour scenes in black and white, as nobody knew how the Technicolor footage would turn out (of the twenty hours of Technicolor rushes, barely more than two hours proved to be usable). Sound recording was equally problematic and the unit had to settle for recording non-synchronized ambient sounds.

Once the carnival was over, Welles was confronted with two major tasks. First, he had to find a way of turning the footage into a proper story. The history of the samba seemed a fruitful prospect given the increasing popularity of Latin American music in the United States. To this end, Welles hired Grande Otelo and Linda Batista, two of the Brazilian music scene's biggest stars, and booked the Cinédia studios, where between April and June he intermittently shot the musical scenes for the film's joyous conclusion on Rio's Praça Onze de Junho. Second, Welles had to develop a complete screenplay and shooting script for what had become the film's dramatic core, the fishermen's epic voyage from Fortaleza to Rio, a passage that covered almost half the Brazilian coastline. At the beginning of March, Welles flew to Salvador de Bahia, and then on to Recife and Fortaleza, in order to scout the stages of their journey. Excited by his meeting with the heroic sailors, he took them back to Rio and booked them into a hotel while waiting for filming to commence.

Besides making his film, Welles had to fulfil his obligations as an informal ambassador and received countless invitations. The atmosphere in the unit was tense, divided as it was between those loyal to the director, technicians with nothing to do, and RKO representatives intent on keeping down costs. In addition, RKO, the CIAA and the Brazilian authorities, all of which had expected the film to celebrate the grand alliance between nation states, were expressing concern over Welles's focus on Brazil's black and mixed race populations. The director of the 'voodoo' *Macbeth* had never made a secret of his hatred of racism in all its forms, and had already attracted considerable hostility at home for demanding that black actors and musicians receive the same respect as their white colleagues. This attitude aroused further opposition in Brazil when, not content with shunning the company of the elite and socializing with popular musicians, he developed a passion for the samba and began researching its African roots. Welles was filming, however, and even fruitfully, since he shot some eighty hours of rushes – a vast amount of footage given that the Brazilian segments would constitute only half the finished film. It was too much for RKO, which also had to fund the protracted stay of a complete unit.

Opportunities to save the project were probably lost during March and April. Welles, still passionate about the discovery of a world previously unknown to him, filmed among the slum dwellers in the hills. This aroused the ire of the local press, previously supportive but now offended by his interest in the 'filthy huts of the *favelas* which infest the lovely edge of the lake where there is so much beauty and so many marvellous angles for filming'. RKO accused him of neglecting his responsibilities as a producer and became even more impatient as shareholders called for the resignation of studio head George Schaefer, formerly his staunchest supporter. At the end of April, six weeks after his arrival in Brazil, Welles had nothing to offer except some carnival scenes and several kilometres of documentary footage, which would not amount to more than a few minutes after the final cut. Moreover, no decisions had yet been taken over the final segment.

In mid-May, Welles began shooting the fishermen's arrival in Rio, although he had not yet filmed the voyage down the coast. On 19 May, Jacaré, the leader of the *Jangadeiros*, was washed overboard and drowned as he re-enacted the triumphant entry into Rio's harbour. Welles was now faced with the problem of filming the bulk of the story without its principal character. Time was running out: on 18 May, Schaefer cabled his representative in Rio and authorized him to cancel the shoot if Welles could not conclude it for less than $30,000. Gambling on shooting the fishermen's voyage with a skeleton crew, Welles concentrated on finishing the carnival scenes, which required considerable technical resources in terms of sound and colour, by 8 June.

FINAL WEEKS ON A SHOESTRING

Most of the crew returned home on 9 June. Welles was now experiencing his first taste of the near-destitution that would become so familiar over the following years. Having arrived with several dozen technicians, he was left with Richard Wilson, Wilson's fiancée Elizabeth Amster, personal assistant Shifra Haran, George Fanto (a Hungarian cameraman living in Brazil) and Reginaldo Calmon, an inexperienced camera operator. His equipment was reduced to the bare minimum: a silent Mitchell camera that Fanto had adapted to take a 25 mm Eyemo lens in order to satisfy the director's love of deep focus. There would be no direct sound and Welles had barely 13,000 metres of black and white film, enough for about seven hours of rushes.

Left:
Welles and George Fanto, cameraman on the last weeks of the shoot.

Opposite page:
Welles and Technicolor cameraman William Howard Greene surrounded by children of Rio.

The tiny unit hired local labour and spent five weeks filming in almost amateur conditions, recording the fishermen's lives in Forteleza, their departure and the landings at Recife and Salvador de Bahia. The iconographic quality of the elaborate, static compositions (there were no dolly tracks) is often evocative of *Que viva México!* while the sculpted cloudscapes, shot through filters, recall the work of the great Mexican cameraman Gabriel Figueroa. Welles experimented with both expanded and reduced framing, photographing numerous close-ups and extreme close-ups of people's faces as well as processions winding their way across wide landscapes. He shot hardly anything of the fishermen's voyage from a boat, but captured it either by filming from the water's edge without showing the shoreline or by placing the sailors ashore and shooting from a low angle so that they were framed against the sky. Their boat was bolted on to a platform rocked by amateur stagehands.

Released from the yoke of a large professional unit, Welles discovered the joys and the inspiration of a location shoot. He could compose silent scenes and worry about adding sound later; or stage action with non-professional actors whose performances he had to 'direct' in some other way. He also learned how to overcome the loss of an indispensable protagonist – in this case the unfortunate Jacaré – by using a double. In effect, he abandoned his usual practices and experimented with another way of filmmaking, which combined the freedom of the documentary and the constraints of a fictional film. He invented the kind of cinema that would eventually reach its apogee with *Othello.*

The six-month stay in Brazil came to an end in late July. Three weeks later, after a final official tour of South America, Welles returned to the United States only to find that things had changed dramatically. RKO, exasperated by a film that epitomized the presumed follies of its former bosses, had lost all interest in the film. The CIAA's withdrawal in May 1943 was the final straw for the studio, which had invested $1.2 million in *It's All True* – far more than for *Citizen Kane* or *The Magnificent Ambersons.* Welles had just had his first encounter with the spectre that was to haunt him for the rest of his life: the possibility of not completing a film in which he had invested all his energy.

THE IMPOSSIBLE DREAM OF FINISHING THE FILM

Welles made repeated attempts to salvage the film until the eve of his departure for Europe in 1947, but potential backers shied away from a vast amount of material that still lacked too many vital elements. In 1944 he managed to arouse the interest of 20th Century-Fox and tried to re-launch the project by buying, on a promissory note, the negative (116,000 metres of Technicolor and 30,000 metres of black and white – seventy and seventeen hours of rushes respectively). He supervised a three-hour cut that included much of the carnival footage, but then defaulted on the debt. The footage reverted to RKO in 1946 and passed from one studio's vaults to another as companies changed hands. Much of the Technicolor carnival footage, unusable since nobody had bothered to acquire the rights to the music, was dumped in the Pacific.

In 1985, an inventory of the material in Paramount's vaults turned up 43,000 metres (about twenty-six hours) of black and white and colour negative, most of it from the *Jangadeiros* segment and Foster's work in Mexico. The following year Richard Wilson put together a twenty-two-minute film, *It's All True: Four Men on a Raft,* in an attempt to persuade potential backers that a film that had never really existed could be restored. The goal was finally achieved in 1993 with the appearance of *It's All True: Based on an Unfinished Film by Orson Welles,* a feature-length work assembled by Wilson, Myron Meisel and Bill Krohn with the support of a French production company.

Besides the contextual material – interviews and archive footage – it includes scenes from the carnival and *My Friend Bonito* and a forty-five-minute cut of *Jangadeiros* with added sound. Although the documentary element constitutes an eloquent tribute to Welles's first adventurous project, the restoration of the *Jangadeiros* segment is a disappointment: the pace is laboured, the editing hesitant, the music uninspired and the sound mix banal and over-reliant on literal synchronization. The restorers might have done the segment more justice by simply guiding us through the rushes, as we will never know how Welles intended to cut his film.

THE STRUGGLE TO REMAIN A PRODUCER

1942–1947

The loss of the battle with RKO was a devastating blow for Welles after the virtually unlimited freedom he had first enjoyed in Hollywood. Having aimed so high he could hardly accept instant defeat, and fought to regain his status as a producer despite the offers of work as a director or actor. After a three-year hiatus, he made three films in a row, although the degree of freedom he was allowed on each of these productions varied considerably.

Once back in the United States in August 1942, Welles and Mercury Productions had nothing to show for their efforts after *Citizen Kane* other than one mutilated film, another whose release had been postponed and a third that RKO refused to edit. All Hollywood directors and producers of high-budget films experience budget overruns and commercial flops; such setbacks do not necessarily spell the end of a career. But Welles's tendency to bulldoze his way through a crisis and his disrespect for the conventions exacerbated the element of risk, which further alienated the studio hierarchy. His public image began to suffer when RKO issued a series of damaging press releases after the split. The dream of an independent production unit operating from the heart of a great studio and lining up film after film had evaporated. In order to stay in the race, Welles had to do some hard bargaining. Most of his future contracts as a director were limited to single films, and those stating a more ambitious programme would result in only one film at the most.

After obtaining another exemption from military service on medical grounds in May 1943, Welles's immediate priority was to protect his status as a producer-director. He had two options: either approach a company with a basic idea or complete script, or accept whatever he was offered. Between the autumn of 1942 and his employment on *The Stranger* three years later, he wrote or co-wrote several scripts, purchased the rights to literary works that could later be adapted for the screen, and assembled a team of writers, some of whom had worked on his radio shows. He turned out scripts for patriotic shorts promoting closer ties with South America and commissioned several feature-length screenplays, often drastically revising the first drafts. None of them found a taker.

The experience with RKO had not led to ostracism and Welles still had many contacts among the major studios and the more ambitious independent producers. The big studios regarded him with suspicion, but their doors were rarely closed. The milieu suited him: he spoke the same language as the producers, while stars admired him and were eager to work under his direction. At one point, in 1943, he even persuaded MGM to distribute an adaptation of Tolstoy's *War and Peace*, which he planned to shoot in London under the aegis of MGM-British in collaboration with Alexander Korda, one of Britain's top producers.

Below:
Make-up test for the role of Rochester in *Jane Eyre* (1943), directed by Robert Stevenson.

Opposite page, top:
The Mercury Wonder Show (1943), Welles and Marlene Dietrich (top), who replaced Rita Hayworth (centre) at the last moment.

Opposite page, bottom:
Joseph Cotten, Hayworth and Welles.

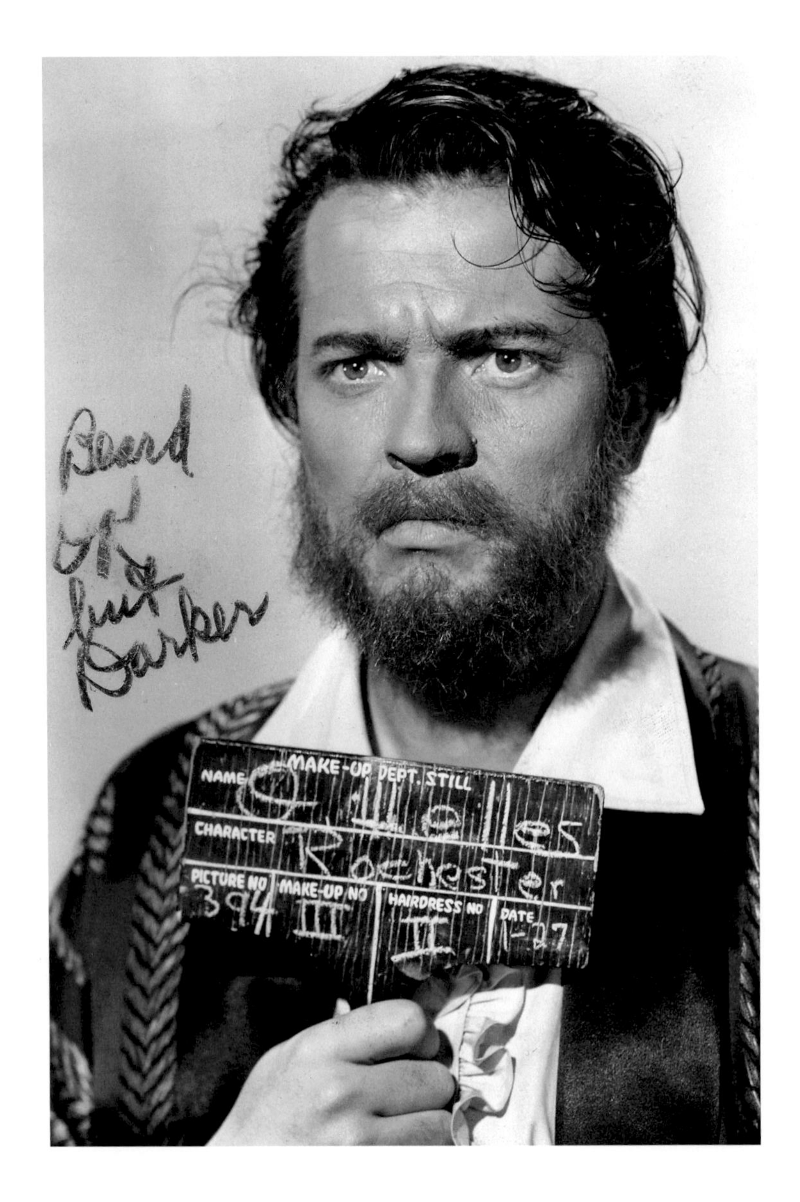

At heart, Welles felt he belonged among the great independent producers. His tendency to bite the hand that fed him had been apparent even before the release of *Citizen Kane*, when he had attacked the Hollywood system in some interviews and articles. In early 1942, shortly before his departure for Brazil and the ensuing conflict with RKO, he had been a founder member of the Society of Independent Motion Picture Producers, an organization set up to combat the monopoly of the major studios. His co-founders were Charles Chaplin, Walt Disney, Samuel Goldwyn, Alexander Korda, Mary Pickford, David O. Selznick and Walter Wanger. Welles looked forward to developing projects with most of these exalted colleagues; Wanger even considered creating a company with him. But none of his proposals, whether pitched to independent producers or studios, bore fruit, while he in turn rejected offers either on script grounds or because they did not grant him what he desired above all else: the restoration of total artistic control.

The major companies were particularly keen to secure Welles's services as an actor: he was offered a variety of parts and a career as a star beckoned. But he resisted the pressure to join a studio star stable for several years, and continued to dismiss most of the single-picture deals, given the insistence on exclusive contracts that would have prevented him from engaging in any other cinematic activity for the duration of the deal. In December 1942, having spent the last six months rejecting offers, he finally agreed to play the male lead in *Jane Eyre*. Selznick had just sold the project to 20th Century-Fox and had suggested Welles for the part. Welles also obtained a position as associate producer, although he would not appear as such on the credits. To the great annoyance of director Robert Stevenson, he took advantage of his star status and meddled in the set design, script revision, casting and editing, besides exerting his influence to bring Bernard Herrmann on board for the music. Over the next couple of years, his screen appearances would be confined to two roles, one for Universal and the other for the small independent company International. The contacts he made on these three films paved the way for his employment as director on *The Stranger* and *Macbeth*.

Welles continued to work as hard as ever despite his steadfast refusal to carve out a career as a Hollywood star. He devoted his energy to promoting the Mercury image in other media and to nurturing his troupe so that he could draw collaborators from the Mercury ranks as soon as a film project materialized.

Welles maintained contact with the public through the CBS radio network. Although his shows had been reduced to thirty minutes, the new industry norm, he was still the producer, director, presenter and star. In the autumn of 1942 he participated in the war effort, directing two weekly radio series over a twelve-week period: one glorified the role of military aviation while the other, sponsored by the CIAA (which had not lost its faith in him), promoted pan-American relations. 1944 saw a six-month run of *The Orson Welles Almanac*, in which Welles, aping the great entertainers such as Jack Benny, presented a medley of dramatic vignettes, comedy sketches, New Orleans jazz, poetry readings and anecdotes that blended fact with fantasy. A drama series followed in 1945, and another in 1946, *The Mercury Summer Theatre of the Air*, which presented new material and revivals of former Mercury hits. Welles secured Herrmann as musical director for two of these programmes. They all featured Mercury players as well as other actors who would later appear in his films. As a star, his salary escalated as he appeared in the most prestigious series of the time. He also responded to an appeal from the Secretary of the US Treasury and organized broadcasts promoting war bonds after the Normandy landings in 1944.

REPUBLIC PICTURES CORPORATION

EXECUTIVE OFFICES

1790 BROADWAY - NEW YORK 19, N.Y.

TELEPHONE COLUMBUS 5-2500

OFFICE OF
THE PRESIDENT

July 18
1947

My Dear Orson:

I am moved to write and congratulate you on the splendid accomplishment of bringing your production of "MacBETH" in on schedule and within budget. The industry has watched this production with great interest, and I am happy to say that from my close personal observation never in my thirty-four years in this business have I seen a job so well done.

I must admit that I was just a shade doubtful when you first told me of your revolutionary plans for the production of "MacBETH". The job of adapting this immortal Shakespearean drama to the screen and translating it to a commercial motion picture seemed to me to be an almost unsurmountable and monumental undertaking. However, I had faith in you. I had confidence in your ability to do what you said, and your integrity to deliver what you promised. Needless to say, you have more than justified my confidence.

From the human side, once again you have made history in Hollywood. The job you have done has not only served as an inspiration to your own cast and crew, but to every other company on the Republic lot — in fact, in every studio in Hollywood. In this day of rising costs and sky-rocketing budgets, it has become mandatory that all of us engaged in the business of making motion pictures do everything in our power to make it possible for us to stay in business. You have demonstrated beyond a doubt that superior product can still be made within reasonable cost and with assurance of a justifiable return.

Again I salute you and congratulate you on the greatest individual job of acting, directing, adapting and producing that to my knowledge Hollywood has ever seen.

Sincerely,
Herbert J. Yates.

Mr. Orson Welles
Republic Productions
North Hollywood.

Above:
Letter from Herbert J. Yates, president of Republic Pictures, written the day after *Macbeth* finished shooting. His satisfaction with the rapidity of the shoot would turn to bitterness during the protracted editing.

Top right:
Welles, associate producer Richard Wilson and Rita Hayworth on the set for *The Lady from Shanghai.*

Right:
In 1945, Mercury's headed paper had to rest on the laurels of productions at least three years old, with the exception of *The Mercury Wonder Show*

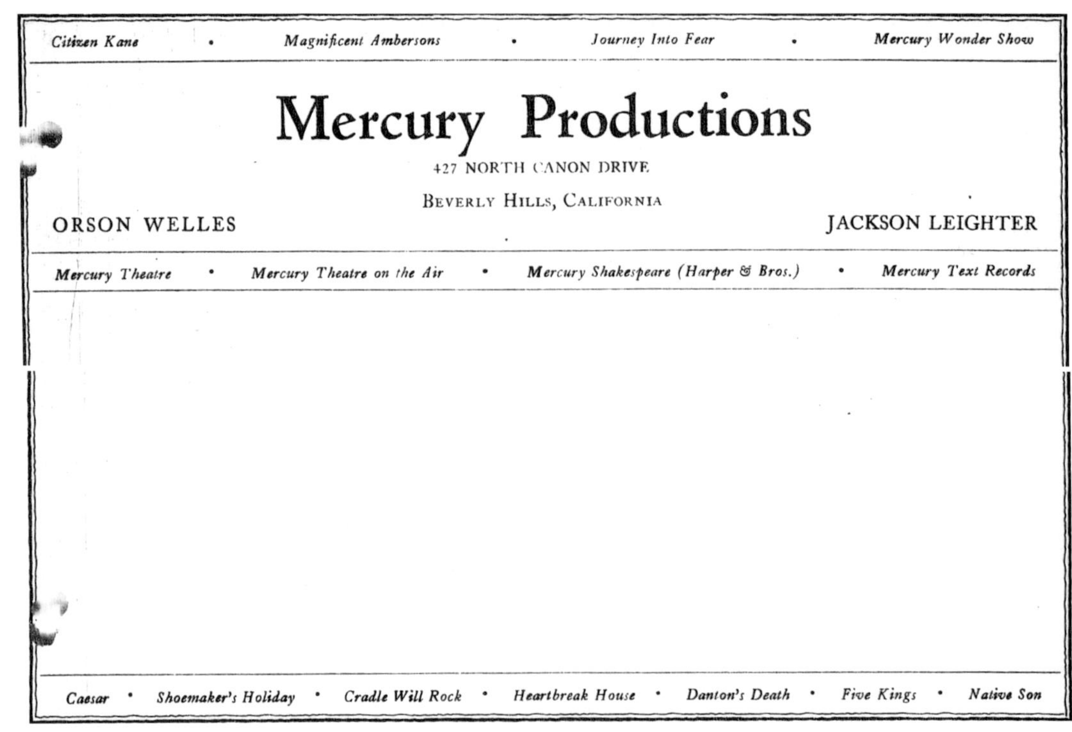
Citizen Kane • *Magnificent Ambersons* • *Journey Into Fear* • *Mercury Wonder Show*

Mercury Productions

427 NORTH CANON DRIVE

BEVERLY HILLS, CALIFORNIA

ORSON WELLES

JACKSON LEIGHTER

Mercury Theatre • *Mercury Theatre on the Air* • *Mercury Shakespeare (Harper & Bros.)* • *Mercury Text Records*

Caesar • *Shoemaker's Holiday* • *Cradle Will Rock* • *Heartbreak House* • *Danton's Death* • *Five Kings* • *Native Son*

On the other hand, Welles did little theatrical work, staging only two productions during the same period. The first of these was not a play at all, but a magic show designed to boost the morale of the troops stationed in Los Angeles. Entitled *The Mercury Wonder Show*, Welles put up most of the money for it himself. A 2,000-seat big tent was erected in the heart of Hollywood in the summer of 1943. Welles took centre stage as the great magician, assisted by Joseph Cotten and Agnes Moorehead. He had planned to saw Rita Hayworth in half but replaced her with Marlene Dietrich when Harry Cohn, the president of Columbia Pictures, refused to jeopardize the image of his only major female star. Welles married Hayworth shortly afterwards and the couple had a daughter, Rebecca. In 1946 he returned to New York to stage *Around the World*, a musical comedy based on Jules Verne's *Around the World in Eighty Days*, adapting it himself and persuading Cole Porter to provide the music and lyrics. The days of non-stop rehearsals were over, however, as union rules now limited actors' working hours. The co-producer and chief backer withdrew before the rehearsals were over, having realized the colossal cost of an extravaganza that required constant, split-second timing from its singers, dancers, orchestra leader and fifty-odd stagehands. Welles refused to accept defeat and invested his own money in the show, which was to plunge him heavily into debt. In 1944, Decca asked Welles to record speeches and texts by American presidents, Pericles and Lazare Carnot, among others, as well as extracts from the *Song of Songs* and an adaptation of Oscar Wilde's *The Happy Prince*, for which Welles commissioned more music from Herrmann.

The possibility of another, more unexpected career loomed on the horizon. Welles's readiness to take a position on social and political issues, evident from the outset of his theatrical career, had gained him a wide audience. After an initial flirtation with the radical left, he rapidly aligned himself with the Democrat party, and his enunciations of injustice and oppression never ceased. His loathing of fascism, asserted long before America renounced its isolationist stance, was as deeply felt as his detestation of racism. In the autumn of 1943, he formed close links with the Free World organization, which defended the rights of nations threatened by fascism. Its pivot was the ex-Comintern member Louis Dolivet, a Romanian with French nationality, who had been living in exile in the United States for the last three years. Dolivet became a close friend as well as a political mentor. Over an eight-month period in 1945 Welles often aired his political views in a daily and then a weekly column in the *New York Post*. The column failed to achieve wide syndication and the experiment was soon abandoned. For three years, much of his time was devoted to political activity. Supported by a team of researchers, he addressed vast crowds, participated in conventions and meetings, and chaired radio discussions. He campaigned for Roosevelt's re-election in autumn 1944, championed the League of Nations and supported the creation of the United Nations Organization. In autumn 1945 he began a twelve-month stint for ABC, presenting *Orson Welles Commentaries*, a patchwork of political analysis, literary readings and anecdotes laced with a campaign against a brutal police beating in America's Deep South. The show came to an abrupt end in the autumn of 1946, when he began filming *The Lady from Shanghai*.

This was the point at which Welles, anxious to continue making films, finally relinquished the total artistic control he had tried so hard to retain. Once he had taken that step, he made three feature films in three years. *The Stranger* (International, 1945) was to be his most conventional film, an attempt to regain Hollywood's confidence by playing its game and accepting a position as a hired hand. *The Lady from Shanghai* (Columbia, 1946), the biggest production of his career, turned into a test of strength. Welles was ostensibly the producer, but was no match for the inflexible Harry Cohn, who eventually mutilated the film. He managed to exercise greater influence over *Macbeth* (Republic, 1947): the studio was a minor player and as the producer he was able to dominate its executives whenever conflict arose. Each of these films involved a struggle to control the final cut.

Right:
Welles and Loretta Young (the future star of *The Stranger*) playing the leading roles in a radio adaptation of *Jane Eyre* produced by Cecil B. DeMille in 1944.

35

THE STRANGER
1946

As *The Stranger* was not a Mercury production, Welles temporarily abandoned his quest for total control. Kept on a tight rein by his producers, he took on a screenplay written by others, filming it with an almost anonymous efficiency. Even so, he managed to take his visual style a step further and created some visually fresh and striking images.

Previous pages:
Welles and the vaudeville comedian Billy House (Potter).

Left:
Welles on the Harper set.

Opposite page:
Welles (Kindler) and Loretta Young (Mary).

PRODUCER POWER

In 1944 Welles had his first commercial success as a screen actor with *Jane Eyre*, directed by Robert Stevenson and produced by William Goetz for 20th Century-Fox. The following year, Goetz joined forces with Leo Spitz to create his own company, International Pictures. He entrusted the distribution of his films to RKO and asked Welles to act in what would become another box-office success – *Tomorrow Is Forever*, directed by Irving Pichel. The good relationship with Goetz was probably responsible for the offer Welles received in 1945: a part in *The Stranger*, a new International production following hard on the heels of Fritz Lang's *Scarlet Street*, starring Edward G. Robinson. Shortly afterwards, Welles was also asked to direct the film. But he found himself under the direct authority of independent producer Sam Spiegel, who had teamed up with International for *The Stranger*.

Spiegel's own company, Eagle Productions, had bought the original story (*The Trap*, written in 1933 by the German director Victor Trivas) the previous year. Eagle had also purchased the screen adaptation by Trivas and Decla Dunning. Spiegel commissioned a new version from Anthony Veiller, an experienced screenwriter and producer. John Huston, already acclaimed as director of *The Maltese Falcon*, had some input but was serving in the armed forces at the time and received no credit for his contribution. *The Stranger* was therefore something of a pet project for Spiegel and he intended to control it from the outset. Welles, far from regaining the independence he had once enjoyed, would have to compromise with a manipulative and authoritarian producer. The terms of his contract reflect the suspicion with which he was regarded in the industry. In effect, Welles had to agree to indemnify the producer if he was unable to finish the film.

Right:
First version of the set for the small town of Harper, which was initially to be built on a lot belonging to 20th Century-Fox. As in the final version, Potter's drugstore (bottom) and the church face each other across the square. Rankin's house and the inn in which Wilson takes up lodgings were part of the same set, but not the judge's house or the river, both of which appear in the film.

Opposite page, top:
Welles directs Edward G. Robinson (Inspector Wilson).

Opposite page, bottom:
The townsfolk search the woods for Meinike.

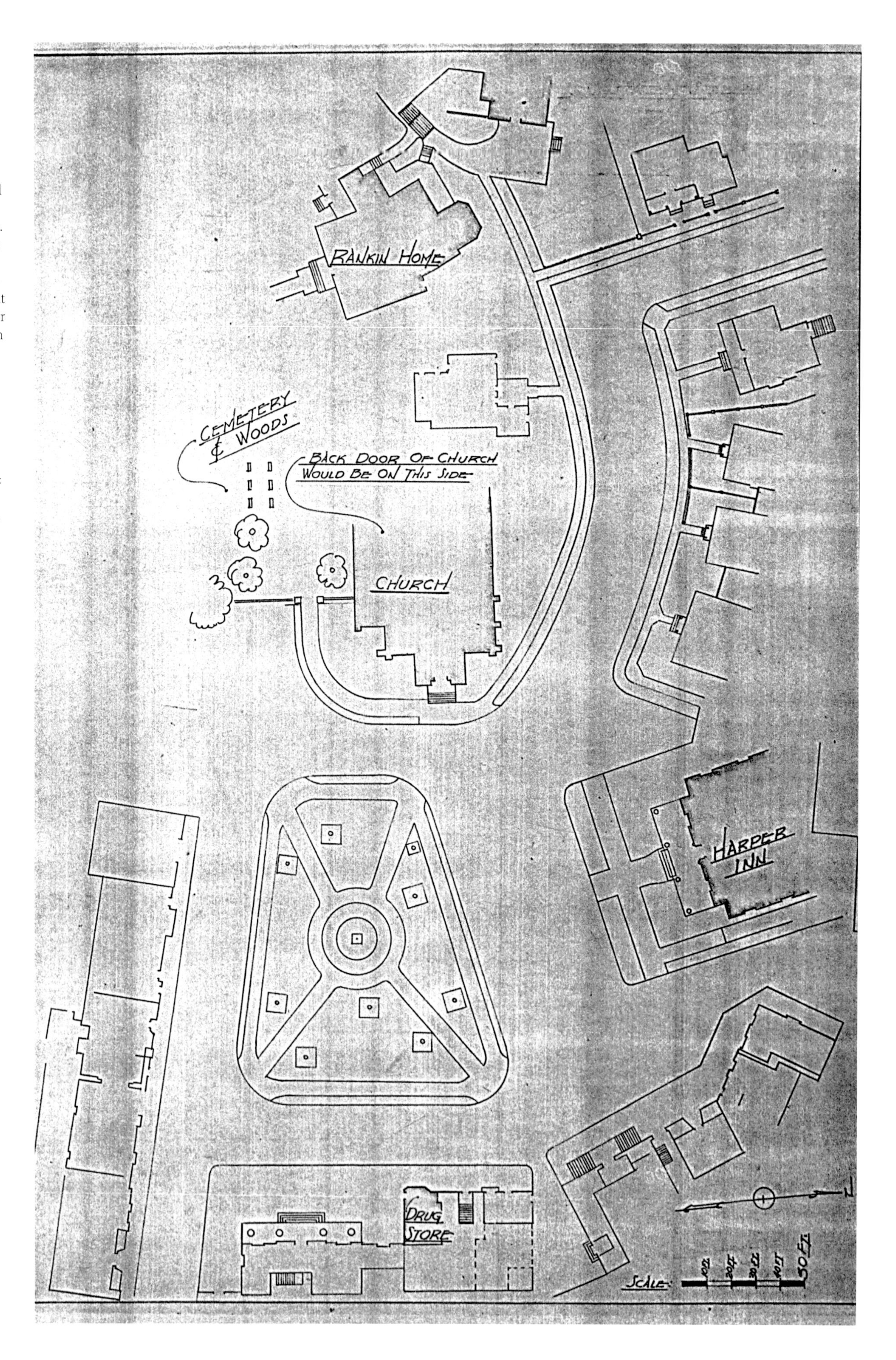

Moreover, if he was removed as director, he would still have to work on the film as an actor, or vice versa. He had no say in casting the leading roles, and was obliged to accept the production company's choice of technicians, although these were all solid professionals. *The Stranger* was also a test of his good behaviour: if Welles respected the shooting schedule and budget, International would give him a four-picture deal. In actual fact this never materialized despite the success of the gamble.

A 'HANDS-OFF' SCRIPT

As usual, Welles tried to impose his personality on the film and meddle with the screenplay. The story concerns a Nazi, Franz Kindler, who assumes a new identity as a teacher named Rankin and settles in Harper, a small New England town. While awaiting the emergence of the Fourth Reich, he teaches in the local school and marries Mary Longstreet, a judge's daughter. When discovered by Meinike, a fellow Nazi, Kindler kills him in order to maintain his cover. But Meinike was himself being pursued by an investigator, Wilson, who was hoping his prey would eventually lead him to Kindler. Wilson soon becomes suspicious of the teacher and persuades Mary to help him. After attempting to kill Mary, Kindler falls to his death from a clock tower. Welles tried, without success, to liven up this banal and predictable plot by introducing two major changes. Given the overly conventional character of the investigator, he suggested substituting a somewhat sour-tempered spinster, to be played by his beloved Agnes Moorehead. Spiegel and Goetz, looking for a box-office draw, overruled him and cast Edward G. Robinson, who turned in a routine performance. Welles also came up with a twenty-minute prologue set in South America: this would clarify the context – the post-war for Nazis – and provide some much-needed visual interest before the action shifted to Harper. Veiller incorporated the prologue into the screenplay, where it did not remain long before attracting the attention of Ernest Nims. Nims, in charge of editing at International, specialized in scrutinizing screenplays in order to detect scenes he considered superfluous: anything that did not advance the plot had to go. Most of the South American scenes were jettisoned before shooting began; in Nims's view, they simply slowed down the action. Some brief scenes of Meinike crossing the border under the surveillance of Wilson and his agents survived the surgery, as did Meinike's visit to the photographer who alerts him to Kindler's whereabouts. Two more scenes from the prologue (about five minutes of footage) were filmed but later trimmed from the final cut. In one particularly striking scene, the body of a female agent is carried into a morgue, the implication being that she has been savaged by dogs belonging to Nazi thugs.

Welles's hand can still be seen in structural elements that were abandoned after shooting started: the attempts to alter the linearity of the narrative by opening with Kindler's death and the puzzlement of the witnesses as to the victim's true identity, followed by a flashback triggered by Wilson's notebook. Welles's influence is even more apparent in an exchange that was eliminated at a very late stage (possibly during the final cut, as it features on a list of scenes still to be shot drawn up nine days before filming ended). Presaging Harry Lime's ironic homage to the Swiss cuckoo clock in Carol Reed's *The Third Man* (1949), Kindler, passionate about old clocks, holds forth on their symbolism: the power that sets the clock in motion is the head of state; the pendulum is his government, which transforms his inspiration into law; the cogs are the toiling masses, striving together without friction; their teeth, individuals 'of good blood, trained and fit physically'.

Two important scenes were deleted after shooting had begun and may not have been filmed at all. One was simply a matter of dramatic economy: instead of showing Rankin's courtship of Mary, followed by the announcement to her father of their engagement, the action would begin on the day of their wedding in Harper. The other, a much more intriguing proposition, concerned Mary's nightmare. Programmed for the very end of the shoot, it would have combined spectacular photography – focal distortions and vertiginous tilts – with a multi-layered soundtrack, a melange of voices, confused echoes and music.

THE DECISION TO FILM IN A STUDIO

The sets for *The Stranger* presented the production company with a major problem. Much of the action unfolded in the streets of Harper (between Potter's drugstore and Dr Lawrence's office on its first floor), Rankin's house, Judge Longstreet's house and the church, the town's central and dominant feature. Street scenes represented no more than five days and six nights – about one fifth of the shooting schedule – but the credibility of the action depended on realistic exteriors, which themselves were of considerable dramatic importance. Hitchcock had been confronted with a similar situation two years earlier when filming *Shadow of a Doubt*, in which much of the action occurred on the streets of a small American town. Departing from his usual practice, he shot all the exteriors in a real Californian town, Santa Rosa. Spiegel was more cautious and decided to build the exteriors on a lot rented from a major company; the interiors would be filmed at the small Goldwyn studio in old Hollywood. A comparative cost appraisal had already established that building sets on 20th Century-Fox property would save a mere $8,000 – an almost negligible sum in relation to the film's total budget. Spiegel obviously wanted to eliminate the possibility of delays due to bad weather, but was probably also anxious to prevent his director from straying too far: Welles's lack of discipline on the *It's All True* shoot in Brazil was still fresh in people's minds.

Even these modest forecasts had to be downwardly revised. All the Harper street scenes were eventually shot on the permanent small-town set that stood on one of Universal's back lots. Curiously, the only spatial relationship clearly established within the set is that between church and drugstore, which face each other across a large central square planted with a few trees. There were, however, enough buildings on the lot to include Rankin's house, Longstreet's house and even the high-school gym which, according to the shooting script, stood next to it. The cemetery adjoining the church – a crucial element in the script – was sacrificed and only appears in a single shot, isolated from its surroundings. Rankin's house lost its direct visual relationship to the rest of the town – all the more so as its curtains are always drawn. The location of Judge Longstreet's house, on the side of the square bordered by a stream spanned by a small bridge, was established by simply stitching together a couple of related shots. The director's choices seem to be at odds with those of his producers. The latter had envisaged a conventional environment, the architectural components of which could be portrayed with relative ease. The film, however, reduces the town's dimensions to a nerve centre – Potter's drugstore – and ensures that the homes of Rankin and Longstreet are physically excluded from the rest of the community. Welles's part in this is now impossible to determine, but spatial dislocation was certainly one of the most characteristic – and striking – elements of his later work.

Right:
Climbing the clock tower.
Welles and Loretta Young.

Below:
Konstantin Shayne (Meinike), seen here with Loretta Young, played the first of the great angst-ridden characters that roam the Wellesian universe. Shayne introduced Welles to his brother-in-law, Akim Tamiroff, who also went on to play many similar characters.

Overleaf, left:
A doomed marriage: Welles and Loretta Young with Byron Keith (Dr Lawrence), Philip Merivale (Mary's father) and Neal Dodd (the minister).

Overleaf, right:
The banality of family life: Edward G. Robinson, Richard Long (Mary's brother), Loretta Young, Martha Wentworth (the housekeeper), Welles, Philip Merivale and Byron Keith.

It was probably chance rather than a considered decision that brought Welles and Perry Ferguson, his art director on *Citizen Kane*, together again. Ferguson had left RKO after *Citizen Kane* and had signed a six-year contract with the Goldwyn company, which, like International, entrusted the distribution of its films to RKO. As all the interiors were to be shot in the Goldwyn studios, Spiegel must have regarded Ferguson as the logical choice for the set design. The result was somewhat mediocre – or at least lacking in the visual inventiveness so typical of Welles's first films – and revealed the inconsistencies of the *mise en scène*. The only decorative element with a touch of originality was the clock at the top of the church tower, an imposing mechanism complete with the medieval statues that were to provide the climax by propelling Rankin to his death. The clock itself, a genuine mid-nineteenth-century timepiece, was borrowed from the reserve stock of a Los Angeles museum, but the audience is allowed only brief glimpses of its face and even fewer of its mechanism, which was hoisted up the tower with considerable effort, according to the publicity department. The statues, an incongruous feature on a New England clock tower, were created in the studio for the final scenes in the tower.

Welles turned self-imposed constraints (which he also clearly inflicted on Loretta Young and Richard Long – Mary and her younger brother – but not Robinson) to spectacular advantage by filming most of his characters' ascents to the mechanism inside the clock tower itself. The tower was completely enclosed and access to the top, a ten-metre climb, was by means of a rickety and near-vertical wooden ladder. Using overhead and extreme low-angle shots he succeeded brilliantly in conveying a sense of danger, whereas the matching shots of the climbs filmed in the studio were much more prosaic.

FURTHER EXPERIMENTATION WITH LIGHT

Fortunately, the visually uninspiring sets were redeemed by Russell Metty's exceptional camerawork. Metty, then a little-known photographer who would begin a two-decade association with Universal-International in 1947, had spent the previous two years working on low-budget independent productions. He had done some minor work on *Citizen Kane* and *Ambersons* while under contract to RKO, but Welles's decision to employ him was probably influenced more by his reputation for speed.

In contrast to Welles's usual preferences, Metty took his inspiration from the bold chiaroscuro effect of the early *noir* films and introduced a more fluid element. Instead of using deep focus and powerful lights, he tended to favour an image that did not extend so far into the background, one in which all the characters' lateral movements were accompanied by sudden transitions from shadow to clarity as they entered the illuminated areas of the set.

This strategy resulted in extremely unstable visual compositions: the lighting often brought the human figure into stark emphasis – even in the brilliant scenes of Rankin alone in the woods at night (shot in day for night) – at the expense of facial detail. The finest example is the two-shot sequence of Rankin and Mary in the church. The first, lasting almost two and a half minutes, opens with a close-up of Rankin, whose sudden movement, which leaves only his hands and arms in the frame, leads to a close-up of Mary. As Mary, still seen from the same angle, gets to her feet, both characters appear in stark outline before their exit towards the rear, which the travelling camera transforms into a shadow play. In the second shot, the shadow figures come together for a kiss, which the play of light renders abstract.

Metty's contribution to the rare long takes (another Wellesian touch on a film in which the abundance of shot-reverse-shots signals adherence to standard filmmaking) is equally arresting. The most complex of these, lasting over four minutes, depicts the meeting between Meinike and Rankin in the woods, from the moment Rankin opens his arms to welcome his former lieutenant to the moment he strangles him. This is a remarkable sequence in which the camera traverses a clearing before penetrating a dense thicket. It begins with a very high overhead shot that follows the characters' movements, then unobtrusively descends to their level before capturing them in a low-angle shot as they fall to the ground, locked in a murderous embrace. The whole scene is infused with dramatic tension yet it is shot discreetly, with none of the bravura evident in Welles's other films.

SUCCESS AND A LESSON

Welles was able to make *The Stranger* in relatively comfortable conditions, although the degree of comfort was in itself responsible for limiting his scope for any real initiative, particularly during post-production. Yet the film, despite its unoriginal editing, bland sound mix and mediocre, studio-imposed score, turned out to be his only commercial success. And it does tell us that Welles was perfectly capable of carving out a lasting career in Hollywood ...had he been willing to stop being himself.

THE LADY FROM SHANGHAI

1947

The methods Welles adopted in shooting *The Lady from Shanghai* were turned upside down by his producers. In the early weeks of the shoot he enjoyed considerable freedom, but then Columbia intervened, demanding that he shoot dozens of retakes and excluding him from the final stages of editing. Columbia's decisions completely distorted the experiment he was trying to conduct: to make a thriller on location for almost the first time in Hollywood history.

FROM NEW YORK TO EXOTIC MEXICO

In spring 1946, when Welles was desperately seeking financial backing for the final weeks of rehearsal of his stage musical *Around the World*, Harry Cohn, president of Columbia Pictures, lent him $25,000, a quarter of his normal salary as a director. An agreement was reached for a shoot. Columbia, one of Hollywood's Little Three companies, specializing in B movies, was not as big as RKO, but Welles would have greater latitude on the set than he had had for *The Stranger*, since he was once again an external producer.

For their text, Welles and Cohn chose a crime novel by Sherwood King, *If I Die Before I Wake* (1938), set entirely in New York and the surrounding area. In April, when preparing his adaptation, Welles wanted to shoot all the exteriors on location in New York, making a low-budget film, without a star, with a reduced shooting schedule. He was therefore a year or two in advance of directors of thrillers such as Anthony Mann, who were looking for an almost documentary realism on the streets of American cities. Welles intended that the young actress Barbara Laage, whom he had taken under contract without being able to employ her, should play the female lead, but Cohn preferred to build the film around his star, Rita Hayworth. Welles was now separated from his wife, acclaimed for her roles in musicals and in Charles Vidor's *Gilda*, which had just opened. Thus *The Lady from Shanghai* was to be a prestigious 'Class AA' film, and the biggest production of Welles's career.

Previous pages:
Columbia's publicity photos did not match the scenes to which they referred: the backless dress worn here by Rita Hayworth is not the much more severe one she wears in this scene in the film.

Opposite page:
Rita Hayworth (Elsa Bannister) in Chinatown.

Above:
Michael (Welles) is hired by Bannister (Everett Sloane), watched by two seamen played by Louis Merrill and Gus Schilling.

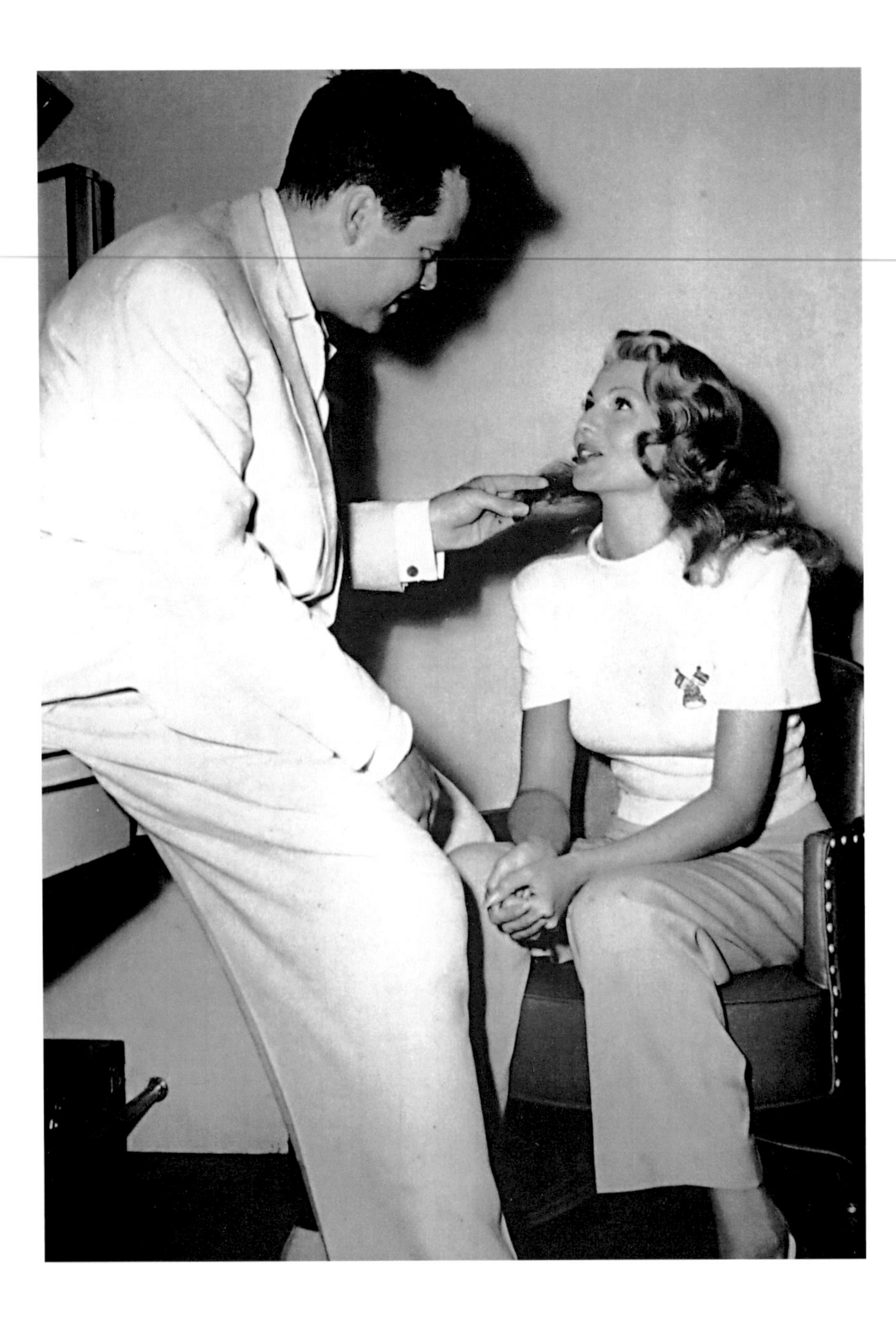

The film was promoted before it was shot, with this visit to the hairdresser, when Welles had Rita Hayworth's red hair cut short and turned her into a blonde.

Welles nevertheless managed to shoot a good part of *The Lady from Shanghai* on location, when, after writing several versions during the summer, he decided to set the screenplay in California and Latin America, mainly in Mexico. The project became what he later called 'an exercise in eroticism and exoticism'. His adaptation retained the book's basic plot: an Irishman (an American in the novel), Michael O'Hara, is recruited by a big-time criminal lawyer, Bannister, and falls in love with his young wife, Elsa. Bannister's associate, Grisby, offers Michael a large sum of money if he will pretend to kill him, allowing him to start a new life. Michael accepts, so that he can run off with Elsa. The story, then, involves murders, the trial of an innocent man and the exposure of the guilty woman. Whereas Welles had Americanized the main characters in his adaptations of English novels (*Heart of Darkness*, *Journey into Fear* and various other projects), here he changed the hero's nationality in the opposite direction, as he would do later in *Touch of Evil*, adding the theme of a culture clash, of which there is no suggestion in his source.

The action still begins in New York, then a cruise takes the characters to Cuba and the Caribbean, through the Panama Canal and up the coast of Mexico, before they disembark at San Francisco, where the threads of the plot finally tie up. Michael, who was the Bannisters' chauffeur in the novel and the early screenplays, becomes the bosun on their yacht, and Welles added many details that make the screenplay more cosmopolitan. Michael, a notorious waterfront agitator, fought for the Spanish Republic, and has seen the inside of prisons in various parts of the world. Echoing *It's All True*, he tells a tale about sharks devouring each other in the waters of the Brazilian port of Fortaleza, and denounces the evils of civilization. Grisby, who supported Franco, fears the atom bomb. The 'Lady from Shanghai' herself has much closer links with China than in King's novel: they are explained in the screenplay, but remain obscure, to say least, in the re-cut film. Welles retained only a few lines of the novel's dialogue.

Once it had been decided that Elsa and Michael were to be played by Hayworth and himself, Welles was able to cast the rest of the roles as he pleased, without favouring actors under contract to Columbia. The jealous Bannister would be played by Everett Sloane, and the nervous Grisby by Glenn Anders, whose extrovert character Welles knew at first hand through having had him play a delightful talking chimpanzee in a 1941 radio broadcast. Welles treated these two actors as equals and gave half a dozen small parts to members of the original Mercury company or to loyal colleagues from recent radio broadcasts. On the other hand, he did not enjoy the same freedom in assembling his crew, since he had to accept the in-house technicians, some of them second-rate, that Columbia provided.

IN THE MEXICAN JUNGLE

The first shoot, beginning on 2 October 1946, took place in Columbia's studios. The sets were designed by Sturges Carné, whose fourth film this was as art director. Carné had not been involved in looking for locations in Mexico, and stayed *in situ* for the following weeks to prepare the studio sets. Then, on 13 October, things got under way. *The Lady from Shanghai* was the first Hollywood production for many years to take so large a unit abroad. It is hard to imagine today what an adventure this expedition was. In the previous year, Columbia had made its major film, *Gilda* (set in Argentina and Uruguay), exclusively in Hollywood. At the very time Welles was shooting, RKO sent only a second unit to take a few long shots of Acapulco for the fifteen minutes in which the action of Jacques Tourneur's *Out of the Past* takes place there.

Welles would have liked to take a small unit and to work quickly, but he found himself leading a veritable Hollywood armada. To judge from the figures supplied to the press, in addition to the actors, around forty technicians flew to Acapulco. Six tons of equipment (out of a total of fifteen tons) was thought to be the largest air cargo consignment ever used in the production of a film. On location, the logistics were complex. Some scenes required the unit to go through the jungle, and hundreds of porters and canoemen had to be hired to transport the equipment. The sound truck and the generators were loaded on to platforms carried on a number of canoes lashed together. Welles actually filmed on board a yacht belonging to Errol Flynn, renamed the *Circe* for the purposes of the film. This meant lining up a dozen or so canoes behind the sailing boat; above this improvised pontoon was stretched a cable that attached the equipment to the boat carrying the generator. For shots that would not make it into the final edit, the camera was placed on board a canoe attached to the one in which the actors stood.

In certain respects, this part of the film could have become another *It's All True*, with a star. But *The Lady from Shanghai* also speaks about corruption in a Mexico invaded by tourists, and the lines they speak contain attacks on frivolousness and an obsession with money. The magical bay of Acapulco, a former fishing port, has become a holiday resort for the privileged. Welles, who again favoured a short focal length and wide shots, made a series of ever-varying connections between his characters and their settings. When he filmed Elsa sunbathing on a rock at one port of call, the yacht and the bay were in the distance. On land, he favoured long takes, some static, others with the camera moving on a crane, ignoring the problems posed by steep slopes, and forcing the actors to hold very precise positions.

The movements of the extras, of whom there were often dozens, including swarms of children, were as complex as those of the seasoned actors, the camera and the sound engineer's boom. Welles shot the conversation between Michael and Grisby about the 'business proposition' that Grisby makes to Michael (a murder for a $5,000 fee) in long takes that meander up and down Acapulco's hills, in order to establish the beauty of the bay at the very moment Grisby expresses his fear that the world will be destroyed by the atom bomb. He took dizzying, almost vertical overhead shots (further distorted by shortening the focal length) over a stone parapet at the top of a cliff: when the camera at last captures the two men in close-up, it is as if they are suspended in mid-air above the sea, with the water shimmering between their faces.

These long takes and wide angles never exclude the local population: Welles's scenes teem with extras, and are full of information about the everyday lives of anonymous people. When Elsa and Michael take a walk at night through working-class Acapulco, the two Hollywood stars pass by arcades through which we can see into bars and the dilapidated homes of families sitting at table. Elsa runs down a street in which pigs are wandering about.

Welles shot the nocturnal picnic – during which his characters tear one another apart – at Pie de la Cuesta, a long, narrow beach of white sand lying between the Pacific and a freshwater lagoon ten kilometres north of Acapulco. (In the screenplay, this was the last stop on the cruise, but Columbia took liberties with the geography and reversed their order.) This spit of sand allowed Welles to have an expanse of water behind the characters in both the shots and the reverses. The depth of field highlights the contrast between the holidaymakers in their hammocks and the fishing community for whom life goes on as usual: the lagoon is full of people on foot, canoemen and people on horseback carrying flaming torches. Welles centred his long takes on his actors' ensemble playing, and on the interaction between Elsa, Bannister and Grisby, and Michael, who joins them. Or, indeed, on their lack of interaction, since Elsa is indifferent, her features unaffected by her husband's drunkenness. Welles filmed in a single four-character shot the moment when Michael tells the story of the ravenous sharks: with his back to the camera in the left of the frame, he faces his listeners and we read the effect of his tale in their expressions.

SAUSALITO, SAN FRANCISCO AND THE STUDIO

Over a month later, in mid-November, Welles returned to the United States and continued shooting until 27 February 1947, with one four-week interruption, for practical reasons, in January and February. He alternated between shooting new sequences in the studio, on location in San Francisco and Sausalito (the small port linked to San Francisco by the Golden Gate Bridge) and, for an insignificant number, in Los Angeles. He had made a careful search for locations: authenticity was still the watchword.

In Sausalito, where the passengers disembark, and where Michael later pretends to kill Grisby, Welles filmed the bay, its wooden wharves and landing-stages with the same care for authenticity as in the Mexican exteriors. He filmed outside the Walhalla Bar & Grill, whose sign can be made out. He emphasized the scene's realism by having the camera roll outside during the course of one of the shots, to show Elsa in line with the jetty leading to the sea.

Opposite page, top:
Errol Flynn's yacht moored in Acapulco Bay. An electrical cable stretched above the line of canoes connected the generator (placed in the furthest canoe) to the shooting gear on board the yacht.

Opposite page, bottom left:
Irving Klein, Everett Sloane and Welles.

Opposite page, bottom right:
Rita Hayworth and, on land, Welles and Richard Wilson (with his arm raised).

Left:
Welles (seen here in Acapulco) was already making systematic use of scaffolding to obtain high-angle shots with the sky as background.

Below:
Welles and the camera operator Irving Klein (on the crane) in Acapulco.

Locations for the Walhalla Bar & Grill and the jetty at Sausalito.

The only difficulty a person would have now in trying to follow the movements of Elsa and Michael in San Francisco is the fact that some buildings have been demolished. There was nothing arbitrary in the choice of these locations, which contrasts with the spatial dislocation that dominated the set design in *The Stranger*. The two steep streets at the top of Nob Hill, which Elsa drives down to reach the courthouse, are in fact near it, in the heart of Chinatown. After making his escape, Michael has only to cross Portsmouth Square to emerge on the avenue that he follows for several hundred metres, with Elsa hot on his heels, as far as the Mandarin Theatre, where he takes shelter. The Chinese Telephone Exchange is a stone's throw away, all the better for taking the scheduled interior shot. The building containing the law office of Bannister & Grisby, outside which Grisby is murdered and Michael is arrested, was one of the most prestigious in the business district, but Columbia eventually decided not to shoot there. Only the Bannisters' house, whose studio-built exterior is completely anonymous, lacks a precise visual location, although the script situates it in San Rafael, about twenty kilometres north of San Francisco.

A few exteriors break the rule of using real settings: Central Park, in New York City, where Michael meets Elsa at the beginning of the film, was built in the studio for the October shoot, and some matching shots of the Mexican lagoon were also planned from the outset. The Columbia Ranch, near Burbank, where exteriors were constructed, provided the street-corners around Central Park, and the street where the law office was situated. A further fifteen or so interiors, such as the New York seamen's hiring hall, where Bannister recruits Michael and which Welles chose to reconstruct, were also shot in the studio. These sets are convincing without being imaginative. Some were made cheaply, like the crude background set that shows the garden through the Bannisters' kitchen door. But the exteriors are powerful enough to make us forget such things.

Three of the San Francisco interiors are even more original than the exteriors and have a quality almost of fantasy. Without naming them, Welles incorporated into the plot three city landmarks: the Steinhart Aquarium, the Mandarin Theatre and Whitney's Playland-at-the-Beach. All that cherished realism, dented in the aquarium and theatre scenes, ends in the excesses of the final scene in the amusement park, closed for the season, where all reference points disappear. For the clandestine meeting between Elsa and Michael, Welles filmed in the Steinhart Aquarium itself, his wide shots of the couple as they pass in front of the glass walls forming its passageways. For medium close-ups and close-ups, he optically enlarged the huge images of fish and an octopus swimming about in their tanks, and filmed Hayworth and himself in front of them, projected on to a process screen. The interior of the theatre was less imaginatively reconstructed in the studio and it was the agreement that Welles extracted from his producers – namely that the Mandarin Theatre company would appear as if giving a performance – that gives the episode its strangely menacing quality.

The interior scenes in the amusement park – the exterior was shot on location – alone absorbed a fifth of the budget for art direction drawn up in October: $8,000 for the diabolical corridor; $6,000 for the crazy house, where Michael has to keep his balance on a double platform, its parts spinning in opposite directions; $4,500 for the hall of mirrors and $4,000 for the Caligari room.

According to the screenplay, after being taken there unconscious, Michael wakes up 'in one of the queerest rooms ever built by man': the floor is sloping and covered in projections that get in the way if you try to walk. The triangular window is criss-crossed by an asymmetrical network of lines, and sharply pointed beams run in all directions. In fact, the edited film keeps only one shot of this room, which Michael enters open-mouthed, then struggles to find his way out.

The hall of mirrors is a transformation set: the mirrors had to be arranged shot by shot to achieve the desired effect and to avoid mistimed reflections, which entailed a much longer and more costly shoot than anticipated. Welles increased the sense of disorientation by using a great many multiple exposures and other effects during shooting and in post-production, and by increasing the number of 'impossible' frames, as in the composite shot in which two Elsas face us, one on either side of Bannister, in close-up, one showing her full-length and the other enlarged, in extreme close-up (the image is frozen), almost dissolving into her husband's face.

The decision to film primarily in long takes also applied to most of the scenes filmed in the United States. Apart from Michael's fight with Elsa's attackers, Welles got most of the night sequence in Central Park into only three crane shots, one of which intermixes the movements of Elsa's horse-drawn carriage, Michael on foot, and a police patrol car, prefiguring the opening sequence of *Touch of Evil*. In Sausalito, he anticipated the end of that film when he had the crane move up and down to follow the nocturnal movements of Michael and Grisby on the stairs and wooden structures of the wharf. After firing his gun in the air to simulate the murder, and at first pretending to make his escape by going up a sloping footbridge, Michael turns right, on to the wharf: the crane, which is mounted alongside it, waiting for him, relentlessly follows him from above as he is held up by a crowd of curious onlookers who have all rushed as one out of the Walhalla. It is this way of cutting in long takes that Welles suddenly abandons in the aquarium and the Chinese theatre, and even more noticeably, in the amusement park, where it shatters like the panels of mirror glass.

FOUR LIGHTING STYLES

For *The Lady from Shanghai* Columbia appointed a cinematographer, Charles Lawton, Jr., whom they had had under contract since the previous year. He had held that position for ten years, but had hardly worked on any major production. Welles complained that he was slow, but he obtained the effects he wanted. The central concept they both applied was to use light to increase the contrast between the various scenes, almost as if several different films were involved.

For the exteriors shot at sea and in Mexico, they made a radical decision: they would rely on natural light sources, using as few reflectors as possible, with the skies heavily filtered. According to a contemporary technical article, reflectors were not even used in the scene in which Grisby and Michael go up and down Acapulco's hills. The bright sunshine in the cruise scenes meant they had to film at specific times of day, and by using a combination of red and green filters they were able to obtain during the day greys that retained their warmth for the evening scenes.

For the daytime scenes on the streets of San Francisco, the same methods produced a range of disturbing greys, with skies of a uniformly pale grey, making the characters melt into their surroundings – very appropriately when Michael is fleeing after his escape. The city exteriors shot at night, whether on location at the Columbia Ranch or in the studio, are bathed in darkness, with exceptionally dense blacks for the sky. In the burgeoning tradition of *film noir*, the bodywork of the cars are shiny, and the beams of their headlamps are reflected in the roadway. Lastly, soft shadows give the studio interiors a different kind of life. The highly expressive chiaroscuro compensates for the unimaginative sets, with their restricted tonal range, although Lawton was less comfortable when creating light from scratch than when adapting what was available. Two other techniques were occasionally used in addition to these four main lighting styles.

The aquarium is in semi-darkness, lit only by sources simulating the scintillating light from the tanks. But, like the couple's reunion in the church in *The Stranger*, Welles ends the sequence with shot-reverse-shot close-ups of Michael and Elsa, in which the black forms of their silhouetted profiles (Michael totally dark, Elsa picked out by the light flickering on her forehead), stand out against shimmering panels of glass, before their profiles merge in the same shot, and they kiss.

From time to time, Welles and Lawton use the two metaphors of imprisonment and the spider's web. It appears at its most basic in the strips of grey shadow cast by the venetian blinds in the courtroom, even when there is no window to explain their presence. More subtly, after the car in which Grisby and Michael are travelling has collided with a truck, the light glinting from the cracks in the windscreen casts a web of fine shadows over their faces.

Opposite page:
This set photograph (apart from the top section) reproduces the composition in the film. But at this point, Elsa is injured and bent double with pain. To take this shot, a painted mirror had to be placed in front of the lens to represent a panel of cracked glass that would create the impression of watching the action through a broken two-way mirror.

Left:
Rita Hayworth poses for a publicity photo in the Caligari Room.

The spider's web motif can also be picked up from the tie Grisby wears in Acapulco, and it reaches a climax in the decoration of the hall of mirrors set (although no such shot appears in the final cut) and the cracks in some of the mirrors smashed by the bullets fired by the Bannisters as they kill one another.

RETAKES BY THE DOZEN

While continuing the main shoot, Welles also did numerous retakes, often under pressure from the producers. For one thing, it had not been possible to film in Mexico everything that had been planned. Columbia sent the unit home a day or two early, which meant making up the work in the studio and taking process shots. The scene in which Michael takes Elsa back to her car also had to be finished off in the studio, because a number of events had prevented the shoot being completed in a Los Angeles parking lot. A significant part of the work was therefore carried out by a different cinematographer, Rudolph Maté, who in December began to take over from Lawton, who was ill.

Maté had worked on Carl Theodor Dreyer's French films, and was Hayworth's favourite cameraman, having just showcased her in *Gilda*, but it was probably the need to keep a member of its permanent contract staff occupied that was Columbia's primary motive in replacing a less well-known cameramen by one of his two most highly regarded colleagues.

The second factor was that, apart from the aquarium scene, Welles made hardly any concessions to conventional shooting styles, nor to the star system. He kept his few close-ups and medium close-ups for his minor characters, to the great annoyance of Cohn and the editor, Viola Lawrence, who was working as filming proceeded. Otherwise, he avoided using traditional close-ups by resorting to a series of variations: he would start shooting in close-up before the actors or the camera moved; partly fill the frame with an actor in profile, who would then turn to show what was hidden behind him; end action shots with a close-up; or create amazing compositions of two figures, one in profile, the other in three-quarter profile.

Top:
The picnic on the beach at Pie de la Cuesta (Glenn Anders, Everett Sloane, Rita Hayworth), shot again later in the studio.

Above:
Rita Hayworth in the song sequence insisted on by the producer, Harry Cohn.

Right:
The scene in Central Park. At Harry Cohn's request, Welles did retakes inside the carriage, as in this shot, which fills only a few seconds on screen.

KEEP CLEAR
EXIT
DOOR
OPENS IN
NC34

11. Cuban love song is backed mostly with "Please Don't Kiss Me". I think it has been used in every scene so far.

12. Grisby's "So long" - both sound of motor boat and voice - is not shocking in the least. Fade out of the motor boat likewise over "Bye-bye". No longer lewd or funny.

13. Dialogue in song sequence - while it can be heard - is without any peaks or accents. Grisby is no longer intrusive and the character of the whole scene is flat.

10. The love scene is backed again with "Please Don't Kiss Me". This might be all right if we hadn't heard it so often before. I think it has been used in every scene so far!

11. The shock value of the motor of the boat and the voice have been diminished by the recording so that the intended impact is absolutely lost.

This sort of thing is known as "smoothing out", but the point was not smoothness at all. The effect was supposed to be sudden and startling. Now it is just fuzzy and dull.

The effect of the retreating motor boat formerly similar to a bronx-cheer, has now been flattened out and Grisby's cry of "Bye-bye!" is no longer lewd or funny.

12. SONG SEQUENCE ON THE BOAT: The dialogue, while it can be heard clearly, is without any peaks or accent. This is the result of more of that "smoothing" process. Grisby's voice is no longer intrusive and nagging so that the impact of his character on the scene has been greatly reduced. All the "levels" are so precisely balanced that the sequence achieves, for the first time since I started to work on it, an overall quality of flatness and banality.

MR. COHN'S CHANGES

Reel 1:

Take out dialogue after "We're at the park entrance now - giddap, Rosinanti" to dialogue of taxi driver - Dissolve from carriage to near accident
This cuts out: "Rosinanti - that sounds like my name" thru to "He doesn't know anything about women" Page 15-16

Reel 4:

Put back dialogue Broome and Bannister in canoe: "You can stop worryin' about your wife findin' herself a boy friend - I got something real for you to fret over - this is hot -- the way I figure It's worth a little extra dough --

Reel 6:

Cut out shot of Mike with Broome in background where he says, "Mr. Grisby, are you ready to talk about that money"
Take out cuts of Broome in bar - maybe only have one cut of him overhearing conversation between Mike and Grisby

Reel 7:

Take out cut of Elsa driving car on way to Grisby's murder (too misleading - she couldn't have done the shooting)

Reel 8:

Cut out laughter after "member of the bar"
All laughter lower

Reel 9:

Take out cops-exterior theatre
Lose dialogue about plot of the play: (See attached page)
Take out Chinese talking English when leaving the house

Reel 10:

Take out another shot of cops inside theatre
Insert made showing hand taking gun out of bag
On speech "Don't move" - take out dialogue: "Now I'll finish the story of the play" according to how much dialogue is lost in telling the plot?
Crazyhouse: Go from slide to mirrors, cutting out closeups of girl with mask, also following shots

Top left:
Memo to Welles from Richard Wilson, about the soundtrack of *The Lady from Shanghai*, giving his detailed impressions after the screening of the re-edited version.

Centre left:
Memo from Welles to Harry Cohn, in which Welles takes his assistant's notes, retaining many of his points and filling them out to make them his own. The numbering is out by one.

Bottom left:
List of changes demanded by Harry Cohn. Some of them make the plot confused, as when Cohn cut Michael's conclusions about the identity of the guilty woman: the discovery in Elsa's handbag of the gun used now takes the audience by surprise.

Above:
Elsa's interrogation by the district attorney, Galloway. The camera is on Carl Frank for this over-the-shoulder shot, one of the rare moments filmed in close-up at the first shoot.

Welles's contract was not watertight, and he had to restrain himself. Cohn demanded that he take shot-reverse-shots, reaction shots and, in particular, medium close-ups, close-ups and extreme close-ups of the principal characters, especially Elsa and Michael. He took process shots in the studio, using back projections that were often over-enlarged. He then tried to turn this to good use by giving them a disorienting or dream-like quality. As a result, Welles changed the way he directed his actors, since it was now to be the faces, rather than the background, that claimed our attention. He demanded solo performances from his actors, and encouraged Glenn Anders and Everett Sloane to overplay their anxiety and their suffering, respectively. Anders twists his mouth in all directions just as he twists his words and syllables. Flouting convention, Welles filmed them in close-up or extreme close-up, using a short focal length, while the harsh lighting revealed their facial flaws, or the sweat pouring from their shiny faces to emphasize the heat of the sun, which was no longer the source of light. In contrast, Hayworth and Welles himself are glamourized in diffusely lit close-ups resembling Hollywood portrait photographs. Welles continued to experiment with unusual compositions, but played the game as far as shot breakdown was concerned, and consistently applied the eye-line matching that he had more or less abandoned throughout the first part of the shoot.

On 10 and 11 March, two weeks after the main shoot had finished, Welles buckled down to making the two more days of retakes his producers demanded: close-ups and medium close-ups of himself, sometimes with a body-double of Hayworth in an over-the-shoulder shot. The cameraman was now Joseph Walker, Columbia's other lighting genius. Imagination was out, but Welles demonstrated to the full his prowess as an actor: on the last day, in a half-set-up corner of the studio, or in front of a process screen, he took, in twelve hours, twenty-eight shots from eight different scenes, including the story of the sharks. Watched in sequence, they showcase the powers of concentration of an actor who could move with amazing speed from one dramatic situation to another. It must be said, however, that his performance owed much to his almost nonchalant soberness in his wide shots. In addition, Welles was forced to hand over to a second unit many purely action shots, as well as retakes designed to fill the gaps left by cuts made during editing. (A copy was made at the Columbia Ranch of the exteriors of the theatre into which Elsa's Chinese accomplices rush, and the amusement park where they take Michael.) These shots are crude and cheaply made.

Once all the retakes were in the can, Columbia was able to stitch the incomplete pieces together. The work dragged on through the summer, and the cost of editing the film tripled, while Welles was already working on his next film, *Macbeth*, which he was preparing for and shooting in the same stride. The only scenes completely spared in making the retakes were the one of Michael and Elsa talking about love beside the handrail of the *Circe*, and the one in which Grisby, in his office, explains to Michael how to get himself acquitted of Grisby's faked murder. Almost all the long takes were shortened, Columbia retaining only five lasting longer than fifty-five seconds. The stylistic *tour de force* of the ride in Central Park was cut altogether, five-sixths of the scene with the sharks consisted of retakes, and the vertiginous high-angle shots in the parapet scene were almost entirely eliminated. Many of Welles's intended effects disappeared, either because the shots were over-shortened, or because they lost their relationship with others.

A case in point is the trial scene, and a shot with extreme depth of field, where the obtrusive images of a glass and flask in the foreground become meaningless unless we know they contain Bannister's medication, which Michael will swallow as the verdict approaches. The result is a film in which the editing constantly defies the logic of space and light – a disorienting film, certainly, but not as Welles had envisaged it.

THE SOUNDTRACK SABOTAGED

Welles struggled in vain to make the soundtrack and the music match his visual solutions. He sketched out sound patterns, which can be guessed from his series of screenplays or various working notes, and began to apply them by overseeing a pre-mix. Alongside highly stylized passages (especially some clever sound transitions), he wanted to make the 'real' exteriors more authentic by using ambient sound, recorded on location, or reconstituted, and to create a landscape, a perspective, in sound. For the picnic, he also mixed the Americans' dialogue with the hubbub of the Mexicans going back and forth in the background.

Welles showed the same concern for the music. He edited pre-existing pieces into a version designed for previews, to give the future composer an idea of what was wanted in terms of the atmosphere and the placing of the cues he was to write. Welles's selection put great emphasis on the popular music associated with the Mexican sequences (he tried to discover who held the rights for certain pieces), and suggested that a Latin-American flavour be given to the original music that had to be written for this section of the film. The music for the theatre performance, on the other hand, was recorded by the Mandarin Theatre company.

Welles's hopes to achieve realism in his soundtrack and music were to be dashed by three decisions made by Columbia. The first of these was to give pride of place to the dialogue, and to ensure that it could be understood perfectly. Columbia were looking for clear dialogue, with nothing getting in its way. Their second decision was to try to compensate for the obscurities of the plot, which were accentuated by the cuts, by introducing a first-person narration spoken by Michael. Welles agreed to write and record the text, but he had no say in where it was to be placed. In many cases it detracted from the power and originality of the images, and vice versa, since, given the actor's fast delivery and Irish accent, his final explanations were notoriously lost on most of the audience.

The third decision was to have music during sixty per cent of the film while also making savings in this department, where the amount spent was less than allowed for in the budget. Of all the Hollywood studios, Columbia was the one with the least interest in its musical identity, and the job of writing the score was given to a hack composer, Heinz Roemheld, without his being asked to follow Welles's suggestions. Roemheld had to work fast, and was more like an arranger than a composer: he endlessly used as a leitmotif the melody of the song 'Please Don't Kiss Me', which Elsa sings on board the *Circe*. Welles, at the insistence of Cohn, who was anxious to show Hayworth off to advantage, had agreed at the last moment to insert into the screenplay this sentimental ballad (which was in Columbia's catalogue) but, at the same time, he tried in various ways to give it an element of parody, most of them erased in editing.

Rita Hayworth and Welles.

Roemheld's showy score accompanies and punctuates in a rudimentary way the action we see on the screen. In a sharp nine-page letter about the sound post-production that he sent to Cohn when he saw his film after a stay in Europe, Welles remarked of the ending in the amusement park, where he had wanted to leave everything to the sound effects once the first gunshot is heard: 'Given the faintest premonition of what sort of music was going to be imposed on this difficult and costly sequence, and I would never have gone to the trouble or expense of shooting it.'

Columbia also reduced the amount of Latin-American music. The pieces that were kept are in fact North American, or are made unexciting by dull arrangements, and the volume of the music in the Chinese theatre was perceptibly decreased in the re-recording. With priority given to the dialogue, the addition of the off-screen narration, and the constant presence of emphatic music, the result was that ambient sound and sound effects were reduced to their simplest forms. Columbia destroyed Welles's sound effects and did not create any others, leaving the ambient sound dead, with no reverberation or direction, and even adding as little sound as possible to the characters' movements. Welles, in his letter to Cohn, complained in particular about the lack of atmospheric sound on the *Circe* when it is moored at its first port of call, where a little sound of wind and the lapping of the waves would have been welcome: 'There's no point in photographing a scene on a real boat if you make it sound as though it all happened in front of a process screen.'

In September, Richard Wilson, the film's associate producer and Welles's right-hand man, described the Mercury Theatre company's feelings about the finished film in a letter to Welles's lawyer: 'All the Welles touches have been as effectively removed as if they'd flattened it out with a steam-roller ... It's really a tragedy that the picture is mediocre now. Perhaps I should qualify that. I still think it is good but it is mediocre in relation to its own potentialities.' Welles's reactions were similar. No director's name appeared in the credits.

TOO SOON, TOO LATE

The shooting schedule for *The Lady from Shanghai* had overrun by half and the budget by almost a third. A well-argued and credible memo written by Wilson, intended to refute Columbia's accusations of waste and extravagance, attributed many of its problems to poor management within the company, which Wilson accused of behaving amateurishly in relation to such a costly film. But Welles, who was busy elsewhere, did not fight the war of public relations. When Columbia finally released *The Lady from Shanghai* in May 1948, a realistic image of New York had already been offered in Jules Dassin's *The Naked City*, which had opened in March. This film, like Elia Kazan's *Boomerang!*, shot earlier in a small town in Connecticut, did not aspire to alter fundamentally the traditional Hollywood editing style. In the case of San Francisco, *The Lady from Shanghai* preceded Dassin's *Thieves' Highway* by a year. But Welles's film, in its representations of California and Mexico, only hints at his original intentions. After the abandon of *It's All True*, the revised *Lady from Shanghai* created the image of a Welles who in his Hollywood period aspired to a studio aesthetic, whereas he was in fact trying to subvert it.

EXIT

MACBETH
1947–1950

So far, Welles had adapted Hollywood's methods, sometimes radically, but apart from the final sequences of *It's All True*, shot in Brazil, he adhered to the system. With *Macbeth* he attempted something entirely different: a film consciously designed as a lesson in method. To curb the rise in production costs *Macbeth* would be almost 'pre-shot', most of the work being done at the preparation stage. Thus, this medium-budget project met the crucial demand for speed made by Republic, a small studio specializing in B movies, eager to make a prestige film. Economy of style was dictated by this need to save money: roughness was all.

FILMING SHAKESPEARE IN TWENTY-ONE DAYS

Early in 1947, while he finished shooting *The Lady from Shanghai*, Welles conceived the idea of giving Hollywood a lesson in production by using his own rapid methods to revitalize traditional practices. Nothing seemed simpler than to link a stage production with a film: it would serve as a general rehearsal and use the same cast. Once the approach had been successfully piloted, it could be repeated. Welles failed to persuade the British producer Alexander Korda to support a production of *Othello* at the Edinburgh Festival. However, in the spring he found a backer for *Macbeth*, bringing together the Utah Centennial Festival and the flourishing Hollywood production company Republic Pictures, which specialized in low-budget westerns. Its recent good fortune enabled Republic to compete with the big studios by producing one or two top-quality films annually, directed by people like John Ford, Fritz Lang and Frank Borzage. Another anticipated source of profits was the sale to schools of 16 mm copies of the first Shakespeare film to be made in Hollywood for ten years. Welles signed a contract with Literary Classics Productions, a company set up for the purpose by the former agent, Charles K. Feldman, in association with Republic. He was free to choose his own actors and cinematographer.

Previous pages:
Welles, Edgar Barrier (Banquo), Erskine Sanford (Duncan) and Roddy McDowall (Malcolm).

Opposite page:
Macbeth's helmet suggests the Statue of Liberty.

Above:
Welles (Macbeth) and Jeanette Nolan (Lady Macbeth).

The Celtic cross motif is seen throughout *Macbeth*.

Opposite page:
Welles used the same basic design in his 1947 stage production of *Macbeth* in Salt Lake City (bottom, with John McIntire as the friar) as he had in his 1936 'voodoo' version (top).

This page:
Welles re-created the stage setting in his film, down to the preparatory sketches.

Welles wrote the first versions of his screenplay before turning to his stage production of Shakespeare's text. In order to bring out the theme of the protagonist's free will, he focused his adaptation on the conflict between the chaos of supernatural forces (embodied in the witches, who predict to Macbeth that he will win the Scottish throne) and the new order introduced by Christianity. To give the new religion a weight it does not have in Shakespeare, he created the part of an ascetic friar, whose lines he took from various characters in the play, including Macbeth. This syncretic character appears throughout the screenplay, and even intervenes at key moments: he tells Macbeth of his promotion by the old king, Duncan, attends the execution of the traitor, Cawdor, and leads the prayer to the archangel Michael – a nineteenth-century invention – which greets Duncan as he arrives at the castle. The friar is the only person to suspect Macbeth after the discovery of the king's murder, joins the rebels who attack the castle, and is the first to die at Macbeth's hand during the siege.

For the film, Welles adapted his direction of the stage production, using eight of the same actors and playing Macbeth himself. It was rehearsed in Hollywood and then in Utah, with some actors hired there. The two projects followed one another: Welles and his company performed at the University Theatre in Salt Lake City from 28 to 31 May, and the film was shot between 23 June and 17 July, exactly fitting the schedule of twenty-one days. The foreign exterior locations for his previous films had got Welles into trouble with his producers; hence perhaps his decision this time to meet all his deadlines in the studio, using a limited number of sets. He chose to film using lip-sync, developing an experimental approach he had tried in *The Magnificent Ambersons*, where the dialogue recorded in rehearsal served only as an aide-memoire, soon discarded, and in *The Lady from Shanghai*, of which two sequences retained their pre-recorded dialogue. His intention was to save time during the shoot, while also ensuring from the outset the quality and consistency of the actors' speaking voices. The technicians would be able to talk as shooting continued, while preparing the following shots, and two crews could be at work on the same set. The theatre production had no music, apart from a few fanfares and the spectacular prologue, in which bagpipers passed through the auditorium in complete darkness, before exiting into the nearby street, and Welles did not have the resources to create complex sound effects. The sound post-production would therefore be one of the film's main innovations.

VOICES AND THE SCOTTISH BURR

Welles decided to have all his actors, except those playing the English general Siward and his son, who join the rebellion against Macbeth, adopt Scottish accents. The fact that the drama is set in Scotland was only a pretext, all the more so since English was not widely spoken there until the seventeenth century, six hundred years after Macbeth's reign. The harsh accent was supposed to make the lines easier to understand, by slowing the actors' diction. It would also help to get away from the declamatory style of Shakespearean acting in vogue on the American stage, and heighten the film's grim aspect independently of the meaning of the lines, since even the most innocent words would take on a strange, menacing tone. Welles also knew that, apart from the leading roles, he could not hire a first-rank company, and the rolled 'r's would give the whole cast a similar sound. The stylized diction would eliminate each character's individuality, a feature well suited to a play in which, except for the witches, verse and metre vary little from one character to another.

In selecting his players, Welles turned first to his company of actors from the Mercury Theatre, whose experience in radio had taught them to master a wide variety of accents. Casting did not, however, go entirely smoothly, especially since the old Mercury players who had made the breakthrough into Hollywood were no longer satisfied with the crumbs Republic offered them. In the end, only five loyal troupers came on board, including Erskine Sanford as Duncan, and Edgar Barrier as Banquo. Like them, most of their colleagues had flourishing radio careers. Jeanette Nolan (Lady Macbeth), whose screen debut this was, had been a long-time mainstay of *The March of Time*, on which she imitated the voices of a wide range of celebrities. In 1945 she had been responsible for one of Welles's greatest radio triumphs, *Snow White and the Seven Dwarfs*, in which her voice as the wicked stepmother turned into a witch's, line by line, in an astonishing way. Peggy Webber (Lady Macduff), nicknamed 'the girl with a thousand voices', and Lurene Tuttle (Lady Macbeth's attendant) belonged to the same circle of virtuosos. Alan Napier (the friar) had adopted a strong Scottish accent two years previously, in Welles's radio adaptation of Robert Louis Stevenson's *The Master of Ballantrae*, which brilliantly anticipated the savagery and deafening noise of *Macbeth*.

Before shooting started, and while still revising his screenplay, Welles held two weeks of intensive rehearsals, in addition to those he had directed for the Salt Lake City production. He recorded all the dialogue on disc, often several times over, and made his selection from the results. He would often spend several hours with Nolan, working on a speech and tirelessly trying out new approaches. Even within a single line he was prepared to combine several takes, which often reflected a number of divergent ways of seeing the role. The dialogue was ready and all that remained was to film it.

OUT AND OUT THEATRICALITY

For his Salt Lake City *Macbeth* Welles used a single set, quite similar in conception to the one he had designed eleven years earlier for his 'voodoo' version. In Salt Lake City the scenery amounted to no more than a huge curve, going to the right from centre stage and rising step by step to a circular platform high up on the left. There was an exit underneath it, right at the back. The whole set, so bare that it contained no hint of literal representation, was hung with cloth in different shades of grey, unlike the 1936 production, in which there was a construction on the left, and in which the action took place in front of a painted backdrop suggesting tropical vegetation. The front of the stage extended over the footlights and ended in two staircases leading down on either side into the orchestra pit.

The film version exactly reproduces the basic principle of these two stage sets, although Welles substantially modified their appearance, since bare rock is visible throughout. Over half the action takes place on a single set, built on Republic's stage 11. It consists of a vast flat surface, entirely empty, on the right of which rises a series of steps, almost immediately turning left to reach the high tower that contains Duncan's bedroom. A wide door opens in this structure, seeming all the more incongruous since the set has no other closures. Behind the tower a painted canvas broadly suggests a sky full of lowering clouds. Opposite it, and rarely shown in the film, a simple wall represents a reverse of the set, in front of which Macbeth's throne will be placed. Further to the right of the steps, a few conical lumps of rock form a maze that is all the harder to interpret since they can be moved around at will.

For the first time, Welles chose to make a film in such basic conditions that each shot was a challenge to his imagination. Fred Ritter, the in-house designer assigned to him by Republic, was an obscure hack who, with no deputy to whom he could delegate, had worked on no less than twenty-four films in the two previous years – all low-budget westerns that used the same sets over and over again. Making the best of a bad job, Welles became his own designer, leaving Ritter to carry out his instructions as he thought best.

The remaining sets were reduced to a minimum: only a few props (a window with pointed bars, a bed, two tables and some benches) indicate the dramatic role of the bedrooms or the banqueting hall, all cut into a rock that is so obviously fake that this becomes a virtue. Only one set breaks this rule: the English heath where the friar comes to tell the exiled Macduff (Dan O'Herlihy) that his wife and children have been murdered. It is also the one that reveals most clearly the decisions governing the design, with its exaggerated theatricality and the explicitness with which it brings together the two visual symbols that dominate the film: the witches' pitchfork, suggested by a bare tree, and the cross that represents Christian society.

As with the sets, Welles refused to give the studio control over the costumes, and designed those for the leading male characters himself. He gave his imagination free rein, liberally combining influences and always prioritizing expressiveness over historical accuracy. In this way, the metaphorical aspects of the final duel are made explicit by the bizarre decorations of the combatants' headgear: for Macduff, a tall Celtic cross that Macbeth cuts down almost immediately, and for Macbeth a crown with sharp points that irresistibly evokes the Statue of Liberty and which his opponent will soon send flying with a stroke of his sword.

Welles's choices regarding the sets, and to a lesser degree the costumes, were for the most part harshly criticized when the film opened in Europe: they were seen simply as so much evidence of 'American' bad taste, and an inability to do justice to Shakespeare. They are, in fact, a virtually unique attempt to do something original: to import into the quintessentially realist art of the cinema the abstraction familiar in contemporary theatre. Welles would achieve that abstraction by disconnecting specific elements from their strictly representative function, and by freely establishing inexplicable spatial relationships between these elements. For example, in the scene following the banquet, in which Macbeth calls up the witches, rather than clearly identifying two distinct settings, as Shakespeare's text suggests, Welles has Macbeth go directly, in a single movement and without passing through a wall, from the bench on which he was sitting at the end of the banqueting table, to a vast indeterminate space, a kind of rocky promontory in the middle of nowhere, behind which violent flashes and the mysterious shadows of branches are projected on to a uniformly grey screen.

A SHOOT LIKE NO OTHER

According to Jeanette Nolan, filming began with a real challenge, for both actors and technicians. It involved nothing less than shooting all in one go, at the bottom of the steps leading up to the king's bedroom, a series of scenes between Macbeth and his wife, beginning before Duncan's murder and ending only after his body is discovered by Macduff. It was known in advance exactly how long – ten minutes forty seconds – this continuous take would last, because the dialogue had all been recorded beforehand. Given that a standard reel containing 1,000 feet of negative takes eleven minutes and six seconds to run, there would only be twenty-six seconds to start and stop the camera. Apart from Macbeth and Lady Macbeth, the porter, Macduff, Lennox and Seyton appear in the shot, which involves Macbeth's going up to the royal bedchamber, then his wife's and finally Macduff's. The recorded dialogue was broadcast on the set through loudspeakers, and the actors had to read their lines while maintaining strict timing.

Once again, Welles had chosen a very inexperienced cinematographer – John L. Russell, his cameraman on *The Stranger* – and the baptism of fire that he put him through with this first shot might have terrified many. In fact, Russell had nowhere to put his floodlights other than on the structures overhanging the set, unless he were to move them with the camera. Furthermore, the actors constantly changed their positions on the staircase, or near it, and the camera reacted so precisely to each of their movements that it occupied no less than twenty-five positions during the shot. Work began at nine in the morning and ended after midnight – with the successful completion of a shot that everyone had agreed was impossible to take. The crew's confidence was now boundless, and a crucial impetus had been given to a particularly arduous shoot.

Freed from the constraints imposed by sound recording, Welles could have two crews shooting concurrently on the same set. It was therefore not uncommon for him to have two scenes in progress in different parts of his huge set. Watching out of the corner of his eye what was going on at the other end, he would sometimes break off to bellow his instructions to the second crew, whose job was to film the action scenes or set up the next shot. But although the size of the main stage allowed for these unorthodox methods, which enabled Welles to meet his deadlines, at the same time it created many problems in the use of space. Welles usually solved them by narrowing the frame on to a particular action, and filming scenes with few characters so close to the rocky background that we are not aware of the surrounding space. His way of handling crowds is no less ingenious, as when, for Duncan's arrival and the prayer that follows, he organizes people in groups round the clear visual reference points of the entrance gate and the foot of the great staircase. The problem of animating space, on the other hand, could not be concealed, as when the same set (now representing the throne room, as Banquo departs on the ride that will cost him his life) contains only thin lines of extras and small, scattered groups of figures that look as if they have been put there for no other purpose than to fill a frame that is too big.

True to the principle established on the first day, Welles filmed as much as he could in very long takes, thus reducing to a minimum both the shot breakdown and the need to alter the lighting to fit various camera positions. So how was he to prevent things seeming static? He increased the number of vertical and horizontal camera movements, exploiting the different levels offered by the staircase, and organized the action within a maze of small rock formations, around which the actors could move. The scene that takes place in England shows the limits of this tactic. It was filmed in a single shot lasting over six minutes, without interruption – the film's second-longest after the one taken on the first day. But nothing in its scenery (a horizontal expanse punctuated only by a stone cross and a forked tree) easily justifies the variations in the framing, and the scene's stiffness is accentuated by the arbitrary movements of the characters, whose comings and goings are no longer determined by the scenery.

Above:
The middle witch was played by Brainerd Duffield, who also played one of Banquo's murderers.

Above right:
Costume ideas for the friar (Alan Napier), a part invented by Welles.

Right:
Welles, John McIntire, his wife Jeanette Nolan and Keene Curtis.

Opposite page:
Welles liberally reorganized Shakespeare's text, and added the role of the friar.

Enter MALCOLM and DONALBAIN

MALCOLM. What is amiss?
MACBETH. You are, and do not know 't:
The spring, the head, the fountain of your blood
Is stopp'd; the very source of it is stopp'd.
MACDUFF. Your royal father's murder'd.
MALCOLM. O, by whom?
~~LENNOX~~. Those of his chamber, as it seem'd, had done 't:
Their hands and faces were all badged with blood;
So were their daggers, which unwiped we found
Upon their pillows:
They stared, and were distracted; no man's life
Was to be trusted with them.
~~MACBETH. O~~, yet I do repent me of my fury,
That I did kill them.
MACDUFF. Wherefore did you so?
MACBETH. Here lay Duncan,
His silver skin laced with his golden blood,
And his gash'd stabs look'd like a breach in nature
For ruin's wasteful entrance: there, the murderers,
Steep'd in the colors of their trade, their daggers
Unmannerly breech'd with gore: who could refrain,
That had a heart to love, and in that heart
Courage to make 's love known?
LADY MACBETH. Help me hence, ho!
MALCOLM. Our tears are not yet brew'd.
BANQUO. Look to the lady:

(LADY MACBETH is carried out.)

And when we have our naked frailties hid,
That suffer in exposure, let us meet,
And question this most bloody piece of work,
To know it further. Fears and scruples shake us:
In the great hand of God I stand.
~~MACDUFF~~. And I.
ALL. So all.
MACBETH. Let's briefly put on manly readiness,
And meet i' the hall together.
~~ALL~~. Well contented.
FRIAR. How goes the world, sir, now?
~~MACDUFF~~. Why, see you not?
~~ROSS~~. Is 't known who did this more than bloody deed?
~~MACDUFF~~. Those that Macbeth hath slain.
~~MALCOLM~~. What will you do?
MACDUFF. [illegible]
To show an unfelt sorrow is an office
Which the false man does easy. ~~[illegible]~~
FRIAR. I have seen
Hours dreadful and things strange, but this sore night
Hath trifled former knowings.
ROSS. Ah, good father,
Thou seest, the heavens, as troubled with man's act,
Threaten his bloody stage: by the clock 'tis day,
And yet dark night strangles the traveling lamp:
Is 't night's predominance, or the day's shame,
That darkness does the face of earth entomb,
When living light should kiss it?
FRIAR. 'Tis unnatural,
Even like the deed that's done.

PAGE 13

Another decision, this time strictly cinematographic, confirms the extent to which Welles was determined to free his film from the shackles of realism. When the witches make their predictions after Macbeth has called them together, a vertiginous high-angle crane shot showing only Macbeth's head and shoulders emerging from the darkness suggests the vantage point of a higher power. Then the camera slowly descends, as if with a will of its own, towards Macbeth, whose features are increasingly distorted by the short focal length, until they come to resemble those of the crude clay figure made at the beginning of the film by the very creatures whose treacherous words accompany the camera's movement. The effect is similar when (again filmed from high overhead) Macbeth, leaning out over the castle's forecourt, where a messenger has just announced that Birnam Wood comes to Dunsinane, turns his anguished face towards an invisible presence above him. The effect is repeated for a third time, when, abandoned by his army, Macbeth is pinned to the ground in a high-angle shot that places him in the centre of a monstrous spider's web, formed by the pattern of the paving stones. The fact that Welles, under pressure from a rigid schedule, found ways to take such difficult shots shows how committed he was to inventing a form of anti-realist 'distancing' that owed nothing to the theatre and everything to the methods of cinema.

AN INTERCONTINENTAL CUT

Now that Welles had honoured the twenty-one days' deadline, it seemed on the face of it that if only he kept up the pace he would be able to finish his film in record time. He began work on the editing, dictating detailed notes. At that point he also started dealing with the post-synchronization, since a substantial part of the dialogue had to be re-recorded after all, especially as he had in fact ended up shooting some passages with live sound or silent.

At the beginning of November, however, though his contract stipulated that *Macbeth* be delivered by the end of the year, Welles left for several months in Europe, where the role of Cagliostro in Gregory Ratoff's eponymous film and various directorial projects awaited him. A few weeks later he managed to arrange for his editor, Louis Lindsay, to join him. Lindsay had been hired from outside the studio and, unlike his Hollywood predecessors, his loyalty was to the director rather than the production company. On his own initiative Welles returned to the system of long-distance editing that had been imposed by circumstances for *The Magnificent Ambersons*. But he proved to be much less accessible in Europe than he had been in Brazil. Republic's management were aghast, accusing him of abandoning his film and threatening him with financial penalties. Welles went for broke, preferring to complete *Macbeth* at his own pace – in Italy, Paris or London – during the gaps in an overloaded timetable. He delegated the rest of the post-synchronization and sound effects to his right-hand man, associate producer Richard Wilson, who had stayed in Hollywood.

Wilson sent the post-sync reels to Welles, who asked for certain shots to be retaken and directed his actors by dictating or recording his comments. Again, a particular line might combine fragments of several takes. The voices of some of the actors playing minor roles were replaced by others. In addition to the role of Lady Macduff, Peggy Webber voiced Lady Macbeth's nurse and attendant in the sleepwalking scene, the court ladies at the banquet, the witches, and Macduff's elder son and baby. To fill the gaps, at least temporarily, she spoke two or three of Lady Macbeth's lines in Nolan's absence, and provided a few screams. Other radio actors were called upon for support. Not all this dubbed material was used because several actors sometimes followed each other in one role. Welles recorded his lines in Europe with Lodge Cunningham, the sound engineer on *The Lady from Shanghai*, whose services he had secured. Since Gus Schilling, who played the porter, was unavailable, and Lionel Braham (Siward) proved rather incompetent, Welles introduced a procedure that he enjoyed and would never give up – dubbing the minor characters in his films using his own voice.

Welles was unable to supervise the recording of the sound effects that he had planned to use in unprecedented numbers – twenty times the norm, asserted a contemporary article. On the other hand, he controlled their placement with an iron fist. Returning to the assumptions he had made for the 'voodoo' *Macbeth*, he created a consistent sound 'architecture' by timing his off-screen sounds to fit the rhythm of Shakespeare's verses. The faint alarm bell that sounds for minutes at a time before the attack on Dunsinane is almost always heard at the end of a verse, or at a clear break in it. The same is true of other repetitive sounds: the bell that tolls its invitation to Macbeth to murder Duncan, the banging on the castle gate after he has been killed, and the blows struck by the ram during the siege. Thunder and wind are timed precisely to emphasize a verse or speech, and Welles may cut a noise dead to mark the last line of a speech, or to draw attention to the fact that Macbeth is about to start speaking one of his soliloquies to himself without moving his lips.

CONTROL – FREEDOM – CONTROL: WORKING WITH JACQUES IBERT

For the first time since he broke away from RKO, Welles was able to select his composer. Before leaving Hollywood he approached Bernard Herrmann, but he had had his fingers burnt over the music for *The Magnificent Ambersons*, and was afraid that once again he would not have the final say about his score. Herrmann withdrew the following month when he learned that Welles was moving to Europe with no return date set. Marc Blitzstein, one of Welles's main collaborators in the theatre during the 1930s, could not free himself from commitments. The alternative was to find a composer locally – in Rome, for example, where Welles was staying. In January 1948, Welles asked Wilson, who had briefly joined him there, to contact Jacques Ibert, director of the Villa Medici. In addition to his compositions for the concert hall, the composer of *Escales* and the *Quatre Chansons de Don Quichotte* had produced scores for some forty films. No Hollywood studio had ever before had the music for one of its films written in Europe. This bold initiative on Welles's part brought with it many problems: slow communications, difficulties in understanding the terms of the contract between Republic and a mistrustful French artist trying unsuccesfully to retain his usual privileges, bad feeling on the part of the company, which was losing control. There were delays, disagreements and threats to end the arrangement.

As far as the music was concerned, Welles proceeded in three phases: close control at the beginning, a hands-off approach during actual writing, and control again when editing, mixing and retouching. In February, Welles viewed an almost final cut with Ibert and agreed with him the places where music was needed. After watching each of the twelve reels, they recorded their requirements on tape, to be transcribed as a record. Once he had obtained the company's agreement, Welles allowed Ibert to work alone for five weeks in March and April. He had told him nothing about the composition of Republic's orchestra (it had thirty-six members) and Ibert therefore sometimes wrote for a larger number.

He opted for a leitmotif identified with specific characters, with themes for Duncan, Banquo and the witches, to which he added others, including one for the rebel army on the march. He was closer than Herrmann to the Hollywood model, and varied his recurrent motifs less through melody than through instrumentation and rhythmic structure. His liking for musical development placed him midway between the aesthetics of Hollywood and the concert hall. When Ibert declined to cross the Atlantic to conduct the orchestra, Welles rejected members of the Hollywood inner circle, starting with Morton Scott, the head of Republic's music department, to whose lack of classical training he objected. On Wilson's advice he set his sights on an outsider, Efrem Kurtz, conductor of the Houston Symphony and a pupil of Alexander Glazunov and Artur Nikisch.

Welles resumed finishing the soundtrack when he returned to Hollywood for a few weeks at the end of April 1948. He added percussion solos to Ibert's score, to heighten the tension in certain scenes. Sinister kettledrums add a heavy sense of menace to Lady Macduff's scene with her son, before their murderers arrive. The percussion cues combine with Ibert's music and off-screen sound effects to highlight the same words and key lines as in the 'voodoo' *Macbeth*. In addition, since Wilson had embarked on the sound effects without knowing where the music cues were to be placed, they now had to be co-ordinated.

In the three principal scenes with the witches, Welles makes music and dialogue do battle against the raging of the elements and other sounds introduced into the foreground. For the scene in which Macbeth and Banquo meet the witches, he decided not to use only the music – Ibert had written a subtly unsettling theme for celeste, harp and piano – to identify these creatures. He cut the cue into five fragments, added percussion links and drowned it in sound effects. The bursts of music come all the more frenetically since they do not form part of a continuous decipherable melody, but are hurled at the audience in the same way as the witches shriek at Macbeth and Banquo. By June 1948 Welles considered his work on *Macbeth* finished and planned to concentrate on his new European career.

REVISION AT A DISTANCE

In October, a month after Welles had withdrawn it from competition at the Venice Film Festival for ill-explained reasons, *Macbeth* opened in Salt Lake City and in three other cities. This was a normal trial run before the film was distributed more widely a few weeks or months later. It was badly received, and Republic postponed its national release until it could draw up a battle plan.

In February 1949, after months of hesitation, the company decided to revise *Macbeth*, despite the foreseeable cost. Welles was more or less unavailable (he had started preliminary work on *Othello*) but, better prepared than he had been for *The Lady from Shanghai*, he was in a position to negotiate, even to threaten on several occasions to remove his name from the credits. Republic asked him to re-record all the dialogue in order to remove the Scottish accent, which was considered ridiculous or incomprehensible, and to moderate the excessive levels of sound, especially in the scenes with the witches. In a letter he wrote in March, Welles protested, 'to re-do everything would be quite literally to undo everything'. The best thing, he wrote, would be 'to further reduce the thickness of this burr whenever it is thick, and to re-record all difficult or questioned parts of the film'. He then agreed once again to post-synchronize words, lines, sentences, speeches, even whole characters. He demanded that Wilson be given absolute authority, and that the sound recordings be sent to him in Europe for his approval. Republic accepted these conditions, and when in May they also decided to shorten *Macbeth*, Welles obtained their agreement that he be given direct responsibility for the work, even if he had to negotiate every inch of the way with Republic, who were suggesting their own cuts.

This back and forth process of re-editing in Europe and post-synchronizing in Hollywood lasted until early 1950. With Lindsay always beside him, Welles did most of the job in London, taking advantage of breaks in shooting *Othello*, and reduced the film's length from one hour forty-seven minutes to one hour twenty-six. The easiest decision was to remove a seven-minute sequence following Macbeth's coronation, moving directly to Banquo's departure to his death, and sacrificing in particular the new king's conference with the two henchmen he has instructed to murder him. For the rest, Welles tightened up the middle sections of scenes, not hesitating to prune long takes or the one-shot English scene. Wilson soon realized that he had to re-record whole speeches, not only the lines most affected by the Scottish accent, and, conversely, he found it unnecessary to redo passages in which the accent was less noticeable. Sometimes he was able to avoid returning to the recording studio by sifting through the rejects.

Welles, who also recorded over half his own part again, gave what might be described as a new interpretation: he made Macbeth more inward, more resigned, thus creating a perceptible disjunction in the final scenes, in which the unaltered lines spoken by a wilder, more haunted Macbeth predominate. He gave some of the witches' lines to Fay Compton, a minor participant in *Othello*, where she played Emilia.

In September or October 1949, after looking at a cut that showed the passages that had been redone, and having listened to samples of Wilson's work, Welles wrote a memo in which he took the opposite position to the one he had taken seven months previously. 'Obviously, if the Scots burr was to be taken out, every single evidence of it should go. I am most distressed to discover that this is not the case.' He asked that the characters involved be entirely dubbed, and more generally, that all the dialogue affected by the accent be recorded again. Republic took some of his comments on board, but otherwise ignored them. Roughly sixty per cent of the dialogue in the re-edited version was new, and some of the leading characters retained their accent here and there.

Welles also agreed to reduce the excessive sound, by removing sound effects or enhancing the dialogue. His efforts were almost fruitless. When the film was released in the United States from May 1950, it was by no means a commercial disaster, but the critics were just as hostile as in 1948. The original cut (of one hour forty-seven minutes) was only temporarily lost, since it was available in France in the 1960s and surfaced more widely in the 1980s, eventually supplanting the shortened version.

THE LESSON FAILED, BUT THE WORK SURVIVES

Welles's lesson in method was a one-off. In the *Macbeth* as the American public knows it, experimentation became its opposite: an incredibly long editing process, an actual release three years after filming, long takes butchered, and a film that was supposed to make the case for lip-sync largely post-synchronized. Instead of being the first film in a series, *Macbeth* exists as a unique, staggering prototype – especially as Welles, who by this time had shot most of *Othello*, was now moving in a radically different direction.

Previous page:
Macbeth's throne, in the 'V' shape associated with the witches' pitchforks, is simply placed in front of a wall of bare rock.

Opposite page:
Richard Wilson and Morton Scott, head of Republic's music department, studying the microfilms of the score sent from Italy by Jacques Ibert.

Below:
Welles, Alan Napier and Keene Curtis.

THE FIRST EUROPEAN PERIOD 1947–1955

Welles lived abroad until the end of 1955, involved in a series of interrelated projects in Europe, where he could more easily find work as a film director and at the same time establish himself as an international star. He could also try to make a name for himself in television, then enjoying a boom. He travelled all over Europe, but the only happy results were a few TV broadcasts and two feature films, *Othello* and *Mr Arkadin*.

FIRST STEPS IN EUROPE

Welles's first European period was in the works as soon as 1946, when he was thirty-one. In the spring, the British producer Alexander Korda bought the rights to his musical *Around the World*, inspired by Jules Verne. Then, in September, a few weeks before he began shooting *The Lady from Shanghai*, Welles signed a contract with Korda for three films, according to which he could please himself about combining the roles of producer, director and actor or not. The studios owned by Korda's London Film Productions, which had international standing and whose methods were similar to those of the big American companies, were among the most modern in Europe, and their technicians were first-rate. Throughout the time he was making *The Lady from Shanghai*, Welles was also writing and designing his next projects. It was a race against time, since, under his contract with Korda, he had to shoot *Salome*, based on Oscar Wilde's play, as soon as he finished making *The Lady from Shanghai*, which was actually completed late. The following months saw constant postponements, and Welles found time to film *Macbeth* for Republic.

In summer 1947 the independent producer Edward Small persuaded Welles to take the lead in a film to be directed in Rome later that year by Gregory Ratoff: *Cagliostro* was one of the first major Hollywood productions to look to Europe for locations and savings. Welles also saw in this proposal an opportunity to get closer to Korda, with whom he devised clever arrangements that would allow for three successive shoots, with no real breaks for pre-production or editing. But the only time they actually collaborated was in 1948–9, on a film for which Welles is best known as an actor: Carol Reed's *The Third Man*, which was to determine his public persona throughout the 1950s. Amid the ruins of post-war Vienna, Welles appears on screen for only a few minutes (after the audience has been kept waiting for half the film) but his presence is underlined by Reed's direction and Anton Karas's zither music. For years Welles would be the callous, cynical Harry Lime, a trafficker in adulterated penicillin that spreads death and disease, a figure as strangely attractive as he is repellent. Welles decided to stay in Europe, even though for a time he cherished hopes of returning to Broadway. The zest with which he immersed himself in cultures and mastered languages made him a welcome guest. His professional image was better in Europe than in the United States, where his problems with his last two production companies reinforced his reputation as lacking in discipline. As a result of post-war conditions, his films from *Citizen Kane* onward came to Europe in quick succession, and their impact was all the greater. Europe could take pride in welcoming a supposed rebel, while reaping the benefits of his international star status. Welles, however, had mixed feelings about Hollywood: one of his plays and one of the screenplays he never filmed were satires on Tinseltown. But his declared aim was indeed to use his time in Europe to bounce back and return one day to the fold with his head held high: 'With the money that I hope my European productions will bring me,' he told the French press in 1949, 'I'll be able to do what I want in Hollywood, and thumb my nose at the banks.'

In the beginning, Welles retained Mercury Productions, watched over by his associate Richard Wilson, as a firm link with Hollywood. After *Cagliostro*, he planned several projects with Edward Small, but they came to nothing. In spring 1948 he tried to repeat the exercise of combining theatre and cinema that he had carried off in *Macbeth*, by getting Small and the Edinburgh Festival to produce together a film of *Othello*. He proposed to shoot it in Italy, in colour, taking advantage of the contacts he had made there. In 1949, Wilson, finding it difficult to get in touch with his partner, had to earn a living and embarked on an independent career, first as a producer and scriptwriter, then as a director. That was the end of Mercury, and for Welles it brought a change of image: he would no longer present himself as head of a production unit or a company of actors. His subsequent films would clearly be his own, and would carry his unique signature, but he would always try to build an organization around himself.

EARNING A LIVING BETWEEN PRODUCTIONS

In Europe, Welles gave priority to his activities as a filmmaker, to the detriment of his other activities. Ambitious as they were, his theatre projects were primarily designed to earn money that could be invested in producing films, or used to support a way of life. He put on four stage productions in different countries, including an *Othello* in London in 1951, before he had finished editing the film begun two years previously. In 1953, again in London, he tried his hand as a ballet story writer and director with *Lady in the Ice*, choreographed by Roland Petit.

Radio, meanwhile, had become for Welles essentially a bread-and-butter affair. He no longer had to appear at the studio every week, since with the arrival of the tape recorder in the late 1940s plays were often recorded and edited before transmission – a far cry from the pressures of live broadcasting. But he did not wait for the decline of the radio play, soon supplanted by television, and ceased working in the medium in 1953. Previously, in 1951–2, he had still been doing work for the BBC, taking part in two programmes consisting of fifty-two episodes each, also broadcast in the United States. The second of these, *The Black Museum*, a tribute to Scotland Yard, demanded only minimal commitment as narrator, but the first, entitled *The Lives of Harry Lime*, in which he was the star and sometimes the acting director, was an opportunity to refine his image. The series softened the protagonist of *The Third Man*, shown before committing the crimes that led to his death in the film, and making him just a boorish crook, witty, cheeky, and a good loser, who visits every corner of the world in the various episodes. Welles also wrote some scripts himself, based on those he had written for the cinema or forming the basis of future projects. For several years he would often try to kill two (or more) birds with one stone by treating the same subject in a script, a play, a novel and/or a radio broadcast. Rather than committing himself permanently to the theatre or the radio, Welles chose to do the opposite of his American practice: to act on a regular basis in other people's productions, for comfortable fees, in European films or Hollywood productions made abroad. He looked to his producers for financial backing as a director, accepting parts in exchange for permission to pursue other projects. This work helped to fill his address book, and brought him into contact with technicians and actors whom he would call on for his own films, sometimes years later. He was also publishing articles and books, and even accepted routine tasks, such as dubbing Italian films into English.

Welles had intermittent contact with Hollywood, in particular maintaining his friendship with Darryl F. Zanuck, head of production at 20th Century-Fox until 1956 and its president a few years later. From 1948 onwards, Zanuck procured some of Welles's most rewarding roles as an actor and sometimes helped him out financially, though he stopped short of officially funding him.

THE NEW ORDER

For his own films Welles now preferred day-to-day financial insecurity to the Hollywood straitjacket. That was the price he had to pay if he was to regain, as the normal state of affairs, control over the final cut. His new choices were to affect the rest of his career. He wasted time trying to sweet-talk producers and financial backers outside the film world, who did not provide concrete support. He met crooks, impecunious producers, and patrons of the arts such as King Farouk of Egypt, whose long-term interest could not be relied on. He sometimes planned shooting in four or five countries in succession, depending on where he hoped to find producers.

Opposite page:
'Cyrano crossing the Pont-Neuf': a drawing by Alexandre Trauner for a 1947 *Cyrano de Bergerac* project with producer Alexander Korda.

Above:
Welles in the title role in Gregory Ratoff's *Cagliostro* (1948), top, and as Cesare Borgia, with Tyrone Power, in Henry King's *Prince of Foxes* (1949), bottom. Both films were shot in Italy.

It became the exception rather than the rule for pre-production, filming and editing to be done in one country. Several of his films had no clear nationality, whether they were co-productions or made under 'flags of convenience'. Financial arrangements fell apart at the last minute, and when a project did come to fruition, the production company or a major co-producer might change during the shoot, or the shoot suffered temporary interruptions. Welles often assembled flexible crews, having a succession of technicians fill the same post, while being responsible for ensuring the project's consistency and cohesion. His choice of actors partly depended on where he was shooting and what country was involved in the co-production, and the cast list often included actors of many nationalities. Two trends emerged: on the one hand, Welles compromised as far as minor roles were concerned, concealing the actors' deficiencies in various ways; on the other, his prestige enabled him to hire stars, who were willing to accept minor roles and derisory payment in return for the privilege of working with him.

Despite his reputation for moving from place to place, Welles retained the idea of launching extended series. He tried to devise economical and logical production arrangements. For example, in 1950, a pioneering co-production of an omnibus film based on his own original screenplays, was to be shot by three directors, including himself, in three countries in Europe or North Africa. He tried self-financing, but resorted to it only in desperation, as previously in the theatre. In 1949 he started work on *Othello*, backed by an Italian production company that soon proved to be collapsing, and decided to carry on with the venture using his own resources. It took three years and, with his back to the wall, Welles learned more directly than ever before how to manage a production and how to make hundreds of savings every day. The film is described in the credits as a 'Mercury production', although there is nothing of the original Mercury in it but Welles himself. In November 1950, Welles asked George Fanto, the cinematographer for the final episode of *It's All True*, who had already been involved in organizing *Othello* before taking over the photography, to manage all his projects. Fanto did so for a few months, travelling round Europe with or on behalf of Welles, despite the fact that he would have preferred to be his cameraman.

In autumn 1953 Welles joined up with Louis Dolivet, his political mentor in the mid-1940s, whom he had met again in France but who had never before been a film producer. They had begun to work together once more in the pages of Dolivet's newspaper, *Démocratie combattante*, and their idea was to collaborate on all their artistic, literary and political projects, especially the establishment of a 'Foundation for a new humanism'. If they could produce a few successful films, starting with *Mr Arkadin*, that should give them the funds they needed to carry out their plans. Dolivet set up a company, Filmorsa, registered in Tangier, using private capital obtained from some of his Swiss banker friends.

Then, in January 1954, he found a Spanish co-producer for three feature films and two television programmes, to be made over a fifteen-month period. When this partner pulled out, he was replaced by another, who would only commit himself to *Mr Arkadin*. Further projects began to accumulate: between April and August 1954, Dolivet signed three co-production contracts with two Spanish and one American company, for a series of shoots at intervals, of which the last was to start in October, when the final matching shots for *Mr Arkadin* had not actually been completed. Another important career choice for Welles was his decision in 1952 to try to establish himself on television, which was then just taking off.

It was obvious: here was a place where he could hope to work in the long term, with shoots timed more closely together and funding more easily available. He expected that television would keep him in the public eye, as radio had done a short time earlier. In any case, the only work he did in the United States during this period was to play, in 1953, the title role in one of the first ambitious attempts to broadcast a play live on television: Peter Brook's *King Lear*. Its warm critical reception reflected audience expectations. Welles envisaged many television series, plays, documentaries and special broadcasts featuring major stars. He negotiated with the big American networks, even offering Apart from a few talks for the BBC, the only one he completed was *Around the World with Orson Welles*, in 1955, for which he shot only a few of the travelogues commissioned by a British network, with Dolivet's logistical support. Throughout this period, one of Welles's aims was to have his programmes broadcast in the United States, so that he could maintain the presence of an expatriate travelling the world on behalf of his compatriots, but who would probably return some day.

Opposite page, top:
With Alexander Korda in 1953.

Opposite page, centre:
Anton Karas recording the zither music for *The Third Man* (1949), produced by Korda.

Opposite page, bottom:
Welles with Louis Dolivet.

Below:
Welles in his costume as Faustus, with Duke Ellington, whom he had asked to write the music for *Time Runs* (Théâtre Édouard VII, Paris, 1950).

OTHELLO
1949–1952

Welles's working methods were to change radically and permanently with the first film he directed in Europe. He started shooting without fixed ideas, changing his methods as he went along and applying new stylistic and technical approaches suggested to him by circumstances. Constant adjustments to constraints would be disguised during post-production. The result is a radically new aesthetic that one could believe emerged from a plan rigorously implemented. Stories told about the shoot, conversely, gave rise to the myth that *Othello* was shot, on the spur of the moment, without a screenplay. In fact, it was prepared with meticulous care, but Welles began keeping his working notes to himself, or shared them with only a handful of loyal colleagues, so that it becomes hard to know when he was improvising and when he was not.

Previous pages:
Michael Laurence (Cassio), Welles and Mac Liammóir on the grand staircase of the Doge's palace in Venice.

Opposite page:
Suzanne Cloutier (Desdemona), Micheál Mac Liammóir (Iago) and Hilton Edwards (Brabantio).

AN INDEPENDENT CRAFTSMAN/PRODUCER

In September 1948, a year after arriving in Europe, and having failed to bring to fruition any of his directorial projects, Welles went to Venice to present *Macbeth*. There, a few weeks later, he made, at his own expense, a series of silent film tests for *Othello*, which the Italian producer and distributor Michele Scalera seemed willing to finance. Welles kept the part of the Moor for himself and cast his then partner, the Italian actress Lea Padovani, in the role of Desdemona. Everett Sloane, who was also in Italy at the time, played Iago.

In Paris, Welles immediately got down to work with Alexandre Trauner, the famous Hungarian designer of films by Marcel Carné and Jean Grémillon, who had been working with him on an unrealized adaptation of *Cyrano de Bergerac*. At that point, Welles planned to film *Othello* at Scalera's studios in Rome and on location in Venice, once he had completed the role in *The Third Man* that he had recently accepted.

But Scalera's financial support was not enough to make the production viable, and in the early months of 1949 Welles proposed to fall back on the Victorine Studios in Nice, where it would be easier to look for a French co-producer. At that point, Micheál Mac Liammóir, Welles's old mentor at the Gate Theatre, Dublin, was cast definitively as Iago. At the same time, the ending of his relationship with Lea Padovani forced Welles to look for another Desdemona.

Everything suggests that in the first five months of 1949 Welles was already taking on, almost alone, the functions of a producer. It was he who selected Mac Liammóir and Trauner, and who was now discussing details of the sets with Trauner, auditioning actors in his suite at the Hôtel Lancaster, having their contracts drawn up by his private secretary and, most important, ever more desperately seeking the additional money required, while a production assistant was making preparations for the shoot.

42—The Merchant

ACT III

Scene III

VENICE—A Street

(*Shylock stands over Antonio. The merchant is in chains and under a jailer's guard. Salarino is with him.*)

Shylock: Tell not me of mercy;
This is the fool that lent out money gratis.
Gaoler, look to him.

Antonio: Hear me yet, good Shylock—

Shylock: I'll have my bond; speak not against my bond.
I have sworn an oath that I will have my bond!
Thou call'st me dog before you hadst a cause;
But, since I am a dog, beware my fangs!
The Duke shall grant me justice. I do wonder,
Thou naughty gaoler, that thou art so fond
To come abroad with him at his request.

Antonio: I pray thee, hear me speak.

Shylock: I'll have my bond; I will not hear thee speak.
I'll have my bond; and therefore speak no more!
I'll not be made a soft and dull-eyed fool,
To shake the head, relent, and sigh, and yield
To Christian intercessors.

He turns to go. Antonio takes a step after him.

Follow not;

The edition illustrated by Welles of *The Merchant of Venice* in the 'Mercury Shakespeare' series (1939) already shows the motif of prison bars that recurs in both the only studio set made for *Othello* (top and centre) and in the exterior locations (bottom).

PRODUCING OTHELLO: A CHRONOLOGY

1948		
18 October	Venice	First film tests, with Lea Padovani (Desdemona).
Autumn	Paris	Set designing by Alexandre Trauner.
Mid-November	Vienna	Welles spends a short time at work on *The Third Man.*

1949		
16–23 January	London	Welles completes his part in *The Third Man.*
9–15 February	Paris	Pre-production with Trauner, Michaél Mac Liammóir (Iago), Robert Coote (Rodergio) and Padovani.
7–28 March	Paris	Rehearsals resume. Betsy Blair replaces Padovani on the 21st.
April – May	Morocco	Welles acting in *The Black Rose.*
9 June	Morocco	Rehearsals start at Mogador.
19 June – 24 July	Morocco	Shooting at Mogador and Safi with Blair, Mac Liammóir, Coote, Michael Laurence (Cassio), Fay Compton (Emilia), Nicholas Bruce (Lodovico), Doris Dowling (Bianca) and Jean Davis (Montano).
		Betsy Blair leaves the shoot on 14 July.
25 July – 23 August		First interruption.
24 August – 3 September	Venice	Shooting resumes with Suzanne Cloutier (Desdemona), Mac Liammóir, Coote, Bruce, Compton and Hilton Edwards (Brabantio).
6 – 17 September	Rome	Shooting in the studio with Cloutier, Mac Liammóir, Compton, Laurence and Bruce.
18 September – 17 October		Second interruption.
18–28 October	Northern Italy	Shooting at Tuscania, Viterbo, etc., with Cloutier and Mac Liammóir.
1 – 17 November	Venice	Shooting with Cloutier, Mac Liammóir, Edwards, Laurence and Bruce.
18 November – 30 January		Third interruption.

1950		
31 January – 7 March	Morocco	End of principal photography with Cloutier and Mac Liammóir.

1950–1		
–	Italy and elsewhere	Close-ups and medium close-ups of Welles, and other matching shots. Editing, post-synchronization, writing and recording the music.
31 August 1951		Welles withdraws the film from the Venice Film Festival.
29 November		A dubbed version opens in Italy.

1952		
10 May		*Othello* presented at Cannes.
19 September		*Othello* opens in France.

1953		
October		Press report that the American and British distributor will be United Artists.

1955		
15 September		A reworked version opens in the United States.

His unfortunate experience with Cécile Aubry, who had been hired in March to play Desdemona but walked out three days later to appear in a major American production, Henry Hathaway's *The Black Rose*, clearly indicates his dilemma: if he wished to avoid seeing actors and technicians deserting an increasingly precarious production, he had no option but to commit himself financially by signing contracts. The project almost foundered when, in mid-March, Scalera withdrew from it. Welles, on the other hand, decided to pursue the project using money he had earned from the roles he had already played in Europe and those he was ready to accept in order to finance the film. As a result, he was forced, throughout the shoot of *Othello*, to divide himself between the roles of actor-director and producer, and had to break off three times to go in search of the money he still needed. He obtained it by selling the Italian distribution rights to Scalera, and the French rights to Edmond Tenoudji, of Films Marceau-Cocinor, and by borrowing the shortfall from his friend Darryl F. Zanuck and others, such as the shady financier Michel Olian, in return for a share of future profits.

This chronic shortage of funds was to have many consequences for the production: a drastic reduction in the size of technical and administrative crews; difficulty in retaining collaborators invited to work on other films; rejection of almost all the sets originally considered, in favour of locations there was hardly any way of altering for the purpose of the film; the impossibility of finding satisfactory conditions for sound recording; the need to retake shots that became unusable as filming progressed; and even the impossibility of ordering from the outset the amount of film stock required – normal practice in order to ensure consistent photography. Under the name Mogador Films, then Mercury, the film of *Othello* eventually sailed under Moroccan colours, but its legal address in Casablanca was a pure formality, and one would be hard put to assign it a clear national identity.

LOOKING FOR LOCATIONS

The action of Shakespeare's play is divided between Venice and Cyprus. The first act, set in Venice, serves only to establish the characters: Othello, a Moorish general in the service of the Venetian Republic; Desdemona, his young wife, who has abandoned her father, Brabantio, for him; Iago, his long-standing subordinate, who harbours a hidden hatred for Othello; and Roderigo, the spurned lover who hopes to win Desdemona's heart with Iago's help. Throughout the next four acts the scene is Cyprus, where Iago accuses Desdemona of adultery with Othello's deputy, Cassio, and so insidiously instills jealousy in her husband's mind that he kills her and then takes his own life.

Welles's original plan was to shoot the first act of *Othello* on location in Venice and to build sets for the Cyprus scenes in the studio. Given the new financial situation, this was no longer possible, but chance was to offer Welles a solution that Trauner enthusiastically accepted. During the two months before he started shooting his own film, Welles too was playing a role in *The Black Rose*, whose exterior sequences were shot in inland Morocco. As he had done before in Italy, he spent all his free time exploring the country with a curiosity that inevitably took him to places normally overlooked by tourist guides. At that time, Morocco's west coast, about two hundred kilometres from Marrakech, received few visitors, but it was there that Welles found, at Mogador (present-day Essaouira), a number of sixteenth-century Portuguese forts that were remarkably well preserved and suitable for use as the Cyprus locations he was looking for.

Trauner was immediately sent for, and continued to explore the coast in search of other locations at Safi and Mazagan (now El Jadida). They provided additional exteriors, but were unsuitable for interiors as they consisted only of battlements, apart from a magnificent vaulted cistern found at Mazagan, where Welles set the altercation between Roderigo and Cassio. Two things followed from this choice of settings for the Cyprus sequences. It was certainly crucial to the decision to shoot an exceptionally high number of scenes (representing well over half of the film) outdoors. It also encouraged Welles to look for other ways of continuing to work outside the studio by similarly increasing the number of ready-made interior locations, which he found later in the cloisters and crypts of churches located north of Rome. There remained only one large studio set, built by Trauner at the Scalera studios, representing a huge antechamber adjoining Desdemona's bedroom. It appears in the film for a total of only nine minutes but it is where almost all the denouement of the drama takes place.

SHOOTING IN FITS AND STARTS

The major part of *Othello* was shot over a period of no less than nine months, from 19 June 1949 to 7 March 1950, punctuated by three long interruptions. The first five weeks of filming reveal both the precariousness of a production launched in haste, and Welles's ability to rally when he came up against obstacles.

Things started with a crisis. The costumes had been ordered from the Peruzzi workshops, the most prestigious in Italy, but in the absence of financial guarantees, only the women's costumes were delivered, and there was now no question of starting, as planned, with the Venetian ambassador's arrival in Cyprus, in which all the male characters are involved. Other costumes were hastily put together, but it took several days to have them altered by local tailors. Completely overturning his plan, Welles decided to make changes to the scene of Roderigo's attempted murder of Cassio, and Roderigo's killing by Iago, which he had intended to shoot in the street, and to set the scene in a Turkish bath instead. Trauner improvised the set in the lower chamber of the great watchtower at Mogador, filled with billowing incense to simulate the steam rising around figures clad only in towels. It proved to be one of the film's most visually memorable scenes. Improvisation did not stop there: Mac Liammóir was suffering from burns to his eyes, caused by the spotlights, and rather than waiting for him to recover, Welles replaced him in long shots by his Italian sound engineer.

The next crisis had a less happy outcome. After three days' shooting, Welles fired the American actress Betsy Blair, who was considered too 'modern' to play Desdemona. That decision meant that a good proportion of the scenes in which she appeared had to be shot again. It may not have done too much harm, since to all appearances the struggle to put a crew together was still going on. There were constant new arrivals: actors, of course, but also – which was more unusual – a French production manager, Julien Derode, more than two weeks after the unit arrived at Mogador, and a Swiss script supervisor, Renée Gouzy, three weeks later. Their presence made work simpler for Welles as producer-director, as he had had only his assistant Michael Waszynski for support.

Despite there being no Desdemona, shooting continued at Mogador, then at Safi, until on 26 July Welles announced that it would stop for a few days: the money had run out. This halt came before Welles had been able to shoot the interior sequences planned for Safi, in the fort of Dar-el-Bahr, impossible without Desdemona. Unless he waited, and returned to Morocco at some point, he had no choice but to look for his locations elsewhere. In fact, shooting was interrupted for a whole month, and resumed in Italy on 24 August with the final choice of Desdemona, the French-Canadian actress Suzanne Cloutier. It proceeded, apparently without a hitch, in Venice and then at the Scalera studios, although there does not seem to have been much usable footage: little more than ten minutes in Venice, where the crew had stayed for over two weeks, and eleven days of studio sequences, where productivity should have been much higher. The fault was no doubt insufficient preparation, as Mac Liammóir suggests when he describes, in the invaluable diary that he published afterwards, the way three lines of text were rehearsed eighteen times, Welles only announcing that he was satisfied with them after seven takes.

There followed a second month-long interruption, in September and October, while Welles went off again in search of funding. That was followed by another month's work, in small towns in Umbria and Lazio, where he shot some exterior sequences (and more importantly, the interiors originally planned for Safi), then in Venice again, before the enterprise came to a further halt in mid-November. This break was the longest of all: ten weeks. Following it, the last five-week period of shooting in Morocco in many ways resembled the end of the adventure of *It's All True*. Of the actors, only Cloutier and Mac Liammóir were still on board. Many changes had been made in the technical crew, which had also been reduced to its bare bones. Anchise Brizzi, the veteran Italian cinematographer, with experience of prestigious film-shoots, refused to continue and left, taking with him his cameraman, Alberto Fusi. They were replaced by George Fanto, cinematographer for the last episode of *It's All True*, who had joined the group a few months previously to help Welles manage his projects, and by Oberdan Troiani, Brizzi's second assistant. From the point of view of design, Trauner and his right-hand man Auguste Capelier had been involved in other films since the summer, and the second assistant, James Allan, had taken over, though in the end he had little to do. Film stock itself had become a rare commodity, and Welles was in favour of holding back the best he had, for use in close-ups and medium close-ups, which he was keeping until last. On 7 March, the main shoot came to an end and the associates dispersed. It took two more years of unremitting work before Welles felt ready to present the film to the public.

TECHNICAL CONSTRAINTS DETERMINE A NEW AESTHETIC

The working method adopted by Welles in making *Othello* and, indeed, the film's overall aesthetic, were to a large extent determined by the circumstances of the initial shoot at Mogador and Safi. The salient feature of the sets was spatial fragmentation as the only way to film the Portuguese forts without also filming the Arab towns around them. There are, therefore, hardly any wide shots, apart from those oriented towards the sea. Nor is there any great depth of field – despite the use of short-focus lenses, which would produce that effect – but, instead, characters are flattened against walls or silhouetted against the sky. Welles enlivens the composition by the frequent use of high- and low-angle shots, which together create a feeling of great instability.

In terms of the image, the main factor was the limitations of Welles's equipment. The harshness of the Moroccan light meant that difficult and time-consuming adjustments would have to be made in order to achieve subtle cinematography. Welles therefore opted for a high-contrast image, with large areas left in shadow. He achieved this by using red filters that darkened the sky and highlighted the few clouds that appeared in it. At the same time, these filters made the cameraman's work more difficult. In the Mitchell camera used initially, the cameraman could see only an image that was considerably darkened by the filter, unless he relied on the external viewfinder, which does not give an accurate image. Welles solved this problem by using, for the rest of the shoot, a somewhat experimental camera, the Caméflex, recently developed for Éclair by André Coutant. It was the first one to provide a reflex mirror system, making it possible to frame shots very precisely. In any case, during the first weeks in Morocco a style of cinematography was established that Welles was bound to retain when shooting the corresponding scenes in Italy. His lack of equipment can also be detected in the lighting (he usually simply reflected natural light to illuminate areas in shadow) and the limited number of camera tracks. The only significant tracking shot in the film, and its sole comparatively long take, was actually taken without the use of tracks. In order to obtain it, Welles mounted the camera in a jeep, which had been hoisted on top of Mogador's Skala, to film Othello and Iago as they passed by a row of canons pointing out to sea. The few other camera movements were essentially restricted to rapid panning shots, for which the camera could be kept in position.

When recording the sound, Welles could not allow shooting to be slowed down by the cumbersome equipment normally used in conjunction with optical film. Eighteen months previously, while making preparations for his first European projects, he had opted for magnetic recording and had commissioned a company in California to make a portable tape recorder that could be synchronized with a camera for takes lasting more than five minutes. With *Othello* he introduced a crude non-synchronous system, which probably accounts for his decision to keep to a minimum the number of lines shot outdoors. Some of the tapes turned out to be unusable because they had been de-magnetized, but the recorded sound could in any case be no more than a guide track, full of intrusive noises from the nearby sea and town. The Caméflex itself made a rattling sound. In the end, Welles shot a great deal of material without sound, including many scenes containing dialogue.

The final constraint on Welles was that he could not use the shots that included Betsy Blair, and had held over the corresponding reverse shots of himself to the end of a shoot that was suddenly cut short. The unforeseen need to shoot in Italy the scenes complementing those begun in Morocco forced Welles to use endless reserves of ingenuity to achieve a match between locations that were 1,600 kilometres apart. Cassio's punishment by Othello had been filmed at Safi on 23 July, and its reverse shot of Othello and Desdemona was taken outside the papal palace in Viterbo on 24 October, in the absence of Michael Laurence (Cassio) and Jean Davis (Montano), whose characters were shot from behind, using body-doubles. But the decision to break up the scenes in this way became deliberate when Welles made use of the Scalera studios to shoot, with all his actors, Lodovico's arrival in Cyprus, and reserved the scenes involving himself, which could just as easily have been shot at the same time, for his return visit to Morocco. Dislocation, which had originally been forced on him by circumstance, now became the film's dominant aesthetic.

Lastly, it was during the first shoot in Morocco that Welles began to use some very simple effects that he seems previously to have left to expert studio technicians. He needed ships to give a suitably dignified impression of the arrival of the Venetian fleet. He could not cover the cost, but instead erected masts and rigging on scaffolding, shooting them from a low angle to create the intended effect. Later, at the Scalera studios in Rome, he developed additional, more elaborate illusions based on the pattern of those created during the shoot. This time, he used models which, when correctly placed in front of the lens, could be made to match the actors. The tall crenellated tower from which Iago's cage hangs, and which Welles made a leitmotif of the film, existed neither in Italy nor Morocco. It was achieved using a simple model, pierced by a hole representing its lighted window. To obtain the stunning low-angle shot in which Cassio and Lodovico appear through a round window mysteriously opening directly above Desdemona's bed, so that they can hear Othello's last words, Welles filmed his actors, perched on a gantry, through an opening in the model of the ceiling in miniature, placed above the camera. A grip manoeuvred a small trapdoor in the top of the model, while Michael Laurence's double carefully co-ordinated his arm movements to make it look as though it was he who was raising it.

Opposite page, top: Shooting tricks. The fortifications and rigging are illusions, achieved using scale models placed between the camera and the extras perched on gantries.

Opposite page, bottom: More illusion: perching on scaffolding, Michael Laurence's double pretends to open the cover from the model of a vaulted ceiling placed a few metres below him.

A JIGSAW PUZZLE OF LOCATIONS

The spatial fragmentation that began in Morocco was to become a ruling principle, governing every choice of setting. One would have expected that in Venice at least – a natural film set if ever there was one – topography would have been treated with due respect. On the contrary, Welles saw to it that the viewer would see no landmarks, usually rejecting wide shots in which the city's tourist spots could be identified.

Brabantio's house, which appears briefly in the Venice prologue, is represented on the screen by parts of three different palaces. Desdemona, fleeing to the canal where Othello is waiting for her, and the servants rushing to find her, were filmed on the famous spiral staircase of the palazzo Contarini del Bovolo; its stone filigree construction reveals every detail of a whirlwind descent, which increases the sense of urgency. Brabantio's appearances on his balcony were shot some distance from there, on the upper floor of the palazzo Contarini Fasan, a very narrow building near the Piazza San Marco.

The fact that legend has it that this palazzo was Desdemona's actual home probably counted for little in Welles's choice of location. The main interest of its gothic facade is that it has richly ornamented balconies on two floors, one above the other. This enabled Welles first to show Brabantio on the large first-floor balcony, then to have him go inside and reappear on one of the smaller ones above, after realizing that his daughter has disappeared. There was one drawback, however: the palazzo has only one very modest entrance from the Grand Canal. Welles made up for this lack of visual interest by shooting the scenes in which Desdemona meets Othello, further up the canal, in the much more grandiose entrance to the famous Ca' d'Oro, whose wide facade, which is also gothic, was substituted for that of the palazzo Contarini Fasan for the long shots. Even Venice did not meet the needs of a director who demanded for each scene, indeed for each shot, a setting that may have had no basis in topographical fact.

The rich set of Lodovico's reception in Cyprus, shot at the Scalera studios in Rome, contrasts with the spareness of the matching shot, taken in Mogador three and a half months later.

He filmed the senators mounting the grand staircase of the Doge's palace, but their council of war was shot elsewhere, probably in Perugia, while scenes showing Iago in the street were shot in Pavia.

The jigsaw puzzle became even more complicated in the case of all the interiors (and some of the exteriors) in Cyprus. Welles filmed many of the interiors about fifty kilometres north of Rome, in the basilica of San Pietro di Tuscania, a magnificent eleventh-century building. Its crypt is a forest of graceful columns, of which Welles made great use, as he did of the two staircases leading down into it, to represent a labyrinthine space whose changes of level defy comprehension. Not far from there, in Viterbo, he took possession of the cathedral of San Lorenzo, still half ruined by bomb damage. He set up the nuptial chamber in the disused church of Santa Maria della Salute, and the great gothic loggia adjoining the papal palace became, for a single shot, the walk where Desdemona meets Cassio. Other scenes were shot in Orvieto, and no doubt elsewhere – it is extremely difficult to identify the pieces of this masterly puzzle. The puzzle re-emerges where one might least expect it: on the single set built by Trauner in the Scalera studios. The designer imagined a disproportionately lofty space (probably ten metres high) both interior and exterior, opening to the outside through two narrow vaulted passages occupying its entire height. It is in the Renaissance style (the rest of the sets and interiors are clearly gothic) and full of doors and passages so low a person cannot pass through them without crouching. In the film, this set connects with a number of others that have nothing in common with it: the bedroom located in Viterbo, the crypt in Tuscania, and lastly, behind a tall iron gate, the battlements, which one guesses are close to the sea. No other set in the entire film shows so clearly the degree to which the idea of disorientation had come to be the driving force of its aesthetic.

THE SCREENPLAY ALTERED: THE PROLOGUE

For a long time Welles claimed that *Othello* was filmed without a screenplay. But a document preserved in the Fanto archives at the Lilly Library, Bloomington, Indiana, contains both the second version of the prologue in Cyprus and the fourth version of the first section, set in Venice. It was written well before shooting began, to judge from the changes that would still be made to it. It was therefore very early on that Welles conceived the idea of starting the action at the end – with the funerals of Othello, Desdemona and Emilia, and with Iago's punishment – as he had done in *Citizen Kane* and the early versions of *The Stranger*.

According to this document, the Cyprus prologue begins with the funeral procession, continues with Iago's interrogation and imprisonment, and ends with Lodovico's departure for Venice, which would make a natural transition to the beginning of the action in Italy. The changes Welles made to this sequence arose from the vagaries of the shoot. The scene described in the screenplay would have required the presence of Lodovico, Cassio, Montano and Bianca, all of them played by actors not involved in the final Moroccan phase of the venture. Welles probably hoped to shoot this passage before the first interruption, in the summer of 1949. The break forced him to rethink his plans, and to postpone it until he returned to Morocco.

As a result, the prologue – which is entirely silent whereas the screenplay contained dialogue – includes only three reaction shots of Lodovico and Cassio crossing themselves as the bodies pass by, filmed in Morocco the previous summer in front of scenery consisting of a crenellated wall. Welles was dissatisfied with most of the Moroccan shots and after the official shoot had ended, he retook, in the studio, a sequence of shots of the funeral procession that opens and closes the film. He wanted the procession to appear in the form of dark silhouettes, at the foot of the massive battlements, against a hard, blanched sky, like a woodcut with powerful, unmodulated contrasts. He achieved this by having a small group of extras pass by on a gantry, behind a model that created in the left-hand side of the frame the appearance of massive fortifications, before falling away into blackness. The use of unusually high contrast film stock helped to conceal the artifice involved. The Venetian scenes described in the same screenplay differ in many respects from what we see and hear in the completed work. They nevertheless accurately evoke their general tone – a picturesque treatment of a city under the pale light of early morning, where the amorous miaowing of cats mingles with the laughter of late-night revellers. In this version, the prelude to the main action is much more fully developed, and much more ambitious, especially in the director's notes.

This outline, like the film, did indeed begin with a few shots designed to set the scene and establish the atmosphere, but they were followed immediately by a feat of great technical virtuosity. As if drawn by a magnet to a lighted window, the camera rises to reveal guests (who include Roderigo) at a noisy party drawing to an end. However, as the screenplay indicates, 'the lead glass through which this is observed seems thick enough to mute most of the noise'. The revellers leave, rousing the neighbourhood, and the camera, as if guided by the chiming of church bells, moves through the sky to the Doge's palace.

Behind windows that again prevent our hearing what is being said, the Doge is in council with his senators, all poring over maps, in lively discussion. The camera leaves them, moving through the sky again, still to the sound of the bells, until it reaches Brabantio's palace, behind one of whose windows Desdemona is preparing her escape. Down below, in front of the entrance to the palace, the revellers seen at the beginning are making their way along the canal. A man conceals himself in the entrance. It is Othello, too concerned about intruders to notice the furtive shape of Iago, who is spying on him. He is joined by Desdemona, and leaves with her in a gondola, while the camera floats away for the last time, revealing the bronze figures of the two Moors striking the clock on its tower to awaken the city. Such a description reveals Welles's breadth of vision and ambition (and also his absolute demands in terms of technical capability), his intention being to establish a high viewpoint very similar to the one that transports the spectator towards the lighted window at the beginning of *Citizen Kane*. It also underlines the importance he gave to sound, which is systematically reduced to noises, as the conversations occurring in this sequence would always be muffled. It is not surprising that he had to abandon this introduction. When he arrived in Venice to shoot it he was already running short of money, and in most cases he had to restrict himself to taking static shots. This original plan was therefore abandoned in favour of a greatly simplified version in which the dominant element was not air, but water.

Below:
Robert Coote (Roderigo) and Micheál Mac Liammóir.

Right:
This sketch by Alexandre Trauner, and others like it, show that the scene of Cassio's attempted murder in the Turkish bath, which was improvised in shooting, had actually been anticipated long in advance.

Bottom right:
Angelo Francesco Lavagnino's manuscript score for the Turkish bath scene. In the film, the bars shown occur after a prelude has introduced the setting.

Opposite page, top:
Robert Coote (Roderigo) and Micheál Mac Liammóir. By choosing the church of Santa Maria dei Miracoli for the marriage of Othello and Desdemona, Welles was able to have them arrive in a gondola.

Opposite page, bottom:
A setting used twice: Welles filmed Cassio's punishment in front of the grand staircase and the entrance of the papal palace in Viterbo, but without showing its famous gothic loggia, where he later set a meeting between Cassio and Desdemona.

MATCH CUTS METICULOUSLY PLANNED

Another myth dispelled by the documents was that *Othello* was filmed without a script, and that only the director's infallible memory kept track of the link shots needed. Welles claimed in his 1977 broadcast, *Filming Othello*, that there 'was no way for the jigsaw picture to be put together, except in my mind. Over a span of sometimes months, I had to hold each detail in my memory, not just from sequence to sequence, but from cut to cut.' However, the Fanto archives contain thirty-three pages of instructions in which, shortly before the last phase of the main shoot, from January to March 1950, Welles listed about a hundred shots to be taken in Morocco, most of them belonging to scenes that had already been shot. Welles would later regularly create documents of this kind. He organized his shots to make maximum savings on extras, technicians and equipment, specified places where spotlights were not needed, and listed separately the few shots for which sound recording was indispensable. Welles thought out his cuts carefully, although he revised some of the shots while filming. He indicated the direction of movements, the limits imposed by the set, and the estimated position in the cut. He used still photographs, and ordered rushes to ensure precise continuity. His notes also show clearly the degree to which the direction depended on the heavy use of doubles: 'In this shot we might arrange to show Iago's face since all other important players are doubled.'

TWO YEARS IN THE EDITING ROOM

The process of editing *Othello* took even longer than the shoot and was plagued by financial difficulties. On arriving in Europe, Welles had intended to equip a trailer with editing tables, so that he could put his films together as he shot them. In the end he edited *Othello* in a more conventional way, but in three cities (Paris, Rome and London), depending on his other activities and the facilities offered by his financial backers. For the first time, he gave the job of editor to a succession of different technicians, who had no contact with each other. Louis Lindsay, his collaborator on *Macbeth*, whom he had persuaded to come to Europe, stayed with him throughout his first tribulations, at least until autumn 1949. Jean Sacha, a director and former editor, took care of the Paris operations, and the experienced Renzo Lucidi, who was familiar with American productions shot in Italy, worked in Rome for some months from the end of 1950. In London, it seems to have been the Hungarian director John Shepridge, whose only known credit as editor this is, and William Morton, who had worked on a short made by Mac Liammóir, who took over. None of these technicians appears to have been able to make his mark on the film and, to all appearances, the editing of *Othello* reflects the vision of only the director himself.

Welles re-created his film on the editing table. The fragmented nature of the shoot is reflected, and accentuated, in the atomization of some 1,300 shots, many of them very short, which collide rather than mesh fluidly together. Welles ruthlessly pruned the scenes he had shot, and broke up shots of a certain length. He made his cuts as forced as possible, invariably expressing disjunction rather than continuity. Between one shot and the next, when there is spatial coherence, disorientation comes from mismatches between eyelines or between location sets. Welles abandoned Trauner's suggested method, which he had adopted while shooting, of linking one set to another by using props, such as tapestries, to conceal doors and passageways. By cutting his characters' entrances and exits, Welles makes them cross spaces at a speed that reflects Othello's mental disorientation. These spaces are sometimes mutually incompatible, as for example in the almost vertical shot in which Desdemona's servant, Emilia (Fay Compton), leaning out of the window, sees her mistress going out into a square, whereas in fact she has just left Emilia in a room that gives every impression of being almost below ground.

Opposite page:
Before the murder. Welles and Suzanne Cloutier.

Above:
Suzanne Cloutier and Fay Compton (Emilia). Desdemona's bedroom was filmed in the church of Santa Maria della Salute, Viterbo.

Right:
Title page of an incomplete screenplay, illustrated by Welles.

Below:
Instructions for the final weeks' filming in Morocco, early in 1950, include codes to show how each shot was to be handled.

Opposite page:
Welles filming Suzanne Cloutier in Safi, February 1950. Behind him is his assistant cameraman, Oberdan Troiani. The camera is a Debrie 300 Parvo.

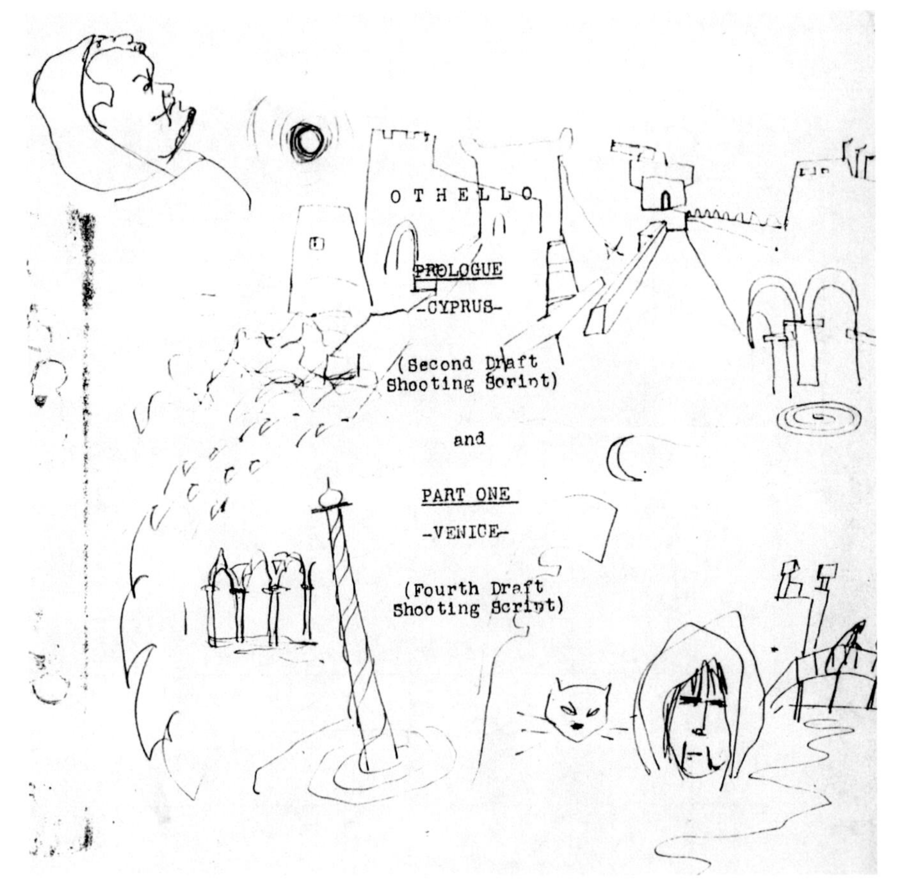

O T H E L L O

PROLOGUE

-CYPRUS-

(Second Draft
Shooting Script)

and

PART ONE

-VENICE-

(Fourth Draft
Shooting Script)

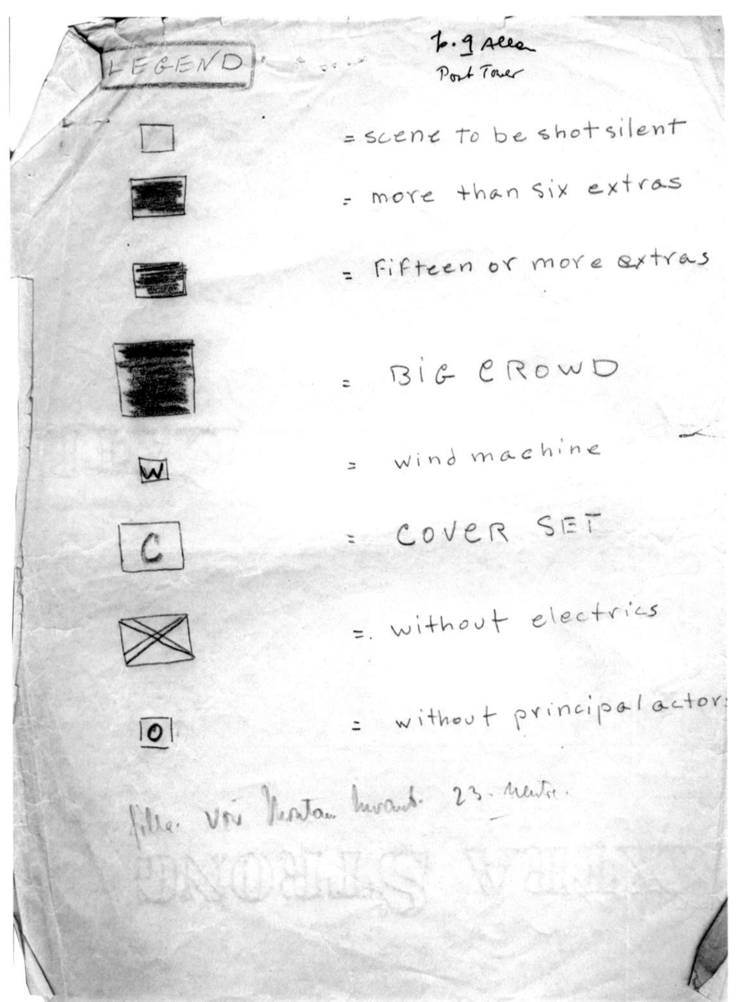

LEGEND

Port Tower

= scene to be shot silent

= more than six extras

= fifteen or more extras

= BIG CROWD

W = wind machine

C = COVER SET

= without electrics

O = without principal actor

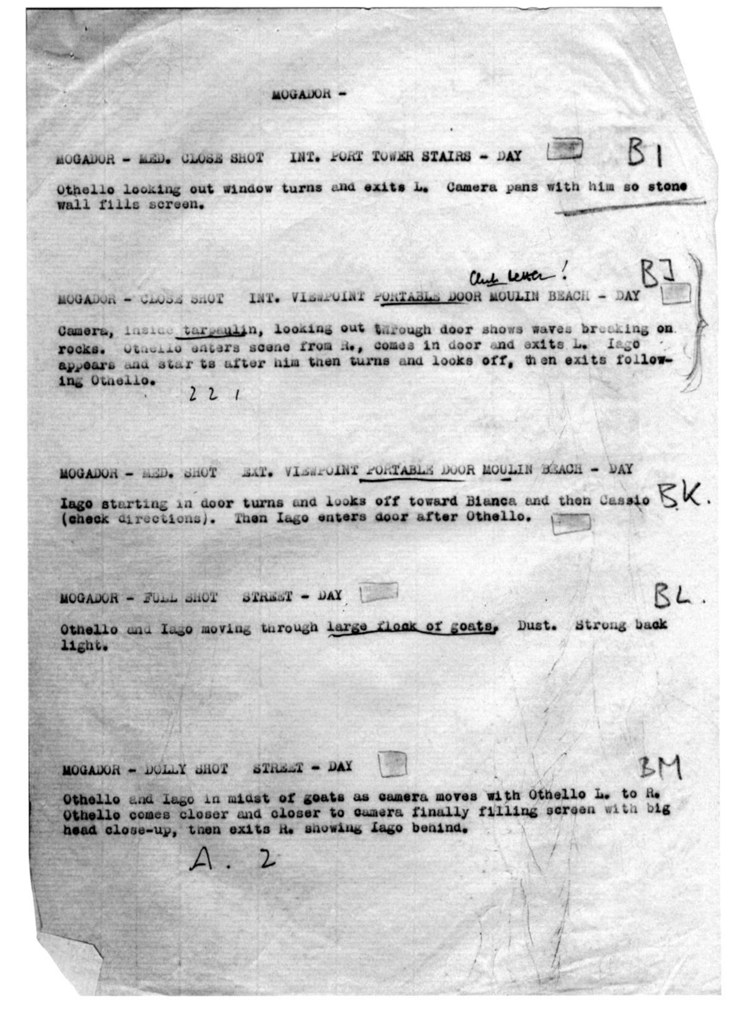

MOGADOR -

MOGADOR - MED. CLOSE SHOT   INT. PORT TOWER STAIRS - DAY   B1

Othello looking out window turns and exits L. Camera pans with him so stone wall fills screen.

MOGADOR - CLOSE SHOT   INT. VIEWPOINT PORTABLE DOOR MOULIN BEACH - DAY   BJ

Camera, inside tarpaulin, looking out through door shows waves breaking on rocks. Othello enters scene from R., comes in door and exits L. Iago appears and star ts after him then turns and looks off, then exits following Othello.

221

MOGADOR - MED. SHOT   EXT. VIEWPOINT PORTABLE DOOR MOULIN BEACH - DAY

Iago starting in door turns and looks off toward Bianca and then Cassio (check directions). Then Iago enters door after Othello.   BK.

MOGADOR - FULL SHOT   STREET - DAY   BL.

Othello and Iago moving through large flock of goats. Dust. Strong back light.

MOGADOR - DOLLY SHOT   STREET - DAY   BM

Othello and Iago in midst of goats as camera moves with Othello L. to R. Othello comes closer and closer to camera finally filling screen with big head close-up, then exits R. showing Iago behind.

A. 2

Temporal continuity is disturbed as much as spatial consistency. Shakespeare's play makes use of a double time-system: everything serves to create the idea that the whole action takes place during the forty-eight hours that are enough for Iago to distil his venom. At the same time, other clues would seem to suggest that several weeks, or even months, pass between the marriage of Othello and Desdemona in Venice and the tragic unravelling of their union in Cyprus. Welles himself goes out of his way to ensure that it is impossible to measure the duration of the action. He conceals the alternation of night and day, or confuses the issue, as in the night scene of the brawl provoked by Roderigo, which ends in front of the Cypriot palace, in blinding sunlight!

During editing Welles was still demanding additional shots, and in November 1950 he drew up a list of those that remained to be taken, in three Italian towns and in the studio. He made it clear that it was pointless to start with his close-ups: 'The longer we delay them the faster I can do them because the surer I will be of what I want to accomplish because of advanced work on the cutting.' The close-ups of Othello that Welles inserted into the scene of Desdemona's murder, where his face barely emerges from total darkness, show a blithe disregard as to whether they match the larger, much less dark close-ups that surround it, but the dramatic tension easily allows for this degree of visual intensity.

AN ABOUT TURN TO POST-SYNCHRONIZATION

Until at least early 1951, Welles edited *Othello* without sound. His decisions as editor are nevertheless inseparable from those he made regarding sound, which also radically altered his aesthetic. He went completely for post-synchronization, which he had previously seen as no more than a stopgap, and created the whole soundtrack in the recording studio, after shooting was finished. This had consequences that went beyond Othello, since this was the method he was to adopt for all his work in Europe.

Despite the fact that this change in approach was the result of circumstances, Welles saw a number of advantages in it. Delaying sound recording allowed costs to be staggered: Welles would pay for what was indispensable on the set and would worry later about how the soundtrack was to be funded. This made shooting more flexible. Welles, who had no time for on-set ritual, liked to talk and laugh while the camera was running. That way he discovered methods similar to those of the silent cinema. He enjoyed total freedom of movement on the set, was in contact with his actors at all times, including the actual moment of the take, and could, if necessary, give them their cues in the place of an absent fellow actor.

By doing without sound recording and limiting himself to a simple guide track, Welles was also able to reduce the size of his crew, or at least not to be held back by it. This feeling of momentum matched his natural impatience and his liking for small crews made up of devoted associates. In the 1960s, he said: 'I don't pay attention during shooting, to any department which may slow things up, because I have found that three departments – sound, continuity, and make-up – together take about an hour between them every day. And if you don't just let them talk, you've gained an hour's shooting. At the beginning, I tell them: [...] [K]now you are going to be a second-class citizen. You're just going to do the sound, and nobody will ever ask you: "Was that all right for you?"'

Welles did not feel bound to stick to the lines spoken on the set. He could alter the dialogue after the event, to fit changes made in editing, placing it off-screen or even inserting new words to coincide with the movements of the actors' lips. Conversely, he could get a sense of the cadence of Shakespeare's lines before completing the cut to fit them. He was still in favour of overlapping dialogue, if on a smaller scale than in his films with a contemporary setting, and made lines recorded months apart overlap.

As with *Macbeth*, Welles had no hesitation in substituting one voice for another. For the secondary roles, he was happy to use doubles for British or American actors who had returned home or had left to shoot another film. He was also willing to hire actors with relatively poor English, or 'casual' actors such as Jean Davis, in charge of international sales of the film, who was rewarded for his services by being given the small part of Montano. Welles himself stood in for some of the minor characters. He did it throughout for his only British actor, Robert Coote (Roderigo), to whom he gave a high-pitched, nasal voice, like a parodic inversion of Othello, Iago's other dupe. He also stood in at times for Cassio and Montano, and even for Iago, for whom he spoke a number of sentences, or a few words within a sentence. He was a virtuoso, the most economical and willing dubbing actor imaginable, but used such opportunities to mark the work with his hidden signature.

Welles did not always post-sync the dialogue using the usual method of checking that the sound is synchronized with the image projected on a screen. Sometimes, during the shoot, he would ask his actors to repeat a scene straightaway for the sound, if the only thing preventing live recording was the noise made by the equipment or the crew. Usually he had them work 'blind' in the recording studio, without having either the image or the guide track to refer to. He believed it was possible to make improvements in the comfort of the studio, and attached only limited value to synchronizing with lip movements. Actors are normally obsessed by this problem, but Welles believed that by freeing them from it he would enable them to give a more expressive performance.

Welles refused to keep the editing stable by giving pride of place in the shot to characters who were actually speaking. When shooting, he often framed the actors in such a way that the words cannot easily be read on their lips. He took many shots in which they are outlined like moving shadows, have their backs to the camera, or are placed at a distance from it. When editing, he placed an unusual amount of dialogue off-screen. When the audience's attention is drawn elsewhere, he has no compunction about having characters seen in three-quarter profile speak lines while their lips do not move, or conversely, remain silent though their lips can be seen moving. This unashamedly casual approach, long familiar in Italian cinema, whose practices Welles often adopted, earned him harsh comments from British and American critics, who made a fetish of synchronicity. The same applied to the placing of sound effects. Live recording of ambient sound would have been a hindrance when making the many changes required in editing: cuts and jumps in the soundtrack would have had to be camouflaged. Welles, however, allows the sounds of rumbling thunder, gunfire or the crash of waves on the citadel's rocky base to come and go as the drama of the scene evolves, and with scarcely a thought as to whether they coincide with the image. The editing of the film, which emphasised the dislocation of space around the characters, encouraged this freedom in placing sounds.

The citadel of Cyprus echoes to the cries of animals that haunt Othello's mind: donkeys, screaming gulls and, above all, the bleating of goats that evokes Iago's venomous remark about the supposed coupling of the adulterous lovers – 'as prime as goats, as hot as monkeys'.

A NEW MUSICAL COLLABORATION

Welles chose the composer for the *Othello* score while editing the film, late in 1950. He had first contacted Jacques Ibert, the composer he used for *Macbeth*, and he also came up with a number of other possibilities. Through the songwriter Alberto Barberis, he met Angelo Francesco Lavagnino, a forty-one-year-old concert composer, whose experience of writing for the cinema was limited to working as a 'ghost writer' for colleagues with better connections. Welles was delighted with his initial ideas, and hired him, but it was agreed that Lavagnino's name would appear in the credits with that of Barberis, who would make no actual contribution to writing the score.

For the first time since making his films with Bernard Herrmann, Welles could collaborate closely with his composer, as editing proceeded. Work extended over an unusually long period, since the drafts that preceded the writing of the score took up two months, from 20 March to 21 May 1951. At first, Welles and Lavagnino worked in the traditional way, watching the film while the composer made precise notes of the passages for which he intended to write music, using stopwatch cues.

Lavagnino was given to writing lush, highly textured music, full of folk rhythms and local colour. His specific task here was to impart a Venetian or 'orientalist' period flavour but, for the most part, the score was in a more contemporary idiom. In order to give his composition cohesion, Lavagnino devised three leitmotifs: Love, Jealousy (these two invariably associated with Desdemona and Iago, respectively) and a third that could be described as the theme of Fate. The Love theme, fervent and lyrical, is fought against by its two rivals, who work doggedly to undermine it. The theme of Fate, inspired by the *Dies Iræ* of the Gregorian Mass for the Dead, rings out during the funeral procession in the prologue, before its tireless recapitulations serve both to presage and to recall to mind the tragedy whose outcome is already known. Welles and Lavagnino were in agreement that, as in *Citizen Kane*, some passages should be very short, sometimes lasting only about fifteen seconds.

Welles's most deliberate interventions again related to the orchestration, which he encouraged Lavagnino to restrain and to vary from one piece to the next. To begin with, the composer expected to write for an orchestra of some seventy musicians, including a strong string section and a full complement of brass, with a tragic chorus that would hum wordlessly, their mouths closed. Later, two important decisions were made about the orchestration. The first was the surprising use of a harpsichord, not only for cues evoking the period, but throughout most of the score. The second was made while Welles and his composer were deliberating about the sequence in the Turkish bath, when they agreed to use mandolins. Lavagnino decided to use a variety of plucked string instruments – including the mandolin, mandolincello and guitar – but progressively to reduce the number of players. All that remained for Welles to do was to take the additional shots, including the opening one in which (against all reality, since steam would slacken the strings and ruin the instruments) Welles shows two musicians beside a masseur.

The music, which at the beginning is supposedly justified by the action, then follows the drama as it unfolds, until the moment Iago kills Roderigo, when the instrumentalists ratchet up the tension and the whole cast goes into a frenzy. Welles was so taken with this idea that plucked strings were eventually used in the orchestration of other pieces. Lavagnino was then able to reduce the number of instruments played with the bow, of whose use in film music Welles was so wary. In its final form, the score often features small, constantly varying combinations of instruments.

Welles and Lavagnino also liked to use music to imitate sounds. The alarm bell of the Cypriot fortress, which rings out at various moments like a disembodied manifestation of fate, was created by a solemn, muffled chord on the harpsichord, hauntingly repeated.

And at the various moments when Othello is wavering in the face of evidence supposedly proving Desdemona's adultery, and when he regains consciousness after fainting, Welles needed the cry of a lone gull in the bass register: Lavagnino provided it, to the amazement of the orchestra assembled in the Scalera recording studios, by asking a vocalist to sing a descending minor third.

Welles did not content himself with making suggestions beforehand. After the initial recording sessions, he would ask for more, either to alter the score itself, or because he was dissatisfied with the sound quality. He re-edited some passages to make them fit the music and, conversely, his tireless reworking of the cut forced him to make changes to the music. In order to counterbalance the fragmented cut and the many moments when there is no dialogue, the music was called upon to create continuity. For this reason, Welles used more music in *Othello* than in any other film. Rather than asking for new performances, recorded at great expense, he decided simply to manipulate the soundtracks as freely as the shots he had taken. He used Lavagnino's pieces as he pleased, moving them from one sequence to another, with the result that only the Love theme seems always to appear in the places for which it was written. And Welles went even further: he sometimes indulged in a kind of musical patchwork, stitching together fragments from different cues to create a single one. The theme of Fate is frequently transplanted in different combinations, highlighting different elements in turn, especially those taken from the prologue: the orchestral melody, the tragic choruses, the regular beat of the percussion or the piano. And it was by cutting up and re-joining these fragments that Welles matched the evolving changes in the music with those in the cut, as if that had always been the intention. Following this successful collaboration, Welles commissioned other scores from Lavagnino, the only musician, apart from Herrmann, who was to work with him more than once. And *Othello* launched the career of one of the most prolific Italian composers of film music.

RETHINKING THE CUT

The post-production vagaries of *Othello* were made more complicated by the fact that Welles had ideas for many versions of his film, even after its commercial release. At one time he proposed to edit two separate negatives, one for the British and American market and the other for Europe. This second version was first to be dubbed into Italian and French, with a deadline of March 1951. In January, Welles temporarily gave up this idea, if for no other reason than that he needed Renzo Lucidi for the English version, which had priority.

One problem was bringing together in one place the reels of film that were scattered around three countries, because one of the investors refused to send abroad the parts that were under his control, while the film-processing laboratories were holding on to the material until outstanding debts were paid. Welles, who still needed the shots that had been held up elsewhere, had to mix duplicates with the negatives and work on different states of the cut at the same time. The version dubbed into Italian finally opened in Rome and Milan in November 1951, but Welles described it as no more than a provisory cut.

Louis Touron, whose job it was to present *Othello* at the May 1952 Cannes Film Festival on behalf of Films Marceau-Cocinor, reported that Welles and his partners argued bitterly for hours until the very last moment, about which version to show: an 'orthodox' one, with written credits; or another, which won the argument, in which Welles spoke the credits after the prologue. But the negative could not leave Rome and they had to show a mediocre print without subtitles, sent from London and made from an obsolete work print. It was in that form that *Othello* was joint winner of the Grand Prix. Four months later, another version with spoken credits opened in France.

Welles continued to retouch his film for distribution in Britain and the United States. United Artists acquired it in 1953, but it was not released in the United States until 1955, and in Britain in 1956. Welles made concessions to meet the presumed expectations of the English-speaking public, and took this opportunity to indulge in the invisible tinkering of an artist who is never satisfied. This version opens with an off-screen commentary taken from the Italian novella that Shakespeare used as his source. In the traditional way, it sets out the play's theme and introduces the characters. Another passage of commentary replaces the lines spoken by the Venetian senators about the war against the Turks, in which there was notably little synchronization with lip movements. Changes in detail are scattered throughout the film. Welles reversed the order of some lines, moved others from one shot to another, and shortened or removed some altogether. His aim in doing this was sometimes to produce a less disconcerting cut, by reducing the number of lines spoken off-screen and thus not clearly related to the characters speaking them. But he would also transplant into one sequence a shot borrowed from another, divide one shot into two (which he would then arrange on either side of a third) and invisibly tighten the cut.

Another, more substantial change was that the parts of Othello and Desdemona were re-recorded, thereby altering their relationship. Meanwhile, Welles had directed the play in England in autumn 1951, with the Scottish actress Gudrun Ure playing Desdemona. He decided to post-sync half of his own role again, producing an Othello who is coarser, more impatient, and in his great soliloquies, more florid and declamatory. He also replaced Cloutier's delicate, refined voice – which suggested Desdemona's disarming innocence and her blind trust in Othello – with Ure's more mature one, so that Desdemona becomes combative and determined to defend herself.

Welles scattered other versions around different laboratories. The National Film and Television Archive in London holds a provisional copy with spoken credits, deposited in 1979 by a London laboratory from which Welles had not reclaimed it. A version with voiceover commentary was discovered in 1989 in a New Jersey warehouse. These various versions confirm that the dislocation of the cut is so thorough going that images and sounds could be assembled in hundreds of other ways without the meanings being seriously distorted.

The story does not stop there, as in 1992 a posthumous revision of the film appeared, produced by an American company with the support of Welles's third daughter, Beatrice, who held the rights to the works in which her father had retained copyright. This version was one of the first major attempts to bring an old film into line with technical progress and changes in aesthetic taste. The aim was not only to restore the material image of the version found in New Jersey, but also to rectify Welles's sound editing and mixing, which were considered unsatisfactory. Words or lines were electronically compressed or lengthened in order to re-synchronize them; all the sound effects and Lavagnino's score were recorded again; some sound effects and music were deleted, shortened or extended while others were invented; and the balance of the mixing was radically altered. In order to establish this new incarnation of the film more firmly, Beatrice Welles banned the commercial distribution of the versions her father had made.

THE PLEASURE OF ARTISTIC FREEDOM

Most of the formal solutions adopted for *Othello* reappear in Welles's later films. Amid all the discomforts of being short of funds, he found methods with which he felt at ease. He was able happily to return to the Hollywood system with *Touch of Evil* but when he worked outside it, rather than trying to imitate its virtues he preferred to do the opposite. The rich visual and aural qualities of *Othello* are very much the result of Welles's ingenious exploitation of the limited production facilities at his disposal, which makes all the more dazzling his illusionist's skill in concealing his lack of resources. On repeated viewings the spectator can try to unpick the pieces of the puzzle, and work out how their improbable juxtapositions were arrived at. The traces of the process are there, before our eyes, and we can observe at one and the same time the work and the artist in the act of creating it.

Suzanne Cloutier,
Fay Compton and
Welles in the cathedral
of San Lorenzo, Viterbo.

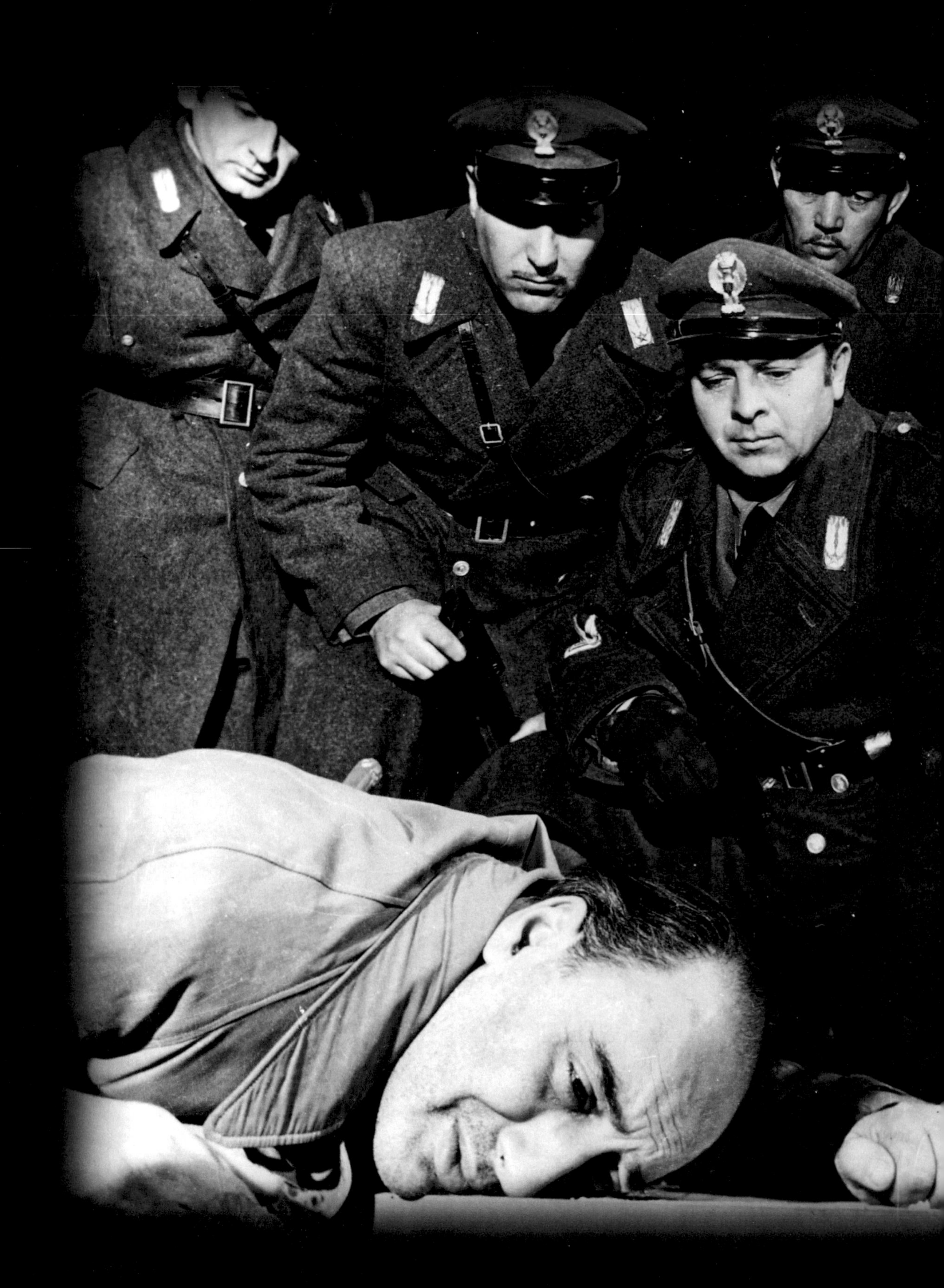

MR ARKADIN

1954—1956

The background to *Mr Arkadin* was even more cosmopolitan than that of *Othello*. Cosmopolitanism is integral to the plot, which takes the investigator Van Stratten and his girlfriend, Mily, to several continents in search of members of the scattered Polish community. Welles began shooting the film without proper financial backing, which forced him to work from day to day in conditions of great uncertainty. As with *Othello*, he continued to defy the constraints, but this time without support from his crew. He also tried out a new idea: his composer was to write the score without seeing a single frame of film.

FROM HARRY LIME TO VAN STRATTEN

As early as January 1952 Welles described in French newspapers a project called *Mr Arkadin*. However, the earliest known screenplay, dated March 1953, was provisionally titled *Masquerade*. In it, Welles developed the plot that he had sketched out in a series of half-hour BBC radio programmes, *The Lives of Harry Lime*, based on *The Third Man*. An episode entitled *Man of Mystery*, recorded in Paris in 1951 and broadcast the following year, already contained the basic storyline. The protagonist and narrator Harry Lime (Welles) introduces a flashback that explains the surprising sight of an aeroplane drifting across the sky without a pilot at the controls. In the flashback, the millionaire Gregory Arkadin, pretending to have lost his memory, hires Lime to investigate his past life, so that he can eliminate undesirable witnesses and prevent his daughter Raina discovering his beginnings as a member of a Warsaw gang. Lime meets the Polish Baroness Nagel, played by Suzanne Flon, who once helped the police break up the gang and is now reduced to working as a saleswoman in a leading Paris fashion house. Lime also describes his encounters with the former leader of the gang, Sophie, and the heroin addict, Oskar, whom he kidnaps in order to extract information from him.

Previous pages:
Grégoire Aslan (Bracco, fatally stabbed) and Patricia Medina (Mily).

Opposite page:
Mischa Auer as a flea trainer.

Above:
Welles (Arkadin) and Robert Arden (Van Stratten).

Much of the dialogue appears almost unaltered in the film. For the film's opening, Welles borrowed from another episode in the series, *Blackmail is a Nasty Word*, in which Bracco, a gangster who had been fatally stabbed, gives Lime (who comforts him in his last moments) the name of an important man he will be able to blackmail.

In autumn 1953, funding for the project, which was soon retitled *Mr Arkadin*, seemed secure. Welles's close friend Louis Dolivet went through a baptism of fire as a producer when in December he set up the company Filmorsa, based in Morocco. Its proxy in Geneva helped to obtain bank loans and private Swiss capital. Welles and Dolivet both invested in the company, and were to receive a share of its profits. Payment to several of Welles's actors would also be wholly or partly deferred. Early in January 1954, Dolivet won the backing of a Spanish minority co-producer, who was to have exclusive distribution rights in Spain. This arrangement led Welles to work in the Madrid studios of Sevilla Films, in order to take advantage of their lower costs. Wishing to film his exterior scenes on location, he then set a substantial part of the action in Spain. The masked ball given by Arkadin, which was originally supposed to take place in Venice, now took its theme from the world of Goya.

Promotional material for the film stated that eighteen nationalities were represented among the crew and the actors. The pre-production and film crews were mostly Spanish, but also included a good number of French technicians, notably the cinematographer Jean Bourgoin, who had worked with André Cayatte, and his assistants. Welles, who played Arkadin (a Georgian) did not attempt to match the actors' nationalities with those of the characters. His first concern was to find his young male and female leads, while most of the minor roles could wait, because they would have only one scene – sometimes a single day's shooting – to make their mark. He was as ready to give these minor parts to seasoned actors or even to stars, as he was to offer the leads to newcomers with no real experience. To play Raina, he chose his young Italian partner, Paola Mori, whom he had met some time before and who had played small parts in Italian films. Welles hired the actor who was to play Van Stratten, an American (Lime in the radio programme and a Frenchman in *Masquerade*), less than a week before shooting started and after an unknown number of others had turned the part down. He chose the British actor Robert Arden, one of Welles's colleagues on *The Lives of Harry Lime*, who often played tough, brutal gangsters or policemen. Arden was allowed a few hours' rehearsal before being thrown in at the deep end.

A NERVE-WRACKING SHOOT

Begun in late January 1954 with a very vague budget and shooting schedule, *Mr Arkadin* should have been filmed by the end of April or early in May, and edited by mid-July, target dates that were missed by a wide margin. Welles described the shoot as 'anguish from beginning to end', seemingly for the first time in his career. An explanation for such bitterness is no doubt to be found primarily in the lack of understanding that soon arose between Welles and Dolivet, who criticized his dilatoriness and behaviour. Welles sometimes ignored timetables, and allowed himself to fall behind schedule in a spectacular way, as he had done in the theatre when he was his own boss. He himself complained about a local lack of organization, and unwillingness on the part of some of the crew. Reports by several of the technicians and actors, as well as letters exchanged between Welles and Dolivet, describe an atmosphere that was tense throughout the shoot. From the outset there was conflict between Welles and his camera operator and sound engineer. Having learned from the best teachers, Welles now knew more than some of his technicians, and now and then took their place, giving them lessons on lighting or design without always being able to get them to do what he wanted.

Furthermore, Welles was not in a strong position when shooting started. The production was very soon beset by financial problems, which only got worse. Shooting had barely started when the Spanish co-producer, who had his own money troubles, withdrew and was replaced at short notice. The new associate did not have the means to come to Filmorsa's aid if the budget was overspent. Dolivet had to ask for extensions of credit in Switzerland, and to look for additional partners in Spain. Welles was exasperated by customs regulations and the bureaucracy entailed in co-production, which held up the movement both of people and equipment, including the rushes that were developed in France and brought back into Spain for editing. Welles radically altered his screenplay, which played havoc with the shooting schedule from the beginning. In the very first days of the shoot, he changed the overall structure by inserting secondary flashbacks within the main one, following the prologue that announces a fictionalized reconstruction of events leading up to the appearance of a pilotless plane over Barcelona. Van Stratten recounts his falling out with Arkadin to the only surviving member of the gang, Zouk, in order to persuade him to flee with him, and his story is shown in several parts. Welles then expanded the role of the dying crook, played by Akim Tamiroff, who was to become one of his favourite actors.

Actors were hired for other minor roles as shooting proceeded. Poles were played by a German, Peter Van Eyck (the smuggler, Tadeus) and the Russian-American Mischa Auer (the flea trainer). Michael Redgrave came from London to play Trebitsch, the Amsterdam fence. Welles gave his Spanish actors many small roles and walk-on parts, but for the time being they played no major characters.

With Tamiroff and his seasoned colleagues trying to outdo each other in their caricatures, Welles filmed rapidly. As a general rule, however, he seems to have used more takes than usual – up to thirty per shot or even more. The rushes held at the Cinémathèque municipale de Luxembourg show Welles shooting ten successive versions of one line in a single shot, directing the novices Mori and Arden while the camera was running and, contrary to his usual practice, whispering to them to indicate how they should deliver their words.

Opposite page:
Welles retouching Akim Tamiroff's make-up for his role as Jacob Zouk.

Below:
The Spanish actress Irene López Heredia (with Robert Arden) played Sophie several months before the Greek tragic actress Katina Paxinou (bottom) was brought in.

In mid-March, Welles suddenly left the Madrid studios before the work scheduled to be done there was finished, to continue it more easily in different parts of Spain. Given his financial problems, he decided to lower his ambitions and to complete in Spain a provisional version that he could use in his quest for investors, or sell to foreign distributors to fund further shooting. However, in the end, he and Dolivet decided to enhance the film by shooting the French and German scenes on location. Welles went back and forth along the French Riviera, back to Spain, then to Munich (to shoot exteriors and to use the Bavaria studios), before finally returning to Spain. Weeks could pass between taking a shot and shooting its reverse somewhere else. Depending on his movements, Welles would sometimes return to material he had already filmed and take advantage of a new setting to try out an alternative version. The scene in which Van Stratten is hitch-hiking and is picked up by Raina was shot no less than three times, at three locations (using three completely different cars) – the first two over a month apart, in Spain, on 12 February and 20 March, and the third probably in April on the Riviera. Welles included his own shots among the last he took, working alone or with a partner.

Because Welles could not obtain the actors he had had in mind for three of the roles of exiled Poles, he postponed shooting the scenes in which they appear. He approached Michel Simon to play the human wreck Oskar, and Alida Valli, Ingrid Bergman and Margaret Leighton for the elegant Baroness Nagel. He obtained an agreement in principle from Marlene Dietrich for the part of Sophie, the former gang leader once in love with Arkadin. He was especially keen to have Dietrich, and endlessly postponed her scene in the hope that she could free herself from other obligations. He went so far as to suggest to her that if she were unable to come to Europe they would film in Mexico – where, in the story, the character rebuilds her life. In the meantime, by filming the two missing female parts in one day each, he preserved the option of editing a complete version that could be released in Spain. The performance of Amparo Rivelles as the baroness is rather weak, while Irene López Heredia plays Sophie unsubtly but with authority. As for Oskar, Welles removed two of his three scenes from the screenplay.

In mid-June, the crisis of confidence between the two led Dolivet to threaten Welles that he would finish the film without him if he continued to ignore deadlines. At the end of the month, when editing was supposed to have been almost finished, shooting stopped. In exchange for an injection of additional funds with which to continue, and a flat-rate salary, Filmorsa secured Welles's exclusive services for two and a half years. Dolivet tried to persuade him to speed things up in post-production, without having a real hold over him, simply because they were friends. In the meantime, the Spanish version of *Mr Arkadin* was virtually completed by August, but some important shots still remained to be filmed for the English version.

BORROWED SETS

A series of designs painted at the time by Jean Douarinou, who as it turned out did not take part in the production, show that Welles initially proposed to film a large number of interior scenes in a French studio. Moving the project to Spain enabled him to use the Sevilla Films studios, but it did not provide the money needed to build large sets. As with *Macbeth*, Welles decided to design the sets and costumes himself, with the help of a Spanish designer, Gil Parrondo, and his assistant, Luis Pérez Espinosa, with whom he did not get on.

Opposite page, top:
Robert Arden with
Michael Redgrave as
the junk-shop dealer.

Bottom left:
Suzanne Flon
(Baroness Nagel)
and Welles.

Bottom right:
Akim Tamiroff
and Robert Arden.

Top:
Welles played opposite Amparo Rivelles (Baroness Nagel in the Spanish version) even when he did not appear in the frame.

Above, left and right:
For the scene on board the yacht, Welles was replaced in several shots by a double (left, in a test shot).

The credits for the English language version mention no names for these jobs, showing that Welles assigned his unlucky co-workers very low status. Parrondo and Pérez Espinosa were experienced technicians, used to studio facilities, and were hardly prepared for the state of constant improvisation in which they had to work. Due to lack of money, the most imposing sets were borrowed from other productions being shot in the same studio or located in existing buildings. The Munich Christmas scenes were filmed on a set of reception rooms for Luis Marquina's *Alta costura*, and at the Hilton Castellana, which Welles filled with a crowd of unpaid extras by inviting them to a 'filming party'. The luxury La Gavina hotel, at S'Agaró, on the Costa Brava, was used for the terraces of Sophie's Mexican residence. The simpler sets were put together using bits and pieces from the studio's storerooms. It is these indescribably chaotic interiors, rather than the sumptuous spaces haunted by Arkadin, that create the film's lasting image and that inspired Welles's most arresting effects: Trebitsch's junk-shop lair, where the action takes place around a skeletal spiral staircase, or Zouk's attic, cluttered with a lifetime's rubbish.

With blithe disregard for plausibility, Welles shamelessly gathers together a heterogeneous collection of exteriors signifying Arkadin's wealth. His hero has to have a castle in Spain, so this will be no less than Segovia's Alcázar, in the shadow of which Welles shot, in best travelogue tradition, the love scenes between Van Stratten and Raina. Its interior, on the other hand, was shot in a variety of different places, with a few studio sets slipped in among them. Arkadin's yacht ('one of the biggest in the world') was most probably filmed in a marina on the Côte d'Azur, which is so unrealistically vast and calm that it is difficult to connect it later with the sparsely furnished cabin, vigorously shaken by the grips to simulate the motion of the sea, where Arkadin is extracting information from Mily (Patricia Medina).

AN UNINSPIRED CINEMATOGRAPHY

If Welles could only rarely expect to provide visual interest by way of the film's sets, he found it no more easily in Bourgoin's lighting, which was strictly functional, completely devoid of dramatic force, and unremarkable in a way unparalleled in the rest of Welles's films. But Welles stamped his mark by frequently filming from unusual angles, taking extreme high-angle shots throughout the film or, at the beginning, shooting at ground-level for Bracco's death and trying again to achieve the spatial distortion produced by using wide-angle lenses.

This time, such effects rapidly became routine, since they were not accompanied by the imaginative set-ups that had constantly unsettled audience expectations in the preceding films. Many of the dialogue scenes in *Mr Arkadin* consist of shot-reverse-shots whose predictable alternation is hardly ever varied by the sudden narrowing of the frame or the unexpected changes of perspective that Welles had turned into a virtual trademark. Whether the fault lay with a mediocre crew or with working conditions that did not allow him to vary the way he framed his shots, Welles gave up trying to be visually innovative and contented himself with repeating some of the most showy effects from his previous films.

AN ON-OFF CUT

Welles began editing the film right from the beginning of the shoot. First of all, he summoned to Madrid William Morton, who had worked on the final stages of *Othello*. In mid-March, he hired as Morton's assistant another Englishman, Derek Parsons, who, like him, had never edited a feature film. One of them worked during the day, the other at night, so that Welles always had somebody at hand when he paid a visit to the cutting room. In addition, union rules required that a Spanish colleague be hired. In May, Morton was replaced by Renzo Lucidi, another *Othello* veteran. In July, after shooting was interrupted, Lucidi resumed work in Paris, where the finishing touches would be put to the English version. One of the assistant directors, José Luis de la Serna, estimated that fifty-five hours worth of material had been exposed thus far, so that cataloguing and organizing the rushes took up an unusual amount of time. According to the assistant editor, Colette Cueille, Welles gave Lucidi very little room for manoeuvre.

Two major difficulties then presented themselves. The first was that some shots were still missing: the inserts of the flea circus, shots of Arkadin at the controls of his plane, various other single shots, stock shots, the scene with Oskar, and the shots of Sophie and the baroness in their respective scenes. Welles filmed the final matching shots in the Paris area and on the Côte d'Azur in September and October, with Roger Dormoy, a cinematographer used to run of the mill French film productions, because Bourgoin was no longer available. The film reached full steam when Welles was finally able to complete the casting of secondary roles. At the Photosonor studio, in Courbevoie, the Greek tragic actress Katina Paxinou and Frédéric O'Brady, who had performed for Welles in the theatre before playing Arkadin in *Man of Mystery*, brought Sophie and Oskar to life. These two actors, like Suzanne Flon, who repeated the part of the baroness that she had played on the radio, seem to have worked for friendship's sake, without a contract.

Welles took advantage of shooting these French matching shots to change the location of one of Van Stratten's stopovers. The restaurant where Arkadin is having dinner with the baroness and the hotel where Raina waits for Van Stratten, situated in Paris in the screenplay but in New York in the shooting script, are relocated in Paris through scenes shot in the city's streets. Another last-minute decision enlivened two edited sequences and, indirectly, the whole film: when Welles filmed, in Paris and its outskirts, Van Stratten questioning 'all over Europe' a succession of witnesses at the beginning of his inquiry and then searching for the baroness, he ended most of those shots with a whip pan, going out of focus and leading swiftly into the next.

The second difficulty was to find a structure for a film whose screenplay had been altered at the last minute, and whose construction in flashbacks had been frequently revised. A connecting thread was soon established for the Spanish section, centred on Arkadin's castle, and for the ending in Munich and at the airport in Barcelona. But for the attempts to follow Arkadin's trail along the Riviera, and the international wanderings of Van Stratten and Mily, the order of the sequences frequently changed. New transitions had to be created and the possible off-screen narration re-written. The drama had to be given a new logic, and obstacles overcome when the coherence of the plot conflicted with that of the cuts, whether the settings or the lighting were involved.

The conditions in which the film was shot, and the changes in editing, led to astonishing mismatches. The characters' respective spatial positions are reversed from one shot to another, and when we see the plane with its cockpit open in the studio shots of Arkadin at the controls, we have to forget it was closed in the shots where it is in flight. All this takes nothing away from the force of a cut that gives an impression of frenzy and constant movement, even though most of the scenes are 'settled' in a fixed space and time, with the minor characters often sitting opposite Van Stratten, Mily or Arkadin.

There was an equal amount of re-working at the post-synchronization stage. Welles rewrote the dialogue as he pleased, and filmed the same lines or the same scenes several times. Some of these changes were designed to remove the contradictions resulting from the changes made to the dramatic structure. The lines spoken by the dying Bracco were totally altered and re-recorded by Welles, who himself stood in for the actor, Grégoire Aslan.

This is the first dubbed version of lines addressed to Van Stratten: You're with me. After all the friends I've had ... You that I've known a few minutes ... You're the only one. I want to give you something ...to show you my thanks.

And here is the second, which is carefully given the same rhythm: You'll be rich. Don't have pity on him, eh? ... You'll see, he'll pay you millions ... Just do what I say. Say Bracco told you all about him ... all about his past.

In the recording studio, Welles again gave Arden hints about his delivery: 'I found,' he wrote, 'that if I didn't "talk" Bob *directly* into the readings, he repeatedly lost what I was after [...] it took a lot of "direct talking" to get any performance out of him at all.' Mori's part was dubbed by a British actress.

Welles commissioned the music from Paul Misraki, whom he had met while making *It's All True*, at the same time as he met Aslan: the two Frenchmen were on tour in Brazil with Ray Ventura's orchestra, and Misraki supplied him with arrangements. He had been a successful songwriter in the 1930s and was now France's most prolific composer of film music and a crucial contributor to French cinema's *qualité française*. Reversing his normal procedure, Welles asked Misraki to write without timings, without seeing a single frame and without even reading the screenplay or being aware of the meanderings of the plot. All he had to guide him were Welles's indications of the atmosphere and style he wanted. Misraki wrote pieces of music based, not on short motifs, like those of Herrmann or Lavagnino, but on a small number of developed themes: a melody full of menace, associated with Arkadin; a nostalgic theme linked with evocations of Poland; a theme for Raina; one suggesting the hurly-burly of the city; and so on. All of this was in a wide variety of musical styles that fitted the nationalities of the characters or the places where the scenes were set. In order to match the recorded score to the details of the editing, Welles cut and pasted all of it in a way he had done with only part of the score of *Othello*. He created a patchwork of long music cues that combined fragments of different pieces: five snatches of music for the sequence on board the yacht; six for the series of witnesses questioned by Van Stratten in his search for the baroness.

The music is written with unparalleled vigour, but it is also this fragmentation, the way it constantly starts and restarts, that gives the film its utmost energy – as the Spanish version, where the pieces retain their original length, confirms.

LOSING THE FINAL CUT, AGAIN

By the end of October 1954 editing was far from complete, although Dolivet had planned to present the film at the Venice Film Festival in September. Before going to Switzerland again in search of funds, he issued Welles with an ultimatum, demanding that it be finished in two weeks, although processes such as recording the sound effects and editing the music had not yet been completed. Relations became soured, though not to the point of preventing Welles and Dolivet preparing the ground for one of their next projects, *Noah*, an original screenplay in which the Flood is caused by an atomic explosion. In January 1955, Welles agreed to stay out of the cutting room and to collaborate with Lucidi from a distance, on condition that he could polish up the work later. During the same month he shot tests for a film version of *Don Quixote*, which were funded by Filmorsa, and from March the company handled, on behalf of a British company, the production of the episodes in the television series *Around the World with Orson Welles* that were to be shot on the continent. However, once *Mr Arkadin* was behind them, Welles and Dolivet decided to dissolve their association amicably.

In April, Lucidi completed a cut that probably fitted the order of sequences that Welles wanted. Welles, meanwhile, continued making his television series and, after marrying Paola Mori in London in May, directed a play there. Dolivet gave up having the sound finished professionally, leaving audible joins between one sound recording and another in the dialogue, a distant hum over Paxinou's lines, the whirring of the camera and other background noises. He did not add to the soundtrack, which Welles had only sketched out. Welles had not finished work on his film but this time neither had the producer. In mid-July he broke with Dolivet over funding for a television project, and after that it was often impossible to meet with him or even to find out his whereabouts.

In August what Welles called a simple 'selling copy' (probably the one finished by Lucidi in April) opened in London, with the approval of the director, who did not wish to exacerbate his conflict with Dolivet. Welles chose the new title *Confidential Report* to avoid those suggested by the distributor, Warner Bros. This version is no longer available. In October, the Spanish version edited a year previously and with sound hastily added, was released in cinemas, to the detriment of another cut that was close to a provisional state of the English version. The same month, Welles wrote to Dolivet: 'My old dream of being able to make enough capital outside of America to pay my debts and get a fresh start before returning to residency there, is completely shattered.' But a few days later he did in fact return to the United States.

Flouting his exclusivity agreement with Filmorsa (and giving up the chance to direct the screenplays for which he had sold the rights to the company) Welles left for New York to direct a theatre production of *King Lear* in the hope of relaunching his career. There Paola Mori gave birth to their daughter, Beatrice.

In November, after *Confidential Report* came out on general release in Britain – in a version that was probably slightly revised and has also disappeared – Dolivet gave way to pressure from Warner Bros., who found the dramatic structure too convoluted. An unidentified editor reshaped the film, eliminating the flashbacks in which Van Stratten tells his story to Zouk, and making various other changes. Some of the dialogue loses its meaning in the process. This version was released on the Continent in spring 1956, also under the title *Confidential Report*, without Welles's being able to see it. Over the coming years other versions of uncertain status were distributed in Spain and the United States and, in 2006, the Luxemburg and Munich film archives collaborated with a publisher of DVDs to make a version that amalgamated three of the earlier ones. However, none of these alternative versions offered a more coherent cut than the 1956 *Confidential Report* – a film that was released prematurely and has an unfinished feel despite all its brilliance.

Van Stratten and Raina (Robert Arden and Paola Mori) in a characterless hotel lobby, set in New York during shooting, but in Paris in the final cut.

DISCOVERING TELEVISION

From 1955, Welles worked in both cinema and television, a medium that offered him new scope for experimentation, and one that he saw not as a dramatic but as a narrative form. In keeping with his radio work, and with the films of Sacha Guitry whose influence he acknowledged, Welles assumed the role of storyteller and presenter, eager to communicate directly with the viewer. This applied both to his first documentary series, *Around the World with Orson Welles*, and to his first completed drama, *The Fountain of Youth*.

HARRY LIME REMAINS OBEDIENTLY YOURS: 'AROUND THE WORLD WITH ORSON WELLES'

The idea for a programme based on Welles's own peregrinations, in which he would be the viewer's guide in different countries, went back to the early 1950s. In spring 1955 he embarked on a series of twenty-six half-hour travelogues, *Around the World with Orson Welles*, for Associated-Rediffusion, one of the production companies within the British commercial network, ITV. They were to be broadcast every other week, starting in September, and would mainly be portraits of major cities. It was quite a coup, since the series was designed to mark the launch of commercial television in Britain. In March, Welles shot the first programme, Vienna, in a few days, on the basis of an informal agreement and without waiting to sign a contract.

Filmorsa, the company headed by Louis Dolivet with which he had committed himself to work exclusively, advanced the costs and handled the production of this broadcast (and of all the rest, apart from the one made in London) in exchange for the rights outside the English-speaking world. Welles and Associated-Rediffusion retained artistic control. Welles granted the company a number of privileges – the right to approve the preliminary synopsis, the shooting script and the music, and to view the rushes and work prints – but in reality, the balance of power remained in his favour throughout pre-production and shooting. The contract demanded an impossible schedule: a further twenty-five weeks' shooting, to be spread over nine months, in addition to the editing. In spite of that, Welles continued his other activities, directing only six programmes in the intervening periods. These episodes took him to the village of Lurs, in Haute-Provence, the scene of the Dominici affair – the murder in 1952 of a British couple and their young daughter, for which a local 'patriarch', Gaston Dominici, was sentenced to death. He then went to Saint-Jean-de-Luz and the surrounding area, and to Madrid, London and Saint-Germain-des-Prés.

The essence of these travelogues, like the other programmes he was to make in the 1950s, was Welles's own personality. Jovial and cajoling in his dinner jacket and bow tie, the gentleman globetrotter played on his cultivated charm, consciously relaxed attitude, good humour and sense of intimacy with the viewer, with whom he seemed to be having a casual chat. On television Welles combined the two public images that he had created for himself through radio. His American persona was still that of the radio producer and presenter who for ten years had signed off with the words 'Until then, I remain, as always, obediently yours', inviting listeners to join him again the following week. One of the episodes of *Around the World with Orson Welles* ends with this phrase, which was adopted for future broadcasts. Welles's British persona, on the other hand, was based on *The Third Man*, since in 1951 and 1952 regular BBC listeners had spent months in his company when he played Harry Lime on the air. His television project was launched with his return to Vienna, seven years after the film was made.

The basic formula was a mixture of commentaries by Welles, scenes shot on location and interviews, often with English speakers. Welles would sometimes ask an American expatriate to be his guide. In Saint-Germain-des-Prés, for example, it was the eccentric octogenarian artist and philosopher Raymond Duncan, wearing a Greek tunic and sandals, who taught in his 'Akademia' that the only things we need are those we can make ourselves, adding that total independence was necessarily the last word in Americanism. Other people interviewed included, in London, residents in a home for poor but deserving widows and in another for old soldiers. In Lurs, where Welles was accompanied by a journalist from *France Soir*, he interviewed the leading witnesses in the Dominici case, at a time when a new inquiry was rekindling strong feelings.

Above:
A fake 'live broadcast', with Caméflex and microphone, for the Madrid programme of *Around the World with Orson Welles.*

Opposite page:
As a globe-trotting presenter in the Basque country programme, part of *Around the World with Orson Welles.*

SIMULATING LIVE COVERAGE

Welles followed the practice, then unusual in television, of recording his interviews live. Hence his use, in the programmes filmed by the French cameraman Alain Pol, of a heavy Debrie camera, weighing around sixty kilos, connected to the soundtrack for synchronization. In addition, a small, silent, news reporter's Arriflex enabled the cameraman to work in comfort when sound was not required. Welles sometimes included himself in the same shot as the person he was interviewing. He gave them priority, but he would ask the cameraman to show his shoulder and ear momentarily in an over-the-shoulder shot, just to establish his presence. But for the most part the interviews consisted of shot-reverse-shots. Whenever he could, Welles used two cameras when filming, even allowing the camera filming his interviewee, or the boom held towards him, to be visible in his own shots. Usually he added the reverse shots of himself later. He also filmed many images *in situ*, or asked the cameraman to do it in his absence, sometimes giving him a detailed list of the shots he wanted taken.

Welles edited some of the programmes in London, with a technician from Associated-Rediffusion, and some in France, with the assistant editor from *Mr Arkadin*, Colette Cueille, or others. When organizing his wealth of material, he would wait until the end before writing the voiceover or the comments he made on the images in his role as presenter. He manipulated the sound recording to reorganize the words spoken by his interviewees and took advantage of off-screen moments, if necessary, to create a new sentence from phrases taken from several different responses, to make the passages flow more clearly. Once these processes had been completed, he was usually left with interviews that were missing their reverse shots and segments with no visible connecting thread. He used his presence, his commentary and the matching shots filmed later to mask any discrepancies, producing a contrast between live broadcasting in its purest form and the most shameless artifice. This daring attempt at illusion was repeated twenty years later in *F for Fake* and *Filming Othello*.

Over a few days, chiefly in Alain Pol's garden beside the Seine, Welles filmed a wealth of matching shots that would fit most episodes: dozens of reverse shots of himself that would give the mangled interviews coherence; dozens of shots in which he speaks directly to the audience, often leaning casually on his camera; and abstract whip pans, of the kind used in the montages of *Mr Arkadin*, providing transitions and enabling him to move freely from one place and topic to the next. Backgrounds – trees, a wall, a plain surface or the sky – that are blurred because Welles often shot the interviews in long focus, draw the attention away from any discontinuity.

In these matching shots Welles simulates the spontaneity of live broadcasting. When he retained the questions he had actually asked, he filmed silent reverse shots, and even shot his questions again, editing them in synchrony with the original sound. But most often he wrote and recorded a new piece of text that would fit naturally with the words of the interviewee that he had already filmed. In a single shot he may look in turn at his interlocutor, presumed off-screen, and then at the camera, to involve the viewer. Even when he speaks to local people in their own language, he turns slightly towards the camera to translate the conversation into English.

When he has let the audience forget about him for a while, he comes into the frame to mark a break by speaking again. When he has been present for some time, he goes boldly off-screen as if to meet whatever awaits him in the next shot. These are all devices that enhance his status as all powerful director/presenter.

For the bravura 'live coverage' of a bullfight in the episode about Madrid, Welles simply had himself filmed entering the packed bullring and watching a fight. Then he filmed all in one go, with a few extras, a series of medium close-ups from the same angle, making two ropes and a post represent two rows of seats. Here, everything can be read on Welles's face and in his gestures. In the first matching shot, having taken a number of wide shots in which he pushes his way through the crowd and makes as if to sit down in his reserved seat, he interrupts the movement; now he is holding a microphone, which will establish him as a 'special correspondent', while also helping to account for the fact that his voice can be heard so clearly despite the hubbub. A few shots later, he picks up from off-screen a camera that he did not have when he arrived. Then he gives 'on the spot' commentary on the *corrida* taking place in front of him, describing the action and anticipating with suppressed excitement what is going to happen next. He brings to life whatever is going on off-camera by nodding his head to let the non-expert understand the place in the arena of every last owner and breeder, every emergency surgeon and *alguacil*.

However, Welles had not completed a single one of these programmes when broadcasting began, as planned, in late September. Since May he had also been working on his play, *Moby Dick – Rehearsed*, which was performed in London, and on his uncompleted adaptation for television, part of a project of 'Sunday Spectaculars' for CBS. He filmed first in London, then, under the false pretext of shooting the Italian episode of *Around the World with Orson Welles*, in a small studio in Turin, where he planned to follow it with a version of Ben Jonson's *Volpone*. This meant that on the evening when his first travelogue was broadcast on ITV, Welles spoke live the linking commentary he had not recorded, while some of the commentary was missing from the second one.

Opposite page:
With Lettrists Maurice Lemaître and Isidore Isou in the Saint-Germain-des-Prés programme of *Around the World with Orson Welles.*

This page:
The programme on the Dominici affair in *Around the World with Orson Welles.*

Left-hand column:
Welles, the journalist Jacques Chapus (an expert on the case) and the crew, filming with two cameras.

Right-hand column:
Gustave Dominici (Gaston's son) and a prosecution witness, Paul Maillet.

Associated-Rediffusion demanded that he return to London, but in October, far from complying, he left Europe altogether, leaving no address. He later asked that broadcasts of the remaining programmes, which he would complete in the United States in his own time, be postponed indefinitely.

For its part, Associated-Rediffusion was determined to keep to the published dates and pressed Filmorsa to deliver the episodes edited in France. Filmorsa completed the work alone. The meetings with Duncan and a trio of Lettrists (writers of concrete poetry) had not provided enough material to fill the programme about Saint-Germain-des-Prés, for which Welles had barely filmed himself as presenter, and for which he refused to record a commentary in New York. Filmorsa resorted to various strategies: they took some of Welles's silent shots from other programmes, or substituted a double, and shot some retakes. They also used scenes from *Désordre*, a short made by Jacques Baratier on the night life of Saint-Germain-des-Prés and its celebrities, including Jean Cocteau, Simone de Beauvoir and Juliette Gréco. The programme also borrowed from another performance of Lettrism, and many shots taken in clubs in the late 1940s.

Filmorsa were also able to add shots of Eddie Constantine, with whom they had recently signed a contract. At Associated-Rediffusion's request, they also edited another version, now unavailable, of the Spanish programme, and given the quantity of material already filmed, assembled an alternative version of the Basque programme, intended for American television, which did not purchase it. Instead of having an American schoolboy and his French-speaking friends talking about the national sport, *pelota*, Welles spoke to an English-speaking Basque and the schoolboy's mother, the writer Lael Wertenbaker, who compare the Basque and American ways of life. For the programme on the Dominici case (banned in France for political reasons), the picture editing, apart from a few final details, was finished without Welles, but part of the soundtrack was not recorded. The programme was carefully completed in 2000 as part of a documentary describing its production history: the director, Christophe Cognet, notes where each of his additions, which he does not claim correspond with Welles's creative decisions, begins.

A TELEVISION FILM WITHOUT A SET: 'THE FOUNTAIN OF YOUTH'

Early in 1956, after directing *King Lear* in New York, Welles found work as an actor in Hollywood, in popular broadcasts exploiting his public image. With his company Orson Welles Enterprises he produced or co-produced low-budget pilots for two half-hour television series – one of plays, the other of documentaries about famous people. None of the three big American networks bought them, and only *The Fountain of Youth*, based on a humorous short story by John Collier, was broadcast two years later; a programme about Alexandre Dumas has not been seen to this day.

Set in the 1920s, *The Fountain of Youth* was meant to inaugurate a programme in which Welles would be a one-man band, much more visible than Hitchcock in the famous series *Alfred Hitchcock Presents*, which had just begun. It was produced by Desilu, a company breaking new ground by specializing in sitcoms, and the programme was shot in one week, in its small studio. In order to get revenge on his fiancée – a young actress played by Joi Lansing, who has left him for a tennis ace (Rick Jason) as much in love with his own good looks as she is with hers – the scientist Baxter (Dan Tobin) gives them as a wedding present what he claims is the world's only dose of a revolutionary elixir of youth: a poisoned chalice, since it cannot be shared. The fickle creature returns to Baxter in the end, having drunk the liquid on the sly. He tells her that her husband has done the same, and that it was actually only water. Apart from the love-triangle, the cast included only three minor and some non-speaking roles. Welles appears regularly as presenter, sometimes on screen and sometimes in voiceover, making his own words alternate with the characters' dialogue, as in his radio plays. The screenplay consists of very short scenes, which follow closely the dialogue in Collier's story. Welles enriched it by using means that exactly parallel Collier's mischievous and unpredictable humour. For the first time since *Macbeth*, everything was planned well in advance.

Welles needed only two sets, reduced to their essentials, representing a landing stage and a night club, where a small part of the action takes place. Apart from that, he adopted the method used in photo-stories or 'picture films', very popular in Europe, in which it is the simplification of the visuals that makes everything comprehensible.

Welles had his cast perform in front of a simple screen, in front of which there also appeared a few stylized pieces of furniture, such as the mantelpiece on which the elixir stands. While shooting, Welles projected on to this screen images shot beforehand: almost abstract silhouettes, like shadow puppets, or slides of the set or the action. At the beginning, an anonymous hand sets the mood by inserting a slide into a projector that immediately swivels to face the viewer. What follows is fleeting images and shifting perspectives. The slides and the lighting, which Welles varied in a decidedly anti-realist manner during the course of a take, allowed for quick transitions from one short scene to the next. Welles combined the transition techniques he had learned from stage and radio to produce an unbroken pyrotechnic display.

Behind Welles – the master of ceremonies – the sideways movement of an image projected on the screen represents an abstract panorama, or suggests in a single shot a transition from Vienna to the skyscrapers of New York. Welles also often plays his voiceover over a series of full-frame slides; the actors, reduced to silence while Welles is in full flow, exaggeratedly mime the situations presented in still photos, sometimes shown in quick succession to simulate movement. This has the effect of constantly disorienting us, because there seems to be no underlying principle. For example, Welles may come into the frame in front of a photo of his characters that fills the whole screen; the assistant cameraman will focus on him, while the slide becomes an out-of-focus background. Or, when Baxter learns that his fiancée loves another man, a 'slide' suddenly comes to life, showing him closing his eyes in mute agony and then, after the image has been held for some time, opening his mouth to demand his rival's name. Each character in turn is seen in both soft and sharp focus, becomes a static image, or starts to move again, and they all lose or recover their voice. The characters may, in fact, unexpectedly take over lines started by Welles, or he will speak a line instead of his characters, although their lips move.

In terms of the lighting, Welles relies on two kinds of transition, similar to those he had used in the theatre. He makes the lights fall, plunging the screen into black following the verbal or visual gag on which certain scenes end. Most of all, he douses the lights in mid-shot to represent a change of time and place, while the actor stays in the same place. At the end of the scene on the landing stage, in which Baxter, returning from Europe, learns of his misfortune, the lights go right off, plunging him temporarily into shadow. The screen behind him is still lighted but using a dissolve this slide turns into another, which places Baxter in a restaurant before he is illuminated again, having visibly changed some of his clothing for the rest of the shot. When this new scene ends, Welles uses the same device to transport Baxter from the restaurant to his office. Welles treats the short scenes making up *The Fountain of Youth* like the pieces of a puzzle that can be endlessly reconfigured as the puppet master's imagination dictates. And he ends by announcing the following week's broadcast: 'Until then, I remain, as always, obediently yours.'

This exercise in virtuosity failed to appeal to advertisers and remained an isolated effort – a clear sign of what Welles could have done in television if he had worked there as frequently as he did for radio. At the same time, *Around the World with Orson Welles* allowed Welles the freedom for formal experimentation which, after some intervening sorties, would be developed on a more ambitious scale in his essay films of the 1970s.

Opposite page:
One of the casual chats in *Orson Welles' Sketch Book*, made for the BBC (1955). Welles was filmed in a single take, apart from the time it took to do a few sketches. He deplored the growing use of an autocue or teleprompter 'because of course I make it up as I go along'.

Top:
Joi Lansing and Rick Jason in *The Fountain of Youth*.

Above:
Welles in *The Fountain of Youth*.

TOUCH OF EVIL 1957–1958

Touch of Evil was a project that Welles inherited, but he made it completely his own. He was excluded from the last post-production stages, but in the meantime he firmly imposed his unorthodox decisions on this studio film, and was always open to the unexpected and the inspiration of the moment. Of all his Hollywood films, *Touch of Evil* is the one in which there is the greatest degree of improvisation, and Welles constantly discovered new possibilities during the course of a shoot that had initially been very carefully planned.

Previous pages:
Welles with Charlton Heston and camera operator Philip Lathrop.

Left:
Searching Sanchez's apartment – Joseph Calleia (Menzies), Welles (Quinlan) and Akim Tamiroff (Joe Grandi).

Opposite page:
Welles (seen here with Janet Leigh and Akim Tamiroff) often used low-angle shots to exaggerate Quinlan's bulk.

BACK IN THE DIRECTOR'S CHAIR

On his return to Hollywood, where he had not worked since he made *Macbeth*, and at the same time as he was trying to establish himself in television, Welles made great efforts to regain a foothold with the major film companies. His chance came in 1956, when Universal-International offered him the second lead in Jack Arnold's *Man in the Shadow* (released in Britain under the title *Pay the Devil*). It was an unpretentious production, but it gave Welles the opportunity to try his hand in the kind of role with which he would become identified: a corpulent, bigoted, small-town potentate. Albert Zugsmith, the producer, in particular, was well satisfied with his performance and immediately suggested he play a variant of the character: a corrupt police officer, in a run of the mill film in which he would appear opposite Charlton Heston.

Heston – who, with Cecil B. DeMille's *The Ten Commandments*, was on his way to becoming one of the biggest American stars – owed Universal another film under the terms of his contract. Why would he wish to appear in a routine crime film when leading roles in films such as *The Big Country* and *Ben-Hur* were waiting for him? No reason, unless drawn by the opportunity to work under the man who had made *Citizen Kane*. And Universal, who had only planned to hire Welles as actor, bowed without demur to Heston's suggestion that Welles should also direct. But the deal was far from perfect on both sides. The project was pretty modest and Universal could hardly refuse to take the risk, yet it is hard to see why its efforts to secure Heston's services were not devoted to a more significant film.

Right:
Shooting schedule approved by the producer, Albert Zugsmith. The search of Sanchez's apartment (scenes 73 to 79 and 90 to 95) was expected to take up the better part of the first three days' filming.

Below:
Welles as Quinlan (left) and as director (right).

Opposite page:
Welles, Charlton Heston and Janet Leigh, whose broken arm was often concealed under a jacket she threw over it.

PROD 29
ac

SHOOTING SCHEDULE

Mr. A. Zugsmith

PROD. NO. 1851 TITLE BADGE OF EVIL
START 2/18/57
CLOSE 3/22/57 CAMERA DAYS 24 plus 1 layoff

DIRECTOR ORSON WELLES
ASST. DIR. PHIL BOWLES
BUS. MGR. T. THOMPSON

Camera Day and Date	Description of Set or Location	Actors Working	Wardrobe Change	Seq	Page	Location or Studio	Day or Night
1st Day 2nd Day 3rd Day Monday Tuesday Wednesday Feb. 18 Feb. 19 Feb. 20	INT. SQUAD ROOM Sc. 135-D Menzies on phone to Quinlan	MENZIES CASEY SANCHEZ			1/4	STAGE 19	N
	INT. SANCHEZ' APARTMENT Scs. 73 thru 79 Questioning Sanchez.	QUINLAN MIKE SCHWARTZ SANCHEZ MARIA CASEY FRANTZ			8	STAGE 19	D
	Sc. 79-C Grandi brought in by Menzies.	SANCHEZ CASEY MENZIES GRANDI QUINLAN SCHWARTZ			2-1/2	STAGE 19	D
	Scs. 90, 90-A, 90-B, 93, 94, 95, 95-A, 95-B Menzies finds dynamite. Mike leaves.	SANCHEZ CASEY MENZIES GRANDI QUINLAN MIKE SCHWARTZ			5	STAGE 19	D
	EXT. CONSTRUCTION JOB Scs. 59-A, 62, 64, 65, 66, 67, 68 Question superintendent. Get flash on radio.	QUINLAN MIKE SCHWARTZ			3-1/2	BACK LOT	D

Albert Zugsmith
$1999.50

As for Welles, he was so eager to be given this new opportunity that he agreed to rewrite the film and direct it without being paid any more than he would have been for just appearing as an actor.

TWO SOURCES FOR A NEW SCREENPLAY

Welles was hired by Universal in the first week of January 1957, and a month later delivered a screenplay (dated 5 February). He claimed later that he made almost all of it up himself, without bothering to look at the original novel (which he said he did not read until several years later) nor at the first adaptation submitted to him. The truth is more complicated, and Welles's final screenplay actually owes a great deal to the two texts that preceded it.

The first was *Badge of Evil*, a crime novel published under the name Whit Masterson, a pseudonym of Robert Wade and William Miller. It was published in 1956 and immediately bought by Universal, who commissioned an adaptation from Paul Monash, a writer of crime series for television. It was his screenplay, dated 24 July 1956, that Welles used as the main source for his rewriting. Masterson's novel, set in southern California, describes the confrontation between Mitch Holt, an honest American police officer, married for the past nine years to a Mexican wife, and a pair of local detectives, over the death of a local worthy, killed when his beach cabaña is blown up. The prime suspect is Shayon, a young shoe clerk whom the murdered man's daughter wanted to marry, against her father's wishes. One of the two detectives, Captain McCoy, is a living legend in the area – a wiry little man, now retired, whose only reason for returning to the force is the importance of the case. His deputy, Hank Quinlan, is a large, fat man, utterly devoted to his chief, whose life he saved some years previously, sustaining an injury that means he still walks with a cane. Furious at not being able to get the better of Shayon, McCoy fabricates damning evidence against him by hiding dynamite in his bathroom cabinet. At the same time, Holt discovers who was really responsible, and comes into conflict with McCoy, who tries to get his own back by falsely implicating Holt's wife in a drug-bust. Holt then persuades Quinlan to allow him to record McCoy's confession, using a hidden microphone. McCoy kills Quinlan, who was trying to arrest him, before committing suicide. With the exception of the first chapter, describing the explosion that starts off the action, the reader experiences the whole novel from Holt's point of view, and has only indirect access, for example, to the final exchanges between McCoy and Quinlan.

Monash's screenplay departed from this outline on several major points, most of which Welles retained. The first was to exchange the positions of the corpulent Quinlan (whose first name is now Thomas) and his more slightly-built deputy, renamed Jack Miller. But at this point it is still the deputy who walks with a limp, the legacy of a bullet that was meant to injure Quinlan. Monash also emphasizes the similarities between Quinlan and Holt, who are equally obsessive in pursuing a truth of which they believe they are the natural guardians, and equally ready to abuse witnesses in order to drag evidence out of them. Another of his changes is to make Shayon the guilty man, thus justifying Quinlan's instincts as a police officer, if not his methods, and to develop a plot-line that is barely sketched in the novel. It involves a gang, made up of members of an Italian family, which is broken up by Holt. They provide a source of constant menace, and are given the surname Grandi in the screenplay itself. Monash was also responsible for the idea that the initial explosion would catch its victim in the company of a lady friend, with the rhythm of a cha-cha in the background. He invents several scenes that appear in the film: the discussion among the officers immediately after the murder, the drive to a construction site to question a suspect, the exchange between Holt and the district attorney in the police records department, Quinlan's dramatic offer to resign following the accusations made against him by Holt, and Holt's fight with members of the Grandi family in the bar.

As in the novel, the point of view is still essentially Holt's, even though in the final scenes of Quinlan's confession at his ranch, shots of Quinlan and Miller alternate with those of Holt, who is recording their conversation from his car. There is no disputing that Welles borrowed freely from these two sources. His screenplay follows the ins and outs of Monash's quite closely, but he also takes from Masterson whole passages of dialogue that do not appear in the 1956 screenplay. This does not mean that his contribution is any the less substantial, and it gives the film, even from the writing stage, an entirely new complexity.

Welles's major change was certainly to move the action to a small border town, divided between Mexico and the United States, where racial tension will be an issue. The settings are confusingly juxtaposed, on either side of the border, and each of the characters intrudes on the territory of the others. Tension is further heightened by Welles's making Quinlan an openly racist brute, while his adversary, now renamed Miguel Vargas, becomes a highly cultured Mexican, 'educated in Switzerland and England', and a senior police officer in Mexico. Furthermore, he is married to a woman from Philadelphia – in others words, the cream of American society, whose racist attitudes she embodies with superb self-assurance. Welles adds to these racial antagonisms by turning the chief suspect in the bombing into Sanchez, a Mexican whose liaison with the victim's daughter is a pathetic counterpart of Vargas's marriage to Susan, and by introducing into Quinlan's distant past the murder of his wife, strangled by a man of mixed race.

Welles's second major contribution to the film lies in its almost total refusal to identify its point of view with that of the hero. Vargas turns out to be just one character among others, a virtuous but slightly dull double of Quinlan, whose ambiguity is of a different order. The decision to use multiple points of view enables Welles to create scenes in which Vargas cannot appear: in particular, all those involving his wife's troubles with the Grandi family, and her moving into the motel. Characters that were previously marginal now become far more central – like Susan, whose personal nightmare (not directly connected with the main action) now takes up a substantial part of the screenplay, and Joe Grandi, whose appearances are scattered throughout the film. Most important, it allows Quinlan to function separately from Vargas, and to explain himself in his conversations with Menzies, Grandi and the brothel-keeper Mother Lupe – a character who did not appear in the earlier versions, was further developed during shooting and eventually became Tana, played by Marlene Dietrich. After reading this version, Heston realized that Quinlan was now the protagonist. As a good loser, he was content not to allow himself to be too much eclipsed by his director's powerful presence. The new treatment also resolved an important point ignored in Monash's version, as in the original novel: the possible reasons why Quinlan's deputy suddenly turns against him.

To explain it, Welles invents a small detail and has Quinlan leave his cane behind on several occasions, the last time near Grandi's body, where Menzies finds it.

A FINE BALANCE OF POWER

Even with the support of his star, Welles found himself in a delicate situation *vis-à-vis* a production company who at first did not want him as director. Good sense suggested that he adopt the low profile of the prodigal son allowed to return to the fold. But that was not to be, and Welles chose, on the contrary, to start the shoot with a bold move that clearly signalled his determination to work in his own way or not at all.

He had planned for the first three days' shoot a series of scenes that were among the most complicated and difficult to organize of any in the film, in which the police search Sanchez's apartment and eventually find the dynamite hidden in his bathroom. The sequence presented many problems, the first being its length: over eleven minutes, divided into three sections, between which Vargas goes out to telephone his wife and comes back into the apartment later. Then there were the many characters involved, eleven in all, constantly coming and going, entering and leaving, and speaking their lines over one another very rapidly. The space was also very small – a simple apartment whose three rooms were arranged in sequence: the front living room, then the bedroom, then the bathroom. The last problem was the number of actions: in addition to the conflictual relationships within constantly reconfigured groups of characters, it has to be established before Vargas goes out that the dynamite that will incriminate Sanchez was not in the place where Menzies will find it when Vargas returns. The whole thing, which represents fifteen pages and about twenty numbered set-ups in the screenplay, was scheduled to take at least two days to shoot.

Contrary to all expectations, Welles decided to film the whole of the action in only three long takes, in the apartment set built on Universal Studios' stage 19. By doing so, he added three new constraints to the difficulties already mentioned. The first of these was that the action had to move smoothly from one room to another. This problem was solved by completely opening one side of the set representing the series of three rooms. The camera and other equipment would thus be free to move between different parts of the set, whose internal walls could slide back as required, to let them through.

The second was that the cinematographer, Russell Metty – who had worked on *The Stranger* and was now with Universal – had to provide a basic lighting scheme that would be suitable for the whole scene. A further complication was the fact that since the low ceilings had to be visible, the action could not be lit from above, as it usually is. Welles and Metty found a brilliant dramatic solution, placing all the lights on the same side, opposite the open part of the set, thereby casting menacing shadows of the actors on the white back wall, but at the same time increasing the risk that those of the crew would also appear. The third constraint forced Welles to find the means of reproducing, within the fluid movement of this single long take, equivalents of what the screenplay had kept for the editing stage: alternation between full shots, medium close-ups and close-ups – such as the crucial one of the empty shoebox in which the dynamite will later be found. Welles handled this last difficulty by choreographing the constant movements of the camera and the actors, who stopped moving only long enough to emphasize an exchange of lines or an action.

Decisions like this demand meticulous execution, and the first half-day was given up to preparation, without a shot being taken. It was the same for most of the afternoon, when the studio bosses, worried about the turn that events were taking, began to prowl round the edges of the set in a threatening fashion. Finally, at a quarter to six, Welles was ready to start shooting. Less than two hours later, he announced that he was satisfied with the result. He had gained a whole day in his schedule.

Quite aside from the pleasure of carrying off a *tour de force* of that kind, there is scarcely any doubt that Welles carefully calculated this spectacular start (he had previously rehearsed the scene at length at home, with his leading actors) as a way of setting the ground rules with his producers. If they would let him work in his own way, he in turn would commit himself to delivering the film on time and within budget. That is what in fact happened throughout the length of the shoot, and Welles made good use of the freedom that Universal gave him to direct the film in the way he chose.

ON LOCATION AGAIN

Welles apparently wanted to shoot *Touch of Evil* near the Mexican border, but in the face of opposition from the studio, he resigned himself to looking in the Hollywood area for the exteriors. He found them near Palmdale, in the Mojave desert (for the motel), and in Venice, a former seaside resort west of Los Angeles, built from scratch in 1905 in imitation of Venice, Italy. It was now surrounded by oil wells and was half derelict: its main streets were lined with tall arcades whose indeterminate style was just right, its old canals were falling into ruin, and it was less than an hour's drive from the studios.

Welles found this amazing location a constant source of inspiration. In the film, aspects of Venice create a visual metaphor on two levels. The first is the image of a maze that is less physical – the city is modern and its plan rigidly geometrical – than psychological: we never know where we are in this network of streets, identical bridges arching over canals and tangled patterns of derricks. The second image is that of a crumbling, decomposing world, where the oil wells seem about to be abandoned and water stagnates instead of flowing. Even the city's residents appear to have deserted, and we are surprised to see them suddenly appear, always in scenes set at night – the opening shot, the crowd under Susan's windows following Grandi's death – like so many ghosts returning from the past. This almost always nocturnal view of the city is an essential feature of the film, since it allows Welles and Metty to fill it with dark nooks and crannies, to cast shadows that give its walls sinister life, and to light its arcades in such a way as to trace through them vanishing points that command the attention.

It was not the physical reality of Venice that Welles was trying to show, in order to ground the action more firmly in an urban setting – as did many Hollywood thrillers of the 1950s and as he had tried to do in *The Lady from Shanghai*. Closer to his approach in *Othello*, Welles took random fragments of the city, which he combined at the editing stage to create Los Robles, a border town made almost abstract by being reduced to symbols. Departing from normal industry practice, he did not use Venice only for his exteriors, but took the opportunity of shooting a considerable number of interiors there, either because chance had led him to a more suitable location than the studio sets that were ready and waiting, or because he wanted to make a visual match between the interior spaces and the exterior appearance of the town.

Welles, Philip Lathrop, Charlton Heston and Janet Leigh. Lathrop was making his last film as a camera operator, before becoming one of his generation's best directors of photography.

It was no doubt the same concern to establish a very strong connection between the action and its setting that explains the solution Welles adopted when filming the dialogue between Schwartz, the assistant district attorney, and Vargas, in Vargas's car. The screenplay and shooting schedule had the scene take place, more conventionally, in the street, before the two men get in the car. If their exchange was to be filmed inside a moving vehicle, good sense would suggest that it be shot in the studio, in front of a process screen on to which a moving road would be projected, in ideal lighting and sound conditions. Instead, Welles demanded that the scene be filmed, in a single shot lasting about fourteen seconds, in an actual car, moving straight down a Venice street. The camera was secured to the bonnet, simultaneously filming the two characters in the foreground and the facades on either side of the street, which seem to be sucked into the background, so greatly does the short focal length exaggerate spatial depth. It is impossible not to feel the car vibrating or the air blowing through the actors' clothes, or to sense the characters' real difficulty in making themselves heard above the ambient noise.

TURNING THE UNEXPECTED TO ACCOUNT

The locations it provided did not exhaust Venice's potential, and new options kept occurring to Welles, who was always ready to revise his schedule to follow the spur of the moment. If torrential rain made it impossible to work in the street, rather than cancel the night's work he would decide to occupy the hotel lobby and Vargas's bedroom, and film there and then the scene in which Vargas tells Quinlan's superiors of his suspicions about him. The exchange takes place in the office of the district attorney, Adair, and the plan was to film it in the studio after all the exteriors had been shot. What was originally simply a response to a problem immediately became a prodigious piece of cinematic inventiveness, based on the slow ascent of the wheezing lift as it takes the visitors upstairs.

The scene starts conventionally enough, in the hotel lobby, where Vargas is inviting Adair, Schwartz and the police chief, Gould, to come up to his room. What follows is in the nature of a *tour de force*, feasible only because Welles, when shooting his exteriors, had insisted on using his favourite camera, a portable Caméflex, little used in the United States, where it was known as a Camerette. The long take that follows begins with the camera already inside the lift into which the three men are packed. Vargas closes the door on them in the lobby, telling them he will meet them upstairs. Their conversation continues until the lift stops, Vargas opens the door ('Well, Vargas, you must be pretty quick on your feet' – 'It's just that the lift's slow') and they all emerge on to the landing, still followed by the camera from inside the lift. What is more, according to Heston the scene was shot with live sound, and the lift cage was connected by the sound and light cables to the crew working at ground level.

Improvisation did not stop there. Once this scene had been shot, at two o'clock in the morning, Welles decided to spend the rest of the night filming, in a basement of the same hotel, the brief scene (which had also been scheduled for the studio) in which Menzies shows Vargas the cane left behind by Quinlan near Grandi's body. Joseph Calleia, who played Menzies, was not on hand that night, and had to be dragged out of bed to do the scene, still half asleep.

AN UNLIKELY SET OF ACTORS

Welles's confidence in the inspiration of the moment was also evident in the casting of some of the actors hired at the last minute for secondary roles. They included Dennis Weaver, familiar to audiences in his role as the deputy sheriff in the television series *Gunsmoke*, who plays the night clerk at the Mirador motel; Marlene Dietrich, whom Welles persuaded to accept the then very small part of Tana; Joseph Cotten, who agreed to make a brief appearance as the medical examiner; and Mercedes McCambridge, with whom Welles had worked in radio and who was hired to play the uncredited role of a disconcertingly androgynous member of the gang that attacks Susan.

The first consequence of these choices was that they divided the cast into two. On one side were the main characters, led by Susan and Vargas and flanked by the predictable figures of local notables and officials. On the other side, a confusing series of bizarre caricatures and menacing figures, dominated by the outlandish characters of Grandi and the night clerk. Between these two poles are three figures that cannot be clearly situated: Quinlan, Menzies and Tana, who also happen to be the only ones who continue to live in a past of which all the other characters seem unaware. Welles had long wished to work with Dietrich, who he had hoped would play Sophie in *Mr Arkadin*. He did not obtain her agreement until half-way through shooting *Touch of Evil*, and then undertook to develop Tana's role for her, based on that of Mother Lupe, who had only one short scene in the original screenplay. When she arrived, she brought her legendary status to the film, and Welles directed her in a manner in keeping with her firmly established image: almost motionless, often in a static medium close-up, like an icon from the past, forgotten by time itself.

Grandi and the night clerk belong to a different world, that of the grotesques that Welles had earlier explored with such enjoyment in *The Lady from Shanghai* and especially in *Mr Arkadin*, where he had already employed Akim Tamiroff, who now played Grandi. With them, there is no place for psychology, and the characters exist only in terms of forms of behaviour that cannot be rationally explained. It would be tempting to convince ourselves that Grandi is no more than the third-rate 'godfather' of a family of gangsters, but Welles does not allow us to do so, giving the character a colourful presence, at once pathetic and menacing, ready at any moment to topple as easily into broad comedy as into nightmare.

When it comes to the night clerk, Welles encourages Weaver to make him a sexual innocent, open-mouthed but always nervously alert, a cackling capon equally terrified of a woman's presence as of the thugs who invade his lifeless existence. Almost all Weaver's scenes are improvised, since his role was developed during shooting. Welles's main instruction was never to let another actor come between him and the camera, so that he is constantly hopping about as he reacts instantly to the slightest movements of his fellow actors, not to mention his unplanned flight from the motel room, poking his head through the window and the door.

This page:
The night clerk, vividly portrayed by Dennis Weaver (below, with Janet Leigh), and Marlene Dietrich as Tana (bottom, with Welles).

Opposite page:
Zsa Zsa Gabor (centre), the star invited at the insistence of producer Albert Zugsmith, appeared on the screen for only a few seconds, and Welles took care not to demand too much of her.

EXTREME CAMERA ANGLES

In *Touch of Evil*, more than ever before Welles expresses a consistently extreme aesthetic through the cinematography, exaggerating the bizarre or ridiculous elements in the performance of some of the actors. Apart from the frequent use of a hand-held camera – notably in the scene of Grandi's murder, or at the end, when Vargas is following Menzies and Quinlan – the three key features are violent contrasts, disorienting angles and the use of wide-angle lenses. The greater part of the film takes place at night, not only on the streets of Los Robles, but also in the interiors, where powerful light sources increase the number of shadows cast by the set, as well as by the actors. And yet this is very different from the mannerist chiaroscuro that was a feature of post-war *noir* films. Here Welles's use of black and white is cruder, less overtly aestheticizing, and his lighting contrasts are always in movement, creating the sense of a world that cannot be grasped because it is constantly being remade. This tendency reaches its height in the scene of Grandi's murder, lit by the regular flashing of a neon sign that suddenly becomes out of control, against all probability, at the actual moment when he is killed. The same goes for the scene of the final chase among the derricks, in which new lights constantly appear as if from nowhere, briefly plucking the characters out of the darkness.

The number of extreme high- or low-angle shots, whether designed to dramatize the balance of power or, less conventionally, to place the characters in a distorting perspective, is less surprising because, since *Citizen Kane*, Welles had made it a kind of formal trademark. However, to use them systematically in association with a very short focal length was far more daring. In fact Welles decided to use as often as he could lenses with a focal length of 18.5 mm, which gave him, in his interior locations, a very wide aperture and great depth of field.

The disadvantage of such lenses is that they produce an apparent curvature of space that distorts the image, especially round its edges, while exaggerating its depth. Far from trying to hide these deviations from the way things actually appear, Welles exploits them to create an image that is more expressionist than realist, in which effects of perspective are heightened, the successive shots of an action are more clearly organized in terms of depth and, most of all, the distortions produced by the lens turn into stylistic devices.

Flouting the elementary rule that prohibits (because of this distortion) the use of short focus for close-ups or pans, Welles uses it systematically. For example, he uses it in the film's first shot to transform into a menacing claw the hand that is setting a timer wired to a bomb, then to exaggerate Quinlan's corpulence in a low-angle shot, to distort the faces of the gang, and to further unsettle our sense of space when Grandi is murdered.

DELIBERATELY DISJOINTED EDITING

When it came to editing *Touch of Evil*, Welles's approach was equally unconventional in that he planned to make use of contrasts and disjunctions that would catch the viewer unawares. At its simplest, this might involve one action being interpolated within another, or the sudden jump that interrupts the long exchange between Susan and Grandi to return to the scene of the explosion, or the deliberately mismatching cuts that create spatial confusion in the final scene. But Welles does not always use sudden breaks, and can also handle transitions as complex as the very slow dissolve linking the end of the search of Sanchez's apartment and the beginning of the following scene in the motel bedroom. It fuses two perfectly symmetrical shots: one of Menzies filmed behind a window in which Quinlan and Grandi are reflected, hatching their plot in the street; and the other of Susan, seen behind another window in which there is a reflection of the desert from which her assailants are about to come.

Welles's plan for the editing is marked above all by the way he breaks up the pace, alternating very long takes and scenes of extreme brevity. The better part of Sanchez's interrogation consists of two shots, each lasting over five minutes, and the film opens with a stunning three-minute twenty-second tracking shot which further increased Welles's technical problems.

In this opening shot, the camera follows, in real exteriors and over a distance of about one hundred metres, the movements of the unidentified man who is putting dynamite into the boot of a car, of the couple who get into the car in order to cross the border, and of Vargas and his wife, who pass it on foot at that moment. The sequence is divided into several set-ups in the screenplay, and it is not until the last of these, when they reach the border checkpoint, that the two couples meet.

DIVORCES

Previous pages:
Valentin De Vargas (back to camera) and Janet Leigh in the streets of Venice.

Top:
The use of short focus dramatically distorts space, but makes it possible to include all the characters in one frame (Charlton Heston, Gus Schilling, Mort Mills and Welles).

Bottom:
Two old Mercury hands, Ray Collins and Joseph Cotten, meet briefly at the scene of the explosion.

The shooting schedule allocated four whole nights to this shot and a few others in the streets, following the explosion. As with the search of Sanchez's apartment, the natural thing would be to retain the breakdown into shots, and film separately the successive stages of a continuous whole that freely changes its point of view: from a close-up of the dynamite the killer is holding, to a full shot of the traffic in the street; and from a high-angle crane shot taken from a height of several metres, to one that returns to ground-level to show a flock of goats. There was all the more reason to do this since the depth of field had to be reduced because of the lack of light, and each stage of the action required its own flood lighting, which was in danger of being exposed to view every time the camera moved. At the very least, the last part of the shot, beginning with the characters' arrival at the border checkpoint, could be separated from the rest, as its great amount of dialogue is in contrast with the silent, choreographed movements that precede it.

Welles, however, decided to shoot it all at once, in one night, after indulging himself by filming two shots of his friend Joseph Cotten in the role of the medical examiner. Why did he take this gamble (whose successful outcome, incidentally, was in itself enough to secure the film's place in cinema history)? The motive was surely the temptation to play God: how better to show that a director was all-powerful than by creating an appearance of happenstance that in fact reflected his intended purpose?

No doubt also for the pure pleasure of scoffing at difficulties that were apparently insurmountable. But dazzling as it is, Welles's technical virtuosity is never gratuitous. This time he had to find a way to avoid breaking down his opening shot, because it is driven by the setting of the timer in the first seconds; it has to run its allotted time, which also marks the end of the shot.

In contrast to these long takes, the gang's invasion of Susan's bedroom is handled in a score of very brief shots, and Grandi's murder by Quinlan consists of forty-two shots taking up less than two minutes in total. What is most remarkable is that the relationship between the long takes and brief shots is not the traditional contrast between slowness and acceleration. The long takes are anything but slow: endlessly varied in their framing, full of often simultaneous actions and constant movement, and, in the Sanchez sequence, of overlapping lines. Welles uses them to preserve the continuity on which the action depends: just as nothing can stop the mechanism that sets off the explosion, the dynamite could only be planted in Sanchez's apartment between the two shots in which Vargas is never far away from Quinlan. The impact of the brief shots depends on the same movements, the same disruption of the frame, the same variations in perspective. However, their brevity means they have no clear spatial location, and makes them symptoms of a general disorientation.

Once shooting was finished, on 1 April 1957, the editing of *Touch of Evil* was at first closely supervised by Welles. The work was not easy, and a number of editors paid the price. Aaron Stell, who replaced them, described the disconcerting methods of a director who never visited the cutting room but, after viewing the edited scenes on the big screen, wrote minutely detailed instructions as to the improvements to be made.

In mid-July a provisional version of the film was shown to the studio bosses, who were not happy with the result and asked Ernest Nims to oversee the corrections. He had been head of post-production on *The Stranger* and was now with Universal, still firmly convinced that it was pointless to retain in a film anything that slowed down the action. Welles reluctantly withdrew, but not before leaving directions as to how the work should continue. It is very likely that he did not see the film again before the end of August, when he returned from Mexico, where he had started filming *Don Quixote*. He then wrote a new set of suggestions which, if they were ever sent, seem not to have reached the studio. Meanwhile, relations between Welles and Universal had turned sour, and when Universal decided in November that some scenes needed to be re-shot to clarify the plot, they refused to allow him to take on the work and gave it to a little-known director, Harry Keller.

On 3 December 1957, Welles viewed the film as edited by Nims, still without the music that was being written by Henry Mancini, using the broad guidelines Welles had given him during a brief consultation. Two days later, he sent Edward Muhl, vice-president and head of production, a fifty-eight-page memorandum, in which he made extraordinarily detailed comments, based on a single viewing. Many of them referred to the soundtrack, suggesting that lines that were not clear be recorded again, and saying that he was available to do the job. Others emphasized his idea of putting together a soundtrack made up of natural sounds and music coming from identified sources – car radios, for example. Welles also argued the case for retaining the alternation between parallel actions: he suggested a certain number of changes to the cut, and insisted that the visual crescendo leading up to Quinlan's death be retained. Far from containing the virulence of the letters exchanged when *The Lady from Shanghai* and *Macbeth* were re-edited, the general tone of the document is calm and reasonable: Welles is careful to acknowledge Nims's improvements, and to avoid creating the impression that he has a moral right over the film. He always puts the case for his suggestions in terms of dramatic effectiveness, although occasionally they are more like entreaties, so much has he taken the correction to heart. Welles was anxious not to poison the atmosphere, and two weeks later made himself available to post-sync the faulty lines. But his film had by now irretrievably slipped his grasp, and Universal, which was in the throes of reorganization, no longer believed in its potential success.

A first version, lasting one hour and forty-nine minutes, was completed, probably in January 1958. But it was a different one that was eventually distributed a month later, with no press launch or exclusive release, and cut by fifteen minutes so that it could be shown as part of a double bill. This shortened version was distributed in the rest of the world in the same year. In 1975, chance produced from the archives the longer, unreleased version. It was shown in that year at the Paris Film Festival, then distributed increasingly widely in place of the earlier one, which almost completely disappeared.

In 1997 the independent producer Rick Schmidlin persuaded Universal to pay for a posthumous revision, on the basis of the instructions given by Welles in his long memo of December 1957. The editor was Walter Murch, one of the best known sound designers in the new Hollywood of the 1970s, but the restorers had only the two existing versions to work from, all the other original material having disappeared. They could therefore incorporate the instructions in the memo only when they simply involved moving scenes around, removing images or altering the mix.

This re-edited version could neither restore cuts that were permanently lost, nor even remove the mediocre scenes filmed by Keller to replace those shot by Welles, which had vanished in the meantime. We now have three versions of *Touch of Evil*, but we still lack the one that only Welles could have edited, and in particular, the soundtrack he was prevented from putting together.

Following the shoot, Welles's relations with Universal looked promising, all the more so since he had made his name good again by going over his thirty-day shooting schedule by only one day and, according to Heston, exceeding his budget by only three per cent. As for Zugsmith, who had left the studio in the meantime, he had enough confidence in Welles to suggest that he make a film for MGM, but Welles's difficulties with his producers at the editing stage once again undermined these good relations, and he never again made a film for a Hollywood studio.

DON QUIXOTE
1958

After the discipline of making a film for a Hollywood studio, Welles shot his next venture, *Don Quixote*, in an even freer way than he had for *Othello*. He used only two actors, both of whom remained committed to the project for years, and a minimal, constantly changing crew. With practically no sets built, no camera tracks laid and no live sound recorded, everything depended on the virtues of improvisation. Throughout both the shooting and editing phases, Welles continually modified his conception of *Don Quixote*, which was to become the archetype of his unfinished films.

Previous pages:
Francisco Reiguera was sixty-nine when the attack on the windmills was shot in Mexico.

Left:
Patty McCormack playing the role of the American girl to whom Welles relates the adventures of Don Quixote, during filming in Mexico.

Opposite page:
Akim Tamiroff had earlier played Sancho Panza in the tests filmed in colour in Paris in January 1955.

AT FIRST, FRANCE AND MEXICO

As he had done for *Othello* after the Venice Film Festival, Welles shot scenes for *Don Quixote* long before he began the filming proper. In practice the early version consisted simply of silent tests for costumes and make-up shot in the Bois de Boulogne in Paris in late January 1955. Judging from the laboratory bills, they amounted to a total of six usable minutes. Having just completed his involvement in *Mr Arkadin*, Welles did not look very far to find his Knight of the Sad Countenance and squire, giving the roles to Mischa Auer and Akim Tamiroff, who had played the flea trainer and Zouk in the previous film. Despite an ongoing dispute between Welles and his producer Louis Dolivet over the editing of *Mr Arkadin*, Filmorsa again financed the tests, which were shot in 35 mm Eastmancolor (probably by Roger Dormoy, who had finished off the photography for *Mr Arkadin*) thirteen years after the Technicolor images of *It's All True*. The idea was abandoned in Europe in 1955, but subsequently re-surfaced in the United States in July 1957.

Welles was two months into cutting *Touch of Evil* when his friend Frank Sinatra offered him the opportunity to drop everything and shoot a version of the second part of Cervantes' *Don Quixote* for television. Charlton Heston at once agreed to be his Don Quixote, but absolutely had to be free at the end of the month, giving Welles only a week's filming in Mexico to do a half-hour drama. Faced with the impossibility of managing such a tight schedule, Welles gave up the idea of the television piece, but his desire to film *Don Quixote* remained so strong that, from late July to September of that year, he divided his time between Hollywood and Mexico and managed to spend four or five weeks shooting his new project. This time it seems he was aiming to adapt three episodes of Cervantes' novel into three half-hour episodes, which soon turned into a ninety-minute feature, in which the stories were told by Welles himself to a young American tourist. The main originality of this adaptation lies in the fact that in it Don Quixote and Sancho Panza appear as Cervantes portrayed them, while the adversaries they face are transposed into the modern world.

So Don Quixote goes into the bullring to defend a bull against the picador who is persecuting him; instead of windmills he now attacks bulldozers; and his combat with the Moors is now directed against a cinema screen showing a projection of larger-than-life images, which Quixote cuts to pieces. The film ends with the inevitable atomic explosion which, for an audience of 1957, could only herald the end of the civilized world, and from which Cervantes' two heroes nevertheless emerge unscathed. Welles ultimately gave the role of Quixote to Francisco Reiguera, a gaunt, sixty-nine-year-old Spanish actor who had been in exile in Mexico since the Spanish Civil War. In that time he had had only minor roles, but had himself directed two films. The role of Sancho remained with Tamiroff, whose recent performance in *Touch of Evil* reaffirmed his natural affinity with the more grotesque aspects of the director's world. Welles himself took on the role of the narrator who relates episodes from *Don Quixote* to the young tourist. She was played by Patty McCormack, who, though only twelve years old, was a seasoned stage and film actress fresh from the success of her performance in Mervyn LeRoy's *The Bad Seed.*

UNSTRUCTURED PRODUCTION

The filming of *Don Quixote* had very little in the way of organization, since Welles had neither a written script nor a shooting schedule, nor even a production manager to organize his work, nor a script supervisor to keep a record of what had been done. Welles personally bore a large part of the cost, which was not covered by the $25,000 advance later reclaimed by Sinatra. Oscar Dancigers, who was already involved in several American and French productions in Mexico and had produced a dozen films by Luis Buñuel, liaised with the local laboratories and technical and professional organizations. The film crew was kept to the minimum. The director of photography was an American, Jack Draper, who had been living in Mexico for over twenty years, making a living on lacklustre productions. Working with Welles he had to learn how to use very short focal lengths (everything or almost everything was shot with an 18 mm lens) and zoom lenses. Use of the latter was only just becoming widespread at the time of shooting and Welles had immediately concluded that they should never be used in an obvious way. So he used them discreetly, either in combination with a very slow tracking shot of no more than a few metres, to create the illusion of a much longer tracking shot, or from time to time to change his framing without wasting time changing lens. The first assistant director was none other than Juan Luis Buñuel, son of director Luis Buñuel, who was then in exile in Mexico. Juan had no experience of the cinema whatsoever, but was nevertheless hired during his university holidays, acting more as an interpreter than an assistant director. To these were added a dozen or so technicians: assistants, make-up artists, electricians and prop assistants, recruited from crews working on short films rather than features in order to save money. The crew also included a sound engineer, whom Welles soon gave up asking for even a guide track because his requirements slowed everything down.

Following his usual practice Welles himself dubbed Reiguera and Tamiroff, provisionally at least, giving them caricatured and contrasting English and American accents. Even with such a small crew, the finances remained precarious and, as Juan Luis Buñuel recalled, Welles often had to interrupt the shooting and go to the United States in search of new money. However, a lot of money was also saved, since the crew had no official art director. Welles planned to shoot the entire film using real exteriors or, for the scene of the charge against the giants, a projection room at the San Ángel studio where he viewed his rushes. In these early days of the *Don Quixote* story Welles's intention to project the knight and his squire into the contemporary world was evidently not yet fully developed, since the shooting locations, all less than an hour's drive from Mexico City, were systematically chosen for their historic character and capacity to provide the director with the period buildings that would become his sets, along the lines of those he found for *Othello* in Italy and Morocco.

'LIKE MACK SENNETT'

The main innovation of this Mexico shoot lies in the way Welles experimented with a highly unusual filming strategy. Some ten months later he described how *Don Quixote* was shot 'with a degree of liberty that one seeks in vain in normal productions, because it was made without cuts, without even a narrative trajectory, without even a synopsis. Every morning, the actors, the crew and I would meet in front of the hotel. Then we'd set off and invent the film in the street, like Mack Sennett.' Nevertheless, this method, which Buñuel confirms, had an underlying discipline. The actors had become familiar with their characters over several weeks of rehearsals and Welles was not so much asking them to improvise as to regain a freshness of invention backed up by their memory of these rehearsals. It nevertheless required a great deal of time, as did Welles's concern to capture on film the extraordinary cloud formations of Mexico, which caused him to wait longer than was reasonable for the right moment to start filming the shots involving them. In mid-September 1957 Welles had to interrupt the shoot to go to Louisiana to take a major role in Martin Ritt's *Long Hot Summer* and to try to resolve the conflicts caused by the finishing of *Touch of Evil.* Tamiroff went back to France, where his next film was already waiting for him. Shooting was suspended on *Don Quixote,* although editing continued in Mexico for another few weeks, overseen by Alberto Valenzuela. According to Welles it would have taken only one more week to complete the whole thing. In practice the filming continued sporadically for a further ten years or so.

CONTINUING IN EUROPE

Early in 1958 Welles went into a new voluntary exile in Europe, settling with his family in a villa in the coastal town of Fregene, to the west of Rome. So it was out of the question for him to finish *Don Quixote* in Mexico in the near future. But no matter: Welles had become expert in creating continuity between the most diverse landscapes and he simply moved his actors to Italy to finish the filming, which began anew near Rome in August 1959. Meanwhile he was also playing Saul in *David and Goliath,* directed by Richard Pottier and Ferdinando Baldi, and shot at Cinecittà. Welles had made an unusual arrangement with the film's producer. Every day he would spend the hours from 6 a.m. to 4 p.m. filming *Don Quixote* in the arid landscapes around Rome. He would follow this, from 5 p.m. to 2 a.m., with his work on *David and Goliath,* on which he had been unofficially invited to direct his own scenes. He had arranged for the production to hire him a private secretary, Audrey Stainton, who in practice was also working on *Don Quixote* and has provided us with an invaluable account of this period. The role of Saul was not very long, but Welles, who was paid by the day, cunningly found ways to slow the filming down, thereby spinning out his performance and so financing his own film.

Mischa Auer and Akim Tamiroff, two of the most colourful actors from *Mr Arkadin*, try out their roles as Don Quixote and Sancho Panza in the Bois de Boulogne.

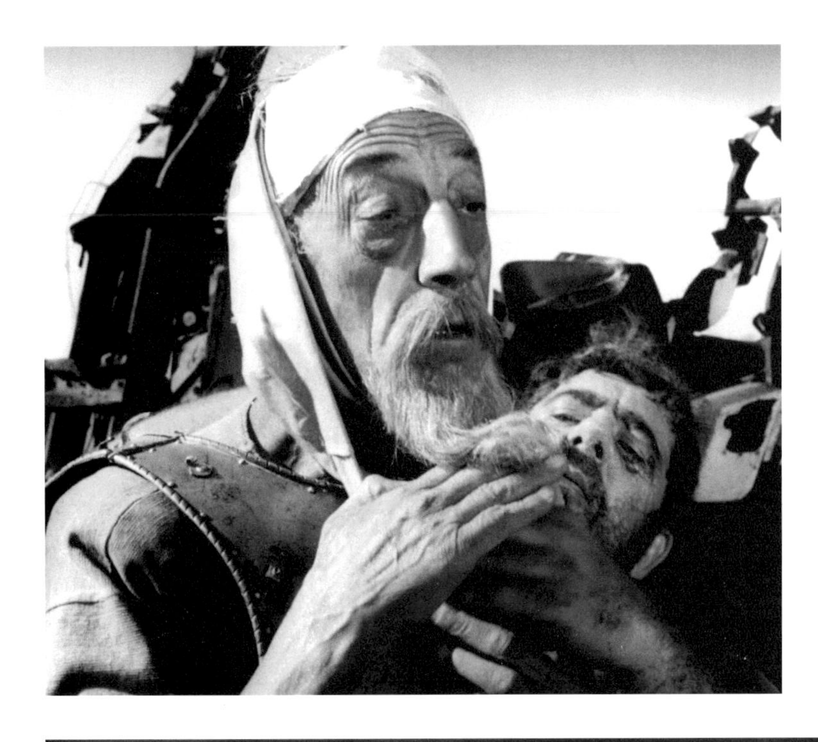

Opposite page:
Don Quixote swaps his sword for a lance in the move from Mexico (top, car cemetery scene) to Italy (below, with Paola Mori).

This page:
Francisco Reiguera (above and left) was not allowed to work in Spain when Welles filmed Sancho's discovery of the modern world in Pamplona (bottom).

Overleaf:
Mischa Auer and Akim Tamiroff in the Paris test shots of 1955.

Welles was joined in Rome by Reiguera and Tamiroff, but not Patty McCormack, who would no doubt have found it difficult to regain her physical appearance of two years earlier in any credible way. At one point Welles thought of hiring someone to double for her, or even of finding a different actress to redo her role. When these ideas proved too complicated he decided to concentrate on the scenes with his two main characters. *Don Quixote* was still unfinished by the end of the summer and was shelved for a further two years until Welles returned to shooting during the summer of 1961. This time he was in Spain, and so without Reiguera, who was banned from Spain by General Franco's government, but with the loyal Tamiroff, who spent most of the 1960s in France and Italy. In subsequent years Welles kept adding to his film, fragment by fragment, in Italy or in Spain, sometimes taking advantage of an official shoot, such as that of *Falstaff*, to divert film stock or a cameraman for use on *Don Quixote*. Just how much was unplanned is clear from the many images showing the dumbfounded reaction of modern crowds to the unexpected appearance of Cervantes' heroes (and also no doubt to that of the camera) or the antics of Sancho Panza wandering through the motor traffic of modern Spain. In July 1966 the images were largely in the can when Welles himself, his own Caméflex on his shoulder, filmed Sancho Panza searching for his master at the fiesta of San Fermin in Pamplona. After that date the additional elements shot in Italy or Spain were no longer acted scenes, but documentary images and landscapes. In 1968 Welles even suggested that a possible Yugoslavian co-producer might finance a few days shooting (in black and white and in colour) on the Dalmatian coast 'with no actors, extras, or doubles', but just a silent camera, a Croatian director of photography and his assistant. In the spring of 1972 he sent his cameraman Gary Graver to film images of the Holy Week procession in Seville. By that time, Reiguera had died in 1969, leaving the role of his life unfinished. Then, Tamiroff died in 1972. The loss of the actor who had become Welles's oldest collaborator seems to have marked the definitive end of the filming, but not of the editing, which, having begun in Mexico in 1957, continued intermittently in Italy, France and the United States until the death of Welles himself almost thirty years later.

POST-PRODUCTION IN SECRECY

The conditions of the filming itself, as drawn out over time as it was fragmented in space, explain the turnover of technical personnel, many of whom worked on the film for only a few days or weeks. They included a succession of no fewer than eight cameramen, equipped with different cameras and using different film stock. Yet, as far as one can tell from the rushes and known edited scenes, the images remain remarkably consistent, no doubt due to the emphasis on wide-angle lenses and the systematic use of red filters that add drama to the clouds. Welles was so aware of this issue that he wanted to shoot only in August and September, when the skies were filled with the superb cumulus masses that give the film one of its visual motifs.

The editing underwent similar vicissitudes. Welles started it in Mexico with Valenzuela. Shortly after arriving in Italy and thanks to Darryl F. Zanuck, he acquired an Italian Prevost editing machine, which he at once had installed in his Fregene villa. From then on, successive editors would come to his different homes; first were Renzo Lucidi and his son Maurizio, followed, in Madrid, by Peter Parasheles, then, back in Rome, by Mauro Bonanni. And there were others besides. For wherever he moved, Welles seems to have taken a few reels of *Don Quixote* with him so that he could polish the cut. When it came to the post-synchronization of the dialogue, at one point with Bonanni, Welles adopted a recording method that he probably could not have imposed on any other editor. Before any editing began he made an initial recording of the dialogue himself, with no reference to the image or to any synchronization, in order to establish a rhythm that would later guide the editor. Then, once the first edit was satisfactory, he returned to the dialogue to take it in the other direction, adapting it to the image and recording a kind of model of the sound on a small portable tape recorder. The next day he further polished the result, firstly by listening to the previous day's recording, speaking the dialogue again, from memory, and finally comparing the fruits of his labours against the images in order to check for synchronization, experimenting until he was entirely satisfied. No one but the editor was allowed to see the successive versions of what quickly became a mythical example of work in progress. In 1959 Stainton was amazed at the secrecy with which Welles surrounded his intentions. The cutting room door was double locked while he was working in order to prevent any intrusions. Welles preferred to cut the film with scissors, frame by frame, or to add clear frames himself one by one, rather than instruct outside laboratories to optically speed up or slow down the image track. He gave his actors and principal crew members loose sheets of paper rather than a complete script. While this certainly reflects a taste for secrecy on Welles's part, it was probably motivated still more by his sense of a work in progress, being constructed as it was shot, and of which nothing could be shown before it was completed, for fear of betraying it.

THE FILMMAKER'S RIGHT NOT TO FINISH

Having failed to come to full fruition immediately – and Welles was possibly very close to it at the end of the first period in Mexico – *Don Quixote* was condemned to become the archetype of an unfinished Welles film, unfinished because it was unfinishable. This was a project that, having begun with no fixed script, was continually changing as the years went by. It started out as three of Don Quixote's adventures told to a twentieth-century girl, who visualized them in her own naive way. As the film progressed it moved away from its original form to become an essay on contemporary Spain and then, more generally, on the conflict between universal values and the realities of the modern world. With *Don Quixote*, produced with greater independence from the industry's structures than any of his earlier films, Welles asserted the artist's rights over his work with a new clarity. The condition of exercising these rights was an acceptance of frugality. At that price the creator could experiment as he chose, changing his mind about his intentions. Welles is almost certainly alone among major filmmakers in having invented the means to allow himself to assert his full right not to show his work to the public until he judged the moment had come, even if that meant he never showed it at all. The so-called completed version, hastily cobbled together in 1992 by Jesús Franco for a Spanish producer, with the title *Don Quijote de Orson Welles*, merely created a sense of regret that posterity does not always respect this right not to finish.

THE SECOND EUROPEAN PERIOD 1958–1970

During the dozen or so years of his second European exile, Welles lived primarily in Italy, the country of his wife Paola Mori, and in Spain, which provided the locations for several of the films he was working on. But he was always on the move, meeting people, taking on commissions, and extending his search for producers to new countries.

After his return to Europe early in 1958, cinema and television became the main focus of Welles's activities. As late as 1960 he put on two plays in Ireland and in London (including *Chimes at Midnight*, an amalgam of several Shakespeare plays out of which the film *Falstaff* would later emerge) and developed a few projects, but after 1966 he does not seem to have attempted anything at all in the theatre. On the other hand he was now acting far more regularly in other people's films. He often accepted, for a large fee, short but flamboyant roles requiring only two or three days filming. Darryl F. Zanuck remained loyal to him, with three Hollywood films shot in Europe in 1958–60, directed by John Huston and Richard Fleischer. And Welles still had enough prestige to be a valuable addition to the cast list of many European productions. He familiarized himself with the process of filming in Eastern Europe, where mainly French or Italian co-productions took advantage of the cheaper labour and production costs offered by the peoples' democracies. His more benevolent producers would provide him with an editing machine or let him borrow equipment, sets and extras so that he could get a few shots of his own outside his official working hours. It was also on his return to Europe that he began to specialize in the lucrative work of the voiceover artist, recording a great many commentaries for both fiction films and documentaries. As a film director he was now mainly dealing with young independent producers, including some novices. He planned co-productions with Eastern European countries, using the contacts he made through his work as an actor, and with Denmark and Australia. He tried to take advantage of the fashion for omnibus films with episodes by different directors with *The Bible* of 1963, which was eventually made by Huston alone, and, in 1967, *Spirits of the Dead*, after tales by Edgar Allan Poe, in which the episode Welles was going to shoot was replaced by that of Fellini. He also kept trying to set up a production company that would be viable in the long term. Early in 1967, a few months after finishing filming in Spain for *The Immortal Story*, he considered applying for Spanish nationality, with a view to setting up a Spanish company consisting of a solid, cohesive team that would produce fourteen feature films in five years.

The first works Welles made during this period, aside from his return to the filming of *Don Quixote*, were television shows. In 1958 he obtained a commission from the American ABC network to make a pilot for a new programme about a journey around the world, a wandering half-hour essay on Italy and Gina Lollobrigida, posthumously baptized *Portrait of Gina*. In it he returned to the shooting principles adopted in *Around the World with Orson Welles* and took as his on-screen guide his wife Paola Mori, who introduces him to her country and to her compatriots. He films himself as both special envoy and 'live' studio presenter, pretending to catch, out of the corner of his eye, the control room people's signal that his time on air is almost over. ABC was not interested in the show and Welles lost his own print, which was rediscovered by chance after his death. In 1961, in the same vein, he filmed a bread-and-butter series of nine documentaries taking a tourist's eye view of Spain – *Nella terra di Don Chisciotte* – this time showing the Welleses travelling with their young daughter Beatrice. After various disagreements the Italian television company that had commissioned the series re-edited and re-recorded the episodes without Welles, dressing them up with commentaries by other writers.

The years 1962–6 saw the production of three feature films: *The Trial* in France and Yugoslavia, *Falstaff* in Spain and *The Immortal Story* in France and Spain. These were the first features since *Othello* that Welles was able to edit as he chose. They were followed in 1967 by *The Heroine*, a project that proved still-born from its first day's shooting in Hungary, and two more that Welles financed himself when his backers withdrew their support along the way, and which he was unable to finish: the thriller *The Deep*, in Yugoslavia, and the television show *Orson's Bag*, filmed in five different countries. As with many of his earlier features, Welles had to take things one day at a time, financing them himself or raising the finance for each stage, since most of these projects were inadequately funded when work began. Welles finished filming *The Trial* ahead of schedule, but the other shoots took longer than planned. Producers were particularly wary of editing that ran over time, leading to equivalent delays in the arrival of the first box-office receipts, since they needed a rapid return on their investments. Their suspicion was heightened by the fact that, as with *Othello* and *Mr Arkadin*, Welles missed every deadline that was arranged with the big festivals. He justified himself as follows in relation to *The Trial*, whose screening at Venice in September 1962 he refused to allow: 'This is my film. I will not bend to any pressure which attempts to force me to expose it to the public until I am completely satisfied that, in its every phrase, it is commensurate with the high standards I have set for myself.'

Whenever possible Welles preferred to rely on a solid director of photography while he did his own production design. But he was using more people than before for the same job, often hiring several camermen or editors. Both to save money and to preserve his unorthodox working methods, he preferred to recruit younger technicians who were not yet used to the ways of the film industry and so were more malleable, rather than experienced professionals who might have too many preconceived ideas and be too much in demand elsewhere to follow his rhythm of work over the long term. In particular he learned to be wary of editors who owed allegiance to the producers rather than to him, and he readily sidelined protégés of his backers to replace them with people he had hired himself. Some of his collaborators performed increasing numbers of different tasks and Welles demanded their unstinting devotion to his cause. He had regular associates in Italy, Spain, France and the UK, including technicians, production managers and lawyers, who were ready to work for him as soon as he gave the slightest signal. His Italian producer Alessandro Tasca di Cutò, whom he met in 1947 on the set of *Cagliostro* and with whom he renewed contact in the early 1960s, remained with him intermittently in this way until the end of his life. For his very last shoots of the decade Welles returned to using smaller crews. With *Falstaff*, and particularly *The Immortal Story*, it was often simpler to work with a few others at home, even though the nomadic Welles had not one home but several.

Opposite page:
Bread-and-butter roles.
Welles as King Saul in *David and Goliath* (1959) directed by Richard Pottier and Fernando Baldi (top), and as King Louis XVIII of France in *Waterloo* (1970) directed by Sergei Bondarchuk (bottom).

This page, top:
With his friend Darryl F. Zanuck, Françoise Sagan and Juliette Gréco at the Cannes Film Festival, 1959.

Centre:
With Pier Paolo Pasolini on the set of *La ricotta* in 1962.

Bottom:
With François Truffaut at the Cannes Film Festival, 1966.

THE TRIAL
1962

Welles had not previously shown any marked interest in the work of Kafka when, in 1961, he chose *The Trial*, a posthumously published novel by the Czech writer, from the list of works out of copyright that the Parisian producers Michel Salkind and his son Alexandre suggested he might like to adapt for the screen. Although the adaptation written by Welles is remarkably faithful to the letter of the original story, it makes no bones about betraying its spirit. The enthusiastic participation in his project of some of the most high-profile young actors of the day reflects the extraordinary status Welles enjoyed in Europe at the time. Partly due to financial constraints, he completed the process he had begun on *Othello* of putting the director in total control of the art direction. He also created a radically new aesthetic of black and white photography and, more than ever before, took control of the music and voices at the re-recording stage, bringing to perfect closure a work that is definitively his alone.

Previous pages:
Anthony Perkins and
Romy Schneider (Leni).

Above:
Jeanne Moreau (Miss
Burstner) and Anthony
Perkins (Joseph Kay).

THE ADAPTATION: UNFAITHFUL FIDELITY

Opposite page:
Welles directs a scene
in the Gare d'Orsay, Paris.

The structure of Kafka's novel, as published in 1925 by his friend Max Brod, is very simple. It is divided into ten chapters of very different lengths and begins in the apartment rented by Joseph K. in Frau Grubach's house. Here K. is visited by two officers, who inform him of his arrest for reasons he does not know. This does not, for the time being, deprive him of his freedom of movement. There follows a series of meetings and actions that are clearly identified in the title of each section until, in a brief final chapter entitled 'End', K. is executed 'like a dog' by two men who initially try to drive him to suicide. The novel always follows K.'s point of view, frequently describing his thoughts and reactions at each successive meeting, but in an indirect style that keeps the reader at a distance. There is a great deal of dialogue in which always brief speeches and questions from the hero alternate with semi-monologues, sometimes several pages long, from Huld the lawyer, Titorelli the painter and, at the end of the book, the priest, who each provide K. with lengthy descriptions of the judicial system or their own interpretations of events. The action is set in an un-named city whose every particularity has been carefully erased, although a few clues suggest that it is in Central Europe. Its topography is abstract, reduced to a few buildings (the bank where K. is chief clerk, the cathedral, the lawyer's house, apartment blocks) and a network of attics and corridors whose incomprehensible structure and space provide a material representation of the labyrinth of the law. The same can be said of the construction of time in the narrative, which is often referred to but never in terms that enable the reader to track its unfolding. The chapters begin 'a few evenings later', 'one afternoon – it was just before the day's letters went out' or 'one winter morning', and only details of clothing indicate that the action takes place in the period when the novel was being written, around 1920. In his adaptation Welles faithfully followed the English translation by Willa and Edwin Muir published in 1935. He sometimes directly borrowed entire descriptions or lines of dialogue but, more often, took different fragments occurring several pages apart and combined them into something new. Often he created lines by simply transposing what Kafka wrote as unspoken thoughts into direct speech.

However, we should note some minor alterations. These relate to the names of characters, starting with the renaming of Joseph K. as Joseph Kay in the French script that we have seen, as though Welles could not bear him to be absolutely abstract. (The text will hereafter refer to Kay only in regard to the script.) Fräulein Bürstner became Mlle Burst (she returned to her original name in the film), her friend Fräulein Montag appeared as Mlle Pittl, the lawyer Huld became Hastler and the painter Titorelli was renamed Tortelli (he too ultimately regained his original identity). There were also slight changes to the tone of the low-ranking officers' speech, which was subtly Americanized to give it the flavour of a formulaic crime movie. In the first scene 'You can't go out. You are arrested' became 'You're not going nowhere. You're under arrest', while the first officer's fisrt name, Franz, was changed to Franck.

Welles added a similar number of characters: a computer scientist who appears briefly; Kay's young cousin, who is only alluded to in the novel; and most importantly, the only main character he invented, 'the scientist' who watches over the great computer. With the latter character Welles added to the extraordinary gallery of women already present in the book, whose protagonist is surprised at his own ability to arouse their interest and their desire to help him.

Clockwise from top left: Max Haufler (the uncle), Fernand Ledoux (the chief clerk of the courts) and Welles (the advocate); Anthony Perkins and Jeanne Moreau; Thomas Holtzmann (the law student), Elsa Martinelli (Hilda) and Anthony Perkins; William Chappell (Titorelli); Madeleine Robinson (the lodger).

Welles made more extensive changes to the structure of the published novel. Usually he confined himself to moving whole blocks of narrative and rearranging them in a different order. Rather than following Brod in placing Kay's first appearance before the examining magistrate immediately before his subsequent return to the empty courtroom, he preferred to separate these two long sequences with the insertion of shorter scenes set in the office and the first visit to the lawyer. These permutations ceased to be solely a matter of dramatic economy when Welles moved the visit to Tortelli to the end, thereby placing this peak of dizzy disorientation within a final crescendo in which it is immediately followed by the little girls' hallucinatory pursuit of Kay, before the pace slows with the cathedral scene and conclusion.

Finally, three major modifications show that Welles meant to make his own presence felt in an adaptation which was otherwise extremely faithful. The first was the invention of one entirely new scene, which was also the only scene indicating Welles's desire to give the action a modern setting. Two thirds of the way through the script, just before the first of the series of big final scenes at the lawyer's and then at Tortelli's, in the office at night Kay meets the keeper of the computer, a woman 'as old as the world. Immutable, vaguely disquieting, this venerable lady of science is the archetype of the priestess serving a powerful, millenary mystery.' When Kay asks her how the machine interprets his case, she cannot answer him: the computer is capable only of analysing facts and solving that which can be rigorously formulated. So notions of conscience, innocence, guilt, Good and Evil are beyond its competence. The sole conclusion, delivered on a perforated strip, is that the crime Kay is most likely to commit is suicide.

The question of Kay's acceptance of his defeat lies at the heart of the second main alteration. At the end of Kafka's novel the two executioners ceremoniously pass each other the knife above their victim's body, as though inviting him to grab it and end the wait himself. If K. does not do so it is because he no longer has the strength, rather than out of any conscious choice. In the script, by contrast, Kay actively refuses to do so ('You'll have to kill me ... I'm not going to do it for you!') before Welles returns almost to Kafka's exact words to describe the executioner's knife turning twice in his heart and the dying man's last words: 'Like a dog!' The adaptation then abruptly concludes, 'as though he were too ashamed to survive', radically overturning the meaning of Kafka's final phrase 'it was as if he meant the shame of it to outlive him'.

The third major change affected the entire structure of the film. It is almost at the end of Brod's edition of the book, just before the appearance of the executioners, that the priest relates and comments on his famous parable about a dying peasant who has spent many long years outside the gate of the Law, which he has not been allowed to pass through, although it has been opened for him alone. Welles chose to split this passage in two. In his adaptation, the film begins with the projection of a series of illustrations of this story, told simultaneously in voiceover. With the last slide the speaker of the commentary steps into the projector beam to address the audience directly: 'This is a story inside a story. Opinions differ on this point. [...] A true mystery is unfathomable and nothing is hidden inside it. There is nothing to explain ... It has been said that the logic of this story is the logic of a dream. Do you feel lost in a labyrinth? Do not look for a way out, you will not be able to find it. There is no way out ...' The film then takes up from the point where the novel begins, in Kay's room. The interpretation of the parable is kept until the end and remains with the priest, whom Welles decided to play himself, and who is identified with the commentator from the beginning through the projection of images of engravings illustrating his speech.

However, this third change to the novel was not definitive. When Welles decided to play the part of the lawyer rather than the priest, he took everything related to the parable's interpretation from the latter and gave it to the former, who mysteriously reappears in the cathedral for this sole end. As Welles had always intended, it was his own voice that related the parable at the beginning. Whether in the role of the priest or, now, the lawyer, he could not allow anyone but himself to conclude with its interpretation. One last addition to Kafka's work sheds light on the adapter's desire to update the meaning of the novel. When Kay is chased from Tortelli's by the girls, Welles intended to make him pass through 'the seven circles of *Hell*' before he gets to the cathedral. This would be a pursuit through a jungle of wood and metal, 'the real entrails of the technical age', filled with the paraphernalia of the modern world: juke boxes, dispensers, rudimentary lotteries, television screens and loudspeakers that 'spew out the usual cries of torture', 'the vast shambles of slot machines, each served by its own zombie', a mad world 'that is no more unbelievable than modern life in Tokyo'. The script concludes with the words: 'Our chambers of horrors are not imaginary constructions but are taken from a world that can be seen by the most lucid eye.' In the end this scene was never filmed.

A DIVERSE CAST

Of all Welles's films, *The Trial* undoubtedly has the most prestigious cast list. There was renewed interest in Europe in a filmmaker whose work was much discussed. This enthusiasm explains why so many young actors were keen to work with Welles, sometimes, as Elsa Martinelli recalls, without asking to see either script or contract. The international character of this co-production, involving France, Germany and Italy, resulted in a cast of actors of very different origins, but all recruited from among those already gravitating towards Paris. It seems that from the outset Welles wrote the main role for Anthony Perkins, an actor whose adolescent-like fragility sits ill with the idea of Kafka's hero generally formed by readers. But this is to forget that the author has Joseph K. die the day before his thirtieth birthday and that Perkins celebrated his own thirtieth birthday while the film was in production. Moreover, Perkins was used to shooting in Europe, where he had acted in *The Sea Wall*, directed by René Clément in 1957, followed in quick succession by Anatole Litvak's *Goodbye Again*, Jules Dassin's *Phædra* and *Five Miles to Midnight*, again by Litvak. It was through *Five Miles to Midnight* that Welles made contact with Perkins, whose immediate acceptance was undoubtedly crucial for the future of the project.

Welles would have liked to give the part of the lawyer to the American actor Jackie Gleason, who had been much talked about for his role in Robert Rossen's *The Hustler* the year before and with whom Welles had long hoped to work. His readily menacing corpulence was at least equal to that of Welles, who could easily regard him as a double. Crucially, he was in Paris, where he was filming *Gigot*, directed by Gene Kelly. When Gleason turned down the role, Welles decided to take it on himself, giving the young Michael Lonsdale the part of the priest, now largely stripped of its substance.

Below and opposite page:
Welles directs Anthony Perkins
(right) and Romy Schneider.

Anthony Perkins with Jeanne Moreau (top left), Paola Mori (top right), Madeleine Robinson (above) and Katina Paxinou (right, in a scene that was cut from the film).

The other cast members were recruited from the three countries involved in the co-production, each of which provided one of the best-known female stars of her generation. From France came Jeanne Moreau, who played Miss Burstner. Welles was hoping Italy would provide him with Claudia Cardinale (almost certainly for the character of the lawyer's servant Leni), but in the end hired Elsa Martinelli to play the courtroom guard's wife Hilda. Romy Schneider from Germany was eventually given the part of Leni, having fought fiercely to play her rather than Hilda. In a detail revealing Welles's desire to Americanize the two brutal officers who come to arrest K., he gave these parts to Jess Hahn and Billy Kearns, two American expatriates living in France, where they had specialized in playing cops and villains. On the other hand, their more refined superior officer was played by the Italian Arnoldo Foà, who had played opposite Welles a few months earlier on the set of *The Tartars*, directed by Ferdinando Baldi and Richard Thorpe.

A more diverse cast is hard to imagine, particularly when they were joined by classical actors such as Madeleine Robinson, Suzanne Flon, Fernand Ledoux and Swiss actor Max Haufler, by the quintessential Wellesian grotesque as incarnated from *Mr Arkadin* onwards by Akim Tamiroff, and, in the role of Titorelli, a flamboyant personality from the London stage, choreographer, production designer and director William Chappell. One of the challenges Welles set himself was to unify this patchwork of a cast, by guiding all his characters towards a new form of the bizarre and unexpected.

When it came to the post-synchronization of the original English version, Welles chose to use his own voice – even for a handful of lines – to replace those of all the male actors in the film except Perkins, Tamiroff and Hahn. This vocal vampirism cannot be justified simply on the grounds that the actors did not all speak perfect English, nor that some actors were not around for the post-production phase, nor by a simple desire to save money. With this decision Welles once again suggests his underlying presence throughout the film, with the result that K., who is present in every scene, continually encounters, in various disguises, the different facets of a law which, Welles implies, originates from a single Word.

SETS COBBLED TOGETHER

The original plan was to film *The Trial* largely in Yugoslavia, where the Salkinds had just shot two films. It was a country Welles knew well, having recently worked there as an actor in *Austerlitz*, directed by Abel Gance, in *The Tartars* and in *La Fayette*, directed by Jean Dréville. Keen to attract prestigious productions, the Yugoslavs facilitated the project by agreeing to put up some of the finance for the co-production.

In the autumn of 1961 Welles scouted locations in the Zagreb region for his exteriors and some real interiors, which were to be supplemented with studio sets built in Paris. His choices already reflected the broad thrust of the production design, which involved combining elements of an urban space that was ill-defined but could be generally characterized as early twentieth-century with architecture representing the more depressing aspects of modernism. In other words, a pot-pourri of twentieth-century architectural aesthetics leading to the abandonment of all creativity, manifest in the housing blocks on the outskirts of Zagreb and the anonymous buildings recently erected nearby for an international exhibition.

The first art director, who was used to creating standard interiors, was given his cards by Welles after a few weeks. His successor, though far more inventive, did not last much longer, resigning two weeks before the shooting proper was due to start because he had not received even minimal assurances concerning the team and budget at his disposal. So the project was taken on at the last moment by a third designer, Jean Mandaroux. Mandaroux too had a long career but an undistinguished one. Crucially, he had almost no experience in the use of natural locations. However, he managed to adapt brilliantly to the demands of a director who had settled all decisions concerning the sets long before Mandaroux's arrival and gave him his instructions in the form of highly detailed sketches.

The inopportune withdrawal of the Yugoslavian finance also undermined the choices for locations. If the country was no longer involved in the co-production there was no point hoping for any major advantages from shooting in Yugoslavia when, on the contrary, the costs of transporting a French crew were building up. However, Welles decided to go ahead and use the exteriors and some of the interiors in and around Zagreb. As planned, all the scenes at Mrs Grubach's house were filmed at the Boulogne studios in Paris. Welles decided to film all the rest, comprising the greater part of the film, at the Gare d'Orsay in the heart of Paris, where several films had already been shot.

This building had opened in 1900 and would be restored in the 1980s to become the Musée d'Orsay. However, in the 1960s it was merely an empty shell (138 metres long and 32 metres high), combining metal structures and stone to stunning effect. The station had lain almost unused for years, housing only the Grand Hôtel d'Orsay in one corner and tons of archives that had never been moved. For Welles, this building, which seemed destined for imminent demolition, became an improvised studio, ready filled with potential sets crying out for a few finishing touches. However there were major disadvantages: the station let in sound from outside and, more crucially, the entire interior was lit by a glass roof that could not be covered. So Welles had no choice but to shoot at night. In the end he moved in completely, living in the hotel next door and setting up an improvised cutting room within the station, jammed in between the train-drivers' dormitory and the toilets, where he could supervise in real time the assembly of a film on which shooting was being completed only a few metres away. He distrusted the French editor imposed on him by the producers and soon relegated her to the LTC studio some distance away in Saint-Cloud. There she had to make do with assembling the French version of the film while Welles honed the English original in Orsay, assisted by very young and almost totally inexperienced Italian and Swiss editors.

Designed and built in less than two weeks, the set of the Grubach boarding house was of exemplary simplicity, well suited to the needs of the succession of long takes in which it would appear, and to the idea of order without imagination that the set had to establish in the opening scenes. It consisted of a row of four parallel interconnecting rooms: first the kitchen and dining room, then the corridor which runs the length of the boarding house, then the rooms of K. and Miss Burstner, and lastly the balcony, which runs alongside the latter two rooms. So together the rooms formed a geometric unit through which the camera could move easily in one direction (from K.'s room to that of Miss Burstner) or at ninety degrees (from the dining room to the balcony via the corridor and Miss Burstner's room).

Each of the cells was differently furnished, from Mrs Grubach's outmoded interior to K.'s monkishly bare room, to the visual clutter of his neighbour. However, the ceiling weighed down in the same manner over all, so close to their heads that K. needed to raise his arm only slightly to touch it.

By contrast, the spaces in the Gare d'Orsay had no bounds beyond those established by arbitrary partitions. The ceilings in the lawyer's house change from one room to the next and sometimes the chandeliers emerge from unfathomable darkness. Here Welles created not so much rooms as the idea of rooms, described not by enclosed spaces but by the objects within them: rows of files to signify offices; a monumental bed on a platform to suggest a bedroom; a stove, a cupboard and a set of shelves to represent a similarly limitless kitchen. Welles located the high-level maze apparently linking these sets in the metal walkways crossing the space above. On the ground he fashioned the corridors and built a multitude of fragments with no more identity than that conferred on them by the editing, which combined them with shots filmed in Zagreb.

Zagreb provided Welles with the location for the brief scene in the opera house, as well as part of the courtroom (the rest was built in Orsay), the rabbit warren of offices, and the lines of computers set up in two pavilions of a large commercial exhibition. He also filmed some of his exteriors there: the deserted streets, the apartment blocks stuck on waste ground, the exterior of the cathedral and its surroundings. In the editing he created a unity out of this puzzle of ill-matched pieces, with little concern for the sacrosanct rules of continuity. From one shot to the next, from shot to reverse shot, the courtroom door doubles in size; the cubby-hole door suddenly opens the other way; a succession of offices unfolds beneath Yugoslavian ceilings and the metal beams of Orsay without distinction. Here continuity is the lack of continuity – proof that, after the reassuring certainties of his apartment, K. has been projected into an unstable universe in which all means of orienting oneself slip away. This sense of vertigo reaches its peak shortly before the end of the film, when K. leaves Titorelli's workshop to be chased by little girls through a series of the most disparate spaces, underground and high in the air, in a pure hallucination of fleeing.

STARK BLACK AND WHITE

Welles's decisions concerning the photography of *The Trial* were equally radical and unusual, starting with the recruitment of his director of photography, an unknown, thirty-three-year-old cameraman who had never previously worked on a feature film. However, Edmond Richard had many strings to his bow. A highly skilled technician, he had worked as an engineer on the development of Éclair's Caméflex, whose ease of use and simple loading made it Welles's favourite camera. Richard subsequently specialized in sensitometry and laboratory work before becoming interested in special effects and working as a colour advisor on several major films. He was exactly the man Welles needed: inventive and resourceful, capable of understanding all the director's requirements and finding ways to meet them.

Where lenses were concerned Welles followed his usual practice, using only lenses with very short focal lengths (25 or even 14 mm, customized to reduce their distorting effects), while the few close-ups were filmed using 75 mm or, in the single case of Romy Schneider, who benefited from special attention, the more flattering 35 mm.

Richard was assisted by a camera crew who speedily met Welles's framing requirements (unusually long takes, very high or low angles). This left Richard free to concentrate on the director's three rules for lighting: the black and white should have the highest possible contrast; light sources should almost never be identified in the shot; it must be possible to cut any two shots together since their order would be decided at the editing stage.

The solutions Richard proposed were as simple in principle as they were difficult to implement. The first solution is based on the fact that the degree of contrast (the 'gamma') of a piece of film, negative or positive, varies according to the sensitivity of the film's stock and the time it is allowed to develop. The usual preference is to shoot for a low-contrast negative: this allows for the recording of subtly different greys and crucially permits a margin of error where the exposure is concerned. Later, when the prints are made, the contrast of the positive emulsion can be increased until it returns to the original levels. Welles and Richard went in the opposite direction: in addition to generally using red filters to heighten contrast still further, they used a very high gamma for the negative (1, where the more usual figure is around 0.6), meaning that the slightest error of exposure would be irreparable. By proceeding in this way they obtained extreme contrasts from which almost every nuance of grey had disappeared. More importantly, they were guaranteed a uniform degree of contrast, which meant that any shot could be cut to any other with no need for correction during development or printing. The result is a totally consistent and unchanging light from the beginning of *The Trial* to its end.

The second key to the lighting resides in the systematic use of high intensity arc lights, where the trend had long been for far less brutal tungsten lights. Richard often used the arc lights in a highly directional way, to create expanses of light and shadow, and sometimes also to create uniform lighting directed towards the action by reflectors. This is true in Mrs Grubach's room, in which the lighting, from arc lights positioned above the set, is far harsher than in the rooms of K. or Miss Burstner where, reflected by white panels arranged outside, it seems to come naturally from the windows. In the scene where the officers are being whipped inside a tiny cubby-hole, the size of the room prohibited the use of arc lights and light was provided by small, boosted Colortran spotlights, positioned by hand, whose light was reflected by tin foil covering both the floor of the room and the sides of the camera. The decision to use arc lights, which almost always locates the light source outside the action, is crucial to the aesthetics of a film that rarely seeks to suggest a source for light, since the lighting is less a matter of spatial logic than of dramatic necessity.

This need for total control over the light also demanded extraordinary conditions for exterior filming. Welles, shooting in Zagreb in spring, had no intention of allowing natural light to interfere with his project and asked Richard to set up three different film units. The first was to film interiors by day, the second, consisting largely of Serbian crew, would film exteriors by night, and the third would film the scenes that were hardest to light, in the twilight of the early morning or at dusk, when there is no clear division between light and shadow.

The finest example of this is almost certainly the long tracking shot that follows Miss Burstner's disabled friend (Suzanne Flon) as she drags her suitcase across the wasteground by the housing blocks. It begins at the foot of a stairway in the pale twilight and ends, almost four minutes later, on a bank leading up to a road.

Opposite page, top:
There is no continuity between the enormous door found by chance in Zagreb and the one through which Joseph Kay leaves the interrogation room in the preceding shot.

Opposite page, bottom:
A wooden pulpit placed among the metal structures of the Gare d'Orsay is enough to suggest a cathedral (Welles and a double for Michael Lonsdale).

Night has fallen, unnoticed, during the course of the shot, which ends with the woman limping away into the darkness beneath the glow of the streetlights. There is a sharp difference between this use of twilight and the moments in which a dynamic contrast of light and shadow becomes the metaphorical expression of a universe in chaos. This is particularly true of K.'s final flight, pursued by little girls. K. runs into a narrow corridor lined with loose wooden boards, in which the combination of movement and the blinding arc light creates an almost stroboscopic effect. In a similarly unexplained variation, subsequent shots show him running through a tunnel in front of a light source that casts before him a long, disjointed shadow.

Edmond Richard has given a detailed description of the technical conditions in which the filming was done and of the method for constructing shots employed by a director so deeply attached to his own Caméflex cameras that he would take at least one of them with him in his luggage wherever he went:

'He could draw very well, but did not like to use a fine point. Instead he used Parker felt-tips, which enabled him to sculpt in light and shadow. He had a sense of synthesis, something few directors possess. He would stylize, he was after effectiveness. He would draw the broad lines, it was a scene rather than a shot [...] With him I used to do the lighting twice: a rough set-up to get the framing, followed by fine-tuning to create the atmosphere. He couldn't frame a shot unless he had an initial lighting set up with the general idea. He would set the framing according to the direction of the light. He would establish the movements of the actors with his hand-held Caméflex – that was his viewfinder – marking it all out: position here, plumb line, cross on the ground; second position, plumb line, cross. And so on. His camera movements were always devised in accordance with particular points in the actor's movements, but you are never aware of that. He had key positions where his actors would stop. What mattered to him was how well the dialogue could be understood, what his actors did at the point where they stopped. In moving from one point to another, every eccentricity was permitted; in the key positions he wanted to see their eyes. This created an extraordinary dynamic and a syncopated rhythm: movement, pause; movement, pause. Even in complicated movements, movements of fifty metres, in an S shape, going up, going down, there would be infernal positions that had to be linked in a single movement. Once he had settled on the movements he would give me time to perfect the lighting. He wanted me to pay a great deal of attention to the actors, so that they could be completely free; it was out of the question for an actor to be immobilized in a small space by the lighting. He always used to say, 'We need broad lighting. You can't bother the actors with light."'

RECOMPOSED MUSIC

From the scriptwriting stage Welles had planned to use Albinoni's *Adagio* as a musical theme. This was to be heard before the title and a small group of musicians was to be seen rehearsing it in a side room in the opera house. Jean Ledrut, the composer hired by the producers, had no choice but to do as he was told, but he did not get on with Welles and the director had no scruples about changing his work beyond recognition in the edit and sound mix.

In addition to two transcriptions of the *Adagio*, Welles asked Ledrut, a classically-trained musician, to provide a series of jazz variations on the piece, most of which were played by the Martial Solal trio. In this way he confined Ledrut to the role of adaptor, allowing him to record only one more personal, original piece, a slow march for orchestra, and two extracts from an earlier operetta of his. Welles then had eleven pieces for a total running time of forty-two minutes.

Opposite page:
Filming at dusk:
Suzanne Flon at the end of the long tracking shot during which night falls.

Right:
Four stages in Kay's walk towards his execution (Anthony Perkins with Raoul Delfosse and Jean-Claude Rémoleux).

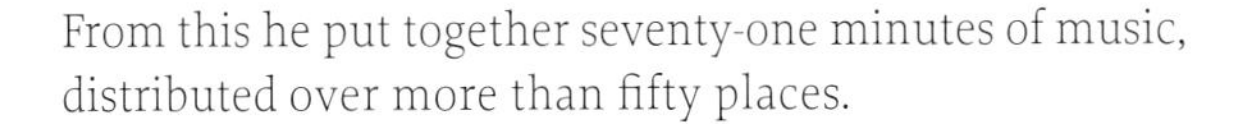

From this he put together seventy-one minutes of music, distributed over more than fifty places.

To an even greater extent than he had done previously, Welles treated Ledrut's music as raw material, which could be endlessly recomposed in the sound edit. Refusing to respect the identity of the pieces, he chopped them up, mixed them together, slowed them down, removed a few bars from the middle of a development and added others that were not designed to be there. The same sections of music are sometimes used in ten different places while others were never used at all. Every now and then two and sometimes three different pieces are superimposed to generate an indefinable malaise. Furthermore, the music seems disconnected from the action, to which, for the most part, it is not linked either by dramatic necessity or by the slightest concern with synchronism. However, because Welles generally mixed this seemingly unstructured patchwork at a very low level, his unusual, not to say aberrant practices go largely unnoticed by the audience.

The deep disagreement between composer and director certainly goes some way to explaining the fate suffered by the composition. However, Welles's radical treatment of the music should not be interpreted as a form of belated revenge against a collaborator who had been foisted on him. The musical framework of *The Trial* – twisted, pummelled, chopped into pieces and stuck back together again – exactly matches a film which is itself a deliberate assemblage of disparate fragments, whose apparently arbitrary juxtaposition provides a striking image of a polymorphous, disorientated world in the process of falling apart, vigorously projecting Kafka into the late twentieth century, rather than locating his work in a historical past.

FALSTAFF

1964–1966

Learning from his experiences on *Othello* and *The Trial*, Welles went to Spain to create another spatial jigsaw puzzle, *Falstaff.* Welles shot fragments of the same scene months apart, in different places, and let enthusiasm and speed of execution take priority over coherent continuity. He allowed creative scope to his director of photography, composer (both of whom he had worked with before) and his virtuoso actors, but laid down the law with his ever-changing Spanish crew and delegated nothing when it came to production design, costumes and editing. This historical film with its on-screen simulations of great wealth was made by a small group akin to a family business.

Previous pages:
Welles with Margaret Rutherford (the innkeeper) and Jeanne Moreau (Doll Tearsheet).

Left:
Welles's sketch for Falstaff's battledress.

Opposite page:
Falstaff in the streets of the medieval village of Calatañazor.

AN ADAPTATION HONED AND POLISHED FOR THE STAGE

Of all Welles's films, *Falstaff* is almost certainly the most deeply rooted in a long-standing desire. In 1939, when he was not yet twenty-four, Welles directed *Five Kings* (*Part One*), a stage production in which a combination of fragments from three Shakespeare plays – *Henry IV Part I* and *Part II* and *Henry V*, all centring on the characters of Prince Hal (the future Henry V) and Falstaff – were linked by a commentary taken from Holinshed's *Chronicles*. Despite his youth Welles himself took the role of Falstaff, the colourful drunkard whom Prince Hal temporarily adopts as his companion, before repudiating him in favour of virtues worthy of a king. The critics were full of praise, hailing the cinematic qualities of a stage production whose key scene was the battle of Shrewsbury, played out before a single, bare tree, in a kind of muddy no man's land reminiscent of the First World War. This production was to be continued in a second part comprising an amalgam of two of Shakespeare's other history plays, Henry VI and Richard III. The failure of the early performances meant that the play closed on its trial run, before it could reach New York, and the second part was never staged.

Welles had trouble reconciling himself to this failure and kept the sets and costumes for his production in storage for almost ten years, hoping to have an opportunity to stage it again. Welles revived *Five Kings* (*Part One*) in 1960 for the Gate Theatre, Dublin, with the title *Chimes at Midnight*, in a new, tighter adaptation focused around the two sections from *Henry IV*. As in the earlier version, but more clearly, the central issue is the choice offered to Prince Hal between the values embodied by Falstaff – which include gentleness and friendship as well as bawdiness and deception – and the self-denial and submission to the higher interests of the kingdom demanded by the exercise of power. The play's run of a few weeks again proved commercially unsuccessful, but provided Welles with an opportunity to showcase a hitherto unknown young Welsh actor, Keith Baxter, in the role of Prince Hal. On the night of their return to London, Welles was already arranging for him to reprise the role in a further production: 'This is only a rehearsal for the movie, Keith, and I'll never make it unless you play Hal in that, too.'

This page:
Welles painted a set design for the inn himself (left) before building it as a small-scale model (below).

Opposite page:
The inn was built in a warehouse on the outskirts of Madrid, but its wooden entrance was erected in the countryside facing the ramparts of Ávila.

Left and opposite page:
Like the royal apartments, the interior of Hotspur's castle was created in the monastery at Cardona (Marina Vlady, Norman Rodway and Welles).

Early in 1964 Welles took advantage of a new stint in Yugoslavia, where he was playing a minor role in *Marco the Magnificent* directed by Denys de La Patellière and Noël Howard, to set up the production of *Falstaff* with the authorities in Belgrade. The project came to nothing, but Welles at once transported it to Spain where, on 30 May, he signed a contract to make the film with Producciones Cinematográficas M.D. He himself was co-producer, accounting for half the finance with his contribution as author, director and star, valued at a total of $200,000 at the time, plus an additional $50,000 to cover the remainder of his share of the production costs, set at a total of $500,000. However, the deal never materialized and the project was eventually taken over at the end of the summer by Internacional Films Española, a company led by the young Emiliano Piedra. To keep him on board Welles committed himself to making a colour adaptation of Stevenson's *Treasure Island* alongside *Falstaff*, which he insisted must be in black and white, using the same sets and actors.

STONE AND WOOD

Although José Antonio de la Guerra was officially in charge of the sets for *Falstaff*, the English language version credits him only as executive art director. Meanwhile, the only mention for costumes goes to the Cornejo workshop in Madrid, which had simply supplied and adapted them. Even though he did not want to claim credit for them himself, Welles did not intend to allow anyone else to put their names to designs for which he regarded himself as solely responsible.

From the start of the project, as shown by his many letters to the producers during the summer of 1964, Welles was worried about the sets and costumes, always crucial to the costs of a historical film. This concern became more complicated when the production was taken over by Internacional Films Española, because Welles was also supposed to be preparing *Treasure Island*, set three centuries later and shot in colour. Only two sets were usable for both films, one the streets of London and the other the inn, which is as important in Stevenson's novel (The Admiral Benbow) as in *Henry IV* (The Boar's Head). The other sets and all the costumes had to be prepared separately.

In reality Welles seems to have paid almost no attention to *Treasure Island*, but his visual plans for *Falstaff* were extremely detailed, as shown by the many sketches for costumes that he sent to the producers.

These drawings, based on reference works describing medieval dress, are very simple and plain, with almost no ornamentation. In them we can already see Welles's aspiration towards a kind of realism grounded less in a respect for history than in a rejection of any picturesque qualities that might prove distracting: the audience might regard a too magnificent costume as inauthentic. This decision, along with budgetary constraints, led the production to seek out usable secondhand garments, starting with the remnants of the recent big budget production of *El Cid*, directed by Anthony Mann and shot in Madrid. Welles offered his actors a selection of these costumes and suggested they should take whatever they wanted. But still they had no armour. When none could be found in the main European costume warehouses, it was decided to have a few dozen pieces cast in fibreglass. These could not be ready in time for the first scenes with John Gielgud (Henry IV), with which the filming started; yet these were the scenes immediately preceding and following the battle. Undaunted, Welles solved the problem by deciding to keep the armour for the battle itself, which would not be filmed until several months later, long after Gielgud's departure. In the meantime the king and his son could stay in lighter clothing, which left the actors freer to use their whole bodies. This bold conception of costume is even more apparent in Gielgud's other scenes where, instead of relying on the splendour of royalty, Welles decided – for reasons of economy as well as drama – to wrap the king in plain robes, and austere coats, and even in simple shirts, which would help to create the striking image of an ascetic who had already renounced all the vanities of this world.

As for the sets, from the start Welles had decided to adopt the method he had used in *Othello* and use some of the very old buildings to be found at a reasonable distance from Madrid. These were medieval rather than the Renaissance architecture of the previous film, expressions of Romanesque rigour rather than the impetuosity of the late gothic, in keeping with two films whose visual styles contrast in every way.

The most striking location was provided by the San Vicente abbey church of the fortified monastery of Cardona, high in the mountains north-west of Barcelona. This was used both for the apartments and scenes such as the death of Henry IV and part of his son's coronation (the interior of the rebel leader Hotspur's castle was set up at the back of the building). The abbey church is huge and Welles planned to use smaller-scale columns to change its perspectives, so that only part of it had to be lit. However, he was unable to communicate his ideas to the set construction team and had to abandon them, wasting – if we are to believe his complaints to the producer – several days on lighting set-ups. Later, once the production had returned to Madrid, he gave up the idea of going back to Cardona to finish the coronation scenes and shot them much closer to the capital, in the church of Santa María de Huerta in Medinaceli.

The preparations for the battle of Shrewsbury and the scenes that follow it were shot in the desert area around Colmenar Viejo, about thirty kilometres north of Madrid. Aside from its proximity, this location had the advantage of offering a horizon closed off by hills, blocking out any glimpses of the nearby modern world. It was also here, on the first day's filming, that Welles shot Richard II's funeral procession, with which the film was to open and which he abandoned at the editing stage. The battle itself was staged in the heart of Madrid, in the Casa de Campo, a vast park which had long been used as a location for a great many different films, where Welles also shot the ambush of the pilgrims carried out by Falstaff and his henchmen in the Gadshill woods. The crenellated ramparts of Ávila represent the walls of London, while the city's streets are the alleyways of the medieval villages of Calatañazor (200 kilometres north-east of Madrid) and Pedraza (130 kilometres north of Madrid), where Welles also recruited local extras. To find the snow around Judge Shallow's house they had to go all the way up to Lecumberri, in the heart of the Basque country. In nearby Lesaca they had the good fortune to find a house with extraordinary beams, where Welles at once decided to set the last scene between Falstaff, Shallow and Silence, and the arrival of Pistol, who has come to announce the death of Henry IV.

All that remained to be decided upon was the set of the inn, whose profusion of beams, platforms, benches, tables and wooden partitions set the seal on a visual language that is rigorously developed throughout the film. Like the Gadshill forest, the tree-filled battlefield of Shrewsbury and Shallow's house, the inn belongs to the world of wood and earth, to the world of nature, in other words to an organic disorder, which contrasts with the bare stone of the royal castles or the desolate ground on which the armies line up before falling upon one another. So it is easy to understand why Welles should have written a letter absolutely insisting that the wooden porch representing the entrance to the inn must be built facing the ramparts of Ávila. This porch can exist only outside London, away from its stone walls, which call Prince Hal back to the inexorable order of the city.

The inn plays such an important role, its functions are so complex that, from the outset it had been agreed that it would be built in the studio. Again, Welles made this a personal issue and, not satisfied with proposing several designs, he had a three-dimensional model made so that the camera crew and set designers would gain a better understanding of all its tricks and possibilities, starting with the exits, which were designed using forced perspectives to give them a depth they did not really have. Once again, there was not enough money to build the set. Eventually it was built in a large warehouse in Carabanchel, a satellite town south of Madrid, where the production team worked through the icy cold of winter, without dressing rooms for the actors or any kind of comfort, amid the roar of neighbouring traffic, which rendered the recording of any usable sound completely impossible. When it was delivered the set was still too new and clean to suit Welles, who wanted it to be more realistic. He settled this problem by organizing an evening of 'music and *tapas*' there for the technicians and actors, during which each armed with a hammer, soldering iron or pot of paint, cheerfully helped to 'distress' the set before it was used.

Opposite page:
Edmond Richard, the film's director of photography, was also hired to play a recruit under Falstaff's command.

Right:
Welles, Margaret Rutherford and Jeanne Moreau.

Overleaf:
Welles as Falstaff.

THE SHOOT: EVER-CHANGING ORGANIZATION

For his producer's benefit, until the first days of shooting *Falstaff* Welles maintained the illusion that he was indeed going to make two films at once. Filming even started with *Treasure Island*, on 5 October 1964, in the port of Alicante, where Internacional Films Española had hired from the American producer Samuel Bronston a sailing ship that had previously featured in many films to become the *Hispaniola* of Stevenson's novel. Welles left a second unit to film the scenes at sea, with Jesús Franco directing, while he started work on *Falstaff*. He was then to proceed by shooting both films at the same time and, wherever possible, on the same sets. He promised to complete the second film after *Falstaff* was finished. This curious method was evidently put into operation immediately, since Baxter, who was also hired to play Dr Livesey in *Treasure Island*, arrived in Alicante just before Tony Beckley, who was to play Poins in *Falstaff* and was currently the pirate Israel Hands. While the ship sailed away with Beckley and a small crew, Welles took advantage of a return to Madrid to rehearse Baxter in his role as Hal. Filming on *Treasure Island* continued without conviction, directed by Franco, until he too was called to carry out more important tasks on *Falstaff*.

Three months earlier, on 13 July, a detailed letter from Welles to his intended producer of that time had asked for a small second unit for *Falstaff*, consisting only of a silent camera and three technicians for the photography, an assistant director, a dresser, three electricians and a dozen grips. He added, to explain the latter number, which might have appeared excessive given the modesty of the rest of his request, 'I need men to move the scaffolding and platforms', already formulating what would be a repeated request throughout the shoot. Having failed to obtain this second unit, he then stole it from *Treasure Island*, which was quickly abandoned as a result. Its technicians, who were still under contract, came to swell the numbers working on *Falstaff*.

This doubling of the teams, crucial for the action scenes and particularly for the battle, also made it possible to preserve the spontaneity of the actors' work by filming their longer, more difficult scenes with two cameras using different focal lengths. The complex shots in the inn were filmed this way, in one take that could then be cut in the editing stage. So was Henry IV's long monologue on insomnia – simultaneously filmed in long shot and medium close-up and for which the first take was so perfect that Welles decided to keep the medium close-up in its entirety, framed by two brief shots locating the king in space.

The shooting schedule was heavily dependent on the availability of the actors, who were once again recruited from a wide range of European countries. Jeanne Moreau could be free for only three or four days to play the woman of easy virtue Doll Tearsheet. Gielgud arrived on 11 October, only to fly out again on the 27th to rehearse a play on Broadway. His entire role was thus concentrated in the first two weeks of filming: first the preparations and conclusion of the battle at Colmenar Viejo, then his scenes in Cardona, representing the major part of his involvement. Work continued in Cardona after Gielgud's departure, with the scenes in Hotspur's castle and the coronation of Henry V. Logically it was there too that Welles should have filmed the repudiation of Falstaff, which interrupts this ceremony. He did not, however, instead returning to Madrid, where he went on with the scenes that required the presence of Beckley: the attack in Gadshill woods, then the scenes at the inn, including the scene following the death of Falstaff.

There are several reasons why Welles may have adopted his singular practice of saving parts of a scene, particularly his own lines, for later, rather than shooting them at the same time as the rest. The first, and most often suggested, is his dislike, as an actor, of speaking dialogue to another actor placed out of shot. This was no doubt real, since one finds it even in films that he had not himself directed. Richard Fleischer – who directed him in *Compulsion* and *Crack in the Mirror* – admiringly describes his unique ability to speak all his lines in one go, leaving the exact pauses necessary for his absent partner's lines to be included later. Another reason is probably that this method allowed Welles, in his own films, to concentrate entirely on his work as director.

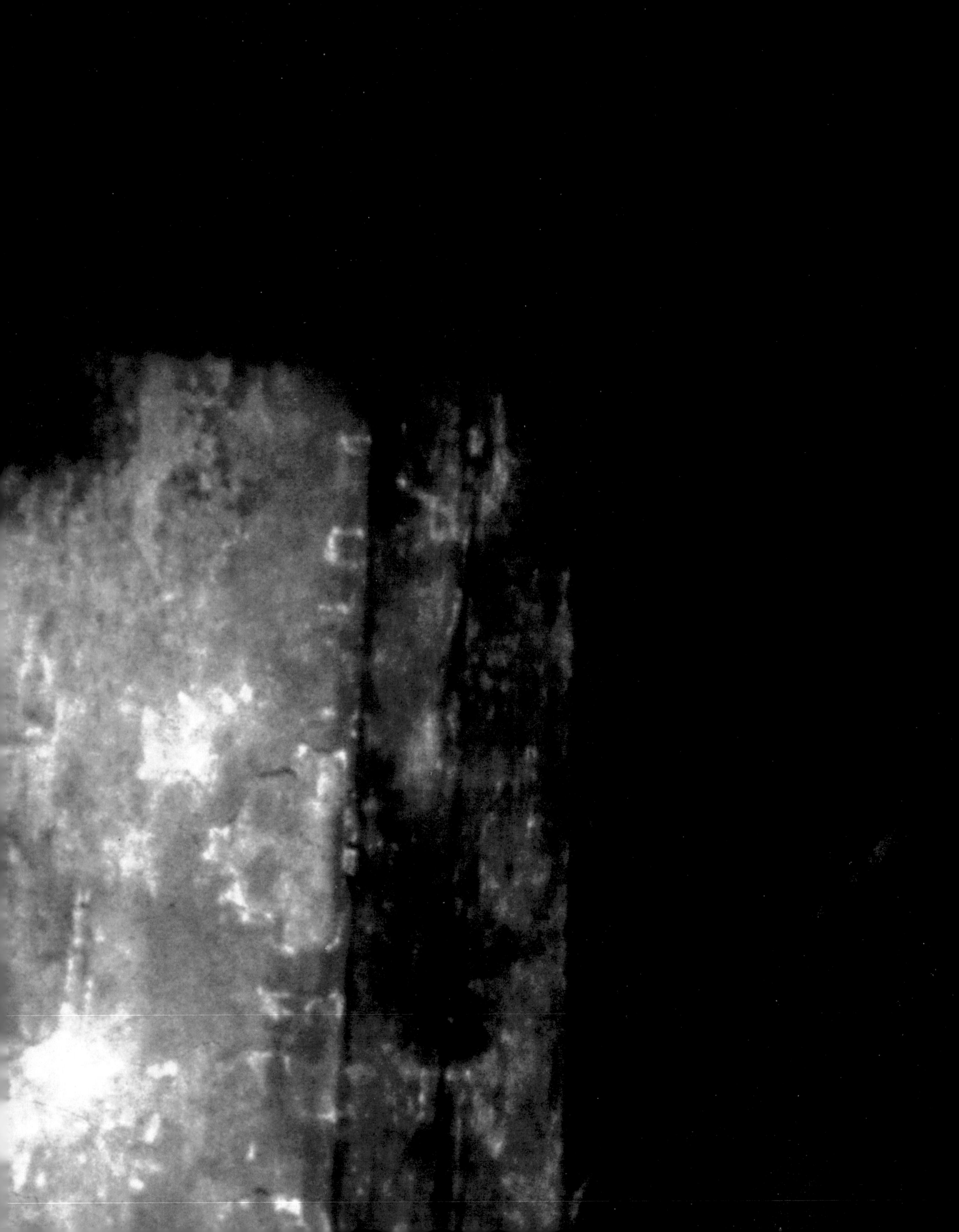

A third reason, and by no means the least in productions as impoverished as his own, is that it enabled him to free actors sooner, rather than having to pay their expenses and fees over a longer period. So Welles would keep his own shots until the end because he was the only one who was not being paid by the week or the day. On *Falstaff* he shared this status with Baxter, who was also present from the first minute of filming to the last, whether or not he was present in the scenes, even staying with Welles over Christmas rather than going home. Their complicity was total and they were together again, alone with the camera in a corner of the Carabanchel warehouse, surrounded by flags and a half-made stone pillar, to play the last exchange of looks between Hal and Falstaff, concluding the coronation scene previously started in Cardona and continued in Medinaceli.

So throughout the shoot many scenes were left unfinished, needing more reverse shots with doubles to replace actors who had left, or else put off until later because it had proved impossible to do them as Welles had wanted. The scene in which Hal is sitting on a low parapet with Poins and receives a letter from Falstaff should have been the first to be filmed in Barcelona, before Gielgud's arrival, when Welles and Baxter were preparing to send Beckley off on the *Hispaniola*. But the little cloister planned as a location had filled with people and Welles had to abandon it. A month later, when he was filming the Gadshill sequence one morning in the Casa de Campo, he suddenly called a halt. The mist was rising over a small pool: the light was magical. Luckily the costume truck travelled with them to every location and in a couple of minutes Baxter and Beckley were dressed in the clothes planned for the letter scene. Fifteen minutes later the scene was shot, the mist had lifted and the little pool had returned to its usual condition – a horrible cement basin sixty centimetres deep surrounded by the noise of traffic and car horns.

There are a great many stories of Welles's amazing capacity to seize any unexpected opportunities he was offered. This required the actors to know their lines perfectly and be endlessly willing to adapt. It also required the crew to act quickly and faultlessly. It was out of the question for Welles to have his impetus or that of the actors halted on technical grounds. On the other hand he never pressured the actors and Baxter mentions the unusual instance of a shot that was retaken around forty times until Welles got the very subtle nuance he was after. However, he had total confidence in his actors and, once he had planned out their movements with them and the lights were set up, he wanted to be ready to shoot at once: 'Let's rehearse on camera.' If rehearsals there had to be, the camera might as well make use of them.

BLACK AND WHITE ENGRAVINGS

As with *The Trial*, the director of photography on *Falstaff* was Edmond Richard, whom Welles had insisted on bringing from France with his own crew. While the overall technical approaches he proposed to Richard remained the same as for their earlier film, his visual aims differed from those of *The Trial* in at least three ways.

First, for what was to be his last black and white film, Welles decided to re-create the atmosphere of wood engravings and their elementary contrasts. Crucially, for the first time in his career, leaving aside the unfinished attempts of *It's All True* and *Don Quixote*, he wanted to show the action within the context of a wider landscape that continually echoed it.

Faked heights:
Either the bottom third of the frame is invisible on screen (above and right), or else Welles (below) raises the horizon by aligning the two soldiers seen from behind with Hotspur and the line of soldiers silhouetted in the background.

The battle of Shrewsbury: To avoid having to bring back Norman Rodway, the conclusion of the duel between the two princes (below left) was filmed long before in the warehouse studio in Carabanchel

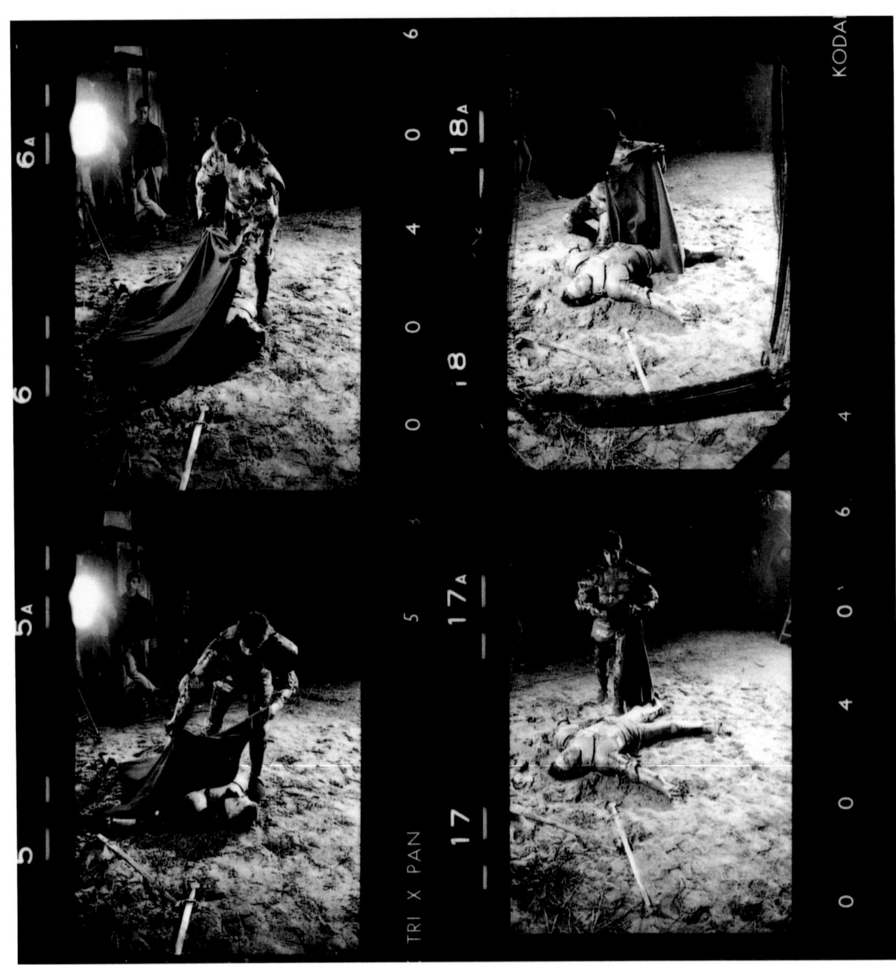

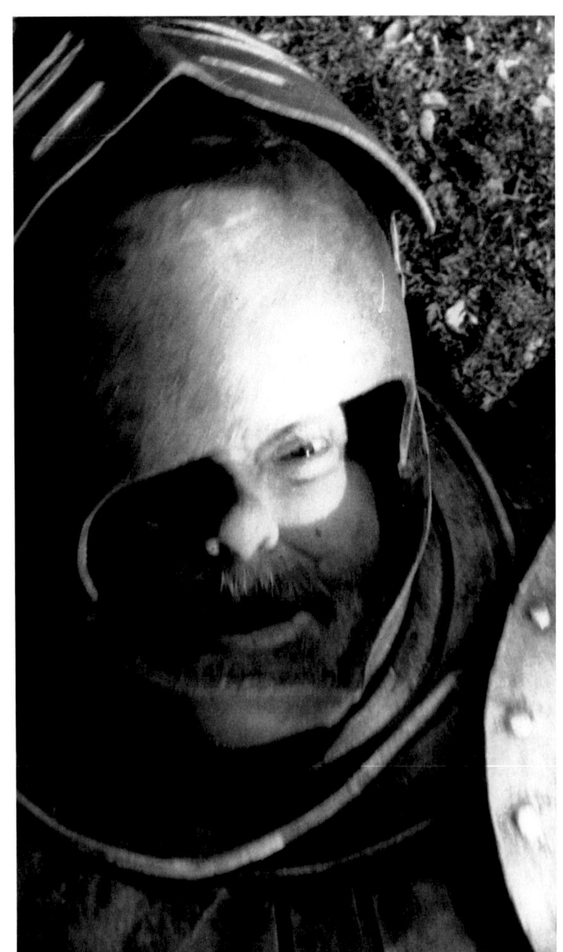

Once again Richard used red filters to remove nuances, but this was to make the silhouettes of trees stand out all the more strongly, to trace the uneven lines of the wood in the beams of buildings and to magnify the clouds hanging heavily over the battlefield. The winter of *Falstaff* is a winter of dead trees standing out against the snow, of prints made using only the contrast between the hollow and the flat.

Second, and more than ever, the power of the electric arc lights is justified here by the vastness of the natural sets to be lit. Particularly in Cardona, where Welles could not use any set-design tricks to alter the perception of space, the lighting lends structure to a space that was designed to be theatrical, making it all the more realistic. The main light source, often suggested as the only one, is the thin beam falling from a high window. A large, five by five metre mirror behind the window reflected the light from half a dozen large arc lights into the interior, all concentrated into a single ray filled with aluminium powder. Everywhere in *Falstaff* the lighting creates a composition that is clearly pictorial, whereas in *The Trial* it was intended only to be expressive.

Third, the lenses were the same as those used for *The Trial* (14 mm, 25 mm and 75 mm), but used in a visibly different way, which helps to contrast the world of royalty with that of Falstaff. In the royal realm, as though respectful of the nobility of both Shakespeare's speeches and the actors that speak them, Welles films in medium close-up using long lenses (which he also used for Hotspur's wife, played by Marina Vlady, the only actress to benefit from a blue filter, which softens her image). In this world of order Welles uses very short focal lengths only to cover entire spaces, or to accentuate their depth. Meanwhile, high and low angles are rare, used only discreetly to signify an apparently natural inequality. By contrast, in Falstaff's world – at the inn or in Shallow's house – wide-angle lenses regain their ability to distort bodies, pushing them into the realm of disorder, as do the brutal high and low angles, which often create breaks in an always unstable equilibrium.

Beyond the elementary contrast of the interiors, Welles had to deal with the matter of the landscapes. All the work on the photography was intended to abstract these, emptying them of their physical peculiarities to retain only an essence that is also the dramatic essence of the film. The landscapes form the third space, implacably horizontal, where the space of power is vertical and the space of disorder has no clear direction. This third space is not that of the ambush in Gadshill or of the hand-to-hand fighting of Shrewsbury, both of which clearly belong to disorder, but that of the armies lining up before battle, shared equally between heaven and earth. It was in order to construct this space, scorning the natural slopes of the Spanish landscape, that Welles so obstinately insisted that his set crew should have scaffolding that was light enough to be moved around according to need and to the light. On its platforms he perched lines of soldiers and the silhouetted figures he used so often. Carefully aligned with a horizontal foreground, they create the rectilinear horizon that is neither that of England nor of Spain, but is so crucial to his vision of *Falstaff*.

THE BATTLE

Objectively speaking, the battle of Shrewsbury is the heart of *Falstaff*, as its seventeen minutes occupy a precisely central place in the film's running time. It is also a bravura piece, unique in Welles's work, comprising no fewer than 392 shots, almost a third of the entire number in the film. Welles chose to portray the battle in four sections of different lengths, which succeed each other like the movements of a musical composition. First, a slow, tense prelude in which challenges are exchanged and the armies prepare for combat. Then the battle itself, its pace always increasing, starting with cavalry charges and ending in a confused muddle of twisted bodies in mud. Then the single combat between Hal and Hotspur, seemingly distanced from a tumult which has died down. Last comes the return to order and calm, with the king's reappearance and his proclamation of victory.

The first and last part were filmed in Colmenar Viejo, when shooting had only just begun, to take advantage of Gielgud's presence. They were supplemented later by a few shots filmed in the Casa de Campo, including those where the knights are hoisted on to their mounts. Concerned to establish continuity with the battle that was to follow, Welles began to fill the plain with a thick fog, which he would allow to disperse at the battle's end.

All the rest was filmed in Madrid, in the Casa de Campo. Some was done in November, while Norman Rodway was still there to perform the death of Hotspur, including the end of the duel filmed in the Carabanchel warehouse; and some in February, when most of the battle was filmed in extremely difficult conditions of cold and bad weather. Rodway had gone by then and a double wore his armour for the combat between Hotspur and Hal. Welles had all 150 horsemen granted him by the producers for only one day. On that particular day the rain was bucketing down, so rather than allow shooting to be called off, Richard used all his ingenuity to light the scene through the rain. After this Welles had to make do with half a dozen horsemen who rode back and forth in front of the camera. It was the same with the infantry of whom, after the first two or three days, only a handful remained, to be used in many different ways. Fortunately Welles had foreseen this gradual reduction from collective to individual action, and also the intractable problem of weather continuity, which he solved through the extensive use of fog machines. Unlike the rest of the film, this ever more confused battle section is treated like a reportage, the four cameras following the action very quickly, one mounted on a highly mobile small crane and the other three hand-held. Welles knew that he wanted the cutting to become faster and faster. He even drew all the details in a pile of sketches, which he gave to his camera operators. Aware how hard it was for the extras to perform only their expected movements, he filmed shots that were longer than necessary, leaving the combatants time to carry out their action. At the editing stage he cut the shots down, speeded them up by removing every other frame, and had the laboratory reverse them. In the film this part of the battle lasts five and a half minutes, with no dialogue. It comprises 214 shots, each of an average length of one and a half seconds. Welles later said that it had taken six weeks to get them exactly right.

POST-PRODUCTION FROM HOME

In the house he had been occupying since shooting in Aravaca, a few kilometres north of Madrid, where he was always happy to have his actors to stay, Welles set up three editing machines. As for *The Trial*, two of these were Prévosts imported specially from Italy; a flatbed model through which the film passed horizontally, which Welles liked for its precision and silence, despite the reputed difficulty of loading it up. Instead of having a frame stopping in front of the lens twenty-four times per second, which implies frame by frame advancing of the film, the Prévost ran the film continuously in front of a hexagonal rotating mirror, thus alleviating the mechanical tension and allowing the editor to run the film very fast or to stop it almost instantaneously. The machine had several plates, allowing several soundtracks to be run at once. Early in January 1965, when most of the filming with the actors was finished and Welles himself was immobilized by illness for around two weeks, he brought in Fritz Mueller, who had previously been involved in editing *The Trial*. Rather than a professional editor, Mueller was a multi-skilled technician whose prime quality for Welles was almost certainly his availability. There were still several weeks' filming remaining, during which Mueller put the film together following the very precise instructions left by his director. Given the scale of the task, he was later joined by a Spanish editor, Elena Jaumandreu, and Welles even sent him to Rome for a couple of days to hone the more difficult passages with Renzo Lucidi, one of the editors who had worked on *Othello*, then on *Mr Arkadin* and *Don Quixote*.

Above:
Fernando Rey (the rebellious Worcester), Keith Baxter (Prince Hal) and John Gielgud (Henry IV). As he did not yet have the necessary armour, Welles decided that doublets would do for scenes before and after the battle.

Following pages:
Keith Baxter and Welles.

According to several witnesses, Welles's now habitual editing technique was rather surprising. Unlike most directors, who tend to watch the film in the projection room and confine themselves to giving instructions orally or in note form, Welles worked at the editing machine himself. He would watch the film at double speed, hardly ever slowing it down, marking in chalk directly on the film as it passed to indicate the cuts. When a scene was finished he would leave the machine to the editor, who then had to carry out his orders, and he moved to the next machine, where another scene had been made ready and waiting for him. It was not unusual for him to notice during this process that he was missing a shot. This would then be added to the list of disparate fragments which the second unit would be asked to film as shooting progressed, or held back for its final days.

During the first stage of the editing process Welles was looking for an essentially musical rhythm and edited the sequences to recordings of medieval music. In his letter of 13 July 1964, before filming began, he was already worried that the first producer wanted to saddle him with a highly popular arranger of classical pieces: 'Who is he? Am I to understand that he's a composer? I'm sure you aren't intending to dictate my choice of musician and I hope you're mentioning his name only as an example of prices in Spain.' Welles called in Angelo Francesco Lavagnino, the Italian composer of the score for *Othello.* His task was both to arrange authentic medieval pieces, such as the dances at the inn, and to write original pieces, some of which could also be distantly inspired by medieval music, in order to bridge the gap between the early and the more modern. Welles and Lavagnino did not keep to English music, believing that music circulated from one country to the next: hence the presence of, for example, a French *estampie* and an Italian *saltarello.* The music was recorded in Rome in July 1965. Welles took a few liberties with it, but nothing in comparison to his treatment of the music for *The Trial.*

Almost all the dialogues had to be post-synchronized. Firstly, because the direct sound was of such poor quality that it was generally unusable; secondly, because of the number of French, Italian and Spanish actors, who were inadequately prepared for the nuances of Shakespearean prosody. The budget did not allow bringing back to Spain those who could dub themselves. Baxter took on the task of directing his English colleagues in London, while Mueller flew to New York to record Gielgud's lines and Peter Parasheles, the film's sound editor, did the same with other actors in Paris. They all followed the very detailed instructions given to them by Welles, who supervised the whole thing from Spain and, in Madrid and Paris, dubbed his own lines and those of a few of his fellow actors.

Stretched across four countries, with four or maybe more sound engineers, the post-production of *Falstaff* seemed as though it would never end. After initial hopes that it would be screened in Cannes in May 1965, then in Venice that autumn, it was not ultimately seen until the Cannes film festival of the following year. For anyone seeking to understand Welles's working methods, the final months of post-production are always the most mysterious, seeming to extend beyond the limits of the reasonable. This almost certainly comes down to the financial difficulties of a production that has exhausted all its resources and is living on its wits.

THE IMMORTAL STORY 1966–1968

Co-produced by French television but shot in 35 mm and intended for simultaneous release on the big and small screens, *The Immortal Story* respects the constraints of television. Welles made an intimist film whose apparent simplicity suited the economical prose of the Isak Dinesen story he was adapting. Everything had to appear clear, smooth and fresh, although the conditions in which the film was made proved almost as rugged as those for the films with intentionally jarring editing. For the first time since *It's All True* Welles experimented with colour, taking the opportunity to expand his approach to photography. And, after asking his composers to draw on existing melodies, he eventually went the whole hog and used existing recordings of music by Erik Satie.

Previous pages:
Jeanne Moreau filmed in the Castilian village of Pedraza.

Left:
Welles as Mr Clay.

Opposite page:
A shot by the initial director of photography Walter Wottitz of Roger Coggio (Levinsky) and Jeanne Moreau (Virginie).

RULES OF THE GAME

In 1966 Welles wrote an adaptation of five stories by Isak Dinesen (one of Karen Blixen's pen names), for which he was planning different kinds of assortments according to the various financial arrangements he tried to make. He had known Jeanne Moreau, actress in *The Trial* and *Falstaff*, since 1950; their friendship led to *The Immortal Story*, based on a story of around eighty pages, which would make a film lasting less than an hour. Moreau's agent, Micheline Rozan, who started out as a producer at Albina Films, joined forces with French television to set up the project. This was the first time that the state-run Office de Radiodiffusion-Télévision Française (ORTF) had become involved in an undertaking on such a scale; it had chosen the project for a broadcast to mark the advent of colour to its second channel. The film was to be released simultaneously in the cinema. The ORTF retained broadcast rights for France in perpetuity while, rather than working for a flat fee, Welles, Moreau and Albina Films retained the theatrical distribution rights and broadcast rights for countries other than France. Welles obtained the lion's share since, after the sums invested had been recovered, seventy per cent or, above a certain level, sixty per cent of the profits were to go to his Swiss company, Ropama.

The plot of *The Immortal Story* concerns four ill-matched characters who have found themselves washed up in the Chinese port of Canton in the late nineteenth century. Impervious to the charms of fiction, rich old merchant Mr Clay (an Englishman in Dinesen's story, American in Welles's script) orders his accountant Levinsky, a Polish Jew, to stage the enactment of a legend that all the sailors in the world relate as though it had actually happened to them: a rich old man pays a sailor to make his young wife pregnant. The sailor and the single girl recruited to act out this story are a young Danish man, Povl, who is a virgin, and a young French woman, Virginie, who is nothing of the kind. The two lovers-for-a-night must part at dawn and Levinsky is convinced that turning the legend into reality will be the death of his master.

Initially Welles's adaptation retained the overall structure of Dinesen's story and included voiceover comments from a narrator (Welles himself) throughout the film. At the risk of a rather static approach, the plot unfolded in only half a dozen scenes, almost all interiors. Welles then transformed this script in three major ways. First, he increased the number of scenes and set more of them as exteriors. To do this he cut certain episodes in two, including the first conversation between Levinsky and Virginie, whose initial location was shifted to the street before it later continued in Virginie's apartment. Welles also added short sequences with dialogue, created by turning indirect speech into spoken lines or by shifting portions of text. So the scenes where Virginie is getting ready for the night while commenting on the events with Levinsky were entirely formed from elements taken from different places in Dinesen's story. The second transformation was to reduce the role of the voiceover narration. The narration was largely given to the characters and the voiceover was used on only a few occasions at the beginning of the film. In addition, as in *The Magnificent Ambersons*, Welles created a prologue in which speeches were shared between the narrator and a chorus of anonymous passers-by who describe Clay's commercial ruthlessness. One consequence of these two initial transformations was an expanded role for Levinsky, who from time to time becomes the source of wisdom represented by the narrator in Dinesen's story. Beyond that, all the characters are given a greater role as interpreters of their own stories. The third transformation was to remove many of the indications of dates and places, reinforcing the timelessness of a drama whose audience cannot tell how many days it takes to play out. The cast list was quickly established.

Above:
Welles on the main square in Pedraza.

Left:
Welles and director of photography Willy Kurant.

Opposite page:
In Chinchón, preparing to film the recruitment of the sailor, using day for night. (Norman Eshley, Roger Coggio, Willy Kurant, Welles.)

Top:
The port of Macao, re-created by placing a few miniature ships' masts in front of the facades at Brihüega.

Above:
A low wall suggests the harbour basin.

Opposite page left, top to bottom:
Playing with lenses. Shots taken using focal lengths of 18.5 mm, 25 mm, 32 mm, 75 mm, 100 mm and 150 mm (taken with a telephoto lens, which blurs the background).

Opposite page, middle:
Two shots taken with a 90 mm lens, reserved for details.

Opposite page right, top:
Yellow lighting is used to accentuate the depth of field

Opposite page right, bottom:
Misty photography.

Jeanne Moreau would play Virginie, opposite Roger Coggio (Levinsky) and the British actor Norman Eshley (the sailor), but would have no scenes with Welles (Clay). The ORTF would broadcast the film in French, but an English language version would be made for theatrical release. So it was agreed to shoot in two languages. Novelist Louise de Vilmorin, an old friend of Welles's, was commissioned to write the French dialogue. Moreau and Coggio would do their scenes in both languages. Eshley and Welles would perform only in English. Filming was to take place on a limited number of sets, none of which would be built in a studio. So Welles did not hire an art director and set decorator André Piltant was to work with the chosen locations. A few weeks before filming was due to start, Welles decided to film in Spain as well as in France. He shifted the action from Canton to the Macao peninsula, as the exteriors of the former Portuguese colony would be well represented by medieval Castilian architecture.

ELEVEN DAYS IN RUEIL

The main set for the filming in France, which began on 21 September 1966, was a house in Rueil-Malmaison, a western suburb of Paris. Welles used this house as Clay's residence surrounded by grounds, and also as the location for Virginie's apartment.

Welles had recruited as director of photography Walter Wottitz, who had just finished work on Jean Gabin's last films with Denys de La Patellière and Jean-Paul Le Chanois, and had worked on French shoots for big-budget American films such as *The Longest Day*. The cramped set, not to mention the slender budget, ruled out any use of arc lights along the lines of *The Trial* and *Falstaff*. Wottitz used more classic incandescent Fresnel lights that give hard shadows. After four days of filming, Welles fired him. Camera operator Adolphe Charlet, who had worked on the previous two films, left with his director of photography. Of the five and a half 'useful' minutes shot by the pair, as noted by script supervisor Suzanne Schiffman, less than three remained in the final cut.

Welles urgently needed a new director of photography and began looking for someone younger, more used to lighter equipment and hand-held camerawork. The man eventually chosen was a thirty-two-year-old Belgian, Willy Kurant, former globe-trotting cameraman on news coverage as well as documentaries by directors such as Maurice Pialat. *The Immortal Story* was Kurant's third feature, following films by Agnès Varda and Jean-Luc Godard. After twenty-four hours Wottitz's focus puller, who had initially taken over the camera, gave up, and Welles asked Kurant to operate the camera as well. Cinematography on *The Immortal Story* is the fruit of Welles's precise instructions combined with the inventiveness of this representative of the new European approach of the 1960s, who favoured directional lighting rather than the uniform, ambient lighting of the early New Wave.

Filming continued for a further seven days in Rueil, until 3 October. Welles often did very few takes (two or three), though he would do ten or fifteen when necessary. This speed made it possible to film variants of simple shots when the original takes had been in the can for some days. The shooting order of the English and French version of shots was not at all systematic and they were sometimes filmed several days apart. Welles gave more time to the English version. In relation to one of Coggio's lines Schiffman noted: 'Sorry, I didn't get a French version of this shot.' This trend increased as time went by.

Before and after the night of love. Jeanne Moreau (top) and Norman Eshley (bottom).

At the start Welles ensured he had the means to record high-quality direct sound. Nevertheless he preferred to abandon the heavy, sound-proofed camera in favour of the lighter Caméflex whenever a shot had no dialogue. By the end he was satisfied to record a guide track during shooting, some in sync, some not. Ultimately almost all the dialogue was post-synchronized and, despite everything, Coggio was dubbed into English.

CHINA IN CASTILE

Welles moved the shoot to Spain earlier than planned. He also filmed interiors there, instead of confining them all to the initial sets. Only the actors, Kurant and the production manager Marc Maurette travelled to Spain, where they were joined by a Spanish crew to form a smaller team than the one in Rueil.

The idea was to turn Welles's own villa near Madrid into Clay's house. So, even more than with *Falstaff*, Welles worked from home, in a little group, with his actors and cameraman staying with him. The villa's huge rooms provided new interiors, such as the office and terrace where Clay sits with Levinsky at the start of the film, or the dining room where he receives the sailor. Welles also shot many supplementary elements to the scenes filmed in France. He had to create matches between the Rueil villa and his own in Spain using props such as red wallpaper (colour would provide enough continuity for everything else), lattice partitions or a bed surrounded by tulle curtains. He did not film the facade (the Rueil facade had been filmed half-hidden behind the trees in the grounds), since the vast residence had to seem smaller in the film. The layout of the rooms in Clay's house is not clear to the viewer, creating around the enormous room that is the setting for the night of love a space that is more mythical than real.

Welles used his knowledge of Spain for the exteriors. He created a haunted, empty Macao, combining at least three medieval Spanish villages within a hundred-kilometre radius of Madrid: Pedraza to the north (where he had previously located some of the English alleys of *Falstaff*), Brihüega to the north-east and Chinchón to the south-east.

The main square in Pedraza, with its colonnades and single-storey buildings, was the setting for the meeting between Levinsky and Virginie (the shot in which the accountant passes through the market crowds, shot in Rueil, was printed in reverse to ensure continuity) and it is here that Virginie lives, filmed on her wooden balcony. Here as elsewhere, Welles took care to remove any sign of verticality, framing the scene so that the church tower that rises above the square was always just out of shot.

Welles filmed the recruitment of the sailor in Chinchón and went back there after the principal photography was over, without Kurant, who was unavailable, but with Edmond Richard, director of photography on his two previous films. They filmed the shots from the prologue with Fernando Rey and two colleagues on the main square lined with arcades and wooden balconies. Meanwhile the port, portrayed only in the film's first two wide shots, was entirely created on the main square in Brihüega, in the way that effects were created in *Othello*. In the foreground, ragged sails on improvised masts represent tired old ships. By shooting the square from a low angle, as though from the bridge of a ship, Welles transformed a low, time-worn wall into a harbour basin of which we see only the upper part. The discreet addition of signs in Chinese and Portuguese makes the illusion complete. The extras were a mix of east Asians and Castilians.

Welles, who had not filmed any of the shots in which he himself appeared in Rueil, went before the camera this time. Unwilling to learn his lines, he often used cue cards or slates, a long-standing practice of his. In the scene of the sailor's dinner, he used cue cards for close-ups while adopting the Italian practice of mumbling meaninglessly in wider shots, leaving the dialogue to be definitively established while editing. So the shots were simply the support on which all could be reinvented at the editing stage.

LONGER FOCAL LENGTHS AND HAND-HELD CAMERAS

Before this film it was only in *Mr Arkadin* and a few passages of *Falstaff* that Welles had used the system of filming shots in several different scales to give the editor room for manoeuvre. However, he developed this practice for the dialogue scenes of *The Immortal Story*, reframing and filming different versions of the same shot. The sole noteworthy exception is the one-shot sequence of the discussion between Virginie and Levinsky in the dressing room before the night of love, filmed by Wottitz and Charlet, which lasts just over seventy seconds in the final cut.

One noticeable innovation can be seen in Welles's choice of lenses. He had returned to short focal lengths for wide shots: 32 mm and particularly 25 and 18.5 mm. But the intimist nature of the story, combined with the need for the film to work on the small screen, led him to move in closer than usual. He had shown a liking for long lenses in filming for television before but here, in addition to a 50 mm lens, he used 75 mm more than he had ever done previously in a film for cinema.

Most importantly, he went for telephoto lenses. Although it had seemed unlikely that he would need them for work with Welles, Kurant had brought with him a range of his own long lenses. For extreme close-ups of objects he used a German 90 mm lens, the kind used in advertising and scientific films, because it was able to focus on a detail. The love scene, started in Rueil and finished in Madrid, required many medium close-ups and close-ups, often shot several times using different lenses. Kurant would use 50, 75 or 100 mm lenses, or the 90 mm lens for the very big close-up in which Virginie's eye slowly opens. He even used 150 mm for the shot (cut in two in the final edit), with a background of greenery that is delicately out of focus, in which the sailor puts to his ear the shell brought back from his desert island that he wants to give to Virginie.

In another manifestation of his new, flexible approach, Welles encouraged Kurant to film some shots with a hand-held camera. Some of these are isolated, almost fixed shots, such as the silent ballet of Clay's Chinese servants bustling around the sailor, or Virginie blowing out the forest of candles by the bed, where the hand-held camera adds to the private, human vibration of the images. The others are tracking shots, again demonstrating Welles's capacity to change his method. When they were in Pedraza filming the scene where Levinsky accosts Virginie and they talk as he walks back with her through the arcades, the truck bringing the electrical equipment, track and dolly had not yet arrived. Welles gave up waiting and trusted to the skill of Kurant. Lacking the lights needed to film the next scene on the schedule, he shot another, the recruitment of the sailor, using day for night. And for the end of the scene he shot rapid pans with a 150 mm lens, similar to those used by Kurosawa, which look just like tracking shots of Clay's carriage with the sailor following quickly behind.

REDISCOVERING COLOUR

Welles always said he preferred black and white: he thought colour showed off the set and costumes to best advantage, but was not so good for actors. He did experiment enthusiastically with cumbersome Technicolor cameras for the carnival in *It's All True* and vainly argued that he should be able to film the voyage of the *Jangadeiros* in the same way. But here colour was stipulated by the ORTF and Welles initially saw it as a concession. He reacted by limiting variations of colour in both shots and sequences, using a restricted range. As in his black and white films, he favoured back-lighting, unrelated to light sources in the set, and made the foreground stand out against the background. But he kept contrast down and went for unsaturated colours that would merge and soften.

During his initial interview with Welles, Kurant suggested radical changes to the electrical equipment. He used Colortrans, the small, boosted lights that Richard had previously used for a handful of particular effects in *The Trial*. These lights offered speed, mobility and economy, but the photography still had to be softened. Kurant set up the key lights behind transparent panels. When pastel tones were required, particularly for the shots of Virginie, he used a box covered in slightly bluish photocopy paper to create atmosphere. He also improvised tricks on the spot, as when he covered the pages of the book of accounts Levinsky is about to close in aluminium foil and lit them from above so that the foil reflected light on to the accountant's face.

Welles and Kurant were also seeking a 'coloured depth of field'. In Madrid, Welles caught Kurant off guard by asking him to get coloured filters to project rays of yellow light on to the white wall of the office in which Clay and Levinsky have their first scene. At the editing stage Welles took out the shot in which Levinsky opens the glass door separating this room from the next and which more explicitly revealed the source of a light which, in the finished film, appears as a purely compositional element. In one of the recurring perspectives from the same scene, in which the camera faces the office from the terrace, Clay's armchair is right in the foreground, a pillar and a lamp give shape to the middle ground and the yellow, in the background, highlights the depth. Welles needed simply to have Coggio move around this space to increase the sense of depth.

The love scene is particularly stylized. Kurant composed a very soft light for it, with the slightly blue photocopy paper and the long focal length further flattening the image. Going against his usual aesthetics, Welles went for diffused light. He filmed many shots through the white tulle curtains around the bed, with a nylon stocking in front of the lens to add to the effect, and asked for some shots to be filmed without nets, to leave himself a choice at the editing stage. The shot of the sailor savouring the sounds of Virginie's name before their first kiss was filmed in eleven takes. Welles printed the last take without nets and the last one with, ultimately selecting the latter for the film.

PENELOPE'S FOUR HANDS

Editing began at the end of October, shortly before filming finished early the following month, at Jean-Pierre Melville's Jenner studios in Paris. Welles recruited an editor, the wife of the production manager, for whom this was her first film, but she soon found herself sidelined. From then on Welles was his own editor, accompanied by two young assistants working in the next two rooms, on both the English and the French versions. Welles often did drawings of the shots in the desired order for them. Françoise Garnault, who soon replaced one of the assistants, explained that Welles reserved the right to try absolutely anything, including going back over something whenever he chose. The order of scenes could not easily be changed, yet there were countless variations because Welles would constantly change the order of shots within a scene or match shots that had not originally been designed to go together. The fact that shots had been filmed from different angles or at different scales allowed for endless different combinations. And Welles often kept several takes of the same shot so that he could use part of this one or that elsewhere. The rejected shots were not regarded as 'outs' which would only be used if he wanted to correct a mistake; instead he called them his 'sources', signifying that they represented possible choices. Depending on how the editing was going, Welles was also filming additional shots of his character in a small Paris studio. He asked for unusual precautions which, in the days before digital editing, represented a great deal of work and money. Because he wanted to preserve the traces of each edited version, his assistants used marks of different colours on the film's optical track to indicate the version to which this or that shot or take belonged. Trims were not simply kept separately, they were used to reconstruct the rushes, which could then be consulted in their entirety. Where there were mismatches between shots, Welles provided his editors with a theory: the bigger the mismatch, the more easily it is accepted. Go for it.

MUSICAL CONJURING TRICKS

Five months after editing began, a programme about Erik Satie happened to be broadcast. Aldo Ciccolini, who had just started work on a complete discography of Satie's works for piano, participated. The next day Welles announced his idea for the film music: Erik Satie. He would use recordings of the three *Gnossiennes*, a *Gymnopédie* and three other pieces. He explained this choice by his desire not to be dependent on what a composer might write after signing the contract.

Satie, with his taste for understatement, light harmonics and *piano* or *pianissimo* nuances, offered a musical simplicity that reflected the modesty of the film. The brevity of his motifs, his rejection of development and his liking for *ostinato* and repetition all act to suspend time and generate a sense of inevitability, creating pieces that can easily be cut into sections. In a sense Satie set the seal on the film's French nationality, while the orientalist flavour of many of the compositions used in the film are in keeping with the setting in Macao. Furthermore, the pieces written between 1888 and 1914 are close to the 'end of the last century' mentioned by the narrator. Welles used music over only a fifth of the film, two or three times less than was his usual practice. He placed it over moments of transition and passages of narration, in which there is a secret complicity between the piano and the speaker, but very seldom combined it with dialogue. He treated Satie's music as he had treated the original scores for his earlier European films, using most of the pieces several times and, at the start of the film, working a new musical sleight of hand, putting together a two-minute piece out of four fragments taken from three pieces composed twenty-five years apart. The pieces were even played by different pianists, since Ciccolini had not yet recorded *En habit de cheval*, a work for four hands from which Welles took a two-handed passage from a recording by Jean-Joël Barbier that had also just been released. The changes of piece are so well matched to the images and voiceover that the trick is imperceptible to anyone unfamiliar with the pieces.

At the same time Welles was busy post-synchronizing the English dialogue and editing the sound, since he was working with Jean Neny, whom he called 'the Paganini of mixing'. He hired a cutting room near the auditorium in order to do any last-minute tweaking. The quietness of the sound effects diverts attention from their expressiveness. What Welles does not show in the night of love he makes audible: a modulation in the song of the crickets translates the emotions of the lovers; the meeting of two sound tracks when a second insect joins the first signifies the union of bodies. When, with a jolt, Virginie relives the exact moment when she lost her virginity, the chirping of the crickets is speeded up in the sound mix to become very shrill, outdoing Virginie's own cry in its intensity, as though driving her pain or ecstasy to new heights. In its sound as everywhere else, *The Immortal Story* demonstrates that the art of manipulation goes hand in hand with simplicity.

BROADCAST BLOCKED

The Immortal Story, whose first version was finished in June 1967, went fifty per cent over budget, causing difficulties for Albina Films, particularly as Welles absented himself on other business during the editing and missed the delivery date promised to the global distributor by five months. The distributors, a subsidiary of Philips, withdrew and asked for their advance to be returned. Their potential replacements were wary of the unusual length of a film that was neither a feature nor a short, while the intermediary for a possible sale to American television suggested among other things the need for self-censorship where nudity was concerned. Welles returned to Paris to put the final touches to the film in September. He ended up with a fifty-minute French version to suit the television schedules and an English version of fifty-seven minutes. Although only about twelve minutes in the two versions use different takes, they vary in many other ways, like two competing cuts between which it is impossible to choose.

France's second channel was moving to colour in early October, but the delays in finishing the film led to its removal from the schedule, with a new date set for May 1968. An all-out strike at the ORTF then meant broadcast had to be delayed again for several months.

Arriving at Clay's house after recruiting the sailor.

Rozan eventually found a new distributor, a German company specializing in small-scale European genre films, which covered part of the deficit and ensured the film would be released in several countries, including the United States. However, this company then collapsed, with the result that neither Welles, nor Moreau, nor their producer received a penny from a film they had made for the love of cinema. Rozan gave up producing films to concentrate on theatre with Peter Brook. *The Immortal Story* was not released in French cinemas until 1976 and has never been broadcast on American television. During the editing stage and while the fate of the film remained in the balance Welles tried to mount shorter adaptations of Dinesen stories that could act as programme supplements, but none of them came to anything. *The Immortal Story* remains the only real public manifestation of his pioneering and passionate love for the work of the Danish writer.

THE HEROINE, THE DEEP & ORSON'S BAG

1967—1970

After *The Immortal Story*, Welles consolidated both his move to colour and his use of a single cinematographer by combining the functions of director of photography and camera operator. He adopted techniques that would enable him to complete comparatively inexpensive films, without art directors, shot freely and with small crews. Yet the three projects he began for cinema and television in 1967–8 remained unfinished – the first after a single day's shooting with no possibility of continuing later, while the other two he worked on for several years.

HIS LAST TWO PROFESSIONAL FILMS

In 1967 Welles began shooting two films in Hungary and Yugoslavia. In April he started *The Heroine*, after a story by Isak Dinesen, and in September a film eventually called *The Deep*, after a thriller by Charles Williams entitled *Dead Calm*. Welles wrote both scripts before his reunion with Olga Palinkas (the future Oja Kodar), a young sculptress he had met in Zagreb while making *The Trial*, who was to share the last nineteen years of his life, although he never divorced Paola Mori. Kodar had played minor characters in films directed by Roger Vadim and Jean Becker, but Welles's scripts offered her an opportunity to take on leading roles. She subsequently worked as a writer with him on most of his fiction projects, assisted him on set and acted in front of the camera.

Without waiting to finish editing *The Immortal Story*, Welles hoped to film one or two other adaptations of stories by Dinesen for cinema release either on their own or as part of a programme with *The Immortal Story*. Alexander Paal, a Londoner of Hungarian origin, joined forces with the Hungarian state film production board to provide him with the necessary means. *The Heroine* is about twenty pages long and set at the start of the Franco-Prussian war of 1870. A young widow from a high-ranking French family is arrested in a town in the Sarre region near the German border,

but eventually continues to France; a Prussian officer offers to give a passport to all the prisoners if she will come to collect it naked. Kodar would be acting with English-speaking Hungarians but, as Welles explained when shooting was about to start, 'a lot of it is dubbed in the respect that I speak for them, I'm a sort of storyteller in sync with their voices'. The linchpin of the crew was Willy Kurant, cinematographer on *The Immortal Story*, who had been contacted at the last minute. The other technicians were recruited in Hungary. The low cost of equipment and crew enabled Welles to return for one last time to the use of arc lights when he began shooting in the opera house in Budapest. But Paal proved a weak partner, while the Hungarians spectacularly inflated the bill for the first day's shooting. Alarmed at the prospect of paying so much, Welles sneaked out of the country that same night. Meanwhile he was sitting on another script, a mixture of two stories by Edgar Allan Poe – *The Masque of the Red Death* and *The Cask of Amontillado*. He had written this with Kodar as a contribution to an omnibus film, *Spirits of the Dead*, whose other two segments were to be directed by Louis Malle and Roger Vadim. The Franco-Italian co-production was headed by *Othello*'s French distributor Edmond Tenoudji. Welles planned to film on the Dalmatian coast, again with Kodar and Kurant, but pulled out of the project in June.

After this, Welles managed to have *The Deep* indirectly co-financed by the state-owned film production boards of Croatia and Bosnia-Herzegovina. These provided logistical support and most of the crew, in return for Welles's participation as an actor in the big-budget, patriotic Yugoslavian production *The Battle of the Neretva* directed by Veljko Bulajić. The company headed by Micheline Rozan, producer of *The Immortal Story*, acted as an intermediary for Welles's own company where the costs of film stock and equipment bought in France were concerned. The Yugoslavian costs again went over budget, leading Welles to continue alone.

The Deep is a film with five characters, whose plot unfolds over less than a day aboard two sailing boats. While honeymooning on their yacht, a young married couple (Kodar and Michael Bryant) pick up a survivor from a shipwrecked schooner (Laurence Harvey). When the husband boards the wreck to inspect the damage, the stranger seizes the opportunity to make off with the young woman and the yacht. Jeanne Moreau and Welles completed the cast list in the roles of the wife and the captain left abandoned by the stranger. Welles began filming off the Dalmatian coast, not far from Kodar's home.

Previous pages, left:
Jeanne Moreau and Welles on the set of *The Deep*.

Previous pages, right:
The prologue of *The Heroine* in the Budapest opera house.

Opposite page:
Filming *The Deep*.
Script supervisor Ljuba Gamulin, the second cinematographer Ivica Rajković, and Welles (left).

Welles, Michael Bryant, Jeanne Moreau and the first cinematographer Willy Kurant (right).

Welles and Oja Kodar (bottom).

Right:
Oja Kodar, Laurence Harvey and Michael Bryant in *The Deep*.

From the outset he decided to use two cinematographers in succession, asking Kurant to work for the first weeks, although he was already contracted for another job and would subsequently have to leave. Every morning the small crew set out to sea, returning only at sunset. They were entirely at Welles's disposal and he took things one day at a time, with no shooting schedules for either the day's work or the whole project. A confirmed enemy of production paperwork, he even preferred not to keep log sheets for use in the edit, referring, when the time came, to a copy of the script annotated by script supervisor Ljuba Gamulin. Where sound was concerned Welles simply recorded a guide track since, leaving aside the noise from the Caméflex, shooting at sea ruled out the recording of any usable direct sound. He reworked the script as he went along and often gave the dialogue to the actors during the first take, obliging them to make something of their lines on the spot. And he had to get everything right first time since, as the rushes were to be developed in France, he was unable to see them.

As in *The Immortal Story*, Welles covered the scenes with different angles and lenses. Kurant filmed in natural light with a hand-held camera, which he stabilized with a harness. Visual choices were made in response to the difficulty of shooting at sea. Kurant suggested keeping the side of the yacht in line with the sun in order to film against the light, with a soft, reflected light on the faces of Moreau and her co-stars Bryant and Welles. Then, before getting to the scenes with Kodar and Harvey on board the second yacht, Kurant made way for his assistant Ivica Rajković, who had to implement these ideas. Welles himself did the framing, particularly for the shots of Kodar that used the subtle movements of her body, before handing the camera over for the actual filming. Unlike Kurant, Rajković did not systematically film against the light, leading to a somewhat hybrid visual style apparent in the edit. During the second part of the filming, Welles revised his own rules and adopted the zoom, sacrificing the better definition provided by fixed-focus lenses. He gained time by not changing lens between two shots and even used zoom-ins and zoom-outs now and then. After *The Deep*, he was all the more ready to add the zoom to his range because most of his projects adopted some kind of documentary style. At the end of the shoot some elements still remained to be filmed. Later, Welles gave other cameramen and even smaller teams the task of obtaining additional shots. He edited *The Deep* in three European countries, through 1970 and beyond, and had some positives printed only in black and white to save money. To help him find the rhythm of the edit, he temporarily dubbed Bryant and Harvey himself, so that the work prints use the guide track sound and this provisional dubbing. For legal and customs reasons, he failed to gather all the reels of *The Deep* in a single place, and never even saw some rushes, which he was unable to print. Today the same obstacle hinders the work of the Munich Filmmuseum, where Kodar has deposited most of the reels of unfinished films from the 1960s to the 1980s, which Welles bequeathed to her. The Filmmuseum started to complete the editing of *The Deep* under the supervision of Stefan Droessler, but cannot finish until it can access the missing material.

A TELEVISUAL MEDLEY

In 1968–70 Welles put together a special show for American television known as *Orson's Bag*, a series of sketches about London and Vienna, combined with a miniature adaptation of *The Merchant of Venice*. This should have seen the globetrotting Welles back up to strength on the American screen after ten years away. But CBS could not legally pay his company in Luxemburg, perhaps because of reprisals from the American government after Welles had performed on a satirical record attacking Presidents Johnson and Nixon. So he continued to film *Orson's Bag* at his own expense.

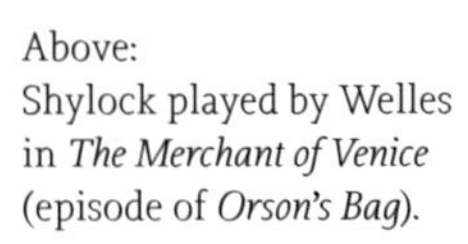

Above:
Shylock played by Welles in *The Merchant of Venice* (episode of *Orson's Bag*).

Right:
Shylock painted by Welles. After CBS pulled out, composer Angelo Francesco Lavagnino offered to write and record the score for *The Merchant of Venice* for no pay other than a dozen watercolours of Shakespearean characters painted on the bottoms of cigar boxes.

Opposite page:
Three faces of Welles in the London episodes of *Orson's Bag*.

The programme was a festival of Orson Welles. The actor at last had an opportunity to play Shylock, as he had often hoped to do in the theatre, and, in the Vienna section, he became a tourist guide before donning the garb of a magician. Above all, in the five robust and juicy London sketches, he played all the parts himself, including Churchill, a fallen aristocrat and his interviewer, four rambling old lords in their club, a one-man band on a street corner, a bad-tempered old woman, a woman selling dirty postcards and four other speedily-drawn characters, not forgetting a caricature of himself as an obese victim of the cruel snobbery of Savile Row tailors.

The scenes are shot with a total freedom and the dislocation between different places is more accentuated than ever. The London episodes were also filmed in Italy and France, the Vienna episode in the streets of Zagreb and a Los Angeles theatre, and *The Merchant of Venice* on the Dalmatian coast. The different shoots merged, so that Eleonora Duse's palazzo near Venice provides the settings for the club library, the London tailor's shop, a Viennese interior and a Viennese residence. Welles also completely transformed the courtyard of the Safa-Palatino post-production studios in Rome, where he was cutting both *Orson's Bag* and *The Deep*. Three cameramen – Yugoslavians Rajković and Tomislav Pinter and the Italian Giorgio Tonti – followed by a fourth for the last matching shots and sequences, worked in relays to film images in 35 mm and 16 mm. In the London and Vienna sketches zoom shots were sometimes a real stylistic choice, sometimes an easy solution executed without grace. As in other later pieces for television, which would foreground him as an orator, conjuror or presenter, Welles started from the principle that the image could remain impersonal as long as he himself was the focus of all attention. Four editors came and went, without Welles being able to finish the piece.

The London and Vienna episodes were completed in 2000 by the Munich Filmmuseum. Here is evidence that unfinished works function best if they are allowed to retain their status as work in progress, with no attempt to hide the raw nature of the direct sound or to add shots where they are missing. On the other hand, the unexplained disappearance of reels from the work print and other elements make it impossible to put together the forty minutes of *The Merchant of Venice*, of which only nine minutes are known today. This footage features subtle colours and music commissioned from the faithful Angelo Francesco Lavagnino, reinforcing its links to *Othello* and *Falstaff*.

In 1970, with *The Deep*, *Orson's Bag* and also *Don Quixote*, Welles found himself with three pieces of work on which filming was more or less complete, but which he could not finish for lack of money. The negatives and positives were scattered in different places while continuity demanded the filming of shots in which the actors were present. For the rest of his career Welles would be, on the one hand, constantly struggling to finish films while, on the other, constantly starting work on new ones – most of which would also remain unfinished.

THE LAST YEARS
1970–1985

Both in Europe – where he was now a visitor rather than an exile – and in the United States, Welles started work on a great many short films, features and television shows, which he shot and edited simultaneously, either at his own expense or with uncertain sources of finance. Only *F for Fake* and *Filming Othello* were shown to the public, while a completed talk-show pilot was never broadcast. In 1970, when he was fifty-five, Welles moved to Los Angeles with Oja Kodar, but regularly returned to Europe, sometimes for long periods. In 1967 he had begun making regular appearances on Dean Martin's very popular talk show on NBC, which led to frequent plane trips back and forth. Back in his native land, his guest appearances on Martin's show and those of Martin's rivals such as Dick Cavett and Johnny Carson provided Welles with a regular income. They brought him centre stage once more in the character of a benevolent intermediary between classical art and mass entertainment, sometimes light-heartedly authoritative, sometimes self-mocking.

He performed magic tricks, recited Shakespeare and passages from *Moby Dick*, sang songs with his host and other celebrities, and related colourful anecdotes from his own life. These appearances on talk shows and in television advertising for products of all kinds became the easiest way for Welles to make a living and to amass money to invest in his personal projects, and in 1975 he settled more permanently in California and Arizona.

Welles also continued to work as a screen actor, with a four-year break from 1972 to 1976. He performed in television dramas and officiated as master of ceremonies in episodes of various series. He continued to supply voiceovers for films and television, and for occasional recordings of both classical and rock music. He maintained his persona as a magician by filming conjuring shows. In 1975 he received a Life Achievement award from the American Film Institute. However, the ripples from this were not enough to enable him to get his stalled projects back on the road.

It was all the easier for Hollywood to forget Welles's work as a director because *Mr Arkadin*, *Falstaff* and *The Immortal Story* had seldom been seen in the United States. In the last fifteen years of his life he rarely had contact with the big Hollywood companies other than to propose, in vain, that they should distribute *F for Fake*. He also discussed a few projects with Paramount. According to Joseph McBride, who has written extensively on Welles, when one of the heads of Warner Bros. called Welles in the late 1960s he is said to have replied that he could no longer respect the daily constraints of official productions. He preferred tiny budgets, or the risk of never finishing, to dependency.

Yet he was always trying to set up new projects, writing new scripts. He had four possible sources of finance in mind. The first, from which nothing concrete ever came, would have involved him working with young, independent cinephiles in the United States, in thrall to Welles's films and charisma and ready to fight on his behalf. In 1970–2, he was in discussion with Bert Schneider – producer of *Easy Rider*, Bob Rafelson's first films and *The Last Picture Show* by Welles's protégé and supporter Peter Bogdanovich – and the short-lived Directors Company, which united Bogdanovich, Francis Ford Coppola and William Friedkin. The idea was to shoot using non-union technicians, with neither minimum crew nor collective agreement. The projects of Welles's that Bogdanovich planned to produce were blocked by various obstacles. In 1980 Welles teamed up with director Henry Jaglom to found Weljag, a company based in Liechtenstein. The pair failed to find financial backers for their two main projects, *The Dreamers*, another adaptation of a story by Isak Dinesen, and *The Big Brass Ring*, an original script on a political theme. Arnon Milchan, future producer of Sergio Leone's *Once Upon a Time in America*, was willing to take on *The Big Brass Ring*, but Welles was unable to find the necessary male lead from the generation of Warren Beatty and Jack Nicholson to play opposite him. In 1984 Michael Fitzgerald, fresh from his first two films directed by John Huston, *Wise Blood* and *Under the Volcano*, tried hard to put various partnerships in place to finance a modest project, *The Cradle Will Rock*, set in 1937 and telling the story of Welles's staging of Marc Blitzstein's proletarian opera and his difficulties with the government. The complex financial arrangements fell apart a few weeks before shooting was due to begin.

The other three financing possibilities were sources Welles had drawn on before: self-financing, television, Europe (and, often, a combination of all three). Hitherto Welles had filmed at his own expense only after an initial production or co-production deal had collapsed. Self-financing as a deliberate choice began in 1970 with *The Other Side of the Wind*, the most ambitious of Welles's projects of the period. This time it was the American administration, which disputed the right of his Luxembourg-based company to produce films, that obliged him to find new backers. As he was still trying to make his presence felt on television, Welles also self-financed a few projects for shows that never found buyers. The only one to be completed was a pilot for *The Orson Welles Show*, with which he tried to launch his own talk show in 1978. He also shot low-cost demonstration footage to promote scripts and rough sketches for his own use, filmed from day to day, that could later be inserted into larger projects.

In addition, Welles took on bread-and-butter roles for British and American television, filming brief chats himself when he was living abroad, rather than coming back in order to go into the studio. The support of a producer at NBC and future executor of Welles's will, Greg Garrison, was not enough to open doors to him as a director. On the other hand, in 1974 he was commissioned to make a piece for German television about the difficult birth of *Othello*: this became *Filming Othello*.

Welles's projects with Europe date mainly from the first half of the 1970s. *F for Fake*, a short television film begun in 1971, which then became a cinema feature, was produced by François Reichenbach before being bought up in 1973 by Les Films de l'Astrophore, which had already taken over production of *The Other Side of the Wind*. Around the same time, according to Andrés Vicente Gómez, Spanish co-producer for both films, Welles signed an exclusive deal with him, in which he undertook to complete the unfinished films to which he retained the rights, without accepting other commissions in the meantime, while Gómez would act as his private producer. Their association came to a stormy end in 1974, with the producer accused of embezzlement. It was not until 1984 that Welles successfully set up another co-production, this time for *King Lear*, with the French television channel TF1, two other European television companies and a film producer. The conditions that were laid down, including a deadline for delivery, payment on completion of the film and a ban on Welles leaving Paris during the editing stage, led to the project's collapse. In the same year, as part of its policy of supporting great foreign artists, the French Ministry of Culture granted finance to *The Dreamers*, but this was subject to half the budget being provided by a producer, whom Welles was unable to find.

At his death in 1985 Welles left a great many unfinished works, which are gradually being rediscovered through the efforts of his friends and family, those who have studied and written about him, and certain institutions, primarily the Munich Filmmuseum. He also left *F for Fake* and a television programme exploring his working methods, *Filming Othello*.

Opposite page:
As a failed magician in *A Safe Place* by Henry Jaglom (1971).

Top:
In *The Magic Show* (1976–82).

Above:
With his guest Burt Reynolds in the unaired pilot for *The Orson Welles Show* (1978–9).

ROUGH SKETCHES & LAST UNFINISHED WORKS

In the years 1970–85 Welles made many different kinds of work: films for his own use, shorts made purely for the money, and even an unfinished feature, *The Other Side of the Wind.* However, the different categories are blurred, since he was increasingly filming and editing at home, and, when necessary, travelling with his work in tow.

SHOOTING ANYWHERE, WITH A STABLE BASE

Two main factors enabled Welles to shoot regularly and freely in the last fifteen years of his life. The first was his frequent use of 16 mm, a lighter and less expensive film gauge. He also began using video in the late 1970s, and died the day before a Betacam shoot. The second was the arrival, one summer's day in 1970, of a twenty-eight-year-old director of photography, Gary Graver, who offered Welles his services free of charge if necessary. Used to working quickly on derisory budgets, Graver undertook to obtain the best conditions for buying film stock and the best payment deals with the laboratory, and brought in non-union crew who were prepared to work at the drop of a hat without fixed hours. He also brought along his equipment, supplementing Welles's own. Filming on *The Other Side of the Wind* could start. While pursuing a prolific career as a cameraman and director in porn and horror films, Graver faithfully followed Welles for fifteen years, longer than any of his other collaborators aside from Kodar. Welles called on him for all his self-financed or low-budget projects, in both the United States and Europe. On the other hand, when he had more upmarket projects in mind, none of which ever reached the shooting stage (such as *King Lear* in 1984, which he and Edmond Richard planned to shoot in France in 'black and white in colour'), he sometimes left Graver out or offered him the second unit.

Shooting was most often organized around a central core of Welles, Kodar and Graver – as in the short advertisements for a Japanese whiskey where Welles appears with Kodar. Technicians and actors would be invited to join the family on what were almost home movies. Welles would shoot one day at a time, at his own pace, with no schedule. Filming was often interrupted, to begin again at a later date, as priorities required. Welles had to work with variations in lighting and different emulsions, which he combined, to the dismay of the laboratories. Filming ill-matched fragments in very different places and cutting them together to create a single unified space had become a process as natural to him as breathing. This was also the period of recycling, when a scene intended for one television show would find its way into another.

Everywhere he lived, in both the United States and Europe, Welles had 16 and 35 mm editing machines installed, including one allowing pre-mixing. In 1974 the co-producer of *The Other Side of the Wind*, Les Films de l'Astrophore, offered him a portable machine. He was able to travel with his reels of film, editing machines and a few accessories for matching shots together.

Secretiveness had by now become a well-established aspect of Welles's work, to the point where the very existence of films or television pieces in a very advanced state was not revealed until long after they had been made and indeed after Welles's death. He filmed almost on the sly, did not give the script to those working with him and forbade all access to the cutting room. He did not want to add credence to the grim legend of a director incapable of finishing his films. And after so many projects had been ruined by others, he wanted to prevent anyone from reconstructing the cut or even the plot or main thread without him.

PRIVATE FILMS, BREAD-AND-BUTTER WORK, SHOW REELS

Welles used film like a notepad. He accumulated material and would spontaneously ask Graver to film his conversations with friends and his public appearances. Some of these fragments remained in a raw, unedited state, including the discussion after a screening of *The Trial* at a Californian university in 1981. Others, including short episodes of *F for Fake* and the discussion with students in *Filming Othello,* were integrated into larger works. Welles also used this technique to build up an omnibus film called *The One-Man Band,* for which there is no known written plan.

For purposes that were sometimes commercial, sometimes private, Welles filmed himself reciting passages from the Bible, Shakespeare, Oscar Wilde, G. K. Chesterton and Ring Lardner, and made sound recordings of similar readings on vinyl and cassette.

The filmed recitations include half-hour readings for a supermarket chain, a poem for an award ceremony sponsored by an insurance company, an extract from Lindbergh's journal for the birthday of Welles's administrator and accountant, and what are perhaps the first sections for his anthology film. He also started work on a condensed version of *Moby Dick*, in which he read Melville's narrative and played all the parts himself, appearing in both shot and reverse shot for dialogues. For all these recitations he was dressed in a suit or indoor attire, without make-up, on a bare set or in everyday surroundings, without any kind of effects, and would work the clapperboard himself. If different atmospheres were required these were created using coloured lighting. He used cue cards all the time, placing his text in different locations out of shot in order to conceal the trick and direct his gaze in a great many unpredictable directions.

Welles's bread-and-butter work included brief presentations for television. In 1971 he hastily shot the intros and outros for twelve classics of the silent cinema broadcast in the series *The Silent Years* for an American network. He used a plain coloured background with rudimentary lighting and editing and occasionally cut without changing angles, at the expense of fluidity. In 1972–3, while living in France he was commissioned to do introductions to twenty-six episodes of the series *Orson Welles Great Mysteries* for the British ITV channel. One Thursday he asked a young editor, Yves Deschamps, to work all-out on a set of introductions for which no image had yet been shot but which absolutely had to be sent to London the following Monday. Welles filmed himself in the Luxembourg Gardens in Paris and in his house in Orvilliers in the suburbs, in front of back-projected stills from the shows. The editor got the laboratory to agree that rushes delivered before midnight would be printed the following morning and that a composite print would be ready on the Sunday night. On another set of pieces the cameraman Serge Halsdorf described how Welles, running late, pretended that he had completed the job with a highly skilled crew in Spain. Then, the day before the producer was due to come to Paris to collect the film and take it back to London for editing, he hastily shot it, with Kodar recording the sound, faking the bustle of a busy Spanish set.

Between 1976 and 1982 Welles shot the conjuring tricks for the unfinished television film *The Magic Show* at his California home and in different theatres in Los Angeles and Atlanta. For the pilot of *The Orson Welles Show*, his foray into talk shows made in 1978, Welles credited himself as director under a pseudonym. The future show was to be recorded live by several cameras, but for the moment Welles sought to obtain the same spontaneity by filming a great many takes. The audience's questions and reactions were repeated and directed. Welles filmed himself responding to his main interviewee Burt Reynolds weeks after filming their actual conversation. And he totally restructured the material in the edit.

Between 1980 and 1985 Welles continued intermittently to shoot a few scenes for *The Dreamers* in order to pre-visualize the project. The film was to be a feature combining two stories by Isak Dinesen set in the nineteenth century: *The Dreamers*, in which three men from different countries each talk about an old flame before realizing they have all loved the same woman, and *Echoes*, in which we learn more about this woman's own wanderings. Welles transformed his California home into a Milanese period villa and filmed Kodar as 'the greatest singer in the world' in the hope of enabling her to act opposite someone other than himself. For *King Lear*, around1983, he simply videoed his pitch in a single static shot, replacing paper with film.

IMMERSION IN BOUNDLESS CREATION: 'THE OTHER SIDE OF THE WIND'

Welles filmed *The Other Side of the Wind* between 1970 and 1975, mainly in the United States, but also in France and Spain. He began the film at his own expense in Los Angeles, with a tiny crew and a cast of friends, then, when the American government caused difficulties for his production company, he began looking for financial backers. For a while he thought of continuing in Spain with Andrés Vicente Gómez, or in France with an associate of the Taittinger family, but eventually the production was taken on by Les Films de l'Astrophore, a company set up in Paris in 1972 to make prestige co-productions with Iran, from where most of the money came. Welles, Astrophore and Gómez were all involved with the film, until disputes led Gómez to withdraw.

Welles and Kodar reworked the original script, whose first version, entitled *The Sacred Beasts* and set among the foreign bullfight enthusiasts in Spain, dated from 1962. The action unfolds over less than twenty-four hours. Hollywood director Hannaford (played by John Huston, who was nine years older than Welles), a former star-maker who has set up his cameras all over the world, has just spent a few unproductive years in Europe and is trying to make his big American comeback with an erotic tale, when he dies at the wheel of a car. Was it an accident or suicide? Flashback to the events of the previous day.

In the studio Hannaford uses a look-alike dummy to replace his male lead, who has walked off the set in the middle of a sex scene after being verbally taunted. The shoot has run over schedule and will soon run out of money. Then Hannaford and his crew go to a party at his house organized by a female star whom he directed in the late 1930s. All the media and the new generation that his friend wants him to meet have gathered to welcome the former exile. Long extracts from the work print of the film in progress are shown in the private projection room, then, due to a power cut, at a drive-in cinema. Hopes of finding the rest of the finance are further compromised when, at the same time, the young studio boss views a rough cut in the projection room and quickly realizes that the director is working without a script. At dawn Hannaford is drunk and, after leading a life of successful machismo, is feeling humiliated by his male star. He drives away – in the sports car he was hoping to offer his protégé as an end-of-film bonus – towards his meeting with death.

The overall conception of Welles's film is bound up with the difficult and fragmented conditions under which it was shot. Most of the images and sound of the party are intended to unify the heterogeneous, clumsy material produced by the journalists and guests who have been wandering round with cameras in their hands for hours, shooting away in different formats (television news report cameras, amateur Super 8, 16 mm and Super 16 cameras, in both colour and black and white) or taking still photographs and making sound recordings. This great range of supposed sources makes for an edit that is more fragmented than ever before. The extracts from Hannaford's 35 mm film that are seen, shot with a camera on a tripod, have a rhythm that is as slow as that of the film around them is fast. Hannaford's new style is insistent and pretentiously symbolic, reminiscent of some American disciple of Antonioni and European art cinema. As the reels go by two young people (Kodar and the television actor Bob Random) pursue each other through a deserted modern city, then through the courtyard of an abandoned film studio. As they never open their mouths, the sound of the framing story is allowed to overflow over Hannaford's images.

Welles dissolves his own visual style into a double pastiche of reportage and of Hannaford. Meanwhile, the power cut during the party conceals the sparseness of the set.

Over the years Welles filmed at his homes in Los Angeles and Orvilliers, in other European countries, in a house perched on a rock face in the Arizona desert (close by the house that acts as a metaphor for the consumer society at the end of Antonioni's *Zabriskie Point*), in the Hollywood villa of his friend Peter Bogdanovich and also on modest studio sets. He asked a technician to rent the Arizona house on the pretext of a holiday and asked his crew to pretend to be film students when he was shooting in public places without authorization. In the early years he concentrated on the 'film within the film' and the multitude of secondary characters, then, early in 1974, confirmed Huston's engagement for a few weeks. Always willing to sacrifice swathes of footage, he would rework the plot according to the way the filming was going, and also following developments in his relationship with the industry or with members of his team.

Welles counted on the love felt for him by a great many actors, and on the fascination felt by actors he did not know when they were offered the possibility of acting for him. Alongside *Falstaff, The Other Side of the Wind* is the film in relation to which actors have spoken of their director in tones of the greatest wonder and devotion. Welles explored every avenue to build up his cast: people he had worked with at the Mercury Theatre or on his first films (Richard Wilson, Paul Stewart, Edmond O'Brien, Benny Rubin, Norman Foster) and Mercedes McCambridge who played the old guard of the Hannaford clan undermined by the new Hollywood. Young filmmakers such as Claude Chabrol, Curtis Harrington, Dennis Hopper, Henry Jaglom and Paul Mazursky play themselves. Bogdanovich plays his fictional double, a fashionable director in pursuit of commercial success and admirer of Hannaford, with whom he is trying to write a book of conversations and whom he is seeking to draw back into the industry. The crew members appear in front of the camera, as does a twenty-two-year-old critic, Joseph McBride, who asked for an interview for his book on the director a few days before shooting started. Welles welcomed anyone that his supporters would bring with them. The old hands simply got on with helping the young actors who turned up. Some roles that had been partially filmed changed hands along the way. Welles had to find ways of dealing with the ageing or death of his actors.

Welles wrote numerous versions of the script and constantly changed the dialogue, moving lines from one character to another. In particular, he got his actors to improvise, basing the scenes on situations that he had thought about for years. Mazursky, a former cabaret comic famous for his improvisational ability, arrived on set after being contacted that day, only to discover that he would be working with Jaglom, with whom he had a difficult relationship. Filmed by two cameras and generously plied with alcohol by Welles, the two spent three hours competing to see who could produce more contradictory judgements of Hannaford. Mazursky later learned that the scene had been reduced to ten minutes. In the edited version known today only one minute remains.

Welles supervised the lighting very closely, or reworked it after Graver had done the basic set-up, and often held one of the cameras himself. Everyone, right down to the French producer Dominique Antoine and people just visiting for the day, took a turn on the lights, coloured filters and reflectors made from silver foil.

Previous pages, left:
Filming *Moby Dick*.

Right:
Filming at home. Oja Kodar as the former opera singer in *The Dreamers* and Welles as an old storyteller in the black and white prologue.

Opposite page, top:
John Huston on the set of *The Other Side of the Wind*.

Bottom:
Pat McMahon, Benny Rubin and John Huston in a 16 mm shot from *The Other Side of the Wind*.

This page, top:
Shooting *The Other Side of the Wind* in Arizona.

Above:
Welles, Gary Graver, Peter Bogdanovich and Oja Kodar.

Below:
Welles, Oja Kodar, (unidentified), Peter Bogdanovich and Norman Foster.

Above and opposite page: The 'film within the film' from *The Other Side of the Wind*, with Bob Random, Oja Kodar and Robert Aiken.

Post-production began in California and was then interrupted to allow Welles to cut *F for Fake*, before continuing in Paris in 1973 once the co-production deal had been settled with Astrophore. The first task was to make an inventory of the abundant material and to organize it. The three editing machines of *The Trial* and *Falstaff* and the four of *Orson's Bag* now became five, arranged in a semicircle, at which five editing assistants worked simultaneously while Welles moved from one to the next, marking out his orders, which were then implemented. Yves Deschamps, officially the chief editor, described himself simply as the chief assistant at the head of a swarm of assistants, since the director kept the content of the plot to himself. Welles put off choices as long as possible: he started by sticking together all the usable takes of a shot, then gradually whittled the selection down until he reached the heart of the sequence, knitting fragments of shots together. During the editing in Paris, which had to be interrupted in order to film with Huston, the different stages of the creative process began to merge. Welles was rewriting the script while also editing in order to shoot new elements to enhance the scenes. In Orvilliers, Los Angeles and Arizona he would write, film and edit in the same house.

In 1974 Welles and Deschamps established the sequences of Hannaford's film. Things started to go wrong when Welles began to suspect his editor of reconstructing dramatic continuity and to perceive him as the producers' ally rather than his own. Welles retreated to Orvilliers and continued working, while the assistant editors became just couriers, shuttling back and forth between the cutting room and the laboratory. Then, fearing that Astrophore might confiscate the film to have it finished by someone else, one night Welles took the print and all the film positives out of France without the producers' knowledge. Once relations had been restored he began work once more in Paris and, for a few weeks, in Rome, with his editor from *F for Fake*, Marie-Sophie Dubus. He honed a twenty-minute section with a sound mix in order to show part of it during the special evening saluting his work at the American Film Institute in February 1975, where he hoped to find financial support. It is a version created for demonstration purposes (a scene shown all of a piece was to have been intercut by others), to be revised according to the development of a project on which shooting continued intermittently over several months. Welles stayed in the United States and asked Dubus to join him. When she refused, he approached at least two American editors. Astrophore was affected by the political tensions in Iran and ceased production in 1976. When the film fell victim to a legal entanglement following the fall of the Shah three years later, a few scenes still remained to be filmed. The editing was still largely at the rough-cut stage, often including several takes per shot. The foreseeable complications caused potential backers to shy away. And when the legal judgement finally went in Welles's favour, it stipulated that he had to cut *The Other Side of the Wind* in France, a condition that had by then become unfeasible.

THE IMPOSSIBILITY OF FINISHING

For those trying posthumously to shape *The Other Side of the Wind* and other, more minor, unfinished works into versions that could be presented to the public, the first problem would be to disentangle often inextricable legal and financial situations. Secondly, the visual material and sound, which is scattered through several different countries, will have to be identified and collected in one place. Then there is the problem of the co-existence of different versions of both isolated scenes and long sections, which had been edited in parallel by Welles and were mutually incompatible.

However, the greatest obstacle lay elsewhere. In his later period Welles made the editing stage the crucial phase of his creative process. His liking for fragmented cutting and rejection of the literal synchronization of dialogue and sound make it impossible to imagine how he might have linked pieces of film between which no link is apparent, inserted dialogue that he would rewrite during post-synchronization, or mixed atmosphere, sound effects and music that had never been recorded. No finished version, however scrupulously made, can ever offer more than a distant approximation of a vision that we can know only in fragments.

F for Fake and *Filming Othello* eloquently prove the efficacy of Welles's late working methods, in situations where he was able to complete the last details. In other cases he did all he could to ensure that no one could finish his projects without him, preferring the risk of incompletion to that of completion by someone else.

F FOR FAKE & FILMING OTHELLO

A small-scale commission accepted at a time when all Welles's big projects had ground to a halt, *F for Fake* looked as though it would be no more than a minor addition to the director's filmography. A sequence of chance events led him to transform the project completely. Freely reworking material from diverse origins, Welles reduced the role of his collaborators still further to the status of simple underlings as he turned the cutting room into the site of the film's true creation. In so doing, he reinvented the notion of the 'essay film', which he would further explore with the television piece *Filming Othello*. In this he describes the sleights of hand of his *Othello* of 1952, while simultaneously weaving new illusions. With his last two works to be shown to the public, Welles first set out his art of poetry then his discourse on method.

Previous pages:
Oja Kodar in *F for Fake*.

Opposite page:
Gary Graver (as all-powerful host) and Oja Kodar in the original trailer made by Welles for the American distributor of *F for Fake*. It was never used due to its unusual length.

'F FOR FAKE': FROM FORGER TO FORGERY

F for Fake was born out of Welles's meeting with French documentary-maker François Reichenbach. Reichenbach had interviewed Welles in 1965, when he was playing the Swedish Consul Nordling in René Clément's *Is Paris Burning?*. Three years later Reichenbach joined forces with Frédéric Rossif to make a half-hour television portrait of Welles, during the shooting of *The Immortal Story*. The two men got to know and like each other, and in the late 1960s Welles would often rub shoulders with Reichenbach in the cutting rooms of Antégor. This small Paris company was particularly well-equipped to make the compilation films with which Rossif, one of its founders and owners, had made his reputation. It was also a place of intense intellectual ferment, which, from May 1968 onwards, generously opened its doors to political filmmakers who used its facilities to put together many of the films made during that period. By the time Welles arrived there, Antégor had become a nerve centre for independent documentary-makers and talented young technicians looking for something out of the ordinary.

It was probably at Antégor that Welles discovered a documentary of around forty minutes, *Elmyr: The True Picture?*, produced and directed by Reichenbach and the American journalist Richard Drewett and broadcast by the BBC on 30 May 1970. The main character was a brilliant forger, Elmyr de Hory, whom Reichenbach had filmed on the Spanish island of Ibiza in 1968, shortly after he had finished a short term in prison. In the documentary Hory talks to Clifford Irving, another of the island's inhabitants, relating the elements that later provided the basis for Irving's highly romanticized biography of Hory, *Fake!*, which was published the following year.

Reichenbach wanted Welles to do the voiceover for the film. Welles declined, but, fascinated by the material, suggested reworking it in his own way. In 1971 Welles and Reichenbach agreed that the latter's production company, Les Films du Prisme, would finance a half-hour programme about Hory, directed by Welles and based on the hour of rushes that Reichenbach had not used.

Left, from top:
Oja Kodar and Laurence Harvey, taken from one of Welles's old home movies.

Editing turns Picasso into a voyeur spying on Oja Kodar.

Opposite page:
Oja Kodar waves to the camera in the real Gare d'Austerlitz in Paris (left), but Welles is photographed in Spain where he pretends to be outside Howard Hughes's hotel in Las Vegas (right).

Welles started work with an editor, supplementing the footage already shot with new scenes filmed with Hory in Ibiza, and others, shot in a Paris restaurant, where he discussed the forger's personality with his producer. However, Welles seemed unsatisfied with the result and radically reoriented the enterprise when the affair of the fake biography of Howard Hughes broke early in 1972. A brilliant con man had managed to sell the so-called memoirs of the most secretive of all millionaires to a prestigious American publisher for an advance of $750,000. The forger was none other than Hory's neighbour and biographer, Clifford Irving. Now the material already assembled featured not one but two forgers, since Irving appeared several times and indeed professed, with disarming sincerity, his total confidence in Hory's honesty. Welles went back to work assisted by a new editor, Marie-Sophie Dubus, to make a ninety-minute feature whose subject was now the very notion of forgery in the creative process.

INTERWOVEN SUBJECTS

For the first time in a feature film, Welles was not telling a story. He unfolds not a plot but an abstract subject, very difficult to formulate in words, which starts from the notion of falsification and branches out to touch on sometimes distantly-related subjects. To the extent that the script has a structure, it is rhizomatic, like tubers that multiply underground throwing up shoots, no one being more important than any other.

The underlying thread of the script is the magician's power over the credulous mind and its corollary – the desire to believe in the improbable. The visible expressions of this in the film include both the true stories of Hory and Irving and Welles's own mystifications, such as getting himself hired by a Dublin theatre when he was only sixteen or terrorizing America by making it believe that the Martians had invaded Earth. Then there is Hughes's invention of his own legend and the illusionist (Welles again) who turns keys into coins, shuts his partner in a suitcase and makes bodies levitate. Last comes the two-part fake story of the real Oja Kodar, in which first Kodar bewitches Picasso so that he gives her twenty-two new paintings, which are destroyed and replaced by brilliant fakes, regarded by posterity as the representation of a previously unknown period of the ageing artist's work. All these stories and situations are inextricably intertwined according to an order decreed by Welles alone, in the role of supreme magician who sets all these illusions in motion.

DISPARATE MATERIAL

The material from which *F for Fake* is made can be split into four categories, depending on whether the images were specifically shot for the film or not, and whether or not they were directed by Welles. The first group, that of existing images filmed by other people, includes all the material filmed by Reichenbach in 1968, archive documents on Hughes and clips from an American science-fiction film *Earth vs. the Flying Saucers* (1956).

Welles also drew on the store of images that he himself had accumulated over the years. The most notable example is the magic trick in which he compresses Kodar to make her fit into a suitcase. His private store of images also provides Kodar's meeting with the actor Laurence Harvey, her co-star in *The Deep*, at Orly airport, and shots of passers-by filmed in Italy and Yugoslavia.

Images specially shot for the film by Welles include firstly his own supplements to the Ibiza interview with Hory and his discussion with Reichenbach in the La Méditerranée restaurant. Filmed before the project's change of orientation, these are very similar to the initial documentary material. The same cannot be said of the new scenes, filmed by three different cameramen, which are much more elaborately staged. Some were filmed in Paris, on the platform of the Gare d'Austerlitz, in the Champ-de-Mars and a cutting room at Antégor; others in Welles's house at Orvilliers, in Chartres and in a small Normandy village; others in Spain, while Welles was there playing Long John Silver in yet another adaptation of *Treasure Island*. For these scenes Welles abandoned documentary-style 16 mm for the far more subtle qualities of 35 mm, but made extensive use of the zoom, as Reichenbach had previously done, thereby helping to give the whole a stylistic unity.

To complete the film Welles commissioned his contacts in the United States, and particularly his cameraman Gary Graver, to shoot scenes whose place in the film he had precisely planned. These were short interviews with former members of the Mercury Theatre – Joseph Cotten, Paul Stewart and Richard Wilson – and shots of bungalows, apartment blocks and urban landscapes to illustrate the story of Hughes. Added to these were still photographs, press cuttings and similarly heterogeneous sound elements. The declamatory voiceover of a fake newsreel about Hughes was specially commissioned from William Alland, who had recorded the narration of 'News on the March' for *Citizen Kane*, from which this ironic pastiche borrowed both its style and its title.

A FILM CREATED IN THE CUTTING ROOM

During the year that it took him to cut his feature, Welles more or less lived at Antégor. At five in the morning he had the cleaner open up for him and waited there, writing his scripts or reading, until Dubus arrived at nine. From then on they worked continuously, seven days a week, often until eleven at night. The editing was done on a German Kem machine, which Welles explored with all the enthusiasm of a child with a new toy. It ran at three speeds, up to eight times normal speed, could take both 16 mm and 35 mm, and its five modules, each of which could be disconnected, made it possible to view three image tracks and two sound tracks either simultaneously or separately. Welles would sit behind the editor, telling her where to cut, without even giving her time to take notes, then leave her to carry out his orders while he got on with something else.

For the first time he built up his film entirely in the cutting room. As the film gradually took shape, Welles would take one scene as a basis on which to imagine another, which he would then interrupt the editing to film, unless he commissioned it from his cameramen or took the shots from an existing document. The sounds and images he assembled in this way were simply raw material, which Welles was always ready to transform. He accelerated some shots, slowed others down, froze images or had part of a shot enlarged by the laboratory to make it look like a different shot in the edit. And, as in Dziga Vertov's *Man with a Movie Camera*, which is the most obvious model for part of the film, the same images sometimes appear full-screen, sometimes refilmed on the screen of an editing machine, often without any break in the continuity of their projection. It is the same for the soundtrack: Welles laid new sound effects over the footage he borrowed from *Earth vs. the Flying Saucers* and himself insidiously dubbed Cotten in the middle of a line to make him say something that had proved to be missing from the brief interview filmed in California by Graver. He also fabricated a version of his radio programme *The War of the Worlds.* Even changed in this way, the sounds and images seem little more than fragments of a mosaic that has yet to be put together. Welles set about this with a skill in making connections that also reflects his prodigious visual and aural memory. For example, he linked Kodar's meeting with Harvey at Orly to the trick where he himself shuts Kodar into a suitcase, almost certainly shot several years earlier, using Harvey's goodbye wave which, judiciously edited, becomes an attempt to catch Kodar's shoe that Welles throws out of shot in the other scene.

The peak of this manipulation by editing, which enabled him to make shots say something quite different from their initial meaning, is reached in the astounding conclusion to the episode devoted to Hory and Irving. Irving is interviewed at his house and Hory seems to be answering him from his own home, but in fact these shots were all filmed on different occasions, as proved by the variations in the two men's clothing. Their manufactured exchange of glances lasts only about fifty seconds, but comprises nineteen shots for only six short lines of dialogue. First come five denials from Hory, who insists that he never signed any of the fakes, apparently in ever angrier, more pathetic response to the shots of the silently incredulous Irving. A variation is introduced when Welles links a shot showing Irving looking out of the frame towards a (real? fake?) drawing by Modigliani, at the bottom of which the artist's signature can clearly be seen. Then, like a truth too long held back, comes Irving's only speech – 'Of course they were signed' – followed by a shot of Hory reduced to silence, obstinately wrapped in his certainty.

Welles was the first to say that his entire film was just a fake, like the above sequence, which invents an exchange that never took place and is perhaps all the more real for that. So can one talk about truth in art if everything can be counterfeited in this way? Welles believed one could, but this is not the truth of a signature but the truth of the work itself. And this idea, which he holds dear, leads him to introduce a moment of calm meditation, marking a complete stylistic break with the rest of the film. He places this not at the end but two thirds of the way through, before starting the story of Kodar and Picasso. It is just two and a half minutes of footage of Chartres cathedral, bathed in a soft light – the light of the 'magic hour' that Welles liked so much, of the separation between night and day. There are far more superimposed images here than anywhere else in the film and Welles, himself filmed in the gardens of the Champ-de-Mars, sets out his credo as an artist: his faith in the eternity of the work of art, his unchanging wonder at this product of thousands of anonymous craftsmen and his personal belief that 'Maybe a man's name doesn't matter that much...'.

'FILMING OTHELLO': SELF-PORTRAIT IN THE MIRROR

F for Fake is the director's art of poetry and also his first complete experiment in inventing a new form of cinematographic essay, combining the discipline of the montage film with a refusal to abandon fiction altogether. A commission from German television gave Welles the means to make a second 'essay film', which was also to be the last of his works to be shown to the public.

The ARD (German public television) asked him, almost certainly early in 1974, to provide a filmed presentation to precede a broadcast of his *Othello.* The financial proposal was generous and Welles responded by shooting in the United States, while he was also filming *The Other Side of the Wind.* The result is an introduction of about twenty minutes in which, out of a concern for the picturesque rather than historical truth, he relates the turbulent circumstances of the shooting of his film of 1952. He is seen seated behind a book-laden table or in an armchair addressing the viewer in a conversational tone. The shots, filmed with a single camera, are long and almost all static, occasionally enlivened by a zoom-in.

Unsatisfied with the result, Welles decided not to send it to ARD as planned and managed to persuade the German producers Klaus and Jürgen Hellwig to fund a more ambitious project, conceived along similar lines to *F for Fake.* His idea was once again to combine filmed material of diverse origins to discuss not only his own cinematographic version of *Othello*, but also the diversity of possible interpretations of Shakespeare's play. In addition to the twenty minutes or so initially filmed, the eighty-five-minute piece, which he took almost four years to make, includes a long discussion with Micheál Mac Liammóir and Hilton Edwards, the actors who played Iago and Brabantio in the film, a discussion with the audience following a screening of Welles's *Othello* at the University of Boston and many extracts from the film itself. The whole is linked by Welles's commentary, which is staged at an editing machine, and by his performance, in the same surroundings, of two long extracts from the play. Other images, according to Graver, who filmed them in Venice, were to show the authentic Italian exteriors used at the time. There is no trace of these in the final version of the film.

After the pyrotechnics of *F for Fake*, *Filming Othello* seems very restrained. Rather than being intertwined, the three main sections are juxtaposed: first comes Welles's monologue on the filming of *Othello*, then his discussion with Mac Liammóir and Edwards, and lastly his performance of the two extracts from the play, followed by the discussion with the Boston audience. But the illusionist's art remains intact, apparent primarily in the way that Welles manipulates the material filmed in Paris during the summer of 1974 with his actor friends. The camera seems to have been focused entirely on them, as though Welles, true to a long-standing habit, already knew that he would have all the time he needed to film his own shots later. And this is what he does – in a minimalist setting (a table with tablecloth and two bottles) that shows little concern for credible continuity – allowing himself to interrupt his colleagues peremptorily with a long monologue or giving their words more weight just by showing the attention he is paying them. The most work had to be done on the sound in order to achieve the continuity of lines recorded months apart.

Equally impressive is the manipulation of the original film, from which all the so-called quotations have in fact been radically reshaped. The process is apparent from the prologue which, just like *Othello*, opens *Filming Othello* with the funeral procession for the bodies of Othello, Desdemona and Emilia and with Iago's punishment. But what takes a little over four minutes and thirty-eight shots in the original here requires only a minute and a half and twenty-six shots. Meanwhile the musical accompaniment to the scene has been discreetly recomposed using fragments from the original soundtrack. No subsequent quotation is untouched, not only because Welles systematically removes the sound to leave room for his own commentary, but because his new edit consists of shots taken from the whole of the film, which he often shortens and freely reorganizes so that they become no more than illustrations of his comments. To borrow fragments from a work to evoke its essence and not to illustrate its physical reality is, indeed, a bold move.

In late summer 1977 Welles chose to have himself filmed at his editing machine, as he had done in *F for Fake*, to record words that are no longer those of the famous presenter, but those of the artist reflecting on his own creative work. At the very beginning of the film it is the editing machine that Welles chooses to introduce, even before he talks about *Othello* or Shakespeare: 'Here films are salvaged, saved sometimes from disaster, or savaged out of existence. This is the last stop on the long road between the dream in a filmmaker's head and the public to whom that dream is addressed.' And, at the end, it is the light of this same editing machine that Welles first extinguishes, before returning to his role as presenter to wish the viewer a good night. He then exits the frame, leaving the camera to linger over this machine on which so many dreams have taken shape. Filmmakers come and go. Cinema lives on.

Micheál Mac Liammóir and Hilton Edwards in Paris, and Welles in Los Angeles three years later, come together around the same table in a final show of trickery.

BIOGRAPHY 1915—1985

6 May 1915: George Orson Welles is born in Kenosha (Wisconsin). His mother Beatrice and father Richard were married in 1903 and the following year had their first son, Richard, who dies in 1975.

1918: the Welles family moves to Chicago.

1919: Welles's parents separate.

10 May 1924: Welles's mother dies at forty-three.

1926: Welles enters the Todd School for Boys in Woodstock (Illinois), where he stages many amateur productions. His talents are encouraged by one of the teachers, Roger Hill, who is also the headmaster's son.

6 July 1928: first article published (an opera review) in the *Highland Park News.*

28 December 1930: Welles's father dies at fifty-eight. Dr Maurice Bernstein becomes Welles's guardian.

June 1931: Welles finishes secondary school and soon enrols at the Chicago Art Institute.

August 1931: Welles travels to Ireland to paint.

13 October 1931: first professional acting role in *Jew Süss*, after the novel by Lion Feuchtwanger, at the Gate Theatre, Dublin, where he appears in other plays.

Summer 1932: writes the plays *Marching Song* (with Roger Hill) and *Bright Lucifer.*

May 1933: makes amateur film of his staging of *Twelfth Night* at the Todd School.

29 November 1933: first professional acting work in the United States, in plays toured by Katharine Cornell's theatre company.

1934: publication of *Everybody's Shakespeare*, edition of *The Merchant of Venice*, *Julius Caesar* and *Twelfth Night*, established, prefaced and illustrated by Roger Hill and Welles.

12 July 1934: launch of the Woodstock Summer Festival directed by Welles, where he stages *Trilby*, after the novel by George du Maurier.

July 1934: films the amateur short *The Hearts of Age* in Woodstock.

14 November 1934: secret marriage to Virginia Nicolson in New York (ceremony 21 December).

20 December 1934: first professional role on Broadway, in Katharine Cornell's production of *Romeo and Juliet.*

15 March 1935: first professional leading role in the theatre, in *Panic* by Archibald MacLeish.

22 March 1935: first confirmed participation in the radio show *The March of Time*, on which he worked for three years. Performs in many other shows.

14 April 1936: first job as professional theatre director, for *Macbeth* at the Federal Theatre, where he also puts on two other productions.

23 October 1936: last appearance in a theatrical production that he has not staged himself, *Ten Million Ghosts* by Sidney Kingsley.

16 June 1937: independent staging of Marc Blitzstein's opera *The Cradle Will Rock*, produced by the Federal Theatre, but a victim of last-minute censorship.

23 July 1937: first work as a radio director with a seven-part adaptation of Victor Hugo's *Les Misérables.*

August 1937: founds the Mercury Theatre with John Houseman.

26 September 1937: first appears in *The Shadow*, a very popular radio show in which he plays the lead role for over a year.

11 November 1937: *Julius Caesar* is the Mercury Theatre's first production. Five others follow.

1 March 1938: records long extracts from *Julius Caesar* for Columbia Records with actors from the Mercury Theatre. Over the next two years he records longer versions of *Twelfth Night*, *The Merchant of Venice*, *Julius Caesar* and *Macbeth.*

11 March 1938: first participates in a round table political discussion. Many public appearances follow until 1946.

27 March 1938: birth of Christopher, daughter of Welles and Virginia Nicolson, in New York.

11 July 1938: launch of his first weekly radio show, *The Mercury Theatre on the Air* (twenty-two broadcasts).

30 October 1938: radio adaptation of H.G. Wells's *The War of the Worlds* for *The Mercury Theatre on the Air* causes panic in the United States.

9 December 1938: launch of the radio show *The Campbell Playhouse* (fifty-six weekly broadcasts).

8 June 1939: appears on tour in an abridged version of William Archer's *The Green Goddess* for the RKO Orpheum vaudeville circuit.

21 July 1939: contract with RKO, for whom he is to produce, write and direct two feature films.

November 1939: first tests for *Heart of Darkness*, a project abandoned the following year.

1 February 1940: divorces Virginia Nicolson.

1 April 1940: starts his first lecture tour.

30 July 1940: filming officially begins on *Citizen Kane.*

24 March 1941: stages the play *Native Son*, after the novel by Richard Wright, in New York.

1 May 1941: release of *Citizen Kane.*

3 September 1941: appears as a magician at the Sacramento Fair. He continues to work as a magician occasionally throughout his career.

15 September 1941: launch of the radio show *The Lady Esther Show* (nineteen weekly broadcasts).

25 September 1941: filming begins in Mexico for *My Friend Bonito*, a section of the film *It's All True*, which Welles asks Norman Foster to direct.

28 October 1941: filming begins on *The Magnificent Ambersons.*

6 January 1942: filming starts on *Journey into Fear*, which Welles asks Foster to direct.

14 February 1942: filming of the carnival episode of *It's All True* begins in Rio de Janeiro. Filming on the following episode, *Jangadeiros*, continues in Brazil until the end of July.

28 June 1942: RKO breaks with Mercury Productions.

9 and 15 November 1942: launch of two weekly radio shows, *Ceiling Unlimited* (thirteen broadcasts) and *Hello, Americans* (twelve broadcasts).

December 1942: Welles acts for the first time in a film that he has not directed, Robert Stevenson's *Jane Eyre.*

3 August 1943: premiere of *The Mercury Wonder Show*, a magic show to entertain American troops, in Los Angeles.

7 September 1943: Welles marries Rita Hayworth in Santa Monica (California).

October 1943: publishes the first of a dozen articles in the magazine *Free World.*

26 January 1944: launch of the radio show *The Orson Welles Almanac* (twenty-six weekly broadcasts).

23 August 1944: begins recording the *Song of Songs* for Decca. This is followed by other recordings for the same company.

1 September 1944: the first of about ten speeches campaigning for the re-election of Franklin D. Roosevelt.

17 December 1944: birth of Rebecca, daughter of Welles and Rita Hayworth, in Los Angeles. She dies in 2004.

22 January 1945: first article of a daily column in the *The New York Post*, which continues until June. On the same day, begins a tour of anti-fascist lectures.

13 March 1945: launch of the radio show *This Is My Best* (seven weekly broadcasts).

16 September 1945: launch of the radio show *Orson Welles Commentaries* (fifty-one weekly broadcasts).

Autumn 1945: filming of *The Stranger.*

27 April 1946: start of try-out tour for *Around the World*, a musical comedy by Welles (adaptation) and Cole Porter (lyrics and music), after Jules Verne.

7 June 1946: launch of the radio show *The Mercury Summer Theatre of the Air* (fifteen weekly broadcasts).

2 October 1946: filming begins on *The Lady from Shanghai.*

16 October 1946: last political lecture in the United States. Welles makes few public speeches after this.

7 May 1947: release of King Vidor's *Duel in the Sun*, the first film in which Welles is credited as narrator.

28 May 1947: the first of six exceptional performances of *Macbeth* in Salt Lake City as part of the Utah Centennial Festival.

23 June 1947: filming begins on *Macbeth.*

November 1947: goes to Italy to act in *Cagliostro* by Gregory Ratoff, his last lead role in a film he does not direct. Spends most of the next eight years in Europe.

18 November 1948: Welles's first day's filming on Carol Reed's *The Third Man.*

1 December 1948: divorces Rita Hayworth.

19 June 1949: shooting begins on *Othello* in Morocco. Filming also carried out in Italy.

19 June 1950: staging in Paris of *The Blessed and the Damned*, an English-language production bringing together two plays by Welles.

7 August 1950: touring the show *An Evening with Orson Welles* in Germany and then in Brussels.

3 August 1951: launch of the British radio show *The Lives of Harry Lime*, in which he takes the leading role (fifty-two weekly broadcasts).

1 October 1951: first performance of *Othello* in Newcastle. It later transfers to London.

1 January 1952: launch of the British radio show *The Black Museum*, which Welles narrates (fifty-two weekly broadcasts).

June 1952: publication of the French versions of his plays *The Unthinking Lobster* (first part of *The Blessed and the Damned* in 1950) and *Fair Warning* (never performed).

January 1953: filming begins on Steno's *L'uomo, la bestia, la virtú* (*Man, Beast and Virtue*) the first non-English language film in which he performs.

8 June 1953: publication of the first novel Welles put his name to, *Une grosse légume*, in Paris.

7 September 1953: premiere in London of the ballet *The Lady in the Ice*, based on a libretto by Welles, with music by Jean-Michel Damase and choreography by Roland Petit.

18 October 1953: plays the lead role in *King Lear*, directed by Peter Brook for American television and performed live.

January 1954: shooting begins in Spain on *Mr Arkadin.*

14 January 1955: first appearance as a personality on a television show in *Press Conference* for the BBC.

March 1955: filming in Vienna of one of the documentaries for *Around the World with Orson Welles* for the British television network ITV. Continues filming other shows until September.

24 April 1955: broadcast of the first of the series of six talks *Orson Welles' Sketch Book* for the BBC.

8 May 1955: marries Paola Mori, the female lead in *Mr Arkadin*, in London.

16 June 1955: premiere in London of his play *Moby Dick – Rehearsed.* In July – August films an unfinished adaptation of the play for American television.

October 1955: returns to the United States.

13 November 1955: birth of Beatrice, daughter of Welles and Paola Mori, in New York.

12 January 1956: first performance in New York of *King Lear.*

March – April 1956: performs in a Las Vegas hotel with a routine combining Shakespeare with conjuring.

8 May 1956: filming begins on the television piece *The Fountain of Youth*, pilot for a show that does not find a buyer.

14 June 1956: filming begins on an episode of *I Love Lucy*, the first television series in which he appears as a guest star.

18 February 1957: filming begins on *Touch of Evil.*

25 July 1957: self-financed filming of *Don Quixote* begins in Mexico.

January 1958: returns to Europe, where he spends most of the next twelve years.

1959: filming begins again in Italy on *Don Quixote*, continuing sporadically in Italy and Spain until 1966.

13 February 1960: first performance in Belfast of *Chimes at Midnight*, an amalgam of *Henry IV* and other Shakespeare plays, which transfers to Dublin.

28 April 1960: first performance in London of Eugène Ionesco's *Rhinocéros*, the last play Welles directs.

April 1961: filming begins on *Nella terra di don Chisciotte*, a series of nine shows for Italian television.

26 March 1962: filming begins on *The Trial* in France and Yugoslavia.

12 October 1964: filming on *Falstaff* begins in Spain.

21 September 1966: filming begins on *The Immortal Story* in France and Spain.

14 April 1967: filming of *The Heroine* in Hungary abandoned after one day. The main character was to have been played by Olga Palinkas (Oja Kodar), who remained Welles's partner until his death.

14 September 1967: first appearance on Dean Martin's talk show in the United States.

October 1967: filming begins off the Croatian coast on *Dead Reckoning* (future *The Deep*), which remains unfinished.

1968: filming begins on the unfinished television show *Orson's Bag.*

Late 1968: starts working with Peter Bogdanovich on a book of conversations that subsequently appears in 1992 with the title *This Is Orson Welles.*

Spring 1970: moves to Los Angeles, while returning frequently to Europe in the following years.

August 1970: filming begins in Los Angeles on the unfinished feature *The Other Side of the Wind*, which continues in the United States and in Europe until 1975.

1971: starts work in France on a short television show, which later becomes the feature film *F for Fake.*

June 1971: unfinished filming of a version of *Moby Dick* in France.

January 1974: settles permanently in the United States.

1974: commissioned by German television to make a short filmed introduction, which becomes the television piece *Filming Othello.*

June 1976: filming begins on the unfinished television programme *The Magic Show.*

7 September 1978: filming begins on *The Orson Welles Show*, a talk-show pilot which no television network buys.

26 April 1980: filming begins on a few scenes of *The Dreamers* and continues intermittently in the following years.

10 October 1985: Welles dies.

FILMOGRAPHY

This filmography of Orson Welles as a director contains a great deal of new information, but gives only the main credits for each film or television piece. We have sought to identify those who genuinely carried out the functions mentioned, without necessarily reproducing the original credits, which are not always trustworthy. In the case of films whose production extended over several years, the photography, sound recording, editing and production were often carried out by a series of different people, whose role cannot always be established.

Secondary characters whose names are not used in Welles's Shakespeare films appear here with the names they have in the original plays.

Release and broadcast dates are given for the countries of production, as well as for the countries of first release or broadcast, if different. In the United States release dates differ from one city to the next and so, sometimes, from one source to the next.

Titles in categories at the end of the filmography – such as occasional film fragments, amateur shorts and rough sketches – remain at the margins of Welles's film and television oeuvre, although they have gained a degree of legitimacy since his death.

* Actors marked with an asterisk have been partially or wholly dubbed by the voice of Welles.

COMPLETED FEATURE FILMS: CITIZEN KANE

1941. USA. 35 mm, black and white. *Production and direction*: Orson Welles. *Original screenplay*: Herman G. Mankiewicz, Orson Welles. *Director of photography*: Gregg Toland. *Camera operator*: Bert Shipman. *Production design*: Perry Ferguson. *Set decoration*: Al Fields. *Costumes*: Edward Stevenson. *Assistant directors*: Edward Donahoe, Fred A. Fleck. *Script supervisor*: Amalia Kent. *Choreographer*: Arthur Appel. *Sound recording*: Hugh McDowell, Bailey Fesler. *Sound effects*: Harry Essman. *Editor*: Robert Wise. *Special effects*: Vernon L. Walker. *Dubbing mixer*: James G. Stewart. *Original score and musical direction*: Bernard Herrmann. *Additional arrangements*: Conrad Salinger, Nathaniel Shilkret, Roy Webb. *Production company*: Mercury Productions for RKO Radio Pictures. *Cast*: Orson Welles (Charles Foster Kane), Joseph Cotten (Jedediah Leland), Everett Sloane (Bernstein), Dorothy Comingore [singing dubbed by Jean Forward] (Susan Alexander Kane), George Coulouris (Walter Parks Thatcher), Ruth Warrick (Emily Monroe Norton Kane), Ray Collins ('Boss' Jim W. Gettys), William Alland (Jerry Thompson), Agnes Moorehead (Mary Kane), Erskine Sanford (Herbert Carter), Paul Stewart (Raymond), Harry Shannon (Jim Kane), Fortunio Bonanova (Matiste), Buddy Swan (Charles Foster Kane aged 8), Philip Van Zandt (Rawlston), Gus Schilling (John, head waiter at El Rancho), Georgia Backus (Miss Anderson, curator of the Thatcher Memorial Library), Sonny Bupp (Kane's son). *Principal photography*: 30 July – 23 October 1940. *Running time*: 119 mins. *Released in USA*: 1 May 1941 (RKO Radio Pictures).

THE MAGNIFICENT AMBERSONS

1942. USA. 35 mm, black and white. *Production, screenplay and direction*: Orson Welles, based on the novel by Booth Tarkington (1918). *Directors of photography*: Stanley Cortez, Harry J. Wild. *Camera operator*: James Daly. *Production design*: Mark-Lee Kirk. *Set decoration*: Al Fields. *Costumes*: Edward Stevenson. *Assistant director*: Fred A. Fleck. *Script supervisor*: Amalia Kent. *Sound recording*: Bailey Fesler. *Editor*: Robert Wise. *Special effects*: Vernon L. Walker. *Dubbing mixer*: James G. Stewart. *Original score and musical direction*: Bernard Herrmann. *Additional music*: Roy Webb. *Production company*: Mercury Productions for RKO Radio Pictures. *Credits for refilming imposed by the studio*: *Direction*: Fred A. Fleck, Jack Moss. *Screenplay*: Joseph Cotten, Jack Moss. *Director of photography*: Nicholas Musuraca. *Assistant directors*: Harry Mancke, G. Rogers. *Sound recording*: Terry Kellum, Earl B. Mounce. *Cast*: Tim Holt (George Amberson Minafer), Anne Baxter (Lucy Morgan), Agnes Moorehead (Fanny Minafer), Joseph Cotten (Eugene Morgan), Dolores Costello (Isabel Amberson Minafer), Ray Collins (Jack Amberson), Richard Bennett (Major Amberson), Erskine Sanford (Roger W. Bronson), Don Dillaway (Wilbur Minafer), Dorothy Vaughan (Mrs Johnson), Bobby Cooper (George as a child), J. Louis Johnson (Sam, the butler), Drew Roddy (little enemy of George as a child), Gus Schilling (drugstore clerk), narrator (Orson Welles). *Principal photography*: 28 October 1941 – 22 January 1942. Running time: 88 mins. *Released in USA*: 10 July 1942 (RKO Radio Pictures).

JOURNEY INTO FEAR

1942. USA. 35 mm, black and white. *Direction*: Norman Foster. *Additional direction*: Orson Welles. *Screenplay*: Joseph Cotten, Orson Welles, based on the novel by Eric Ambler (1940). *Director of photography*: Karl Struss. *Camera operator*: George Clements. *Production design*: Mark-Lee Kirk. *Set decoration*: Ross Dowd. *Costumes*: Edward Stevenson. *Assistant director*: Dewey Starkey. *Sound recording*: Richard Van Hessen. *Editor*: Mark Robson. *Special effects*: Vernon L. Walker. *Dubbing mixer*: James G. Stewart. *Original score*: Roy Webb, conducted by Constantin Bakaleinikoff. *Producer*: Orson Welles. *Production company*: Mercury Productions for RKO Radio Pictures. *Cast*: Joseph Cotten (Howard Graham), Dolores Del Rio (Josette), Eustace Wyatt (Dr Moeller), Jack Moss (Peter Banat), Orson Welles (Colonel Haki), Ruth Warrick (Stephanie Graham), Everett Sloane (S. Kopeikin), Edgar Barrier (Kuvetli), Frank Readick (Mathews), Agnes Moorehead (Mrs Mathews), Jack Durant (Gogo Martel), Stefan Schnabel (purser), Richard Bennett (ship's captain), Frank Puglia (Colonel Haki's aide), Hans Conried (the magician), Robert Meltzer (the steward with the moustache). *Principal photography*: 6 January – 12 March 1942. *Running time*: 68 mins. *Released in USA*: 12 February 1943 (RKO Radio Pictures).

THE STRANGER

1946. USA. 35 mm, black and white. *Direction*: Orson Welles. *Screenplay*: John Huston, Anthony Veiller, Orson Welles, based on a story by Victor Trivas, adapted by Trivas and Decla Dunning. *Director of photography*: Russell Metty. *Camera operator*: John L. Russell. *Production design*: Perry Ferguson. *Set decoration*: Howard Bristol. *Costumes*: Michael Woulfe. *Assistant director*: Jack Voglin. *Script supervisor*: Kay Phillips. *Sound recording*: Arthur Johns. *Editor*: Ernest Nims. *Dubbing mixer*: Corson F. Jowett. *Original score*: Bronislaw Kaper, arranged by Harold Byrns and Sidney Cutner. *Producer*: S.P. Eagle [Sam Spiegel]. *Production company*: Haig Corporation for International Pictures. *Cast*: Loretta Young (Mary Longstreet Rankin), Edward G. Robinson (Inspector Wilson), Orson Welles (Franz Kindler / Charles Rankin), Billy House (Solomon Potter), Richard Long (Noah Longstreet), Konstantin Shayne (Konrad Meinike), Philip Merivale (Judge Adam Longstreet), Martha Wentworth (Sara), Byron Keith (Dr Jeffrey Lawrence), John Brown (the photographer, and the voice of the comedian on the radio), Erskine Sanford (Randall, a guest at the party). *Principal photography*: late September or early October – 21 November 1945. *Running time*: 95 mins. *Released in USA*: 2 July 1946 (RKO Radio Pictures, Independent Releasing Corp.).

THE LADY FROM SHANGHAI

1947. USA. 35 mm, black and white. *Production, screenplay and direction*: Orson Welles, based on *If I Die before I Wake* by Sherwood King (1938). *Director of photography*: Charles Lawton, Jr. *Additional photography*: Rudolph Maté, Joseph Walker. *Camera operator*: Irving Klein. *Production design*: Sturges Carné. *Set decoration*: Wilbur Menefee, Herman Schoenbrun. *Costumes*: Jean Louis. *Assistant director*: Sam Nelson. *Script supervisor*: Dorothy B. Cormack. *Sound recording*: Lodge Cunningham. *Editor*: Viola Lawrence. *Special effects*: Lawrence Butler. *Original score*:

Heinz Roemheld, arranged by Herschel Burke Gilbert, conducted by Morris W. Stoloff. *Song*: 'Please Don't Kiss Me' by Allan Roberts and Doris Fisher. *Production company*: Columbia Pictures. *Cast*: Orson Welles (Michael O'Hara), Rita Hayworth [singing dubbed by Anita Ellis] (Elsa Bannister), Everett Sloane (Arthur Bannister), Glenn Anders (George Grisby), Carl Frank (District Attorney Galloway), Erskine Sanford (the Judge), Ted De Corsia (Sidney Broome), Gus Schilling (Hiram Goldfish, a.k.a. Goldie), Louis Merrill (Jake Bejornson), Evelyn Ellis (Bessie), Wong Show Chong (Li), Joe Recht (parking attendant), Maynard Holmes (lorry driver), William Alland, Byron Kane (reporters at the trial), Richard Wilson (Fasbender, Galloway's assistant), and the players of the Mandarin Theatre, San Francisco. *Principal photography*: 2 October 1946 – 27 February 1947. *Running time*: 87 mins. *Released in USA*: 9 May 1948 (Columbia Pictures).

MACBETH

1947–1950. USA. 35 mm, black and white. *Screenplay and direction*: Orson Welles, based on the play by William Shakespeare (*c.*1606). *Director of photography*: John L. Russell (Second Unit: William Bradford). *Production design*: Fred Ritter. *Set decoration*: John McCarthy, Jr., James Redd. *Costumes*: Adele Palmer, Orson Welles. *Assistant director*: Jack Lacey. *Sound recording*: John Stransky, Jr., Gary Harris. *Editor*: Louis Lindsay. *Special effects*: Howard and Theodore Lydecker. *Original score*: Jacques Ibert, conducted by Efrem Kurtz. *Producers*: Charles K. Feldman, Orson Welles. *Production companies*: Literary Classics Productions and Mercury Productions for Republic Pictures. *Cast*: Orson Welles (Macbeth), Jeanette Nolan (Lady Macbeth), Dan O'Herlihy (Macduff), Alan Napier (Holy Father), Edgar Barrier (Banquo), Roddy McDowall (Malcolm), Peggy Webber (Lady Macduff and the voice of a witch), Erskine Sanford (Duncan), Brainerd Duffield (first murderer and a witch), William Alland (second murderer), Christopher Welles (Macduff's son), Morgan Farley (the doctor), Mary Gordon (lady in waiting at Lady Macbeth's sleepwalking scene), Keene Curtis (Lennox), John Dierkes (Ross), Lionel Braham* (Siward), George Chirello (Seyton), Gus Schilling* (the porter), Jerry Farber (Fleance), Lurene Tuttle (lady in waiting who discovers Lady Macbeth's suicide, and the voice of a witch), Archie Heugly (young Siward), Basil Tellou (Thane of Cawdor), Mary Brewer, Thais Wilson (witches), and the voice of Orson Welles (narrator in the 1950 version). *Principal photography*: 23 June – 17 July 1947. *Running time*: 107 mins (1948 version), 86 mins (1950 version). *First version released in USA*: 1 October 1948 (Republic Pictures). *Second version released in USA*: September 1950 (Republic Pictures).

THE TRAGEDY OF OTHELLO OR THE TRAGEDY OF OTHELLO, THE MOOR OF VENICE

1949–1952. Morocco. 35 mm, black and white. *Production, screenplay and direction*: Orson Welles, based on the play by William Shakespeare (*c.*1603). *Directors of photography*: Anchise Brizzi, G.R. Aldo, George Fanto. *Camera operators*: Alberto Fusi, Oberdan Troiani. *Production design*: Alexandre Trauner. *Costumes*: Maria De Matteis, Alexandre Trauner. *Assistant directors*: Michael Waszynski, Patrice Dally, Lee Kressel. *Script supervisor*: Renée Gouzy. *Sound recording*: Umberto Picistrelli. *Editors*: Louis Lindsay, Renzo Lucidi, Jean Sacha, John Shepridge, William Morton. *Original score*: Angelo Francesco Lavagnino, conducted by Willy Ferrero. *Production companies*: Mogador Films, Mercury. *Cast*: Orson Welles (Othello), Micheál Mac Liammóir* (Iago), Suzanne Cloutier (Desdemona), Fay Compton (Emilia), Robert Coote* (Roderigo), Michael Laurence* (Cassio), Hilton Edwards (Brabantio), Nicholas Bruce (Lodovico), Doris Dowling (Bianca), Jean Davis* (Montano), and the voice of Orson Welles (narrator). *Principal photography*: 19 June 1949 – 7 March 1950. *Running time*: 93 mins (*The Tragedy of Othello*, 1952), 90 mins (*The Tragedy of Othello, the Moor of Venice*, 1955). *Released in USA*: 13 September 1955 (United Artists). In 1992 the American company Intermission Productions replaced the music and sound effects of the 1955 version with new recordings and resynchronized the dialogue, modifying the diction electronically. This is the only version now legally in distribution.

MR ARKADIN OR CONFIDENTIAL REPORT

1954–1956. Spain. 35 mm, black and white. *Original screenplay and direction*: Orson Welles. *Director of photography*: Jean Bourgoin. *Additional photography*: Roger Dormoy. *Camera operator*: Louis Stein. *Set design*: Gil Parrondo (in Spain), Orson Welles. *Set decoration*: Luis Pérez Espinosa (in Spain). *Costumes*: Orson Welles. *Assistant directors*: José María Ochoa, José Luis de la Serna, Isidoro M. Ferry (in Spain). *Script supervisor*: Johanna Harwood. *Sound recording*: Jacques Lebreton, Terry Cotter. *Editors*: Renzo Lucidi, William Morton. *Dubbing mixer*: Jacques Carrère. *Original score*: Paul Misraki, conducted by Marc Lanjean. *Producer*: Louis Dolivet. *Production companies*: Filmorsa (Tangiers), Cervantes Films (Madrid). *Cast*: Robert Arden (Guy Van Stratten, a.k.a. Streitheimer or Streeter), Orson Welles (Gregory Arkadin, a.k.a. Wasaw Athabadze), Paola Mori (Raina Arkadin), Patricia Medina (Mily), Akim Tamiroff (Jacob Zouk), Jack Watling (Bob, Marquis of Rutleigh), Michael Redgrave* (Burgomil Trebitsch), Katina Paxinou (Señora Jesus Martinez, a.k.a. Sophie Radzwieckz), Suzanne Flon (Baroness Nagel), Mischa Auer* (Professor. Radzinski), Grégoire Aslan* (Bracco), Peter Van Eyck (Tadeus), Frédéric O'Brady* (Oskar), Tamara Shane (Zouk's neighbour), Eduard Linkers (the English-speaking German policeman), Gert Fröbe (the other German policeman), Manuel Requena (General Jesus Martinez), Gordon Heath (pianist in the bar), Anne-Marie Mersen (customer in the bar), Louis Dolivet (man who reveals Baroness Nagel's occupation), Maurice Bessy* (the man from London in the bowler hat), and the voices of Antoñita Morena (the song of holy week) and Orson Welles (narrator, and voice announcing the flight to Barcelona and Madrid). *Cast of material shot for the Spanish version*: Irene López Heredia (Señora Jesus Martinez, a.k.a. Sophie Radzwieckz), Amparo Rivelles (Baroness Nagel). *Principal photography*: January – June 1954. *Running time*: 100 mins ('selling copy' entitled *Confidential Report*, 1955), 96 mins (Spanish version titled *Mr. Arkadin*, 1955), 98 mins (re-edited version titled *Confidential Report*, 1956). *Released in the UK*: 11 August 1955 in London, then 20 November nationally (Warner Bros.). *Released in Spain*: 20 October 1955 (Chamartín). *Released in France*: 8 June 1956 (Warner Bros.). A version titled *Mr Arkadin* (99 mins) was distributed in New York in October 1962 and is currently available on video. A shortened version with the same title (92 mins) is also available on video. In 2005 the *Cinémathèque Municipale de Luxembourg*, the *Munich Filmmuseum* and *The Criterion Collection* brought out a reconstructed version on DVD, combining material from several of the competing versions currently available. (*Mr. Arkadin*, 105 mins).

TOUCH OF EVIL

1957–1958. USA. 35 mm, black and white. *Screenplay and direction*: Orson Welles, based on the novel by Whit Masterson *Badge of Evil* (1956). *Director of photography*: Russell Metty. *Camera operators*: John L. Russell, Philip Lathrop. *Production design*: Alexander Golitzen, Robert Clatworthy. *Art Direction*: Russell A. Gausman, John P. Austin. *Costumes*: Bill Thomas. *Assistant director*: Phil Bowles. *Sound recording*: Leslie I. Carey, Frank Wilkinson. *Editors*: Edward Curtiss, Ernest Nims, Aaron Stell, Virgil W. Vogel. *Original score*: Henry Mancini, conducted by Joseph Gershenson. *Producer*: Albert Zugsmith. *Production company*: Universal-International. Credits for refilming imposed by the studio: *Direction*: Harry Keller. *Dialogue*: Franklin Coen. *Director of photography*: Clifford Stine. *Cast*: Orson Welles (Hank Quinlan), Charlton Heston (Miguel Vargas), Joseph Calleia (Pete Menzies), Janet Leigh (Susan Vargas), Akim Tamiroff (Joe Grandi), Mort Mills (Al Schwartz), Valentin De Vargas (leader of the Grandi nephews), Dennis Weaver (the night clerk), Ray Collins (District Attorney Adair), Victor Millan (Manolo Sanchez), Marlene Dietrich (Tana), Harry Shannon (Chief of Police Gould), Lalo Rios (Risto Grandi), William Tannen (Howard Frantz), Joanna Moore (Marcia Linnekar), Gus Schilling (Eddie Farnum), Michael Sargent ('Pretty Boy'), Phil Harvey (Blaine), Mercedes McCambridge (masculine woman in leather jacket), Joseph Cotten (medical examiner), Billy House (construction site foreman), Rusty Wescoatt (Casey), Wayne Taylor (drug-taking member of the Grandi gang), Arlene McQuade, Eleanor Dorado (Grandi gang blonde and brunette, at the motel and the Ritz), Joe Basulto, Yolanda Bojorquez, Jennie Diaz, Ken Miller, Ramón Rodriguez (Grandi gang members), Zsa Zsa Gabor (nightclub manageress), Joi Lansing (Zita, Linnekar's passenger). *Principal photography*: 18 February – 2 April 1957. *Running time*: 95 mins. *Released in USA*: May 1958 (Universal-International). A version (109 mins) used for test screenings was rediscovered in the 1970s and distributed in the 1980s. A version (109 mins) produced by Rick Schmidlin for Universal City Studios, re-edited by Walter Murch following working notes written by Welles in 1957, was released in the USA in September 1998.

THE TRIAL

1962. France / Federal Republic of Germany / Italy. 35 mm, black and white. *Screenplay and direction*: Orson Welles, based on the novel by Franz Kafka (1914). *Pin-screen animation prologue*: Alexandre Alexeieff, Claire Parker. *Director of photography*: Edmond Richard. *Camera operator*: Adolphe Charlet. *Production design*: Jean Mandaroux. *Set decoration*: André Labussière. *Costumes*: Hélène Thibault. *Assistant assistant directors*: Marc Maurette, Paul Seban. *Script supervisor*: Marie-José Kling. *Sound recording*: Guy

Villette. *Editors*: Fritz Mueller, Yvonne Martin. *Dubbing mixer*: Jacques Lebreton. *Original score and arrangements*: Jean Ledrut, played by Tommy Desserre (organ), the Martial Solal Trio and the orchestra of the Association des concerts Colonne conducted by André Girard. Non-original music: Adagio (apocryphal) and Concerto a cinque op. 5 no. 12 by Tommaso Albinoni. *Producers*: Alexandre and Michel Salkind. *Production companies*: Paris Europa Productions (Paris), Hisa-Films (Munich), Fi-C-It (Rome). *Cast*: Anthony Perkins (Joseph K.), Romy Schneider (Leni), Orson Welles (Albert Hastler), Akim Tamiroff (Rudi Bloch), Max Haufler* (Max K., the uncle), Jeanne Moreau (Marika Burstner), Arnoldo Foà* (the Inspector), William Chappell* (Titorelli), Elsa Martinelli (Hilda), Billy Kearns* (Frank, the first Assistant Inspector), Jess Hahn (the other Assistant Inspector), Madeleine Robinson (Mrs Grubach), Suzanne Flon (disabled woman who drags Marika Burstner's trunk), Maydra Shore (Irmie), Wolfgang Reichmann* (courtroom guard), Maurice Teynac* (deputy manager), Michael Lonsdale* (the priest), Paola Mori (employee who helps K. to leave the Court premises), Karl Studer* (man with a whip), Thomas Holtzmann* (Bert, the law student), Max Buchsbaum* (examining magistrate), Fernand Ledoux* (chief clerk), Roger Corbeau* (computer guard), Raoul Delfosse, Jean-Claude Remoleux (executioners), narrator (Orson Welles). *Principal photography*: 26 March – 5 June 1962. Running time: 118 mins. Released in France: 21 December 1962 (Ufa-Comacico).

FALSTAFF (CHIMES AT MIDNIGHT)

1964–6. Spain / Switzerland. 35 mm, black and white. *Screenplay and direction*: Orson Welles, based on the plays by William Shakespeare *Henry IV, Parts I and II* (*c.*1596–8), also *Richard II* (*c.*1596), *Henry V* (1599) and *The Merry Wives of Windsor* (*c.*1598–1602). *Director of photography*: Edmond Richard. *Camera operator*: Adolphe Charlet. *Production design*: Orson Welles, José Antonio de la Guerra. *Costumes*: Orson Welles. *Assistant directors*: Juan Cobos, Juan Estelrich, Tony Fuentes, Alfredo Hurtado. *Editors*: Fritz Mueller, Elena Jaumandreu. *Dubbing mixers*: Jean Neny, Jacques Maumont. *Original score*: Angelo Francesco Lavagnino, conducted by Pier Luigi Urbini. *Producer*: Emiliano Piedra. *Co-producer*: Ángel Escolano. *Production companies*: Internacional Films Española (Madrid), Alpine Productions (Basle). *Cast*: Orson Welles (Sir John Falstaff), Keith Baxter (Henry Monmouth, 'Hal', Henry V), John Gielgud (Henry IV), Norman Rodway (Henry Percy, 'Hotspur'), Alan Webb (Justice Robert Shallow), Tony Beckley (Ned Poins), Margaret Rutherford (innkeeper), Jeanne Moreau (Doll Tearsheet), Paddy Bedford (Bardolph), Walter Chiari (Justice 'Silence'), Marina Vlady (Kate Percy), Fernando Rey (Worcester), Michael Aldridge (Pistol), Andrew Faulds (Westmoreland), Jeremy Rowe (Prince John), Beatrice Welles (Falstaff's page), Alessandro Tasca di Cutò (the archbishop), José Nieto (Northumberland), Edmond Richard (Francis Feeble), Juan Estelrich* (sheriff), and the voice of Ralph Richardson (chronicler). *Principal photography*: October 1964 – April 1965. *Running time*: 116 mins. *Released in Spain*: 22 December 1965, in a dubbed version (Brepi Films Distribución). *Released in France*: 20 July 1966 (CFDC). The film is sometimes found in an early version with similar running time entitled *Chimes at Midnight* that shows some minor variations.

THE IMMORTAL STORY

1966–8. France. 35 mm, Eastmancolor. *Screenplay and direction*: Orson Welles, based on the story by Isak Dinesen in the book collection *Anecdotes of Destiny* (1958). *Director of photography and camera operator*: Willy Kurant. *Production design*: André Piltant (in France). *Set decoration*: Maurice Jumeau (in France). *Jeanne Moreau's costumes*: Pierre Cardin. *Assistant directors*: Olivier Gérard (in France), Tony Fuentes (in Spain). *Script supervisor*: Suzanne Schiffman (in France). *Editor*: Yolande Maurette. *Dubbing mixer*: Jean Neny. *Non-original music*: Erik Satie, played by Aldo Ciccolini and Jean-Joël Barbier. *Producer*: Micheline Rozan. *Production companies*: Albina Films, ORTF. *Cast*: Roger Coggio (Elishama Levinsky), Jeanne Moreau (Virginie Ducrot), Orson Welles (Mr Clay), Norman Eshley (Povl Velling, the sailor), Fernando Rey (a European), and the voice of Orson Welles (narrator). French version: Dialogue: Louise de Vilmorin. English-speaking actors dubbed by: Philippe Noiret (Mr Clay), Denis Manuel? (the sailor), Jean Topart (narrator). *Principal photography*: September – November 1966. *Running time*: 57 mins. (English version), 50 mins. (French version). *First broadcast in France*: 30 September 1968, French version (ORTF, 2nd channel). *Released in France*: 19 May 1976, English version (Studios Action).

F FOR FAKE

1973. France / Iran / Federal Republic of Germany. 35 mm, 16 mm enlarged to 35 mm, Eastmancolor. *Concept and direction*: Orson Welles. *Photography*: Christian Odasso, Gary Graver, Serge Halsdorf, Tomislav Pinter. *Oja Kodar's costumes*: Beaulieu. *Editor*: Marie-Sophie Dubus. *Dubbing mixer*: Paul Bertault. *Original score and musical direction*: Michel Legrand. *Producer*: Dominique Antoine. *Production companies*: Les Films de l'Astrophore (Paris), Saci (Tehran), Janus Film und Fernsehen (Frankfurt). *Cast*: Orson Welles, Elmyr de Hory, Clifford Irving, Oja Kodar, François Reichenbach, Edith Irving, Joseph Cotten*, Paul Stewart, Richard Wilson, Richard Drewett, Laurence Harvey, Christian Odasso, David Walsh, Jean-Pierre Aumont, Adam Karol Czartoryski-Borbón (as themselves), Mark Forgy, Françoise Widhoff (as themselves, not identified), Julio Palinkas (Oja Kodar's grandfather), Gary Graver (English-speaking TV announcer), Andrés Vicente Gómez (as himself, not identified, and as the Spanish-speaking announcer), Sasa Devcic (a little boy), the voices of William Alland (narrator of *News on the March*) and of Peter Bogdanovich (the radio journalist reporting the arrival of the Martians in *The War of the Worlds*), the supposed voice of Howard Hughes. *Principal photography*: intermittently, from 1971 to 1973. *Running time*: 88 mins.

UNCOMPLETED FEATURE FILMS: IT'S ALL TRUE

1941–2. USA. 35 mm, black and white and Technicolor (16 mm black and white for part of the carnival). *Producer*: Orson Welles. *Production company*: Mercury Productions for RKO Radio Pictures.

Episodes: *My Friend Bonito*. *Direction*: Norman Foster. *Screenplay*: Orson Welles, Norman Foster, John Fante, based on *Bonito the Bull* by Robert Flaherty. *Director of photography*: Floyd Crosby (black and white). *Camera operators*: Alfred Gilks, Alex Phillips, Jr. *Cast*: Jesús Vásquez Plata (Chico), Domingo Soler (Miguel), Jesús Solórzano, Silvério Pérez, Fermín Espinosa (the bullfighters). *Principal photography*: 25 September – 18 December 1941. Filming not completed.

Carnaval. *Direction*: Orson Welles. *Additional direction*: Lynn Shores. *Screenplay*: Orson Welles, Robert Meltzer. *Directors of photography*: William Howard Greene (Technicolor), Harry J. Wild (black and white). *Camera operators*: Henry Imus (Technicolor), Joseph Biroc, Edward Pyle (black and white). *Sound recording*: John Cass. *Cast*: Grande Otelo, Odete Amaral, Linda Batista, Emilinha Borba, Horacina Corrêa, Chucho Martínez Gil, Pery Martins, Moraes Netto, Eladyr Porto (as themselves), and the people of Rio de Janeiro. *Principal photography*: 14 February – 8 June 1942, with interruptions. Not edited.

Jangadeiros. *Screenplay and direction*: Orson Welles. *Director of photography*: George Fanto (black and white), preceded by William Howard Greene (Technicolor). *Cast*: Manuel Olímpio Meira, a.k.a. Jacaré, Jerônimo André de Souza, Raimundo Correia Lima, a.k.a. Tatá, Manuel Pereira da Silva, a.k.a. Preto (as themselves), Francisca Moreira da Silva (the young bride), José Sobrinho (the young husband). *Principal photography*: mid-March – 24 July 1942, with interruptions. Not edited. An edit of *Jangadeiros* with sound added, retitled *Four Men on a Raft* (46 mins), appears in *It's All True: Based on an Unfinished Film by Orson Welles* (1993), a film by Bill Krohn, Richard Wilson and Myron Meisel.

DON QUIXOTE

1957– Country of production unknown (filmed in Mexico, Italy and Spain). 35 mm, black and white. *Production, screenplay and direction*: Orson Welles, based on the novel by Miguel de Cervantes (1605–15). *Photography*: Jack Draper, Ricardo Navarrete, José García Galisteo, Juan Manuel de la Chica, Manuel Mateos. *Additional photography*: Edmond Richard, Giorgio Tonti, Gary Graver. *Assistant directors*: Juan Luis Buñuel, Tony Fuentes, Maurizio Lucidi. *Editors*: Alberto E. Valenzuela, Renzo Lucidi, Maurizio Lucidi, Peter Parasheles, Mauro Bonanni. *Original score*: Juan Serano, Angelo Francesco Lavagnino. *Cast*: Francisco Reiguera* (Don Quixote), Akim Tamiroff* (Sancho Panza), Orson Welles (as himself, and narration), and in some versions, Patty McCormack (Dulcie and Dulcinea), Tamara Shane (Dulcie's governess), Paola Mori (woman on a motorcycle). *Principal photography*: 1957–66, intermittent. Final additional shots filmed in 1972. Two versions based on Welles's material have been shown publicly. The first (44 mins) was produced by the Cinémathèque française in 1986, based on a work print, and shown at the Cannes Film Festival 1986. The second, *Don Quijote de Orson Welles* (116 mins), produced by El Silencio and edited by Jesús Franco in 1992, has been released. This version also uses shots from the television series *Nella terra di don Chisciotte* (see below).

THE DEEP

1967–9. Country of production unknown (filmed mostly in Yugoslavia). 35 mm, Eastmancolor. *Production, original screenplay and direction*: Orson Welles, based on the novel by Charles Williams *Dead Calm* (1963). *Directors of photography*: Willy Kurant, Ivica Rajkovic. *Additional photography*: Giorgio Tonti. *Script supervisor*: Ljuba Gamulin. *Editor*: Mauro Bonanni, X. *Production company*: Ropama. *Cast*: Michael Bryant* (John Ingram), Olga Palinkas [the future Oja Kodar] (Rae Ingram), Laurence Harvey* (Hughie Warriner), Jeanne Moreau (Ruth Warriner), Orson Welles (Russ Brewer). *Principal photography*: September – November 1967. The Munich Filmmuseum has begun work on an edit based on various materials.

THE OTHER SIDE OF THE WIND

1970–5. France / Iran. 16 mm and Super 8, colour and black and white (for the main story), 35 mm, Eastmancolor (for the film within the film). *Direction*: Orson Welles. *Original screenplay*: Orson Welles, with Oja Kodar. *Director of photography*: Gary Graver. *Editors*: Yves Deschamps, Marie-Sophie Dubus. *Producer*: Dominique Antoine. *Production companies*: Les Films de l'Astrophore

(Paris), Saci (Tehran), Avenel (Liechtenstein). *Cast*: John Huston (Jake Hannaford), Peter Bogdanovich (Brooks Otterlake), Oja Kodar (the actress), Bob Random (John Dale), Lilli Palmer (Zarah Valeska), Norman Foster (Billy Boyle), Mercedes McCambridge (Maggie, Hannaford's secretary), Cameron Mitchell (Zimmer), Tonio Selwart ('the Baron'), Edmond O'Brien (Pat), Susan Strasberg (Juliette Rich), Cathy Lucas (Mavis Henscher), Geoffrey Land (Max David), Dan Tobin (Bradley Pease Burroughs), Paul Stewart (Matt Costello), Joseph McBride (Charles Pister), Howard Grossman (Higgam), Robert Aiken (the driver of the car), Benny Rubin (Abe Vogel), Gregory Sierra (Jack Simon), Cassie Yates (Cassie), Gene Clark (the projectionist), Pat McMahon (Marvin P. Fassbender), Felipe Herba, Eric Sherman (the cinéma-vérité film crew), Larry Jackson (a documentary film-maker), Paul Hunt (a sound recordist), Kevin C. Brechner, Rick Waltzer (film buffs), Cameron Crowe (a journalist), Claude Chabrol, Curtis Harrington, Dennis Hopper, Henry Jaglom, George Jessel, Paul Mazursky, Richard Wilson (as themselves), Stéphane Audran, Jack Boyce, John Carroll, Gary Graver, Peter Jason, Pat McMahon, Frank Marshall, Nina Palinkas, Stafford Repp, Lily Tomlin. *Principal photography*: August 1970 to June 1975, intermittent.

COMPLETED TELEVISION PROGRAMMES: AROUND THE WORLD WITH ORSON WELLES

1955. UK. 35 mm, black and white. *Concept and direction*: Orson Welles. *Photography*: Alain Pol, X. *Editors*: Colette Cueille, Michelle David, Lael Wertenbaker, Stanley Willis, X. *Producer*: Roland Gillett. *Production company*: Associated—Rediffusion for ITV, in collaboration with Filmorsa. *Filmed*: 21 March to end of September or early October 1955, intermittently. *First broadcast in the UK*: from 23 September 1955 (ITV).

Episodes: *Revisiting Vienna. With*: Orson Welles, Anton Karas. No known copy in existence.

Lurs: see uncompleted television programmes.

The Land of the Basques. With: Orson Welles, Chris Wertenbaker, Beñat Toyos, Father Ibarburu. *Running time*: 28 mins.

The Land of the Basques. With: Orson Welles, Lael Wertenbaker, Chris Wertenbaker. *Running time*: 28 mins. Re-edited version of the above by Filmorsa for sale in the USA.

Spain: *The Bullfight. With*: Kenneth Tynan, Elaine Dundy, Orson Welles, Ángel Peralta, Manolo Vázquez. *Running time*: 24 mins.

Madrid. Different version of the above. No known copy in existence. The French company Gray Film, which took over the rights to those films in the series that were completed in France, also produced another version including additional material in 1959 for distribution as a cinema short: *Corrida à Madrid*. (*Direction*: Alain Pol. *Voice of Orson Welles in French*: Bernard Marcay. *Photography*: Paul Rodier. *Editor*: Charles Bretoneiche. *Dubbing mixer*: Jean Neny. *Musical Director*: Jean de Rohozinski. *Production company*: Gray Film. *Running time*: 28 mins. *Released in France*: May 1959, accompanying the film *The Nuremberg Trials* by Felix von Podmanitzky.)

London. With: Orson Welles, Staff Sergeant Deverill, Sergeant Ingram, Private Page. *Running time*: 27 mins.

Paris after Dark: *Orson Welles in St. Germain des Prés. With*: Orson Welles, Raymond Duncan, Maurice Lemaître, Isidore Isou, Jacques Spacagna, Art Buchwald. *Running time*: 25 mins.

THE FOUNTAIN OF YOUTH

1956. USA. Black and white. *Production, screenplay and direction*: Orson Welles, based on the short story by John Collier *Youth from Vienna* published in the collection *Fancies and Goodnights* (1951). *Director of photography*: Sid Hickox. *Production design*: Claudio Guzman. *Assistant director*: Martin Stuart. *Supervising editor*: Dann Cahn. *Editor*: Bud Molin. *Musical director*: Julian Davidson. *Musical arrangements*: Orson Welles. *Production company*: Orson Welles Enterprises for Desilu Productions. *Cast*: Dan Tobin (Humphrey Baxter), Joi Lansing (Caroline Coates), Rick Jason (Alan Brodie), Marjorie Bennett (gossip columnist), Billy House (Albert Morgan), Nancy Kulp (Mrs Morgan), and Orson Welles (as himself). *Filmed*: May 1956. *Running time*: 26 mins. *First broadcast in USA*: 16 September 1958 (programme *The Colgate Palmolive Theater*, ABC).

PORTRAIT OF GINA

1958. USA. 35 mm, black and white. *Concept and direction*: Orson Welles. *Production company*: ABC. *With*: Orson Welles, Rossano Brazzi, Vittorio De Sica, Anna Gruber, Gina Lollobrigida, Gino Lollobrigida, Paola Mori (as themselves). *Running time*: 28 mins. This programme was rediscovered in the 1980's and received occasional public screenings.

ORSON WELLES ON THE ART OF BULLFIGHTING

1961. UK. *Concept and direction*: Orson Welles. *With*: Orson Welles. *Broadcast in the UK*: 26 November 1961 as part of the series *Tempo* (ABC). Current location unknown. This may be a version of the film made in 1955 for the series *Around the World with Orson Welles* (see above).

NELLA TERRA DI DON CHISCIOTTE

1961–4. Italy. 16 mm, black and white. *Concept and direction*: Orson Welles. *Photography*: José Manuel de la Chica, Ricardo Navarrete. *Narration written by*: Gian Paolo Callegari, with Antonio Navarro Linares. *Narration, spoken by*: Arnoldo Foà. *Editor*: Orson Welles, with Mariano Faggiani and Roberto Perpignani. *Production company*: RAI. *With:* Orson Welles, Paola Mori, Beatrice Welles and, in some episodes, Antonio Ordóñez, Ángel Peralta, Manuel Peralta. *First broadcast in Italy*: late 1964 / early 1965 (RAI). Nine episodes of 22 to 27 mins: *Itinerario andaluso*, *Spagna santa*, *La feria di San Fermin*, *L'encierro di Pamplona*, *Le cantine di Jerez*, *Siviglia*, *Feria de abril a Siviglia* (not originally broadcast), *Tempo di flamenco*, *Roma è Oriente in Spagna*.

FILMING OTHELLO

1977. Federal Republic of Germany. 16 mm, Eastmancolor. *Concept and direction*: Orson Welles. *Director of photography*: Gary Graver. *Editor*: Marty Roth. *Producers*: Klaus Hellwig, Jürgen Hellwig. *Production company*: ARD. *With*: Orson Welles, Micheál Mac Liammóir, Hilton Edwards, and the audience of a discussion at Boston University. *Filmed:* 1974 to 1977, intermittent. *Running time:* 83 mins. *First broadcast in FRG*: 10 July 1978 (ARD).

PILOT EPISODE OF THE ORSON WELLES SHOW

1978–9. USA. Video, colour. *Direction*: G. O. Spelvin [Orson Welles]. *Director of photography*: Gary Graver. *Editor*: Stanley Sheff. *Production company*: Idiom. *With*: Orson Welles, Burt Reynolds, Jim Henson, Frank Oz and the Muppets, Angie Dickinson, Patrick Terrail, Stanley Sheff, Roger Hill. *Running time:* 74 mins. Not broadcast. A copy is held by the Munich Filmmuseum.

UNCOMPLETED TELEVISION PROGRAMMES: LURS

1955. UK, for the series *Around the World with Orson Welles*. 35 mm, black and white. *Concept and direction*: Orson Welles. *Photography*: Alain Pol. *Sound recording*: Jacques Carrère. *Editors*: Michelle David, Colette Cueille, Lael Wertenbaker. *Producer*: Roland Gillett. *Production company*: Associated-Rediffusion for ITV, in collaboration with Filmorsa. *With*: Orson Welles, Jacques Chapus, Lucien Besnard, Commissaire Charles Chenevier, Maître Claude Delorme, Clovis, Gustave, Marie and Yvette Dominici, Paul Maillet. A version with additional sound entitled *La Tragé die de Lurs ou L'Affaire Dominici* (27 mins), reconstructed by Christophe Cognet, forms part of his documentary *L'Affaire Dominici par Orson Welles* (2000).

MOBY DICK - REHEARSED

1955. Country of production unknown (filmed in the UK and Italy). *Screenplay and direction*: Orson Welles, based on his play inspired by the novel by Herman Melville (1851) and performed in London on 16 June 1955. *Director of photography*: Hilton Craig. *Additional photography*: Charles Marlborough. *Producers*: Henry Margolis, Orson Welles. *Cast*: Orson Welles (actor manager / Ahab, Father Mapple), Gordon Jackson (young actor / Ishmael), Christopher Lee (Flask, stage manager), Patrick McGoohan (Starbuck). *Filmed*: July – August 1955. Filming not completed. Current location of the camera negatives and workprints unknown.

CAMILLE, THE NAKED LADY AND THE MUSKETEERS

1956. USA. 16 mm. *Production, screenplay, direction, set design and musical arrangements*: Orson Welles. *Production company*: Orson Welles Enterprises. No copy has been found.

ORSON WELLES IN DUBLIN

1960. Country of production unknown (filmed in the Republic of Ireland). Black and white. *Direction*: Orson Welles. *With*: Orson Welles, Anew McMaster and the audience at the Gate Theatre, Dublin. *Filmed*: February or March 1960. An edited version, *Orson Welles in Dublin* (18 mins), was made in 2002 by the Munich Filmmuseum.

ORSON'S BAG

1968–71. Country of production unknown (filmed in Italy, UK, Yugoslavia, Austria, USA, France). 35 mm and 16 mm, colour. *Production, screenplay and direction*: Orson Welles. *Directors of photography*: Tomislav Pinter, Ivica Rajkovic, Giorgio Tonti, X. *Director of photography for the linking episodes set in London*: Gary Graver. *Editors*: Fritz Mueller, Mauro Bonanni, X. *Production*: Orson Welles (initially for CBS).

Episodes: *Churchill. Cast*: Orson Welles (Churchill).

Swinging London or *One-Man Band. Cast*: Orson Welles (one-man band, 'bobby', old battle-axe, old sailor, woman selling violets and dirty postcards, Chinese manager of Ye Olde Strip Club, recorder -player), Tim Brooke-Taylor (television presenter).

Old Club or *Clubmen* or *Four Clubmen. Cast*: Orson Welles (four old English Lords), Jonathan Lynn (butler). *Stately*

Homes. Cast: Orson Welles (as himself, and Count Plumfield), Tim Brooke-Taylor (Algy Plumfield).

Tailor's Shop. Cast: Orson Welles (as himself), Charles Gray (Mr. Michaelton), Jonathan Lynn (Mr. Johnson). These five London episodes above were completed in 2000 by the Munich Filmmuseum, with the title *Orson Welles' London* (29 mins).

Spying in Vienna. Cast: Orson Welles (as himself), Senta Berger (his assistant in the conjuring trick), Mickey Rooney (participant in the conjuring trick), Arte Johnson (the spy with the cigarette). This episode was completed in 2000 by the Munich Filmmuseum, with the title *Orson Welles' Vienna* (9 mins).

The Merchant of Venice. Screenplay: Orson Welles, based on the play by William Shakespeare (*c.*1597). *Original score*: Angelo Francesco Lavagnino. *Cast*: Orson Welles (Shylock), Charles Gray (Antonio), Irina Maleva (Jessica). *Estimated running time*: 40 mins. Unfinished. Material from this production is held at the Cinémathèque française and at the Munich Filmmuseum, which included eight minutes of the material in its compilation film *Orson Welles' Shylock* (2001). Further material is held by private collectors.

THE MAGIC SHOW

1976–82. USA. 35 mm, 16 mm and video, colour. *Concept and direction*: Orson Welles. *Photography*: Gary Graver, Tim Suhrstedt. *Editor*: Jonathon Braun. *Cast*: Orson Welles (as himself, and the old magician), Abb Dickson (the chief of police, the forgetful magician, Abu-Nar the Wizard and others), Peter Jason (the drunk man in the audience), Oja Kodar (the princess in the air). *Production company*: Screen Images. *Filmed*: intermittently, from June 1976 to 1982. This programme was completed in 2000 by the Munich Filmmuseum with the title *Orson Welles' Magic Show* (27 mins).

FILM TRAILERS BY WELLES: TRAILER FOR CITIZEN KANE

1940–1. USA. 35 mm, black and white. *Direction*: Orson Welles. *Director of photography*: Harry J. Wild. *Production company*: Mercury Productions for RKO Radio Pictures. *Cast*: Ray Collins, Dorothy Comingore, Joseph Cotten, George Coulouris, Agnes Moorehead, Erskine Sanford, Everett Sloane, Paul Stewart, Ruth Warrick (as themselves and as their characters in *Citizen Kane*), and the voice of Orson Welles (as himself). *Running time*: 4 mins.

TRAILER FOR F FOR FAKE

1976. USA. 35 mm, colour. *Direction*: Orson Welles. *Director of photography*: Gary Graver. *Cast*: Gary Graver, Oja Kodar, and the voice of Orson Welles (as themselves). *Filmed*: December 1976. *Running time*: 9 mins. This trailer survives only in a black and white print. A colour version was put together in 2002 by the Munich Filmmuseum with the title *Orson Welles' 'F for Fake' Trailer*, replacing black and white shots taken from *F for Fake* by their colour equivalents, and black and white shots made especially for the trailer by other shots in colour held at the museum.

FILM FRAGMENTS MADE FOR STAGE PERFORMANCES: TOO MUCH JOHNSON

1938. USA. 16 mm, black and white. Silent. *Screenplay and direction*: Orson Welles, based on the play by William Gillette (1899). *Photography*: Paul Dunbar. *Production design*: James Morcom. *Editor*: Orson Welles. *Producers*: John Houseman, Orson Welles. *Production company*: Mercury Theatre. *Cast*: Joseph Cotten (Augustus Billings), Howard Smith (Joseph Hadbury Johnson), Mary Wickes (Mrs Batterson), Ruth Ford (Jennie Billings), Eustace Wyatt (Faddish), Edgar Barrier (Leon Dathis), Arlene Francis (Clairette Dathis), Virginia Nicolson (Leonora Aliza Faddish), Guy Kingsley (Henry Mackintosh), George Duthie (steward), Richard Wilson (cabin boy), John Berry (market gardener in a cart), Herbert Drake, John Houseman (cops), William Alland, Marc Blitzstein. *Filmed*: mid-July 1938. Made for Welles's production of the play, but unfinished. The workprint is presumed lost.

THE GREEN GODDESS

1939. USA. Black and white. *Direction*: Orson Welles. *Production company*: Mercury Theatre for the RKO Orpheum Vaudeville Circuit. *Estimated running time*: 4 mins. Prologue to the abridged version of the play by William Archer (1920) toured by Welles in June and July 1939. No print has been found.

AROUND THE WORLD

1946. USA. Black and white. Silent. *Production, screenplay and direction*: Orson Welles. *Photography*: B. Kelley. *Editor*: Irving Lerner. *Production company*: Mercury Theatre. *Cast*: Arthur Margetson (Phileas Fogg), Larry Laurence (Pat Passepartout), Alan Reed (Dick Fix), Julie Warren (Molly Muggins), Brainerd Duffield (bankrobber), Mary Healy (Princess Aouda), Stefan Schnabel (Avery Jevity), Marion Kohler. Made for the musical comedy by Welles (adaptation) and Cole Porter (lyrics and music), based on Jules Verne's *Around the World in Eighty Days*, premiered in Boston on 27 April 1946. No print has been found.

THE LOVES OF SAINT ANNE

1950. France. *Screenplay and direction*: Orson Welles. *Production company*: La Compagnie Les Pléiades. *Cast*: Julia Gibson (Gloria Granger, as St Anne de Beaumont), Maurice Bessy, Frédéric O'Brady, Boris Vian (paralytics), Marcel Achard, Georges Beaume. Made for the play by Welles *The Unthinking Lobster* premiered in Paris on 19 June 1950. The so-called rushes of a Biblical Hollywood epic were screened as part of the play. No print has been found.

OTHER FRAGMENTS MADE FOR PARTICULAR PURPOSES: TWELFTH NIGHT

1933. USA. Colour. Silent. *Narration, recorded on disc*: Orson Welles. *Filmed*: May 1933. *Financed by*: Todd School. Film of a performance of *Twelfth Night* (1601) by William Shakespeare. Direction by Welles for the Chicago Drama Festival. Available for hire by schools and clubs in subsequent years.

LITERARY READINGS

1970. USA. Film transferred to video, colour. *Direction*: Orson Welles. *Director of photography*: Gary Graver. *With*: Orson Welles. *Commissioned by*: Sears Roebuck department stores. *Filmed*: from 31 August 1970. *Running time*: 6 x 30 mins. Readings of a Socratic dialogue, Oscar Wilde's *The Happy Prince*, works by G. K. Chesterton and P.G. Wodehouse, and of a speech for the defence by the attorney Clarence Darrow.

INTRODUCTIONS FOR THE SILENT YEARS

1971. USA. Colour. *Direction*: Orson Welles. *Director of photography*: Gary Graver. *With*: Orson Welles. *Producer*: Ricki Franklin. *Production company*: PBS. *Running time*: introductions lasting 1 to 5 mins, outros lasting 20 seconds to 2 mins each. *First broadcast*: 6 July to 24 September 1971 (PBS). Introductions and outros for twelve classics of the American silent cinema: *The Gold Rush* by Chaplin, *The Beloved Rogue* by Crosland, *The Son of the Sheik* by Fitzmaurice, *Intolerance, Orphans of the Storm* and *Sally of the Sawdust* by Griffith, *The Extra Girl* by Jones, *The General* by Keaton and Bruckman, *The Mark of Zorro* and *Blood and Sand* by Niblo, *The Thief of Baghdad* by Walsh and *The Hunchback of Notre Dame* by Worsley.

INTRODUCTIONS FOR ORSON WELLES GREAT MYSTERIES

1972–3. UK. Colour. *Direction*: Orson Welles. *Directors of photography*: Gary Graver, Serge Halsdorf. *Editor*: Yves Deschamps. *With*: Orson Welles. *Producer*: John Jacobs. *Production companies*: Anglia Television, 20th Century-Fox. *Broadcast in the UK*: 1 September 1973 to 24 February 1974 (ITV). Introductions for a pilot and twenty-six 30-minute episodes of a series of mystery dramas.

REGRETS

1978. USA. *Direction*: Orson Welles. *With*: Orson Welles. *Filmed*: November 1978. *Running time*: 7 mins. Filmed apology sent by Welles to the Chicago Film Festival, which he was unable to attend.

THERE ARE NO HEROES ANYMORE

1979. USA. 35 mm, colour. *Direction*: Orson Welles. *Photography*: Gary Graver. *With*: Orson Welles. *Commissioned by*: New York Mutual insurance company. *Filmed*: 11 January 1979. Reading of a poem by Earl Fultz *There Are No Heroes Anymore* commissioned by The Loyal Guard for its Man of the Year award ceremony. The film was reconstructed in 2000 by the Munich Filmmuseum with the title *Orson Welles' Unsung Heroes* (6 mins).

PITCH FOR KING LEAR

1985. Country of production unknown. Video, colour. *Direction*: Orson Welles. *Camera*: Gary Graver. *With*: Orson Welles. *Running time*: 6 mins.

THE SPIRIT OF CHARLES LINDBERGH

1984. USA. 35 mm, colour. *Direction*: Orson Welles. *Photography*: Gary Graver. *With*: Orson Welles. *Filmed*: February 1984. Reading of extracts of Lindbergh's diary for the birthday of Welles's financial manager, Bill Cronshaw. The film was reconstructed in 2000 by the Munich Filmmuseum with the title *Orson Welles' 'The Spirit of Charles Lindbergh'* (3 mins).

AMATEUR SHORT: THE HEARTS OF AGE

1934. USA. 16 mm, black and white. Silent. *Direction and photography*: William Vance, Orson Welles. *Cast*: Orson Welles (the old man), Virginia Nicolson (the old woman), Edgerton Paul (the hanged man), William Vance (man in a blanket), Charles O'Neal (man with the atlas). *Filmed*: July 1934. *Running time*: 6 mins.

ROUGH SKETCHES AND UNCLASSIFIABLE MATERIAL:

We do not know the purpose of most of the items below. Some of those made in the 1970's may have been intended for a miscellany entitled *The One-Man Band*. Other fragments, about which too little is known, have been omitted.

MATERIAL FOR A FILM ON AN EQUESTRIAN CIRCUS

1948. Country of production unknown (filmed in Rome for a project with Alexander Korda's London Film

Productions). *Director of photography*: Oberdan Troiani. Filming abandoned. The rushes have not been found.

AN EVENING WITH ORSON WELLES

1950. Country of production unknown (filmed in Federal Republic of Germany). *Screenplay*: extracts from *Henry VI, Part III* (*c.*1592) by William Shakespeare and from *The Importance of Being Earnest* (1895) by Oscar Wilde adapted for the show *An Evening with Orson Welles* premiered in Frankfurt on 7 August 1950. *Director of photography*: George Fanto. *Sound recording*: Rolb. *Cast*: *Henry VI, Part III*: Micheál Mac Liammóir (Henry VI), Orson Welles (Richard, Duke of Gloucester); *The Importance of Being Earnest*: Orson Welles (Algernon Moncrieff), Micheál Mac Liammóir (John Worthing), Lee Zimmer (Lane). *Filmed*: 26–31 August 1950. Tests abandoned. The rushes have not been found.

THE HEROINE

1967. Country of production unknown (filmed in Hungary). 35 mm, Eastmancolor. *Screenplay and direction*: Orson Welles, based on the story by Isak Dinesen, in the collection *Winter's Tales* (1942). *Director of photography*: Willy Kurant. *Filmed*: 14 April 1967. Only one day's shooting took place on this short intended to accompany *The Immortal Story*. The rushes have not been found.

SPEECH BY SHYLOCK FROM THE MERCHANT OF VENICE

1970. Country of production unknown (filmed in France). Colour. *Direction*: Orson Welles. *Photography*: Gary Graver. *With*: Orson Welles. *Filmed*: 20 January 1970. Reading of a speech from *The Merchant of Venice* (*c.*1597) by William Shakespeare. Rushes held at the Munich Filmmuseum, which used three shots from the footage, including one complete 90-second take, in its compilation *Orson Welles' Shylock* (2001).

THE GOLDEN HONEYMOON

1970. USA. 16 mm, colour. *Direction*: Orson Welles. *Photography*: Gary Graver. *With*: Orson Welles. *Filmed*: October 1970. Reading of the short story by Ring Lardner (1922). This unfinished short was reconstructed in 2003 by the Munich Filmmuseum, with the title *Orson Welles' 'The Golden Honeymoon'* (17 mins).

MOBY DICK

1971. Country of production unknown (filmed in France). 16 mm reversal, colour. *Production, screenplay and direction*: Orson Welles, based on his play *Moby Dick – Rehearsed* (1955) suggested by the novel by Herman Melville (1851). *Director of photography*: Gary Graver. *Cast*: Orson Welles (as himself, reading *Moby Dick* and playing Ahab, Peleg, Starbuck and other characters). *Filmed*: summer 1971. These fragments were reconstructed in 2000 by the Munich Filmmuseum with the title *Orson Welles' 'Moby Dick'*. (22 mins).

SPEECH BY SHYLOCK FROM THE MERCHANT OF VENICE

1973. Country of production unknown (filmed in Spain). Colour. *Direction*: Orson Welles. *Photography*: Gary Graver. *With*: Orson Welles. Reading of a speech from *The Merchant of Venice* (*c.*1597) by William Shakespeare. Rushes held at the Munich Filmmuseum, which used two shots from the footage, including one complete 90-second take, in its compilation *Orson Welles' Shylock*.

JEREMIAH

1978. USA. 35 mm, colour. *Direction*: Orson Welles. *Photography*: Gary Graver. *With*: Orson Welles. *Filmed*: February 1978. Reading of an abridged version of the Book of Lamentations and of Jeremiah XXXI. Rushes held at the Munich Filmmuseum. In 2002 the museum restored all of one of the three takes of the short with the title *Orson Welles' Jeremiah* (4 mins).

ORSON WELLES TALKS WITH ROGER HILL

1978. USA. 16 mm, colour. *Direction*: Orson Welles. *Photography*: Gary Graver. *With*: Roger Hill, Hortense Hill, Orson Welles. *Filmed*: June 1978. Rushes held at the Munich Filmmuseum (65 mins).

THE DREAMERS

1980–5. A. 35 mm, colour. *Direction*: Orson Welles. *Screenplay*: Orson Welles, Oja Kodar, based on the stories by Isak Dinesen *The Dreamers* (in the collection *Winter's Tales*, 1934) and *Echoes* (in the collection *Last Tales*, 1957). *Director of photography*: Gary Graver. *Cast*: Oja Kodar (Pellegrina Leoni), Orson Welles (Marcus Kleek). *Filmed*: intermittently, August 1980 to September 1985. Some scenes were reconstructed in 2002 by the Munich Filmmuseum, with the title *Orson Welles' 'The Dreamers'* (24 mins).

MATERIAL FOR A DOCUMENTARY ON THE TRIAL

1981. USA. 16 mm, colour. *Direction*: Orson Welles. *Photography*: Gary Graver. *With*: Orson Welles, and the audience at a discussion held at the University of Southern California. *Filmed*: 14 November 1981.

The rushes were edited in 2001 by the Munich Filmmuseum with the title *Filming 'The Trial'* (82 mins).

SOURCES & REFERENCES

THE BASIS FOR AN INVESTIGATION

Orson Welles at Work offers a step-by-step examination of the filmmaker's creative methods and takes into account his own responsibilities, those of his collaborators and those of his production companies. By this means we hope to achieve a more balanced and detailed perception of the mysteries of creation and, ultimately, a fresh understanding of the films themselves. The first chapter deals closely with the principles Welles established when working for stage and radio during the 1930s. The greater part of the book retraces the making of the films and television programmes, including *Journey into Fear*, for which Norman Foster received sole credit as director although Welles's grip as producer was decisive. We also examine the very first unrealized Hollywood project, *Heart of Darkness* – which is crucial to an understanding of the young Welles's desire for total control – and consider the films he was unable to complete, for these also reveal a great deal about his methods. As we proceed, we hope to show to what extent his aesthetic choices were influenced by the conditions under which he was obliged to work and by the human and technical resources at his disposal. Five chapters take a broader look at the major stages of his career and his relations with various production companies.

We have drawn upon four main types of source, all of which have been subjected to rigorous cross-checking. First, we are indebted to all those who have endeavoured to re-create the production history of the works and place them in a broader perspective. Frank Brady, Simon Callow, Robert L. Carringer, Juan Cobos, Bill Krohn, Joseph McBride, Esteve Riambau, Jonathan Rosenbaum and Bret Wood constitute a Wellesian international that also benefits from the participation of German and Italian friends. Our thanks also to Catherine Benamou, who was preparing her monumental work on *It's All True*, and to James Naremore, whose *Magic World of Orson Welles* provided a comprehensive insight into Welles's oeuvre.

Besides Welles's own writings and interviews, we also consulted any published material that contained accounts by the actors and technicians who worked with him. These have been carefully sifted in an attempt to separate myth from reality: some sources are unquestionably accurate, while others are vague or contradictory. A large number of contemporary newspaper articles helped to establish the chronological highlights.

We met many of Welles's collaborators, some of whom have since died. We are deeply grateful to all of them for their generosity, and for the passion with which they shed light on many of the more obscure aspects of Welles's career.

Finally, we studied the production documents. For the European period, we were able to turn to private collections. In the United States, university and institutional libraries are eager to house the archives of major studios and individuals alike. The Mercury Theatre archives, a particularly rich seam for Welles scholars, are housed in the Lilly Library at the University of Indiana. The collection, amassed by Richard Wilson between 1937 and 1949, contains 20,000 documents ranging from 200-page screenplays to two-line telegrams, and includes material on stage and radio as well as on the films.

The bulk of the documents we consulted consisted of written sources: screenplays, shooting scripts, shooting schedules, breakdowns, budgetary material, financial reports, production reports, letters, etc. Visual documents included preparatory sketches and storyboards for the earliest films. We also examined photographs taken during filming, particularly for the Hollywood productions. Even the smallest companies such as Columbia (*The Lady from Shanghai*) and Republic (*Macbeth*) had hundreds of photographs taken on the set.

All these documents had to be interpreted. When attempting to reconstruct the chronology of the filming of *The Magnificent Ambersons* and detect which cameraman filmed which shots, we had to study and interpret the shooting script, alongside daily production reports, requests to exceed deadlines, photographs that revealed the presence of technicians, personal accounts, the work of our predecessors and, of course, the film itself, as shooting and editing conditions can also be deduced from what appears on the screen.

This is one of the lessons we learned during the course of our investigation: the more dislocated Welles's films were – in terms of the places in which they were shot and then edited – the more secrets they will reveal to the naked eye – in terms of the thousand-and-one tricks that the gifted improviser or conjurer has at his disposal. The tricks were not always apparent on a first viewing but would emerge as we returned to the task; they suggested variations in methods that then had to be confirmed by other means. After watching a film ten or even twenty times and discovering so many different facets, one can only marvel at Welles's creative power, a power that flourished in security and, more often, in adversity.

For Welles's career as a whole, see the volume of interviews with Orson Welles and Peter Bogdanovich, edited by Jonathan Rosenbaum (*This Is Orson Welles*, HarperCollins, New York, 1992), as well as the two most reliable biographies, the one by Frank Brady (*Citizen Welles*, Charles Scribner's Sons, New York, 1989) and the one by Simon Callow, of which the first two volumes (*Orson Welles: The Road to Xanadu* and *Orson Welles: Hello Americans*, Cape, London, 1995 and 2006) have been published.

The main documentaries focusing on a particular period in Welles's career are *Rosabella: la storia italiana di Orson Welles* (Gianfranco Giagni and Ciro Giorgini, 1993), *Orson Welles: The One Man Band* (Vassili Silovic, 1995) and *Orson Welles en el país de Don Quijote* (Carlos Rodríguez, screenplay by Carlos F. Heredero and Esteve Riambau, 2000).

For the mutilation of certain films by the production companies and the various existing cuts of his completed feature films, see François Thomas, 'Un film d'Orson Welles en cache un autre', *Cinéma 011, 012* and *013*, Spring 2006, Autumn 2006 and Spring 2007.

As for the present book, we have cited chapter by chapter the most informative published texts on Welles's working methods (historical studies, first-hand accounts and accounts of film-shoots) as well as the archival material and unpublished interviews used. When his collaborators have made several contributions, we have used the most substantial ones.

The edition cited is normally the first. We do not record the sometimes numerous reprints of articles. The archives we have used most extensively are those at the Lilly Library, University of Indiana, Bloomington. Unless otherwise noted, the documents cited are in the Orson Welles collection. A reference 'XXI/17' indicates 'box XXI, folder 17'. Works by the authors of the present book are indicated by their initials, J.-P. B. and F. T.

INTRODUCTION

Quotations: 'Orson was absolutely awful when he was confined to a single project ...': Richard Wilson, interviewed by Bill Krohn, *Cahiers du cinéma*, no. 378, December 1985. 'a minimum of eighteen hours a day': letter from Welles to George Fanto, 14 November 1950 (Lilly Library, Fanto coll., 2). 'For the cinema, accidents are sublime': in French, part of the broadcast *Vive le cinéma!* made in 1972 by Jacques Rozier. 'best script girl that ever existed': *This Is Orson Welles*, *op. cit.*, p. 104. 'If there's something another fellow can or should add to your picture ...': *ibid.*, p. 254. *Miscellaneous*: Virtuoso long take in *The Other Side of the Wind*: Yves Deschamps, interviewed by J.-P. B., *Positif*, no. 536, October 2005. The indispensable Adolphe Charlet: Monique Lefebvre, 'Quatre mois de chasse à l'Orson ...', *Télérama*, 12 January 1974. On the Lilly Library archives: James Naremore, 'Between Works and Texts', in *The Magic World of Orson Welles*, 2nd edn, Southern Methodist University Press, Dallas, 1989; F. T., 'La collection Orson Welles de la Lilly Library', *Cinémathèque*, no. 12, Autumn 1997.

FIRST STEPS IN THEATRE & RADIO

Historical studies: Richard France, *The Theatre of Orson Welles*, Associated University Presses, Cranbury / London, 1977. Paul Heyer, *The Medium and the Magician: Orson Welles, the Radio Years, 1934–1952*, Rowman & Littlefield, Lanham, 2005. F. T., 'Orson Welles metteur en ondes: *The Mercury Theatre on the Air*', *Positif*, no. 332, October 1988. *First-hand accounts*: John Houseman: *Run-Through*, Simon and Schuster, New York, 1972. Paul Stewart: interviewed by F. T., *Positif*, no. 332, October 1988. *Archives of the Wisconsin Center for Film and Theatre Research:* Corrections, notes on lighting, and cues for music and sound effects in *Macbeth*, 1936 (Manuscripts section) and various other documents. *Quotations*: Orson Welles on stage designers, 'The Director in the Theatre Today' (pamphlet, Theatre Education League, 1938), *Positif*, no. 439, September 1997. 'Until that time lighting ...': Abe Feder, 'Lighting the Play', in John Gassner (ed.), *Producing the Play*, The Dryden Press, New York, revised edn, 1953, p. 359. 'humiliate myself to write ...': *Run-Through*, *op. cit.*, p. 192.

CONQUERING HOLLYWOOD

Historical studies: On *Heart of Darkness*: Robert L. Carringer, chap. I, *The Making of 'Citizen Kane'*, University of California Press, Berkeley / Murray, London, 2nd revised edn, 1996. On Welles's Hollywood career: Douglas Gomery, 'Orson Welles and the Hollywood Industry', *Persistence of Vision*, no. 7, 1989; Richard B. Jewell, 'Orson Welles and the Studio System: The RKO Context', in Ronald Gottesman (ed.), *Perspectives on 'Citizen Kane'*, G. K. Hall, New York, 1996. *First-hand account:* Unpublished interview with Richard Wilson by F. T. (27 March 1982). *Lilly Library Archives (XIV/18–19):* 'The desire to know more about him ...': 'Characters from *Heart of Darkness*'. Statement of intent for 'Camera' (not written by Welles). 'Orson Welles Uses Radio and Recording Technics in Readying First Film' (CBS story, 30 November 1939). Various production documents. *Film script: Heart of Darkness*, Revised Estimating Script, 30 November 1939, in *Revue internationale d'histoire du cinéma*, no. 4, microfiche, 1977. *Documentary: Orson Welles and RKO: Two Masterpieces and a Fiasco* (in the series *The RKO Story*, BBC, 1987).

CITIZEN KANE

Principal references: The primary source is Robert L. Carringer, *The Making of 'Citizen Kane'*, *op. cit.* In addition to the biographies cited, two books on film treat Welles's working methods in detail: Harlan Lebo, *'Citizen Kane': The Fiftieth-Anniversary Album*, Doubleday, New York / London, 1990; J.-P. B. and F. T., *Citizen Kane*, Flammarion, 1992. There are too many substantial articles and interviews on the origins of the film to cite here. There is detailed bibliographical information in the books by Carringer and by J.-P. B. and F. T. *Quotation:* 'It can be taught in about two hours ...': *This Is Orson Welles*, *op. cit.*, p. 89. *Documentaries*: *Orson Welles and RKO: Two Masterpieces and a Fiasco*, *op. cit.* *The Complete 'Citizen Kane'* (BBC, 1991).

THREE FILMS ON TWO CONTINENTS

Historical study: Jeff Wilson, 'Jack Moss: The Man Who Ruined Welles?', December 2004, http://wellesnet.com/OWA_index.htm
See also the sources given for the following three chapters. *Quotations*: 'subtract from, arrange, rearrange, revise and adapt ...': contract quoted in a letter from L. Arnold Weissberger to Welles, 16 September 1942 (Lilly Library, Weissberger coll., I/9). 'Educating the people is expensive ...': letter from George Schaefer to Welles, 20 March 1942, quoted in Frank Brady, *op. cit.*, p. 325.

THE MAGNIFICENT AMBERSONS

Historical studies: Robert L. Carringer, chap. VI, *The Making of 'Citizen Kane'*, *op. cit.*; supplements to Criterion laser disk, 1986; *The Magnificent Ambersons: A Reconstruction*, University of California Press, Berkeley/Los Angeles, 1993. Kathryn Kalinak, 'The Text of Music: A Study of *The Magnificent Ambersons*', in *Settling the Score*, University of Wisconsin Press, Madison, 1992. Joseph McBride, chap. IV, *Orson Welles*, Da Capo, New York, 1996. Jonathan Rosenbaum, 'The Original *Ambersons*', in *This Is Orson Welles*, *op. cit.* *First-hand accounts*: Stanley Cortez: discussion, *American Cinematographer*, vol. 57, no. 11, November 1976. Dolores Costello: 'The Unpredictable Orson Welles', *Screenland*, June 1942. James G. Stewart: 'The Evolution of Cinematic Sound: A Personal Report', in Evan W. Cameron (ed.), *Sound and the Cinema*, Redgrave, Pleasantville, 1980. *Lilly Library Archives (XVI/2–12):* Estimating Script, 15 August 1941. Final Script, 7 October 1941 (copies used by Welles and the script supervisor, Amalia Kent). Storyboards (reproduced, block by block, on the laser disk cited). Shooting scripts. Daily reports. Requests for permission to overrun. '*The Magnificent Ambersons*: Vital Statistics'. 'Preview Comment Cards', 17 March 1942. *Miscellaneous*: 'The first time I did it ...': unpublished talk by Agnes Moorehead at the Actors' Laboratory, 3 December 1945 (Wisconsin Center for Film and Theatre Research, A. Moorehead coll., LX/3). *Documentary: Orson Welles and RKO: Two Masterpieces and a Fiasco*, *op. cit.*

JOURNEY INTO FEAR

First-hand account: Karl Struss: interview, in Charles Higham, *Hollywood Cameramen*, Indiana University Press, Bloomington/London, 1970. *Lilly Library Archives (XX/10–19, unless otherwise noted):* 'It is my policy ...': letter from Welles to Joseph Breen, vice-president of RKO, 10 July 1941 (I). Letter from Norman Foster to Welles, 21 April 1942 (II). 'This is probably the first time ...': Perry Lieber, 'RKO Radio Studio Handbook of Publicity Data', 3 February 1942. Partial synopses and versions of the screenplay. Storyboard. List of passages of off-screen narration and revised text of the final scene. 'New Last Scene'. 'Budget of Production Costs', 5 January 1942. 'Preview Comment Cards', 18 and 20 April 1942. *Additional quotation:* 'I have often been wrong ...': letter from Joseph Cotten to Welles, 28 March 1942, in *This Is Orson Welles*, *op. cit.*, p.121.

IT'S ALL TRUE

Historical studies: Catherine Benamou, '*It's All True* as Document/Event: Notes towards an Historiographical and Textual Analysis', *Persistence of Vision*, no. 7, 1989; 'Retrieving Orson Welles's Suspended Inter-American Film, *It's All True*', *Nuevo texto critico*, vol. 11, nos 21–2, January – December 1998. Richard B. Jewell, 'Orson Welles, George Schaefer, and *It's All True*: A "Cursed" Production', *Film History*, vol. 2, no. 4, November – December 1988. Bill Krohn, 'à la recherche du film fantôme', *Cahiers du cinéma*, no. 375, September 1985. Robert Stam, 'Orson Welles, Brazil, and the Power of Blackness', *Persistence of Vision*, no. 7, 1989. On the 1993 documentary and the reconstruction of *Jangadeiros*: J.-P. B., 'Les lambeaux de Fortaleza', *Positif*, no. 396, February 1994. *First-hand accounts*: George Fanto: 'Eu fui o "camera-man" de Orson Welles', *A cena munda*, 18 August 1942. Richard Wilson: 'It's Not *Quite* All True', *Sight and Sound*, vol. 39, no. 4, Autumn 1970 (see also vol. 40, no. 1, Winter 1970–1). *Lilly Library Archives*: Letter from Welles to Joseph Breen, vice-president of RKO, 10 July 1941 (I). *Additional quotations*: 'no script, no actors, no preconceived ideas ...': quoted in Frank Brady, *op. cit.*, p. 336. 'filthy huts of the *favelas* ...' : Gatinha Angora, *Cine-Rádio-Jornal*, 20 May 1942, quoted in Robert Stam, *op. cit.* *Documentaries*: *Orson Welles and RKO: Two Masterpieces and a Fiasco*, *op. cit.* *It's All True: Based on an Unfinished Film by Orson Welles* (Richard Wilson, Myron Meisel and Bill Krohn, 1993).

THE STRUGGLE TO REMAIN A PRODUCER

Lilly Library Archives: Draft agreement with Walter Wanger (XVII/3). *Miscellaneous*: J.A. Aberdeen, *Hollywood Renegades: The Society of Independent Motion Picture Producers*, Cobblestone Entertainment, Palos Verdes Estates, 2000.

THE STRANGER

Historical study: Bret Wood, 'Recognizing *The Stranger*', *Video Watchdog*, no. 23, May – July 1994. *First-hand account:* Ernest Nims: interview, *American Cinemeditor*, vols 32–3, nos 4–1, Winter–Spring 1982–3. *Lilly Library Archives (XXI/11–18):* Screenplays: *Date with Destiny*, 9 August 1945; same title, Final Shooting Script, 24

September 1945; revisions of 31 October 1945; other revisions. Shooting schedule no. 2, 27 September 1945. Breakdown. 'Time Continuity on: *The Stranger*'. 'Daily Schedule'. Plan of Harper set. 'Comparative Cost: Exterior Harper Square – 20th Century-Fox Location and Construction on Studio Back Lot'. 'Work to Be Finished on *The Stranger*'. Various production documents. *Miscellaneous*: Natasha Fraser-Cavassoni, *Sam Spiegel*, Simon & Schuster, New York/London, 2003.

THE LADY FROM SHANGHAI

Historical studies: Adrienne L. McLean, 'I Told You Not to Move – I Mean It!: Cross-Examining *Gilda* and *The Lady from Shanghai*', in *Being Rita Hayworth: Labor, Identity, and Hollywood Stardom*, Rutgers University Press, New Brunswick/London, 2004. James Naremore, 'Between Works and Texts', in *The Magic World of Orson Welles*, 2nd edn, Southern Methodist University Press, Dallas, 1989. Bret Wood, 'Kiss Hollywood Goodbye: Orson Welles and *The Lady from Shanghai*', *Video Watchdog*, no. 23, May – July 1994. *Technical article*: Herb A. Lightman, '*The Lady from Shanghai*: Field Day for the Camera', *American Cinematographer*, vol. 29, no. 6, June 1948. *Lilly Library Archives (XXI/21–XXII/6 unless otherwise noted)*: Screenplays: *Black Irish*, Third Draft, 13 August 1946; *Take This Woman*, Final Draft (for estimating purposes), 17 August 1946, and First Estimating Script (fourth draft), 20 September 1946; *The Lady from Shanghai*, 'Screenplay as Shot', 20 December 1946; untitled and undated screenplay (later than 25 February 1947). 'Set Budget', 14 October 1946. 'Assistant Director's Daily Report', 11 March 1947. Log for 11 March 1947. Statements of accounts for 15 March, 3 May, 14 June and 26 July 1947. 'Retakes'. *Columbia Music Catalogue*. 'Memo to Mr. Welles from Mr. Wilson. Subject: *Lady from Shanghai*' (IV). 'Given the faintest premonition ...' and 'There's no point in photographing ...': 'Memo to Mr. Cohn from Mr. Welles' (IV). *UCLA Archives*: 'All the Welles touches ...': letter from Richard Wilson to Arnold Grant, 30 September 1947 (Department of Special Collections, Richard Wilson coll., XVII/10). *Additional quotation*: 'an exercise in eroticism and exoticism': *This Is Orson Welles, op. cit.*, p. 33. *Miscellaneous*: Finding exterior locations in San Francisco: www.filminamerica.com/movies/theladyfromshanghai The dates in associate producer William Castle's 'log book', reproduced in his *Step Right Up!* (Putnam, New York, 1976), are fanciful.

MACBETH

Historical studies: Bernice W. Kliman, 'Welles's *Macbeth*, a Textual Parable', in Michael Skovmand (ed.), *Screen Shakespeare*, Aarhus University Press, Aarhus, 1994. F. T., 'Les mésaventures d'une bande sonore: les deux *Macbeth* d'Orson Welles', *Cinémathèque*, no. 6, Autumn 1994. *Account of the shoot*: Harold Leonard, *Sight and Sound*, vol. 19, no. 1, March 1950. *First-hand accounts*: Unpublished interviews with Alan Napier and Richard Wilson by F. T. (23 and 27 March 1982). Letters to F. T. from Jeanette Nolan (August 1994) and Peggy Webber (10 September 1994). Jacques Ibert: radio interview by Gérard Michel (1954), quoted in Alexandra Laederich, *Catalogue de l'oeuvre de Jacques Ibert (1890–1962)*, Olms, Hildesheim / Zurich / New York, 1998. Jeanette Nolan: interviewed by F. T., *Positif*, nos 449–50, July – August 1998. *Lilly Library Archives*: Correspondence (IV). Screenplays (XXII/7–14). Miscellaneous production documents (XXII/15–17). Untitled document from the press office, signed Mort Goodman (XXVI/65). Sketches, blueprints, plans and side elevation of the set (oversize folder 18). *UCLA Archives*: Department of Special Collections, Richard Wilson coll.: correspondence, screenplays, post-production scripts, miscellaneous production documents (X–XII). 'to re-do everything ...': letter from Welles to Charles K. Feldman, 6 March 1949 (XI/6). 'Obviously, if the Scots burr ...': 'Memorandum' (XI/6). *Additional document*: Autograph score by Jacques Ibert (1 March – 4 April 1948), consulted in 1981 with the permission of the composer's family. *Miscellaneous*: Twenty times more sound effects than usual: *The Hollywood Reporter*, 22 June 1948, quoted in *American Film Institute Catalog: Feature Films, 1941–1950 (Film Entries, M–Z)*, University of California Press, Berkeley/Los Angeles/Oxford, 1999, p. 1441.

THE FIRST EUROPEAN PERIOD

Lilly Library Archives: Plan for a three-part omnibus film: letters from Pierre Béteille (14 November 1950) and Peter Margaritoff (26 August, 7 September and 2 October 1950) to George Fanto (George Fanto coll., 1–2). *Gray Film Archives*: Co-production agreements between Filmorsa and Producciones Hispano Film (7 January 1954), between Filmorsa, Welles and José Luis Duro on the one side, Ángel Martínez Olcoz on the other (1 April 1954), between Filmorsa and Messrs Soifer and Veszi (19 July 1954), between Filmorsa and O. J. Seaman (21 August 1954). Plan for a 'Foundation for a new humanism': letter from Louis Dolivet to Welles, 8 October 1955. *Quotation*: 'With the money ...': Welles interviewed by René Brest, *Les Nouvelles littéraires*, 6 January 1949.

OTHELLO

Historical studies: J.-P. B., 'Les labyrinthes d'*Othello*: légendes et réalités d'un tournage', *Positif*, nos 449–50, July – August 1998. F. T., 'La tragédie d'*Othello*' (about the alternate versions), *Positif*, no. 424, June 1996. *Accounts of the shoot*: Olivier Delville, *Le Soir*, Brussels, date not identified. Jacques Le Prévost, unidentified Moroccan newspaper, 17 July 1949. Simone Mougin, *L'écran français*, no. 213, 25 July 1949. *First-hand accounts*: Conversation between J.-P. B. and Louis Touron (30 April 1996). Micheál Mac Liammóir: *Put Money in Thy Purse*, Methuen, London, 1952. Alexandre Trauner: interviewed by Michel Ciment and Isabelle Jordan, *Positif*, no. 224, November 1979; J.-P. B., *Alexandre Trauner: décors de cinéma*, Jade/Flammarion, 1988. Oberdan Troiani: www.geocities.com/hollywood/location/2017/trojani.html *Lilly Library Archives*: *1.* Orson Welles coll. (IV): Letters from Richard Wilson to Welles, February – April 1948. Building a portable tape recorder: letter from Art Davis (Cinema Engineering Company) to Lodge Cunningham, 8 October 1947; letters from Richard Wilson to Welles, 1 March, 24 March and 19 April 1948; 'Import License for Equipment'. *2.* George Fanto coll.: Correspondence (1–2). 'The longer we delay them ...': letter from Welles to Fanto, 14 November 1950 (2). Screenplay of the Cyprus prologue (Second Draft Shooting Script) and of the 'Part One' in Venice (Fourth Draft Shooting Script) (4). Shooting instructions for Mogador, Safi and Mazagan (5). *Lavagnino family archives*: Autograph score by Angelo Francesco Lavagnino. Preparatory notes. Sketches (Rome, 20 March – 21 May 1951). Additional scattered sketches. *Additional quotation*: 'I don't pay attention during shooting ...': Welles interviewed by Juan Cobos and Miguel Rubio, *Sight and Sound*, vol. 35, no. 4, Autumn 1966. *Miscellaneous*: Italian release, November 1951: communication from Alberto Anile to J.-P. B., 16 February 2006. See also Anile's *Orson Welles in Italia* (il Castoro, Milan, 2006). Welles's dubbing his actors with his own voice: F. T., 'La voix des autres, ou le petit théâtre du marionnettiste', *Positif*, no. 378, July – August 1992. *Documentaries*: *Souvenirs d'"Othello"* / *After "Othello"* (François Girard, 1994). Extracts from interviews with Suzanne Cloutier, Angelo Francesco Lavagnino and Oberdan Troiani, shot for *Rosabella, op. cit.*, on the laser disk of *Othello* (Criterion, 1995).

MR ARKADIN

Historical studies: Barbara Leaming, *Orson Welles*, chap. XXXI, Mazarine, 1986. Tim Lucas, 'Will the Real *Mr. Arkadin* Please Stand Up?' and '*Mr. Arkadin*: The Research Continues ...', *Video Watchdog*, no. 10, March – April 1992, and no. 12, July – August 1992. Esteve Riambau, *Orson Welles: una España inmortal*, Filmoteca de la Generalitat Valenciana/Filmoteca Española, Valencia, 1993 (José Luis de la Serna on the amount of film exposed: p. 70). Jonathan Rosenbaum, 'The Seven *Arkadins*', *Film Comment*, vol. 28, no. 1, January – February 1992. *First-hand accounts*: F. T.'s telephone conversations with Colette Cueille (17 January 2006) and Paul Misraki (3 November 1981). Robert Arden: remarks reported by Tim Pulleine, *Sight and Sound*, vol. 51, no. 1, Winter 1981–2. Frédéric O'Brady: *All Told: The Memoirs of a Multiple Man*, Simon & Schuster, New York, 1964. *Gray Film Archives*: Screenplays dated 23 March 1953 (Spanish translation) and 18 August 1954. Correspondence. Working notes. Contracts. Permits to film on the public highway. Miscellaneous. 'I found that if I didn't ...': undated letter from Welles to Louis Dolivet during editing. 'selling copy' and 'My old dream ...': letter from Welles to Dolivet, 10 October 1955. *BiFi Archives*: Preliminary designs by Jean Douarinou. *Additional quotation*: 'anguish from beginning to end': *This Is Orson Welles, op. cit.*, p. 226. *Miscellaneous*: '*Mister Arkadin*' screenplay, *Temas de cine*, nos 24–5, December 1962. Promotional material for the French and British distributors. Written statement by Welles, reproduced in Juan Cobos, Miguel Rubio and José Antonio Pruneda, 'Antes de las campanadas', *Nickel Odeon*, no. 16, Autumn 1999. Rushes and edited scenes held by the Cinemathèque municipale de Luxembourg (extracts in the DVD *The Complete 'Mr. Arkadin' a.k.a. 'Confidential Report'*, The Criterion Collection, 2006). *Documentary*: *Tutta la verità su Gregory Arkadin* (Ciro Giorgini, 1990).

DISCOVERING TELEVISION

Historical study: Christophe Cognet, 'Comme un conteur arabe: *La Tragédie de Lurs* (Orson Welles, 1955, uncompleted)', *Vertigo*, special issue, 'Faits divers', July 2004. *First-hand accounts*: Telephone interview with Colette Cueille by F. T. (17 January 2006). Rick Jason, *Scrapbooks of My Mind*, Strange New Worlds, Sarasota, 2000. Alain Pol: interviewed by Alexandre Moix, *Le Nouvel Observateur*, 6 December 2000. *Gray Film Archives*: Draft contract between Associated-Rediffusion and Filmorsa for *Around the World with Orson Welles*, 3 May 1955. Declarations of intent. Correspondence. Miscellaneous. *Documentary*: *L'Affaire Dominici par Orson Welles* (Christophe Cognet, 2000).

TOUCH OF EVIL

Historical studies: John C. Stubbs, 'The Evolution of Orson Welles's *Touch of Evil* from Novel to Film', *Cinema Journal*, vol. 24, no. 2, Winter 1985 (see also vol. 24, no. 3, Spring 1985). On the competing versions: John Belton, 'A New Map of the Labyrinth: The Unretouched *Touch of Evil*', *Movietone News*, no. 47, 21 January 1976 (see also no. 48, 29 February 1976); J.-P. B., '*La Soif du mal*: chapter 3', *Positif*, no. 466, December 1999. *First-hand accounts*: Charlton Heston: interview by James Delson, *Take One*, vol. 3, no. 6, July – August 1971; *The Actor's Life: Journals 1956–1976*, Dutton, New York, 1978; debate, in Joseph McBride (ed.), *Filmmakers on Filmmaking*, vol. II, Tarcher, Los Angeles, 1983. Janet Leigh: *There Really Was a Hollywood*, Doubleday, New York, 1984. Mercedes

McCambridge: *The Quality of Mercy*, Berkley, New York, 1982. Henry Mancini: debate, *Dialogue on Film*, vol. 3, no. 3, January 1974; *Did They Mention the Music?*, Contemporary Books, Chicago/New York, 1989. Albert Zugsmith: interviewed by Todd McCarthy and Charles Flynn in T. McC. and C. F. (eds), *Kings of the Bs*, Dutton, New York, 1975; 'Orson Welles: Movie Innovator', in Danny Peary (ed.), *Close-Ups*, Workman, New York, 1978. *Archives*: Screenplay from 5 February 1957, with revised pages from 14 February (private coll.). Shooting schedule (University of Iowa, Special Collections Department). Memorandum from Welles to Edward Muhl, 5 December 1957, available on the DVD *Touch of Evil* zone 1 (Universal) or on www.wellesnet.com/touch_memo1.htm
Documentary: Reconstructing Evil (Laurent Bouzereau, 1998).

DON QUIXOTE

Historical studies: Juan Cobos, *Orson Welles: España como obsesión*, Filmoteca de la Generalitat Valenciana / Filmoteca Española, Valencia, 1993. Esteve Riambau, '*Don Quixote*: The Adventures and Misadventures of an Essay on Spain', in Stefan Droessler (ed.), *The Unknown Orson Welles*, Belleville/Filmmuseum München, Munich, 2004. *Accounts of the shoot:* Daniel Aubrey, *Film Ideal*, no. 150, 15 August 1964. Juan Buñuel and Claude Pierson, *Cahiers du cinéma*, no. 92, February 1959. *First-hand accounts:* Unpublished interview with Juan Luis Buñuel by J.-P. B. (5 February 2005). Mauro Bonanni: interview by Marcello Garofalo, *Segno cinema*, no. 57, September – October 1992. Audrey Stainton: '*Don Quixote*: Orson Welles' Secret', *Sight and Sound*, vol. 57, no. 4, Autumn 1988. *Gray Film Archives:* Invoice from LTC for the development and printing of the tests shots in France, 8 April 1955. *Quotations:* 'with a degree of liberty ...': Welles interviewed by André Bazin and Charles Bitsch, *Cahiers du cinéma*, no. 84, June 1958. 'with no actors ...': letter from Welles to Sime Simatovic, 5 July 1968, in the documentary *Druga strana Wellesa* (*The Other Side of Welles*, Daniel Rafaelic and Leon Rizmaul, 2005).

THE SECOND EUROPEAN PERIOD

First-hand account: Alessandro Tasca di Cutò: *Un principe in America e altrove*, Sellerio, Palermo, 2004. *Quotation:* 'This is my film ...': quoted in Herman G. Weinberg, 'Coffee, Brandy & Cigars XXXVIII', *Film Culture*, no. 27, Winter 1962–3. *Miscellaneous:* On the plan to set up a company in Spain: Juan Cobos, *Orson Welles: España como obsesión, op. cit.*, p. 172.

THE TRIAL

Account of the shoot: Enrique Martinez, *Films and Filming*, vol. 9, no. 1, October 1962. *First-hand accounts:* Unpublished interview with Jean Ledrut by F. T. (23 November 1981). Telephone interviews with Jacques Saulnier by J.-P. B. (12 August 2004) and with assistant editor Chantal Delattre by F. T. (15 April 2005). Conversation between F. T. and assistant editor Roberto Perpignani (10 August 2005). Yves Kovacs: 'Orson Welles, tel qu'en soi-même', *Est Ciné-Club*, no. 20, Autumn 1962. Michael Lonsdale: interviewed by F. T., *Positif*, no. 378, July – August 1992. Elsa Martinelli: *Sono como sono*, Rusconi, Milan, 1995. Anthony Perkins: interviewed by Robin Bean, *Films and Filming*, vol. 11, no. 10, July 1965. Edmond Richard: interviewed by Marc Chevrie, *Cahiers du cinéma*, no. 377, November 1985; interviewed by J.-P. B. and F. T., *Positif*, no. 378, July – August 1992. Michel Salkind: interviewed by Patrick Bureau, *Cinéma*, no. 71, December 1962. *Archives:* Undated screenplay in French (BiFi). Correspondence, preliminary design (archives of Jacques Saulnier).

FALSTAFF

Historical study: Juan Cobos, *Orson Welles: España como obsesión, op. cit.* (Who is he? Am I to understand that ...': p. 82). *Accounts of the shoot:* Pierre Billard, *Cinéma*, no. 96, May 1965. Juan Cobos, *Cahiers du cinéma*, no. 165, April 1965. *First-hand accounts:* Keith Baxter: interviewed by Bridget Gellert Lyons, in B. G. L. (ed.), *Chimes at Midnight*, Rutgers University Press, New Brunswick/London, 1988; interviewed by F. T., *Positif*, no. 378, July – August 1992; *My Sentiments Exactly*, Oberon, London, 1998. Edmond Richard: interviewed by J.-P. B. and F. T., *Positif*, no. 378, July – August 1992. Alessandro Tasca di Cutò: *Un principe in America e altrove*, Sellerio, Palermo, 2004. *Miscellaneous:* Richard Fleischer, *Just Tell Me When to Cry*, Carroll & Graf, New York, 1993, p. 164.

THE IMMORTAL STORY

Historical study: Esteve Riambau, *Orson Welles: una España inmortal, op. cit. Account of the shoot:* Danièle Heymann, *L'Express*, 3 October 1966. *First-hand accounts:* Unpublished interviews by F. T. with Françoise Garnault (5 February 2005), Willy Kurant (5 October 2002) and Micheline Rozan (29 April 2005). Willy Kurant: interviewed by Bernard Payen and Glenn Myrent, *Cinémathèque*, no. 22, Spring 2003. Suzanne Schiffman: interviewed by Bernard Cohn, *Cinémathèque*, no. 20, Autumn 2001. *Archives:* BiFi (Suzanne Schiffman coll.): call sheets, continuity notebooks, lists of o.k and n.g. takes, pre-timing, breakdowns for the shoot in France ('Sorry, I didn't get a French version of this shot': 1 October, third pink notebook). Archives of Micheline Rozan: correspondence, accounting documents, statements of accounts. Undated screenplay, translated into French by Pierre and édith Cottrell (private coll.). *Additional quotation:* 'the Paganini of mixing': quoted by Robert Enrico, untitled tribute to Jean Neny, *Le Technicien du film et de la vidéo*, no. 333, 15 February 1985.

'THE HEROINE', 'THE DEEP' & 'ORSON'S BAG'

First-hand accounts: Unpublished interviews by F. T. with Ljuba Gamulin (10 August 2005) and Willy Kurant (5 October 2002). Tony Fuentes: 'Noticias de *The Deep* en primera persona singular', *Nickel Odeon*, no. 16, Autumn 1999. Oja Kodar: interviewed by J.-P. B., *Positif*, no. 479, January 2001; interviewed by Stefan Droessler, in *The Unknown Orson Welles, op. cit. Quotation:* 'a lot of it is dubbed ...': transcript of a televised interview with Welles by Kathleen Halton, broadcast by the BBC on 10 April 1967 (BFI Film Library). *Documentary: Druga strana Wellesa* (*The Other Side of Welles*, Daniel Rafaelic and Leon Rizmaul, 2005).

THE LAST YEARS

First-hand account: Andrés Vicente Gomez: interviewed by Fabrice Pliskin, *Le Nouvel Observateur*, special issue, 'Profession producteur', May 1998. *Miscellaneous:* Welles, Warner Bros. and the constraints of official shoots: Joseph McBride, 'All's Welles', *Film Comment*, vol. 14, no. 6, November – December 1978.

ROUGH SKETCHES & LAST UNFINISHED WORKS

Historical studies: J.-P. B and F. T., 'Welles à Munich: le voile levé sur les inachevés', *Positif*, no. 479, January 2001. Juan Cobos, *Orson Welles: España como obsesión, op. cit.* Stefan Droessler, '(Re)-constructions: Dealing with Unfinished Films', in Giorgio Gosetti (ed.), *'The Other Side of the Wind': scénario/screenplay*, Cahiers du cinéma/Festival international du film de Locarno, 2005. Barbara Leaming, *Orson Welles*, chap. XXXVII, Mazarine, 1986. Esteve Riambau, *Orson Welles: una España inmortal, op. cit.* Jonathan Rosenbaum, 'The Invisible Orson Welles: A First Inventory', *Sight and Sound*, vol. 55, no. 3, Summer 1986. *Account of a shoot:* Joseph McBride, 'All's Welles', *Film Comment*, vol. 14, no. 6, November – December 1978 (on *The Orson Welles Show*). *First-hand accounts:* Unpublished interviews with Marie-Šophie Dubus by J.-P. B. (9 April 2005) and with Serge Halsdorf by F. T. (29 April 2005). Dominique Antoine: interviewed by J.-P. B., *Positif*, nos 449–50, July – August 1998. Kevin C. Brechner: 'Welles' Farewell, *The Other Side of the Wind*', *American Cinematographer*, vol. 67, no. 7, July 1986. Yves Deschamps: interviewed by J.-P. B., *Positif*, no. 536, October 2005. Gary Graver, Oja Kodar and Alessandro Tasca di Cutò: interviewed by Bill Krohn, *Cahiers du cinéma*, no. 378, December 1985. Oja Kodar: interviewed by J.-P. B., *Positif*, no. 479, January 2001; interviewed by Stefan Droessler, in *The Unknown Orson Welles, op. cit.* Joseph McBride: 'The Other Side of Orson Welles', in *Orson Welles*, Da Capo, New York, 1996. Paul Mazursky: *Show Me the Magic*, Simon & Schuster, New York, 1999. *Dialogue continuities for The Other Side of the Wind:* 'Détaildes séquences pré-montées', 12 December 1974 (private coll.). 'Screenplay' (dialogue continuity added in editing period, followed by unidentified pages from the screenplay, held at the Wisconsin Center for Film and Theatre Research, Joseph McBride coll.), in Giorgio Gosetti (ed.), *'The Other Side of the Wind': scénario/screenplay, op. cit. Documentary: Working with Orson Welles* (Gary Graver, 1993).

'F FOR FAKE' & 'FILMING OTHELLO'

Historical study: Esteve Riambau, *Orson Welles: una España inmortal, op. cit. First-hand accounts:* Unpublished interview with Marie-Sophie Dubus by J.-P. B. (9 April 2005). Conversation between F. T. and Tomislav Pinter (3 August 1984). Marie-Sophie Dubus: remarks reported by Dominique Villain, *Le Montage au cinéma*, Cahiers du cinéma, 1991. Dominique Antoine, Serge Halsdorf and Oja Kodar: see preceding chapter.

INDEX

PROJECTS & PERFORMANCES

OTHER FILMS & TELEVISION BROADCASTS

NAMES

SOURCES OF DOCUMENTS & PHOTOGRAPHS

Authors' collections: endpapers, 6–7, 8, 15, 21 (right), 22 (b, c, d, e), 23 (a, b, c, d, g), 25, 27 (top right, bottom), 28, 35 (Photofest), 36–7, 38, 39, 41, 42, 43 (top), 44–5, 46 (bottom), 47 (bottom), 48, 49, 50 (top/Photofest, bottom left), 52–3, 54 (top), 56 (bottom), 57, 59, 60–1, 62, 63, 67, 70–1, 77 (top), 79 (top), 82 (top), 85 (bottom), 89, 94–5, 99, 101, 104, 108, 113 (bottom), 115, 118, 121 (top/Photofest), 123 (top), 124, 126–7, 128, 129, 140 (right middle), 143, 144–5, 146, 147, 148–9, 150, 151 (bottom), 154 (top left, bottom), 157, 159, 161, 163, 164–5, 167, 168 (top left, middle), 172, 174, 176 (top right), 178, 179, 181, 185, 189, 191 (bottom), 198, 199, 200, 201 (top left, top right, middle right), 204–5, 207, 208 (bottom left), 209, 212, 214 (bottom), 216–17, 218 (top), 220–1 (Opening), 226 (bottom/Opening), 227 (top left/Opening, top right/Opening, middle/Opening), 230, 240 (left middle, right middle), 241, 242 (top right), 247 (bottom), 248–9, 258 (top left), 262 (bottom right), 265, 268–9, 271, 274, 275, 276 (top, bottom), 282, 284 (top right), 285, 287, 288, 292 (bottom), 300 (top, bottom), 301, 303. *BiFi (Paris)*: 158, 162 (top), 168 (bottom), 188, 190, 191 (top), 194, 208 (bottom right), 223, 225, 229, 253 (bottom left, bottom right), 258 (bottom), 262 (bottom left), 273. *Juan Luis Buñuel private archive*: 222, 226 (top). *Cahiers du Cinéma*: 31, 74–5, 90 (top right), 91, 105, 107 (top right, bottom right), 111, 123 (bottom), 138 (top, bottom), 192 (bottom left), 227 (bottom), 231 (bottom), 279, 284 (bottom). *Cinémathèque Française, Musée du Cinéma*: 46 (top left, top right). *La Cinémathèque Suisse (Lausanne)*: 11, 23 (f), 64, 66, 85 (top), 114 (top right), 116–17, 119, 121 (bottom), 125, 130, 132 (bottom left, bottom right), 133, 137, 138–9, 162 (middle), 177 (bottom), 186–7, 215, 231 (top), 232–3, 235, 236, 238, 240 (top, bottom), 242 (top right, middle left, middle right), 244 (bottom), 246, 247 (top, upper middle, lower middle), 251, 253 (top), 254, 255, 257, 258 (top right), 262 (top), 263, 266–7, 296–7, 300 (middle). *Cineteca nazionale (Rome)*: 231 (middle). *Christophe Cognet private archives*: 201 (middle left, bottom). *Filmmuseum München (Munich)*: 202, 203, 272 (top), 280–1, 284 (top left/Ljuba Gamulin), 286 (top left, middle left), 289, 290, (top), 291 (middle), 291 (bottom), 292 (top), 293 (top), 293 bottom, 294 top, 294 bottom, 295, 299. *Finnish Film Archive (Helsinki)*: 22 (a, f), 23 (e), 50 (bottom right), 73, 76 (top), 79 (bottom), 80–1, 90 (top left, bottom), 93, 132 (top), 177 (top), 192 (top, bottom right), 197, 206, 214 (top), 218 (bottom), 242 (bottom), 244 (top), 270. Gray Film: 162 (bottom). *The University of Iowa Libraries (Iowa City)*: 208 (top). *Willy Kurant private archive*: 272 (bottom), 283. *Lavagnino family personal archive*: 176 (bottom right), 286 (top right, bottom right). *The Lilly Library (Indiana University, Bloomington)*: 13, 16–17, 19, 21 (left), 26, 27 (top left), 29, 32 (top left, bottom), 40, 43 (bottom), 47 (top), 54 (bottom), 56 (top), 64–5, 76 (bottom), 77 (bottom), 79 (middle), 82 (bottom left, bottom right), 84, 87, 96, 97, 98, 102–3, 110, 112, 113 (top, middle), 114 (top left), 120, 134, 140 (top, middle left, bottom), 151 (top left), 154 (top right), 155, 180. *National Film and Television Archive (London)*: 136. *Edmond Richard private archive*: 252 (bottom), 256, 258–9. *Alexandre Trauner archives*: 160, 176 (top right). *Wisconsin Center for Film and Theatre Research (Madison)*: 114 (bottom).

ACKNOWLEDGEMENTS

We are grateful to many individuals and institutions for contributing to our researches into Orson Welles, which was conducted jointly or separately over the course of twenty years.

Our knowledge of Welles's working methods owes much to the interviews we conducted with his collaborators. We thank actors Keith Baxter, Michael Lonsdale, Alan Napier†, Jeanette Nolan† and Peggy Webber; actors and assistants Paul Stewart† and Richard Wilson†; assistant Juan Luis Buñuel; cinematographers Serge Halsdorf, Willy Kurant, Tomislav Pinter and Edmond Richard; art directors Jacques Saulnier and Alexandre Trauner†; script supervisor Ljuba Gamulin; editors Colette Cueille, Chantal Delattre, Yves Deschamps, Marie-Sophie Dubus, Françoise Garnault and Roberto Perpignani; composers Jean Ledrut† and Paul Misraki†; producers Dominique Antoine and Micheline Rozan; distributor Louis Touron; and muse Oja Kodar. We are also grateful to the former Mercury Theatre actors George Coulouris† and Elliott Reid for introducing us to other members of the company who, although not quoted in the book, enhanced our understanding of the young Welles.

Some of those we interviewed generously provided us with numerous documents. Micheline Rozan, in particular, lent us material from *The Immortal Story* archive. In addition Véronique Loth and Jacqueline Cirrincione gave us access to the Gray Film archives on *Mr Arkadin* and Welles's later projects with Filmorsa. Mrs Jacques Ibert† and Jean-Claude Ibert allowed us to consult the original score for *Macbeth*. Alessandra, Bianca and Iudica Lavagnino showed us the score for *Othello* and other working documents belonging to their father, Angelo Francesco Lavagnino. Our conversations and exchanges of information and documents over the years with Robert L. Carringer, James Naremore, Esteve Riambau, Jonathan Rosenbaum and other Welles scholars were a great stimulus.

Some of the information came from debates and discussions held at the Welles retrospectives and conferences in Venice (1991), Strasburg (1992), La Rochelle (1999), Munich (1999), Mannheim (2002), Locarno (2005) and Udine (2006), which were attended by Gary Graver, Oja Kodar and other Welles collaborators. These events also gave us the opportunity to discover rare films and documentaries. We are particularly grateful to Stefan Droessler, director of the Munich Filmmuseum, the principal source of information on Welles in Europe, and to Robert Fischer-Ettel and Sylvie Pras.

We are grateful to kind help from Alberto Anile, Catherine Benamou, Françoise Berger, N. T. Binh, Dominique Bluher, Florence Bory, Lorenzo Codelli, Christophe Cognet, Olivier Curchod, Michel Dorati, Bernard Eisenschitz, Frank Garbely, Gianfranco Giagni, Stéphane Lerouge, Jacqueline Moreau, Laura Nine, John Oliver, Floreal Peleato, Jacqueline Perney, Gilles Pierre, Jeannette de Poortere, Pascale Ragot, David N. Rodowick, Philippe Rouyer, Markku Salmi, Nane Trauner and Santos Zunzunegui.

Our researches also benefited from the co-operation of numerous libraries and archives. We thank Valdo Kneubhler at the BiFi (Paris), Jacques Verdier at the Institut Jean-Vigo (Perpignan), the National Film and Television Archive and the BFI Film Library (London), the Department of Special Collections and the Theatre Arts Library of the University of California at Los Angeles (Los Angeles), the Wisconsin Center for Film and Theatre Research (Madison) and especially the Lilly Library at Bloomington, Indiana, where Rebecca Cape, Saundra Taylor, Anthony Tedeschi and their staff responded to our queries with unfailing efficiency.

Many of the images reproduced in the book were provided by individuals and institutions mentioned above. We also thank Catherine Fröchen at Cahiers du Cinéma picture library, Antti Alanen at the Finnish Film Foundation, André Chevailler and Richard Szotyori at La Cinémathèque Suisse, Jacque Roethler at the Special Collections Department of the University of Iowa, Jean-Pierre Vasseur at Opening and Patrick Sonnet at the Alexandre Trauner archives.

We are grateful to the many others whom we have doubtless inadvertently omitted. And finally, a conspiratorial wink to Youssef Ishaghpour.

PICTURE CREDITS

Cover: DR *Heart of Darkness* © The Mercury theatre on the air/DR: 25 *Julius Caesar* © DR: 27 *Too Much Johnson* © DR: 29 *Citizen Kane, The Magnificent Ambersons* © RKO Turner: 6–7, 13, 36–7, 38, 39, 40, 41, 42, 43, 44–5, 46, 47, 48, 49, 50, 52, 53, 54, 55, 56–7, 59, 60–1, 62, 63, 64, 65, 66, 67, 70–1, 72, 73, 74–75, 76–7, 79, 80–1, 82, 84–5, 87, 89, 90–1, 93 *Journey Into Fear* © RKO-Aries: 94–5, 96–7, 98–9, 100–1 *It's All True* © RKO/Paramount/ Les Films Balanciaga: 102–3, 104, 105, 106, 107, 108, 109, 110, 113, 114, 115 *The Criminal* © International Pictures: 116–17, 118, 119, 120, 121, 123, 124, 125. *The Lady from Shanghai* © Columbia Pictures: endpapers, 11, 126–7, 128, 129, 130, 132–3, 134, 136, 137, 138, 139, 140, 143 *Macbeth* © Republic Pictures: 146, 147, 148, 149, 150, 151, 15', 155, 157, 158, 159, 160, 161, 162, 163 (other reserved rights) *Othello* © The Orson Welles Estate: 154–165, 167, 168, 172, 174, 176, 177, 178, 179, 180, 181, 185. *Mr Arkadin* © Filmorsa/Gray Film: 186–7, 188, 189 *Around the World with Orson Welles* © Gray Film: 190, 191, 192, 194,197, 198, 199, 200, 201, 202 *The Fountain of Youth* © DR: 203 *Touch of Evil* © Universal Pictures: 15, 204–5, 206, 207, 208, 209, 212, 214, 215, 216–17, 218. *Don Quixote* © Oja Kodar: 219–20, 222, 226, 227 © Oja Kodar/Klissak: 223, 225, 229. *The Trial* © Paris Europa Film/Roger Corbeau: 232–3, 235, 236, 238, 240 (except top left), 242, 244, 246, 247 © Nicolas Tikhomiroff/Magnum Photos: 240 (top left) *Falstaff* © International Film Espagnola: 248–9, 250, 251, 252–253, 254, 256, 257, 258–9, 260 (top), 262, 263, 265, 267 (other reserved rights) © Nicolas Tikhomiroff/Magnum Photos: 255, 260 (bottom) *The Immortal Story* © ORTF-Albina Film/Gorges Galmiche: 268–9, 270, 271, 272, 273, 274, 275, 276, 277, 279 (other reserved rights) *The Heroine, The Deep, The Merchant of Venice, Orson's Bag* © Oja Kodar/Cinémathèque de Munich: 280–1, 282, 283, 284, 285, 286, 287, 289, 290, 291. *F for Fake, The Other Side of The Wind* © Films de l'Astrophore: 292, 293, 294, 295, 296–7, 299, 300, 301 *Filming Othello* © Klaus et Joachim Hellwig: 303